INTERNATIONAL ECONOMICS

INTERNATIONAL ECONOMICS

Second Edition

ROBERT J. CARBAUGH

University of Wisconsin at Eau Claire

WADSWORTH PUBLISHING COMPANY

Belmont, California

A Division of Wadsworth, Inc.

Economics Editor: Stephanie Surfus

Production Editor: Vicki Friedberg

Managing and Cover Designer:
MaryEllen Podgorski

Designer: Steve Renick

Copy Editor: Elaine Linden

Technical Illustrator: Harry Spitzer

Print Buyer: Karen Hunt

Cover: Map of world trade power
adapted from *The State of the World
Atlas*, by Michael Kidron and Ronald
Segal. Copyright©1981 by Pluto Press
Limited. Reprinted by permission of
Simon & Schuster, Inc.

Printed in the United States of America

1 2 3 4 5 6 7 8 9 10—89 88 87 86 85

ISBN 0-534-03831-X

Library of Congress Cataloging in Publication Data

Carbaugh, Robert J., 1946-
  International economics.

  Includes index.
  1. International economic relations. I. Title.
HF1411.C35 1985   337   84-11836
ISBN 0-534-03831-X

To Cathy, Julie, Mary, and Alice

CONTENTS

PREFACE

My belief is that the best way to motivate students to learn a subject is to demonstrate how it is used in practice. The first edition of *International Economics* arose from this belief and was written to provide a serious presentation of international economic theory with an emphasis on current applications. Adopters of the first edition strongly supported integrating economic theory with current events; the second edition has been revised with an eye to improving this presentation and updating the applications.

Like its predecessor, the second edition is intended for use in a one-quarter or one-semester course for students who have no more background than principles of macro- or microeconomics. This book's strengths are its clarity and organization and its applications, which demonstrate the usefulness of theory to students. The revised and updated material in this edition emphasizes current applications of economic theory and incorporates recent theoretical and policy developments in international trade and finance.

Part 1, "International Trade Relations," has been expanded in the following ways: Chapter 1 delves more deeply into the economics-of-interdependence issue, using illustrations that show the significance of international trade and finance for the United States and other countries. Chapters 3 and 4 explore how the terms of trade can be measured and what impact economies of scale have on world trade patterns. Chapters 5–7 include empirical estimates of the welfare effects of protectionism for CB radios, oil, autos, sugar, steel, and stainless steel flatware. They also consider tariff quotas, local content requirements, export trade associations, export trading companies, services trade, and the welfare implications of the Tokyo Round of Multilateral Trade Negotiations. Chapters 8 and 9 examine the trade strategies of export promotion and import substitution for developing nations, the European Economic Community's system of variable levies and export subsidies, and counter-trade agreements, which have become popular in East-West trade.

Part 2, "International Monetary Relations," has also been expanded. Chapter 11 emphasizes the interpretation of the various balances in the U.S. balance of payments. The trade-weighted dollar and effective exchange rates are discussed in Chapter 12. Chapters 13 and 15 consider the impact of capital flows on the balance of payments and the monetary approach to balance-of-payments adjustments under fixed and floating exchange rates. The international debt problem is covered in Chapter 17.

Though instructors generally agree on the basic content of the international economics course, opinions vary widely about what arrangement of material is appropriate. This book is structured to provide considerable organizational flexibility. Though international trade relations is presented before international monetary relations, the order can be reversed by instructors who choose to start with monetary theory. Instructors can begin with Chapter 1, then move to Chapters 11–18, and conclude with Chapters 2–10. Those instructors who do not wish to cover all of the material in the book can omit Chapters 7–10 and Chapters 16–18 without loss of continuity.

Another new feature is the instructor's manual written to accompany the second edition. It contains: (1) brief answers to the end-of-chapter study questions; (2) multiple-choice questions for each chapter; and (3) a bibliography of articles taken from current publications, which provides additional real-world illustrations of the theories discussed in the book.

I am pleased to acknowledge the help of those who aided me in preparing the second edition. Helpful suggestions and often detailed reviews were provided by Byron B. Brown, Jr., Southern Oregon State College; Miltiades Chacholiades, Georgia State University; Kanjo Haitani, State University of New York, College at Fredonia; Jim Hanson, Willamette University; Douglas Jepsen, Marquette University; John McDermott, University of South Carolina; Al Maury, Texas A&I University; Gary Pickersgill, California State University at Fullerton; Anthony Scaperlanda, Northern Illinois University; and Harold Williams, Kent State University.

My thanks are especially due to my colleague Darwin Wassink, who provided a detailed review of the text and enthusiastically answered my many questions during the past four years concerning the second edition. I am also indebted to Joan Erdman, Janna Johnson, and Jeanne Wolfarth, who assisted in the manuscript's preparation, and to Don Ellickson, Lee Grugel, and Jim Wenner for their support. It has been a pleasure to work with the Wadsworth staff, especially Stephanie Surfus and Vicki Friedberg. Finally, I am grateful to my students who commented on the revisions that are included in this new edition.

I would appreciate any comments, corrections, and suggestions that readers wish to make so I can improve this text in the years ahead.

Robert J. Carbaugh
Economics Department
University of Wisconsin at Eau Claire
Eau Claire, WI 54701

INTERNATIONAL ECONOMICS

1

THE INTERNATIONAL
ECONOMY

In today's world, no nation exists in economic isolation. All aspects of a nation's economy—its industries, service sectors, levels of income and employment, living standard—are linked to the economies of its trading partners. This linkage takes the form of international movements of goods and services, labor, business enterprise, investment funds, and technology. Indeed, national economic policies cannot be formulated without evaluating their probable impacts on the economies of other countries.

The high degree of interdependence among today's economies reflects the historical evolution of the world's economic and political order. At the end of World War II, the United States was economically and politically the most powerful nation in the world. It was sometimes stated that "when the United States sneezed, the economies of other nations caught a cold." But with the passage of time, the U.S. economy became increasingly dependent on the economic activities of foreign countries. The formation of the European Economic Community (EEC) during the fifties, the rise in importance of the multinational corporation during the sixties, and the market power in world oil markets enjoyed by the Organization of Petroleum Exporting Countries (OPEC) during the seventies all resulted in the evolution of the world community into a complicated system based on a growing interdependence among nations.

In recent years, the character of global economic interdependence has become much more sophisticated. Rather than emphasizing only the economic issues of the industrial countries, world conferences are now recognizing and incorporating into their discussions the problems of the less developed countries. For resources such as energy and raw materials, the Western industrial nations rely on the less-developed countries for a portion of their consumption requirements. However, this reliance varies among countries. For Europe and Japan, dependence on foreign energy and materials is much more striking than for the United States. On the other hand, the livelihood of the developing nations' economies greatly depends on the exports of the industrial countries.

Recognizing that world economic interdependence is complex and its effects uneven, the economic community has made widespread efforts toward international cooperation. Conferences devoted to global economic issues have explored the avenues through which cooperation could be fostered between the industrial and the less-developed countries. The efforts of the less-developed countries to reap larger gains from international trade and to participate more fully

1

in international institutions recently have been hastened by the impact of the global recession on manufacturers, industrial inflation, and the burdens of high-priced energy.

Interdependence among nations also applies in the case of foreign debt. Throughout the 1970s, the growth of such middle-income developing countries as Brazil, Taiwan, and South Korea was widely viewed as a great success story. Of particular importance was their success in increasing exports of manufactured goods. However, much of this success was due to the availability of loans from industrial nations. Based on overly optimistic expectations about export earnings and interest rates, these countries borrowed excessively to finance growth. Then, with the impact of world recession on export demand, high interest rates, and tumbling oil prices, countries such as Argentina and Mexico found they had to make annual payments of principal and interest that exceeded their total exports of goods and services. The reluctance of creditor nations to lend as much as in the past meant that debtor countries were pressed to cut imports or expand exports, in spite of a worldwide recession. It was recognized that failure to repay the debt could result in a serious disruption of the international financial system.

During the last decade, the world's market economies became integrated as never before. Exports and imports as a share of national output reached unprecedented levels for most industrial countries, while foreign investment and international lending expanded more rapidly than world trade. This closer linkage of economies can be mutually advantageous for trading nations. It permits producers in each nation to take advantage of specialization and economies of large-scale production. A nation can consume a wider variety of products at a cost less than that which could be achieved in the absence of trade. In spite of these advantages, demands have grown for protection against imports. For indus-

trial countries, protectionist pressures have been strongest during periods of rising unemployment caused by economic recession. What is more, developing countries often maintain that the so-called liberalized trading system called for by industrial countries works to the disadvantage of developing countries. Their reason is that industrial countries are able to control the terms (that is, price) at which international trade takes place.

The economics of interdependence also has direct consequences for a student taking an introductory course in international economics. As consumers, we can be affected by changes in the international values of currencies. Should the Japanese yen or West German mark appreciate against the U.S. dollar, it would cost an American more to purchase a Japanese television set or a West German automobile. As investors, we might prefer to purchase British securities if overseas interest rates rise above U.S. levels. As members of the labor force, we might want to know whether the president plans to protect American workers producing steel or television sets from foreign competition.

In short, economic interdependence has become a complex issue in recent times, often resulting in strong and uneven impacts among nations and among sectors within a given nation. Business, labor, investors, and consumers all feel the repercussions of changing economic conditions or trade policies in other countries. Today's global economy requires cooperation on an international level to cope with the myriad issues and problems.

International Trade Patterns

For the world's economies, international trade has assumed an increasingly important role, as summarized in Table 1.1. In 1950, following five years of postwar reconstruction and development, the value of world exports was slightly less than

Table 1.1   Growth in World Trade* (billions of U.S. dollars)

Area	1950	1960	1970	1980	1981
World	57.9	115.5	284.8	1,868.3	1,837.2
Industrial countries	36.4	83.9	220.3	1,239.4	1,219.8
Oil-exporting countries	4.2	7.2	17.1	296.5	272.8
Nonoil developing countries	17.6	24.7	46.5	312.0	323.8

Source: International Monetary Fund, *International Financial Statistics: Supplement on Trade Statistics*, no. 4, 1982, pp. 2–3.
*Exports.

$58 billion. During the fifties, the value of world exports doubled to nearly $116 billion, growing at an average annual rate of 7.1 percent. The 1960s saw the value of world exports growing at a 9.4 percent annual rate to $285 billion. Although these increases in value were impressive, the decade of the 1970s was even more significant. The value of world exports rose 20.7 percent on an annual basis to a level of $1,868 billion. The increases in the value of exports spread across all parts of the world, although some areas enjoyed higher growth rates than others.

In terms of the volume of exports and imports, world trade has expanded in the post–World War II era, increasing from a 6.4 percent annual rate during the fifties to an 8 percent annual rate in the sixties. However, the seventies witnessed only a 5.5 percent annual increase in world trade volume as economic recession slowed down business activity. Over the 30-year period, 1950–1980, the volume of world trade expanded 6.7 percent per year. This was well above the increase in world production and several times greater than the world population growth, suggesting a growing linkage of national economies.

Table 1.2 summarizes the shares of world exports for various country groupings. From the 1950s until the middle 1970s, the nonoil developing countries' share of world exports fell from 30 percent to 15 percent. This decrease

was offset by increases in the industrial countries' share of world exports. Following the rise in world oil prices, which began in late 1973, the oil-exporting countries' share of world exports increased to 15 percent by 1981, up from a 6 percent level in 1970. This increase was roughly balanced by a reduction in the industrial countries' share of the world export market.

Table 1.3 gives a more detailed breakdown of world export shares. From 1960 to 1982, the U.S. share of the world export market fell from 18.2 percent to 15.4 percent. Even more striking was the United Kingdom, whose exports

Table 1.2   Distribution of World Trade*

Year	Industrial Countries (percent)	Oil-Exporting Countries (percent)	Nonoil Developing Countries (percent)
1950	62.9	7.3	29.8
1960	72.6	6.2	21.2
1965	74.8	6.1	19.1
1970	77.4	6.0	16.3
1975	70.7	13.9	14.7
1981	66.4	14.9	17.6

Source: International Monetary Fund, *International Financial Statistics: Supplement on Trade Statistics*, no. 4, 1982, p. vii.
*Exports.

Table 1.3   Shares of Total World Exports (percentages)

Period	United States	France	West Germany	Italy	Nether-lands	United Kingdom	Japan	Canada
1960	18.2	6.0	10.1	3.2	3.6	9.4	3.6	5.1
1970	15.4	6.4	12.1	4.7	4.2	7.0	6.9	5.9
1980	13.9	6.3	10.5	4.2	4.0	6.0	7.1	3.7
1982	15.4	5.3	10.5	4.3	3.8	5.9	8.7	4.4

Source: U.S. Department of Commerce, *International Economic Indicators*, March 1983.

as a percentage of world exports fell by about a third over the same time period. Conversely, Japan was able to more than double its share of the world export market from 1960 to 1982.

As illustrated in Table 1.4, foreign trade has become increasingly important in recent years. Before the 1970s, the growth of U.S. trade as a share of gross national product (GNP) was moderate. During the 1960s, exports' share of U.S. GNP increased from 4 percent to 4.3 percent. By 1980, this share had almost doubled to 8.2 percent. The rise in the price of oil, from approximately $3 a barrel in 1972 to almost $33 in 1980, increased the significance of trade for the U.S. economy. The payments for oil resulted in expanded flows of dollars out of the United States, which stimulated foreign demand for U.S. exports. Strong economic growth in the developing countries as a group also resulted in increases in

U.S. exports, particularly in capital goods, plant, and equipment. The official dollar devaluations of 1971 and 1973, as well as the inception of managed floating exchange rates by mid-1973, helped restore more realistic currency values for the U.S. dollar, improving the competitive position of American exporters. Finally, it was in the early 1970s that the tariff reductions of the historic Kennedy Round of Multilateral Trade Negotiations were implemented, resulting in greater potential for U.S. exports.

Although the importance of trade to the American economy increased during the 1970s, the United States remains among the countries for which foreign trade plays the smallest role in the domestic economy. This is due to the vast size and wide diversity of the American economy. As illustrated in Table 1.4, other industrial countries tend to find trade representing a greater share of their

Table 1.4   Exports as a Percentage of Gross National Product

Period	United States	France	West Germany	Italy	Nether-lands	United Kingdom	Japan	Canada
1960	4.0	10.3	15.9	10.5	35.8	14.4	9.4	14.1
1970	4.3	12.8	18.5	14.2	37.1	15.8	9.5	19.6
1980	8.2	17.7	23.5	19.7	43.9	22.1	12.5	26.1
1982	6.8	17.9	26.8	20.2	48.9	20.1	13.4	25.4

Source: U.S. Department of Commerce, *International Economic Indicators*, March 1983.

domestic economic activity. Facing many of the same influences as the United States in recent years, these countries also saw increases in their rates of exports as a percentage of GNP. For some small countries, such as the Netherlands, exports account for almost half of national output. On the other hand, with the constant media attention given to the subject of Japanese exports, it may come as a surprise that Japan exported only 13 percent of its national output in 1982!

International Trade and the U.S. Economy

Table 1.5 summarizes the net positions (surplus and deficit)[1] of various U.S. trade sectors for the years 1970 and 1980. The various trade sectors have shown increases, not only in dollar terms, but also as a percentage of gross national product (GNP). As for U.S. exports, manufactured goods

Table 1.5   U.S. Trade Balances: Selected Sectors, 1980 and 1970 (billions of dollars)

Sector	1980	1970
Surplus sectors		
Agriculture	+24.3	+1.6
Crude materials and fuels, except petroleum	+14.6	+2.4
High-technology manufacturers	+39.3	+11.7
Services, including investment earnings	+36.1	+3.0
Deficit sectors		
Petroleum	−75.8	−2.3
Low-technology manufacturers	−34.8	−8.3
Consumer goods	−18.3	−4.7
Automotive products	−11.2	−2.3

Source: U.S. Trade Representative, Office of the President, *Annual Report of the President of the U.S. on the Trade Agreements Program*, 1980–1981 (Washington, D.C.: U.S. Government Printing Office), p. 25.

recently have accounted for approximately two-thirds of total foreign sales, whereas agricultural exports accounted for one-fifth of foreign sales.[2] Of growing significance has been the service sector (for example, travel and insurance). Service-sector exports as a share of U.S. GNP increased from 0.3 percent in 1970 to 1.4 percent in 1980.

Table 1.5 also shows which U.S. sectors faced large trade deficits. By 1980, significant trade deficits existed in petroleum and low-technology manufacturing. The composition of U.S. imports also has changed in recent years. Petroleum imports, which accounted for 7 percent of the value of merchandise imports in 1970, increased to more than 33 percent of U.S. imports by 1980.[3] This led to a decrease in the share of U.S. imports held by other sectors, most notably agricultural products.

Although the U.S. economy is relatively insulated from foreign trade compared with other industrial nations, foreign trade has significant impacts on certain sectors of the economy. For American manufacturers, exports constituted 13.4 percent of total sales (domestic sales plus foreign sales) in 1981. Industries with the highest dollar value of exports included machinery, transportation equipment, chemicals, primary metals, and electric equipment. Table 1.6 identifies leading American exporters in 1981. For firms such as Boeing Inc., whose exports constitute more than two-fifths of total sales, foreign economic conditions play a key role in the firm's profitability.

Exports also influence domestic employment levels. There were 4.8 million jobs in the United States associated with exports of manufactured goods in 1981. These jobs constituted 4.7 percent of the nation's total work force. Within the manufacturing sector alone, exports accounted for 12.8 percent of total manufacturing employment. In addition, there were 2.2 million employees in non-manufacturing industries that supply materials and services that support manufactured exports. In 1981, California led the states with the

Table 1.6   Leading U.S. Industrial Exporters, 1982

Company	Export Sales (billions of dollars)	Export Sales as a Percentage of Total Sales
General Motors	4.7	8
General Electric	3.9	15
Boeing	3.9	43
Ford Motor	3.7	10
Caterpillar Tractor	2.6	40
DuPont de Nemours	2.6	8
United Technologies	2.2	17
McDonnell Douglas	2.1	28
International Business Machines	1.9	5
Eastman Kodak	1.9	17
Top 50 exporters	58.7	9

Source: "The 50 Leading Exporters," *Fortune*, August 8, 1983, pp. 88–89.

largest number of jobs related to manufactured exports, 296,000 jobs. This figure amounted to 14.5 percent of California's manufacturing employment. Ohio was second with 180,000 jobs, followed by New York, Pennsylvania, Illinois, and Michigan.

The traditional view of foreign trade as an exchange of goods (or merchandise) increasingly is giving way to a more balanced view of trade as encompassing services as well. As more and more economies have become service oriented, foreign sales of services such as banking, insurance, construction, and engineering consulting have been gaining recognition as important contributors to a country's exports. For the United States, service industries recorded exports of $39 billion in 1981, 17 percent of total exports.

U.S. agriculture also is tied to international trade. In recent years, two out of every five acres in U.S. agricultural production have grown food for export. U.S. exports of farm products totaled $39.1 billion in 1982. The two leading customers were Western Europe and Asia, and the principal commodities sold abroad were soybeans, feed grains, and wheat. Table 1.7 summarizes the agricultural export position of the top 10 states,

Table 1.7   U.S. Agricultural Exports by Leading States, 1982

State	Agricultural Exports (billions of dollars)	Share of U.S. Agricultural Exports (percent)
United States	39.1	100.0
Illinois	3.3	8.4
Iowa	3.0	7.7
California	2.9	7.4
Texas	2.6	6.6
Minnesota	1.9	4.9
Nebraska	1.8	4.6
Kansas	1.6	4.1
Indiana	1.6	4.1
Missouri	1.4	3.6
North Dakota	1.3	3.3

Source: U.S. Department of Agriculture, *Foreign Agricultural Trade of the United States*, March–April, 1983, p. 68.

which accounted for about 55 percent of U.S. farm product exports in 1982. Whereas in the 1960s, exports represented 14 percent of total farm cash receipts, by the 1980s, cash receipts from exports represented nearly 30 percent of the total farm receipts. However, since the end of World War II, agriculture's share of total U.S. exports has remained at approximately 20 percent. In contrast, agricultural exports were 31 percent of total U.S. exports during the 1930s.

Some Arguments For and Against an Open Trading System

The benefits of international trade accrue in the forms of lower domestic prices, development of more efficient methods and new products, and a greater range of consumption choices. In an open trading system, a country will import those commodities that it produces at relatively high cost while exporting commodities that can be produced at relatively low cost. Since resources are channeled from uses of low productivity to those of high productivity, gains from trade are attained, permitting higher levels of consumption and investment. Competition from imports tends to hold down the prices of domestic substitutes while promoting efficiency among home producers. The advent of relatively low prices for American portable color television sets, for example, has been encouraged by imports from Japan and other countries.

Although the benefits of an open trading system are widely understood, several conditions give rise to arguments against international trade. It is sometimes maintained that import protection should be extended to preserve or strengthen industries that produce strategic goods and materials vital for the nation's security. During periods of national emergency or war, political and military objectives may dominate over the goals of economic efficiency. Arguments against an open trading system also arise during eras of high unemployment and low plant utilization. Displaced labor and capital may find it costly and time-consuming to shift to new industries. Their demands for protection often are stated more effectively than the demands of consumers for a better range of products and lower prices. Imports that might be welcomed during periods of high employment become increasingly condemned as a main cause of domestic unemployment during periods of excess production capacity. To the average citizen, such arguments are often very appealing, even though the gains to a nation from international trade may more than outweigh the losses to particular domestic firms and workers.

The Plan of This Book

This book examines the functioning of the international economy. Although it emphasizes the theoretical principles that govern international trade, it also gives considerable coverage to empirical evidence of world trade patterns and to trade policies of the industrial and developing countries. The book is divided into two sections. Part 1 deals with international trade and commercial policy, whereas Part 2 stresses the balance of payments and adjustment in the balance of payments.

Chapters 2–4 deal with the theory of comparative advantage, as well as theoretical extensions and empirical tests of this model. This is followed by a treatment of tariffs, nontariff trade barriers, and contemporary commercial policies of the United States in Chapters 5–7. Discussion of trade policies for the developing countries, preferential trading arrangements, and multinational corporations in Chapters 8–10 completes the first section of the text.

The treatment of international financial relations begins with an overview of the balance of payments and foreign exchange market in

11–12. Balance-of-payments adjustment under alternate exchange rate regimes is discussed in Chapters 13–16. The last two chapters analyze the role of international liquidity in the world payments system and the implications for economic policy in an open economy.

Summary

1. Throughout the post–World War II era, the world economies have become increasingly interdependent in terms of the movement of goods and services, business enterprise, capital, and technology.

2. Over the period 1950–1980, the volume of world trade increased well above the increase in world production and several times more than world population growth, suggesting a growing linkage of national economies.

3. Largely owing to the vast size and the wide diversity of its economy, the United States remains among the countries for which exports constitute a small fraction of national output.

4. The traditional view of foreign trade as an exchange of goods is increasingly giving way to a more balanced view that recognizes the rising importance of service transactions. Foreign agricultural sales also have significant impacts on economies such as the United States.

5. Proponents of an open trading system contend that international trade results in higher levels of consumption and investment, lower prices of commodities, and a wider range of product choices for consumers. Arguments against free trade tend to be voiced during periods of excess production capacity and high unemployment.

Study Questions

1. What factors explain why the world's trading nations have become increasingly interdependent from an economic and political viewpoint during the post–World War II era?

2. What are some of the major arguments for and against an open trading system?

3. What significance does growing economic interdependence have for a country like the United States?

4. What factors influence the rate of growth in the volume of world trade?

5. Why have service transactions become more important for international trade?

6. Why is it that some countries like the United States are relatively insulated from international trade while economies of other countries are heavily geared toward exports and imports?

Notes

1. A trade surplus results when the value of a country's exports exceeds the value of its imports. A trade deficit implies the opposite.

2. *Agricultural Letter*, no. 1625, 16 March 1984 (Federal Reserve Bank of Chicago), p. 1.

3. *Economic Report of the President* (Washington, D.C.: U.S. Government Printing Office, 1984), p. 334.

Suggestions for Further Reading

Data Sources on International Trade and Finance

Bank for International Settlements. Basel. *Annual Report*.

Board of Governors of the Federal Reserve System. *Federal Reserve Bulletin*, monthly.

Council of Economic Advisers. Washington, D.C. *Economic Report of the President,* annual.

General Agreements on Tariffs and Trade. Geneva. *International Trade,* annual.

International Monetary Fund. Washington, D.C. *Annual Report.*

_____. *Annual Report on Exchange Restrictions.*

_____. *Balance of Payments Yearbook.*

_____. *International Financial Statistics,* monthly.

_____. *IMF Survey,* biweekly.

Morgan Guaranty Trust Co. New York. *World Financial Markets,* monthly.

Organization for Economic Cooperation and Development. Paris. *General Statistics,* monthly.

_____. *Overall Trade by Countries,* monthly.

United Nations. New York. *Commodity Trade Statistics,* quarterly.

_____. *Direction of International Trade* (jointly published with the International Monetary Fund).

_____. *Monthly Bulletin of Statistics.*

_____. *Yearbook of International Trade Statistics.*

United States Department of Commerce. Washington, D.C. *Historical Statistics of the United States.*

_____. *Business Conditions Digest,* monthly.

_____. *International Economic Indicators,* quarterly.

_____. *Statistical Abstract,* annual.

_____. *Survey of Current Business,* monthly.

World Bank. Washington, D.C. *World Bank Atlas,* annual.

Supplementary Readings

Adams, J., ed. *The Contemporary International Economy: A Reader.* New York: St. Martins Press, 1979.

Balassa, B., ed. *Changing Patterns in Foreign Trade and Payments.* New York: W. W. Norton, 1978.

Baldwin, R. E., and J. D. Richardson. *International Trade and Finance: Readings,* 2nd ed. Boston: Little, Brown, 1981.

Cooper, R. N. *The Economics of Interdependence.* New York: Council on Foreign Relations, 1968.

Keohane, R. O., and J. S. Nye. *Power and Interdependence: World Politics in Transition.* Boston: Little, Brown, 1977.

Morse, E. L. *Modernization and the Transformation of International Relations.* New York: Free Press, 1976.

INTERNATIONAL TRADE RELATIONS

2

FOUNDATIONS OF MODERN
TRADE THEORY

A major task of modern trade theory is to answer the following questions: (1) What constitutes the basis for trade—that is, why do nations export and import certain products? (2) At what terms of trade (relative prices) are products exchanged in the world market? (3) What are the gains from international trade in terms of production and consumption? This chapter addresses these questions, first by summarizing the historical development of modern trade theory and next by presenting the contemporary theoretical principles used in analyzing the effects of international trade.

Historical Development of Modern Trade Theory

Modern trade theory is the product of an evolution of ideas in economic thought. In particular, the writings of the mercantilists Adam Smith and David Ricardo have been instrumental in providing the framework of modern trade theory.

The Mercantilists

During the period 1500–1800, a group of writers appeared in Europe who were concerned with the process of nation building. According to the mercantilists, the central question was how a nation could regulate its domestic and international affairs so as to promote its own interests. The solution lay in a strong foreign trade sector. If a country could achieve a favorable trade balance (a surplus of exports over imports), it would enjoy payments received from the rest of the world in the form of gold and silver. Such revenues would contribute to increased spending and a rise in domestic output and employment. To promote a favorable trade balance, the mercantilists advocated governmental regulation of trade. Tariffs, quotas, and other commercial policies were proposed by the mercantilists to minimize imports in order to protect a nation's trade position.[1]

By the eighteenth century, the economic policies of the mercantilists were under strong attack. According to David Hume's *price-specie flow doctrine*, a favorable trade balance was possible only in the short run, for over time it would automatically be eliminated. To illustrate, suppose England were to achieve a trade surplus that resulted in an inflow of gold and silver. Because these precious metals would constitute part of England's money supply, their inflow would increase the amount of money in circulation. This would lead to a rise in England's price level relative to that of its trading

13

partners. English residents would therefore be encouraged to purchase foreign-produced goods while England's exports would decline. As a result, the country's trade surplus would eventually be eliminated. The Hume price-specie flow mechanism thus showed that mercantilist policies could provide at best only short-run economic advantages.[2]

Another attack against mercantilism concerned its static view of the world economy. To the mercantilists, the world's economic pie was of constant size. This meant that one nation's gains from trade came at the expense of its trading partners. Not all nations could therefore simultaneously enjoy the benefits of international trade. This view was challenged with the publication of Adam Smith's *Wealth of Nations* in 1776. According to Smith, the world's economic pie is not a fixed quantity. International trade permits nations to take advantage of specialization and the division of labor, which increase the general level of productivity within a country and thus world output. Smith's dynamic view of trade suggested that both trading partners could simultaneously enjoy higher levels of consumption and production with free trade. Although the mercantilist views of regulated trade have been subject to attacks by free trade proponents, their policies are certainly evident in today's world. This topic is discussed in Chapters 5 and 6.

Why Nations Trade: Absolute Advantage

The next stage in the development of modern trade theory is found in the writings of the classical economist Adam Smith. Smith was a leading advocate of free trade on the grounds that it promoted the international division of labor. Nations could concentrate their production on goods they could make most cheaply, with all the consequent benefits of the division of labor.

Accepting the idea that *cost differences* govern the movement of goods among nations, Smith

sought to explain why costs differ among nations. Smith maintained that *productivities* of factor inputs represent the major determinant of production cost. Such productivities are based on *natural* and *acquired advantages*. The former include factors relating to climate, soil, and mineral wealth, whereas the latter include special skills and techniques. Given a natural or acquired advantage in the production of a good, Smith reasoned that a nation would produce that good at lower cost, becoming more competitive than its trading partner. Smith therefore viewed the determination of competitive advantage from the *supply side* of the market.[3]

Smith's trading principle was the *principle of absolute advantage*. In a two-country two-product world, international trade and specialization will be beneficial when one country has an absolute cost advantage (that is, can produce a good using fewer resources) in the production of one product, whereas the other country has the absolute cost advantage in the other product. For nations to benefit from the international division of labor, each nation must have a good that it is absolutely more efficient in producing than its trading partner.

Smith felt it was far better for a country to import goods that could be produced overseas more efficiently than to manufacture them itself. Countries would import goods in the production of which they had an absolute disadvantage against the exporting country. They would export goods in the production of which they had an absolute advantage over the importing country.

Why Nations Trade: Comparative Advantage

According to Smith, mutually beneficial trade required that each country be the least-cost producer of at least one good that it could export to its trading partner. But what if a nation is more efficient than its trading partner in the production of *all* goods? Dissatisfied with this looseness in Smith's theory, David Ricardo (1772–1823) developed a trade principle to show that mutually beneficial trade could occur when one nation was absolutely more efficient in the production of all goods.[4] Like Smith, Ricardo emphasized the supply side of the market. The immediate basis for trade stemmed from cost differences between nations. These differences were ultimately governed by natural or acquired advantages affecting input productivities. Unlike Smith, however, Ricardo stressed the importance of *comparative* or relative costs.

According to Ricardo's *principle of comparative advantage*, even if a nation has an absolute disadvantage in the production of both goods relative to its trading partner, a basis for mutually beneficial trade may still exist. The less efficient nation should specialize in and export the good in which it is comparatively less inefficient (where its absolute disadvantage is least). The more efficient nation should specialize in and export that good in which it is comparatively more efficient (where its absolute advantage is

greatest). Absolute productive efficiency was thus not a crucial factor governing the basis for trade, according to Ricardo. The Ricardian principle of comparative advantage is today one of the most famous and influential principles of economics. The next sections illustrate the operations of this principle.

Transformation Curves

The operation of the comparative advantage principle can be illustrated with the transformation curve, also referred to as a production possibilities curve. This curve shows the various alternative combinations of two products that a country can produce with the best available technology when all of its resources are fully utilized. The transformation curve hence illustrates the maximum output possibilities of a nation.[5]

Figure 2.1 illustrates a hypothetical transformation curve for the United States. By fully utilizing all available inputs with the best available technology during a given time period, the

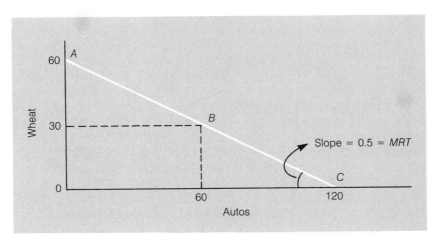

Figure 2.1   Transformation curve.

United States could produce either 60 bushels of wheat or 120 autos, or certain combinations of the two commodities.

Just how does a transformation curve illustrate the comparative cost concept? The answer lies in the transformation curve's slope, which is referred to as the marginal rate of transformation (*MRT*). The *MRT* shows the amount of a product a nation must sacrifice to get one additional unit of the other product, when moving along the transformation curve. This rate of sacrifice is sometimes called the *opportunity cost* of the product:

$$MRT = \frac{\Delta Wheat}{\Delta Autos}.$$

Since this formula also refers to the slope of the transformation curve, the *MRT* equals the absolute value of the transformation curve's slope.

In Figure 2.1, the *MRT* of wheat into autos gives the amount of wheat that must be sacrificed for each additional auto produced. Moving from point *A* to point *B* along the transformation curve, the comparative cost of producing 60 additional autos is the sacrifice of 30 bushels of wheat. This means that the opportu-

nity cost of each auto produced is ½ bushel of wheat sacrificed—that is, the *MRT* = ½.

Trading Under Constant Cost Conditions

This section illustrates the Ricardian principle of comparative advantage under constant cost conditions. Although the constant cost case may be of limited relevance to the real world, it serves as a useful pedagogical tool for analyzing international trade. The discussion focuses on two questions. First, what is the basis for trade and the direction of trade? Second, what are the potential gains from free trade, for a single nation and for the world as a whole?[6]

Constant Costs

In Figure 2.2, the hypothetical transformation curves for the United States and Canada illustrate the capacities of these nations to produce two commodities, autos and wheat. If the United States fully utilizes all of its resources in the most efficient manner possible, it can produce a

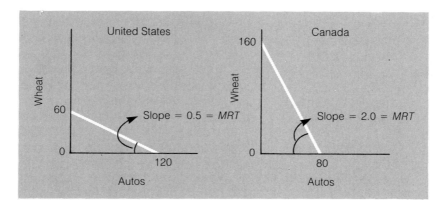

Figure 2.2   Transformation curves—constant opportunity costs.

maximum of 60 bushels of wheat or 120 autos or any combination in between along its transformation curve. Canada, on the other hand, could produce 160 bushels of wheat or 80 autos or some combination in between, if it used all of its factor inputs in the most efficient possible way. Note in this example the transformation curves for both countries are drawn as straight lines. The reason for this is we are assuming constant cost conditions.

Constant opportunity costs suggest that the relative cost of one product in terms of the other will remain the same, no matter where a nation chooses to locate on its transformation curve. In Figure 2.2, we can see that for the United States, the relative cost of each auto produced is ½ bushel of wheat. For Canada, the relative cost of producing each additional auto is 2 bushels of wheat.

There are two explanations of constant costs. First, the factors of production are perfect substitutes for each other. Second, all units of a given factor are of the same quality. As a country transfers resources from the production of wheat into the production of autos, or vice versa, the country will not have to resort to resources that are less well suited for the production of the commodity. Therefore, the country must sacrifice exactly the same amount of wheat for each additional auto produced, regardless of how many autos it is already producing.

The constant cost concept can also be illus-trated in terms of a supply curve. Remember that the law of supply reasons that a producer's supply price rises as he offers more of the commodity for sale on the market. This means that the supply curve slopes upward from the quantity axis. The factor underlying the law of supply is the tendency for marginal production costs to increase as the level of output rises. But what if a producer faces constant cost conditions? What then would be the shape of the supply curve?

Based on the transformation curves in Figure 2.2, Figure 2.3 illustrates the supply curves of autos and wheat for the United States and Canada. Note that on the vertical axes the prices of the commodities are measured in opportunity cost terms rather than monetary terms. The transformation curves of the two countries suggest that the relative price of producing each extra auto is ½ bushel of wheat for the United States, whereas it is 2 bushels of wheat for Canada. Since constant cost conditions imply that these prices (costs) do not change with the level of production, the supply curves of autos are drawn as horizontal lines at the respective supply prices. Wheat production provides similar results. The production conditions are such that the relative price of producing an extra bushel of wheat is 2 autos for the United States and ½ auto for Canada. Given constant cost conditions, the supply curves are drawn horizontally at the respective supply prices.

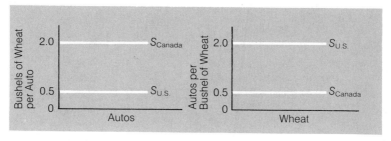

Figure 2.3   Supply curves—constant opportunity costs.

The Basis for Trade and Direction of Trade

In autarky (the absence of trade), a country's transformation curve represents the possible points along which its production as well as consumption will occur. This is because a country can consume only that combination of goods that it can produce. Based on Figure 2.2, Figure 2.4 depicts the output possibilities of the United States and Canada under constant cost conditions.

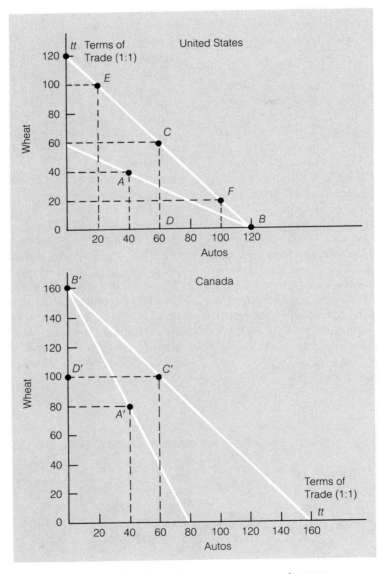

Figure 2.4   Trading under constant opportunity costs.

Assume that the United States prefers to produce and consume at point *A* on its transformation curve, with 40 autos and 40 bushels of wheat. Assume also that Canada produces and consumes at point *A'* on its transformation curve, with 40 autos and 80 bushels of wheat.

The slopes of the two countries' linear transformation curves give the relative cost of one product in terms of the other. The relative cost of producing an additional auto is only ½ bushel of wheat for the United States but is 2 bushels of wheat for Canada. According to the principle of comparative advantage, this situation provides a basis for mutually favorable trade owing to the differences in the countries' relative costs. As for the direction of trade, we find the United States specializing in and exporting autos and Canada specializing in and exporting wheat.

Production Gains from Trade

The law of comparative advantage asserts that with trade each country will find it favorable to specialize in the production of the commodity of its comparative advantage and will trade part of this for the commodity of its comparative disadvantage. In Figure 2.4, the United States moves from production point *A* to production point *B*, totally specializing in auto production. Canada totally specializes in wheat production by moving

from production point *A'* to production point *B'*. Taking advantage of specialization and the international division of labor can result in both production and consumption gains from trade for both countries.

Looking at Figure 2.4, we find that in autarky the United States produces 40 autos and 40 bushels of wheat. But with free trade and specialization, the United States produces 120 autos and no wheat. As for Canada, its production point in autarky is at 40 autos and 80 bushels of wheat, whereas its production point under complete specialization is at 160 bushels of wheat and no autos. Combining these results, we find that both nations together have experienced a net production gain of 40 autos and 40 bushels of wheat under conditions of complete specialization. These results are summarized in Table 2.1.

Consumption Gains from Trade

In autarky the consumption alternatives of the United States and Canada are limited to points along their domestic transformation curves. The exact consumption point for each nation will be determined by the tastes and preferences in each country. But with specialization and free trade, two nations can achieve posttrade consumption points outside their domestic transformation curves. Clearly this would be a more desirable consumption point than that point attainable without trade.

Table 2.1   Production Gains from Trade

	Before Specialization		After Specialization		Net Gain (Loss)	
	Autos	Wheat	Autos	Wheat	Autos	Wheat
United States	40	40	120	0	80	−40
Canada	40	80	0	160	−40	80
World	80	120	120	160	40	40

Under free trade conditions, both countries exchange their export products to attain consumption points outside their domestic transformation curves. The set of posttrade consumption points that a nation can achieve is determined by the rate at which its export is traded for the other country's export. This rate is referred to as the *terms of trade*. The terms of trade defines the relative prices at which two products are traded in the marketplace.

Under constant cost conditions, the slope of the transformation curve defines the domestic rate of transformation. But the domestic rate of transformation represents the relative prices at which two commodities can be exchanged at home. The slope of the linear transformation curve therefore defines the domestic terms of trade for two commodities. For a country to consume at some point outside its transformation curve, it must be able to trade its export good internationally at a more favorable terms of trade than can be attained at home.

Assume that the United States and Canada are able to agree to a terms-of-trade ratio that permits both trading partners to consume at some point outside their respective transformation curves (Figure 2.4). Suppose that the terms of trade agreed upon are at a 1:1 ratio, whereby 1 auto is exchanged for 1 bushel of wheat. Based on these conditions, let line *tt* represent the international terms of trade for both countries (note that the terms-of-trade line is drawn with a slope having an absolute value of one).

Suppose now that the United States decides to export, say, 60 autos to Canada. Starting at postspecialization production point *B*, the United States will slide along its international terms-of-trade line until point *C* is reached. At point *C*, 60 autos will have been exchanged for 60 bushels of wheat, at the terms-of-trade ratio of 1:1. Point *C* then represents the U.S. posttrade consumption point. Compared with autarky consumption point *A*, point *C* results in a net consumption gain for the United States of 20 autos and 20 bushels of wheat. The triangle *BCD* showing the U.S. exports (along the horizontal axis), imports (along the vertical axis), and terms of trade (the slope) is referred to as the *trade triangle*.

Does this trading situation provide favorable results for Canada? Starting at postspecialization production point *B'*, Canada can import 60 autos from the United States by giving up 60 bushels of wheat. Canada would slide along its international terms-of-trade line until it reached point *C'*. Clearly this is a more favorable consumption point than autarky point *A'*. With free trade Canada experiences a net consumption gain of 20 autos and 20 bushels of wheat. Canada's trade triangle is denoted by *B'C'D'*. Note that in our two-country model the trade triangles of the United States and Canada are identical. Table 2.2 summarizes the consumption gains from trade for each country and the world as a whole.

Table 2.2   Consumption Gains from Trade

	Before Trade		After Trade		Net Gain (Loss)	
	Autos	Wheat	Autos	Wheat	Autos	Wheat
United States	40	40	60	60	20	20
Canada	40	80	60	100	20	20
World	80	120	120	160	40	40

The Distribution Problem

The preceding example assumed that the terms of trade agreed to by the United States and Canada resulted in both trading partners benefiting from trade. Both countries were able to achieve posttrade consumption points outside their domestic production possibilities curves. However, the distribution of the consumption gains from trade may not always be favorable for both countries. The closer the international terms-of-trade line is located to the U.S. transformation curve, the smaller are the U.S. consumption gains from trade. At the extreme, if the international terms of trade was to coincide with the U.S. domestic rate of transformation, the United States would experience no gains from trade. This is because the U.S. posttrade consumption point would lie along its transformation curve. With trade, the United States could not achieve a higher level of consumption than could be attained in the absence of trade. The same also applies to Canada.

The domestic transformation rates of the United States and Canada clearly represent the limits within which the international terms of trade must fall. But where will the international terms of trade ultimately fall? As we explain in the next chapter, the actual location depends

on the relative bargaining strengths of the two nations.

Complete Specialization

One implication of the foregoing trading example was that the United States totally specialized in auto production, whereas Canada produced only wheat. To see why complete specialization in production occurs under constant cost conditions, consider Figure 2.5. The figure depicts the autarky cost conditions and production points for the United States and Canada based on the trading example. The United States is assumed to have the cost advantage in auto production, whereas Canada is more efficient in the production of wheat.

As the United States increases and Canada reduces the production of autos, both countries' unit production costs remain constant. Since the relative costs never equalize, the United States does not lose its comparative advantage nor does Canada lose its comparative disadvantage. The United States therefore totally specializes in the production of autos. Similarly, as Canada produces more wheat and the United States reduces its wheat production, their production costs remain the same. Canada totally specializes in

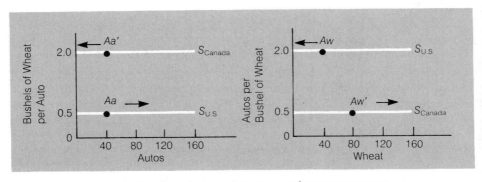

Figure 2.5   Complete specialization under constant costs.

the production of wheat without losing its advantage to the United States.

Trade Restrictions

The preceding analysis suggests that trading nations will achieve the greatest possible gains from trade when they completely specialize in the production of the commodities of their comparative advantage. One factor that limits specialization and the international division of labor is the restrictions imposed by governments on the movement of commodities among nations. By reducing the overall volume of trade, trade restrictions tend to reduce the gains from trade.[7]

Assume that for reasons of national security, the United States establishes restrictions on the amount of oil that can be imported from the OPEC cartel. Rather than importing all of its oil from OPEC, suppose the United States wishes to produce at least some oil itself, even though its production costs exceed those of OPEC. The United States chooses to produce some of the commodity of its comparative disadvantage in return for a greater degree of national security.

Figure 2.6 illustrates this trading situation between the United States and OPEC. Because the United States has the comparative advantage in the production of manufactured goods, it would benefit by specializing in manufactured goods production. The United States thus moves its production location from autarky point *A* to point *B*. By exporting, say, 175 manufactured goods at the international terms of trade *tt*, the United States would import 275 barrels of crude

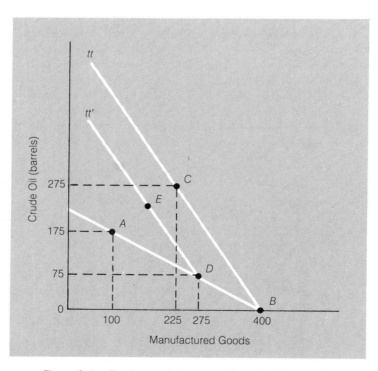

Figure 2.6   Trade restrictions and the gains from trade.

oil. At posttrade consumption point C, the U.S. consumption gains from trade total 125 manufactured goods and 100 barrels of crude oil.

Suppose instead that for national security reasons, the United States wishes to produce some crude oil as well as some manufactured goods. Assume that the United States locates at point D, producing 275 barrels of crude oil and 75 manufactured goods. Given terms of trade tt' (assumed to be the same as terms of trade tt), the United States will achieve a lower posttrade consumption point than would exist under free trade. The U.S. posttrade consumption point will lie along tt', (note that tt' is drawn parallel to tt) at some location, say point E. Clearly point E is inferior to point C.

Trading Under Increasing Cost Conditions

The preceding section illustrated the comparative advantage principle under constant cost conditions. But in the real world, a good's opportunity cost may increase as more of it is produced. The workings of the Ricardian principle of comparative advantage should thus be shown in a slightly modified form.[8]

Increasing Costs

Increasing production costs give rise to a transformation curve that appears concave, viewed from the diagram's origin. In Figure 2.7, with movement along the transformation curve from A to B, the opportunity cost of producing autos becomes larger and larger in terms of wheat sacrificed. Since the real cost of producing autos rises as more autos are produced, the auto supply curve is positively sloped. Auto producers will offer more autos on the market only if they are compensated for their rising costs of produc-

tion. Changes in the quantity supplied and product price are therefore directly related. This is shown in the lower part of Figure 2.7.

Increasing costs mean that the MRT of wheat into autos rises as more autos are produced. Remember that the MRT is measured by the

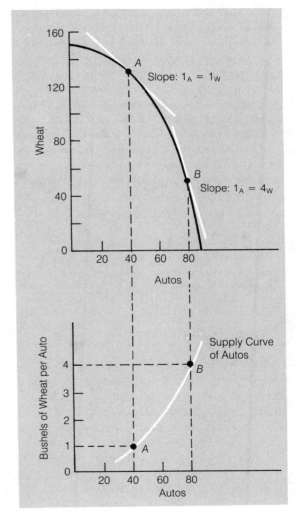

Figure 2.7   Transformation curve and supply curve under increasing cost conditions.

absolute slope of the transformation curve at a given point. With movement from production points A to B, the respective tangent lines become steeper—their slopes increase in absolute value. The MRT of wheat into autos rises, indicating that each additional auto produced requires the sacrifice of increasing amounts of wheat.

Increasing costs represent the usual case in the real world. Looking at the overall economy, increasing costs may result when inputs are imperfect substitutes for each other. As auto production is increased in Figure 2.7, inputs that are less and less adaptable to autos are introduced into that line of production. To produce more autos requires more and more of such resources and thus an increasingly greater sacrifice of wheat.[9]

Under increasing costs, the slope of the concave transformation curve varies as a nation locates at different points on the curve. Since the domestic MRT equals the transformation curve's slope, it also will be different for each point on the curve. In addition to considering the supply factors underlying the transformation curve's slope, one must also account for the role of tastes and preferences, for they will determine the point along the transformation curve at which a country chooses to consume.

Increasing Cost Trading Case

Figure 2.8 gives the transformation curves of the United States and Canada under conditions of increasing costs. Assume that in autarky the United States is located at point A along its transformation curve, producing and consuming 5 autos and 18 bushels of wheat. Assume also that in autarky Canada is located at point A' along its transformation curve, producing and consuming 17 autos and 6 bushels of wheat. For the United States, the relative price of autos for wheat is indicated by the slope of line $t_{U.S.}$, tangent to the transformation curve at point A (that is, 1 auto = 0.33 bushels of wheat). In like

manner, Canada's relative price of autos for wheat is denoted by the slope of line t_C (that is, 1 auto = 3 bushels of wheat). Because line $t_{U.S.}$ is flatter than line t_C, autos are relatively cheaper in the United States and wheat is relatively cheaper in Canada. According to the law of comparative advantage, the United States will export autos and Canada will export wheat.

Both countries will continue to specialize in the production of their export goods until the relative costs of producing the goods equalize. Assume this occurs where both countries' domestic rates of transformation converge at the rate given by line tt. The United States produces more autos until it reaches production point B, where its relative cost of producing autos reaches that of Canada. In like manner, Canada produces more wheat until its relative cost of producing autos moves to the U.S. level. This occurs at production point B'. Line tt is the international terms-of-trade line for both nations (that is, 1 auto = 1 bushel of wheat). The international terms of trade are favorable to both, since tt is steeper than $t_{U.S.}$ and flatter than t_C.

The United States can now choose its posttrade consumption point along tt. Assume that the United States prefers to consume the same number of autos as it did in autarky. It will export 7 autos for 7 bushels of wheat, achieving a posttrade consumption point at C. The U.S. consumption gains from trade are 3 bushels of wheat. The U.S. trade triangle, showing its exports, imports, and terms of trade, is denoted by triangle BCD.

In like manner, Canada can choose to consume at some point along tt. Assuming that Canada holds constant its consumption of wheat, it will export 7 bushels of wheat for 7 autos and wind up at posttrade consumption point C'. Its consumption gains from trade total 3 autos. Canada's trade triangle is depicted by triangle B'C'D'. Note that Canada's trade triangle is identical to that of the United States. Table 2.3 summarizes these results.

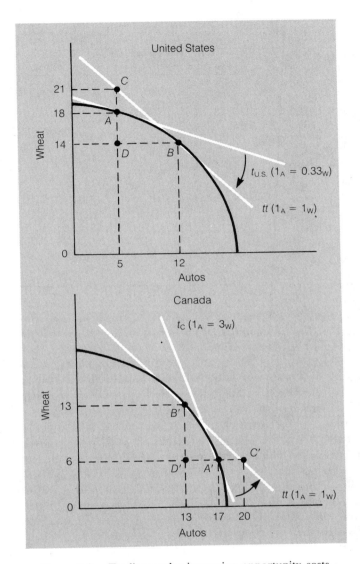

Figure 2.8   Trading under increasing opportunity costs.

Partial Specialization

One feature of the increasing cost models analyzed here is that trade generally leads each country to specialize partially in the production of the good in which it has a comparative advantage. The reason for partial specialization is that increasing costs constitute a mechanism that forces costs in two trading nations to converge. When cost differentials are eliminated, the basis for further specialization ceases to exist.

Figure 2.9 assumes that in autarky the United States has a comparative cost advantage in auto production, whereas Canada is relatively more

Table 2.3   Gains from Trade

	United States		Canada	
	Autos	*Wheat*	*Autos*	*Wheat*
Before trade				
Production	5	18	17	6
Consumption	5	18	17	6
Exports	—	—	—	—
Imports	—	—	—	—
After trade				
Production	12	14	13	13
Consumption	5	21	20	6
Exports	7	—	—	7
Imports	—	7	7	—
Gains from trade	—	3	3	—

efficient at producing wheat. With trade, each country produces more of the commodity of its comparative advantage and less of the commodity of its comparative disadvantage. Given increasing cost conditions, unit costs rise as both nations produce more of their export commodities. Eventually the cost differentials are eliminated, at which point the basis for further specialization ceases to exist.

When the basis for trade is eliminated, there exists a strong probability that both nations will be producing some of each product. This is because costs often rise so rapidly that a country loses its comparative advantage vis-à-vis the other country before it reaches the endpoint of its transformation curve. In the real world of increasing cost conditions, partial specialization is a likely result of free trade.

Summary

1.   Modern trade theory is primarily concerned with determining the basis for trade, the direction of trade, and the gains from trade.

2.   Current explanations of world trade patterns are based on a rich heritage in the history of economic thought. Among the most important forerunners of modern trade theory were the mercantilists Adam Smith and David Ricardo.

3.   To the mercantilists, stocks of precious metals represented the wealth of a nation. The mercantilists contended that the government should adopt trade controls to limit imports and promote exports. One nation could gain from trade only at the expense of its trading partners, since the stock of world wealth is fixed at a given moment in time and because not all nations could simultaneously have a favorable trade balance.

4.   Adam Smith challenged the mercantilist views on trade by arguing that with free trade, international specialization of factor inputs could increase world output, which could be shared by trading nations. All nations could simultaneously enjoy gains from trade. Smith maintained that each nation would find it advantageous to specialize in the production of those goods in which it had an absolute advantage.

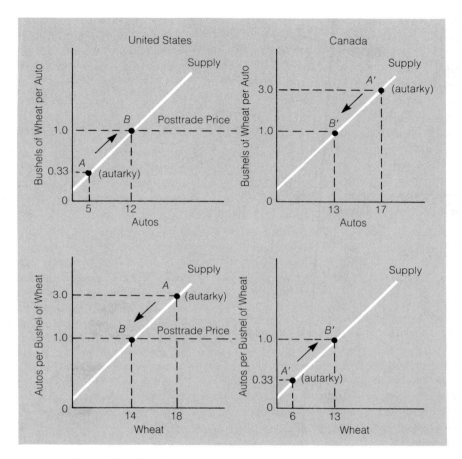

Figure 2.9   Partial specialization: increasing opportunity costs.

5.   David Ricardo argued that mutually gainful trade is possible even if one nation has an absolute disadvantage in the production of both commodities compared with the other nation. The less productive nation should specialize in the production and export of the commodity in which it has a comparative advantage.

6.   Modern trade theory reasons that if in the absence of trade the comparative costs (prices) of two products differ between nations, both nations can benefit from international trade. The gains from trade stem from increased levels of production and consumption brought about by the international division of labor and specialization.

7.   Comparative costs can be illustrated with the transformation curve, also called the production-possibilities curve. This curve indicates the maximum amount of any two products an economy can produce, assuming that all resources are used in their most efficient manner. The slope of the transformation curve provides a measure of the marginal rate of transformation, which indicates the amount of one product that must be sacrificed per unit increase of another product.

8. Under constant cost conditions, the transformation curve is a straight line. Domestic relative prices are exclusively determined by a nation's supply conditions. Complete specialization of a country in the production of a single commodity may occur in the case of constant costs.

9. In the real world, nations tend to experience increasing cost conditions. Transformation curves thus are drawn concave to the diagram's origin. Relative product prices in each country are determined by both supply and demand factors. Complete specialization in production is improbable in the case of increasing costs.

Study Questions

1. Identify the basic questions with which modern trade theory is concerned.

2. How did Adam Smith's views on international trade differ from those of the mercantilists?

3. Develop an arithmetic example that illustrates how a nation could have an absolute disadvantage in the production of two goods while at the same time having a comparative advantage in the production of one of them.

4. Both Adam Smith and David Ricardo contended that the pattern of world trade is determined solely by supply conditions. Explain.

5. How does the comparative cost concept relate to a nation's transformation curve? Illustrate how differently shaped transformation curves give rise to different opportunity costs.

6. What is meant by constant opportunity costs and increasing opportunity costs? Under what conditions will a country experience constant or increasing costs?

7. Why is it that the pretrade production points have a bearing on comparative costs under increasing cost conditions but not under conditions of constant costs?

8. What factors underlie whether specialization in production will be partial or complete on an international basis?

9. The gains from trade are often discussed in terms of production gains and consumption gains. What do these terms mean?

10. What is meant by the term *trade triangle*?

11. With a given level of world resources, international trade may bring about an increase in total world output. Explain.

Notes

1. See E. A. J. Johnson, *Predecessors of Adam Smith* (New York: Prentice-Hall, 1937).

2. David Hume, "Of Money," *Essays* (London: Green and Co., 1912), vol. 1, p. 319. Hume's writings are also available in Eugene Rotwein, *The Economic Writings of David Hume* (Edinburgh: Nelson, 1955).

3. Adam Smith, *The Wealth of Nations* (New York: Modern Library, 1937), pp. 424–426. For a discussion concerning the logical possibility of the absolute advantage concept, see Royall Brandis, "The Myth of Absolute Advantage," *American Economic Review* (March 1967).

4. David Ricardo, *The Principles of Political Economy and Taxation* (London: Cambridge University Press, 1966), chap. 7.

5. See Gottfried Haberler, *The Theory of International Trade* (New York: Macmillan, 1950), chap. 10.

6. A more rigorous treatment of the comparative cost principle is found in H. Robert Heller, *International Trade: Theory and Empirical Evidence* (Englewood Cliffs, N.J.: Prentice-Hall, 1968), chap. 3.

7. See Klaus Friedrich, *International Economics: Concepts and Issues* (New York: McGraw-Hill, 1974), pp. 20–21.

8. A discussion of trade under decreasing cost conditions is found in Miltiades Chacholiades,

"Increasing Returns and the Theory of Comparative Advantage," *Southern Economic Journal,* 77 (1970), pp. 157–162.

9. From the perspective of a single product, increasing costs can be explained by the principle of diminishing marginal productivity. The addition of successive units of labor (variable input) to capital (fixed input) beyond some point will result in decreases in the marginal production of autos that is attributable to each additional unit of labor. Unit production costs therefore rise as more autos are produced.

Salvatore, D. *Theory and Problems of International Economics,* 2nd ed. New York: McGraw-Hill, 1983.

Suggestions for Further Reading

Balassa, B. "An Empirical Demonstration of Classical Comparative Cost Theory." *Review of Economics and Statistics,* August 1963.

Baldwin, R. E., and J. D. Richardson, eds. *International Trade and Finance,* 2nd ed. Boston: Little, Brown, 1981.

Bhagwati, J. *International Trade: Selected Readings.* Cambridge, Mass.: M.I.T. Press, 1981.

Brandis, R. "The Myth of Absolute Advantage." *American Economic Review,* March 1967.

Haberler, G. *The Theory of International Trade.* London: William Hodge, 1936.

Heller, H. R. *International Trade: Theory and Empirical Evidence.* Englewood Cliffs, N.J.: Prentice-Hall, 1973.

Krauss, M. B. *A Geometric Approach to International Trade.* New York: Halsted-Wiley, 1979.

Meade, J. E. *A Geometry of International Trade.* London: Allen & Unwin, 1951.

Meier, G. "The Theory of Comparative Cost Reconsidered." *Oxford Economic Papers,* June 1949.

Ohlin, B. *International and Interregional Trade.* Cambridge, Mass.: Harvard Economic Studies, 1933; rev. ed., 1967.

3

MODERN TRADE THEORY: DEMAND AND THE TERMS OF TRADE

This chapter examines how *demand* affects the basis for trade, the composition of the products consumed, and the gains from trade. The indifference curve technique is introduced to analyze these topics. Analysis then turns to the role that demand plays in establishing the equilibrium terms of trade. The chapter also discusses how the terms of trade are empirically measured. The chapter appendix uses offer curve analysis to illustrate the terms-of-trade determination.

Indifference Curves

Modern trade theory contends that the pattern of world trade is governed by international differences in supply conditions and demand conditions. Therefore, the role of demand must be developed and introduced into the trade model. Economic theory reasons that an individual's demand curve is based on several underlying determinants, among them (1) the level of disposable income and (2) personal tastes and preferences. Discussion of income as a determinant of demand is undertaken in Chapter 4. Here we consider the role of personal tastes and preferences in demand analysis.

The role of tastes and preferences can be illustrated graphically by a consumer's indifference curve.[1] An *indifference curve* depicts the various combinations of two commodities that are equally preferred in the eyes of the consumer—that is, yield the same level of satisfaction. The term *indifference curve* stems from the idea that the consumer is indifferent among the many possible commodity combinations providing him with identical amounts of satisfaction. Figure 3.1 illustrates a consumer's indifference curve. The consumer is just as happy consuming, say, 6 bushels of wheat and 1 auto at point *A* as he is consuming 3 bushels of wheat and 2 autos at point *B*. All combination points along an indifference curve are equally desirable, since they yield the same level of satisfaction. Besides these characteristics, indifference curves have several other features.

Inspection of Figure 3.1 reveals that an indifference curve tends to be negatively sloped—that is, sloped downward to the right. This is assured by the assumption that a consumer always desires more of a commodity than less of it. Because each combination of goods along an indifference curve provides the same level of satisfaction, it follows that should a consumer increase his auto holdings, he must decrease his wheat intake by some amount if the initial level of satisfaction is to be maintained. If he did not

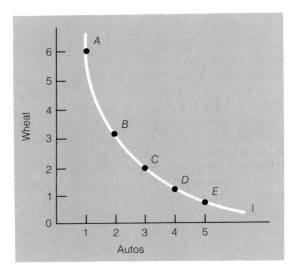

Figure 3.1   A consumer's indifference curve.

$$MRS = \frac{\Delta\ Wheat}{\Delta\ Autos}.$$

The marginal rate of substitution is equal to an indifference curve's absolute slope. Moving downward along the indifference curve, autos become relatively plentiful while wheat becomes relatively scarce. With less wheat and more autos, the less valuable each additional auto becomes to the consumer. For each additional auto consumed, the consumer is willing to sacrifice smaller amounts of wheat. This means that the marginal rate of substitution of autos for wheat decreases as more autos are consumed—hence, the convex nature of an indifference curve.

An indifference curve shows the various combinations of two commodities that yield equal amounts of satisfaction to a consumer. An *indifference map* is a graph that illustrates an entire set of indifference curves. Figure 3.2 illustrates a consumer's indifference map. Although the figure contains only three indifference curves, an infinite number can be drawn. Note that each higher indifference curve denotes a greater amount of satisfaction. This is because any point

decrease his holdings of wheat, the new market basket would include more of the combined amount of both commodities, resulting in a higher level of satisfaction. Since changes in the consumption of one commodity are inversely related to changes in the amount consumed of another for a given level of satisfaction to be maintained, it follows that an indifference curve slopes downward to the right.

Indifference curves are also generally convex (bowed in) to the diagram's origin. The negative slope of an indifference curve indicates that, for any given level of satisfaction, some amount of one good must be sacrificed if more of another is to be acquired. The rate at which the substitution occurs is called the *marginal rate of substitution* (MRS). In terms of Figure 3.1, the marginal rate of substitution indicates the extent to which a consumer is willing to substitute autos for wheat (or vice versa), while maintaining a given level of satisfaction. The marginal rate of substitution of autos for wheat is algebraically expressed as:

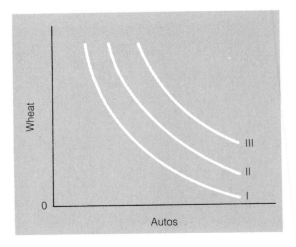

Figure 3.2   A consumer's indifference map.

on a higher indifference curve suggests at least the same amount of one commodity plus more of another commodity.

Indifference Curves and International Trade

Having developed an indifference curve for a single person, can we assume that the preferences of all consumers in the entire nation could be added up and summarized by a *community indifference curve*? Strictly speaking, the answer is no. This is because it is impossible to make interpersonal comparisons of satisfaction. For example, person A may desire a lot of coffee and little sugar, whereas person B prefers the opposite. The dissimilar nature of individuals' indifference curves results in their being noncomparable. In spite of these theoretical problems, a community indifference curve is nevertheless useful as a pedagogical device that depicts the role of consumer preferences in international trade.[2] Community indifference curves can be used to analyze several important topics that have not yet been discussed.

Autarky Equilibrium

In this section, we derive the optimal level of production and consumption for a nation. The central question that will be addressed is, at *what point on its transformation curve will a country choose to locate in the absence of trade?*

Assuming that a nation wishes to maximize satisfaction, it will attempt to consume some combination of goods on the highest indifference curve that it can reach. But an indifference curve only tells what a consumer would "like to do." Given the availability and quality of resources and the level of technology, there is a constraint on how many goods will actually be available to consume. For a nation, this production constraint is represented by its transformation curve. A nation in autarky will maximize satisfaction if it can reach the highest attainable indifference curve, given the production constraint of its transformation curve. Since there are an infinite number of indifference curves in an indifference map, this will occur when the transformation curve is tangent to an indifference curve.

Figure 3.3 illustrates the transformation curve and indifference map for a single country. In autarky, the country will maximize satisfaction if it produces and consumes at point E, where indifference curve II is tangent to its transformation curve. Any point on a higher indifference curve, say F, is unattainable since it is beyond the economy's capacity to produce. Any point on a lower indifference curve, such as G or H, does not represent maximum satisfaction. This is because a higher indifference curve can be reached with the existing transformation curve. Point E then represents the autarky equilibrium location of production and consumption.

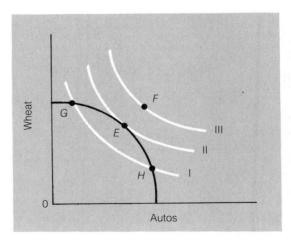

Figure 3.3   Indifference curves and international trade.

A Restatement: Basis for Trade, Gains from Trade

In this section, we develop a trade example to restate the basis for trade and the gains from trade issues. Figure 3.4 depicts the trading position of the United States. Assuming that the United States attempts to maximize satisfaction, its autarky location of production and consumption will be at point A, where the U.S. transformation curve is just tangent to indifference curve I. At point A, the U.S. relative price ratio is denoted by line $t_{U.S.}$.

Suppose that the United States has a comparative advantage vis-à-vis Canada in the production of autos. The United States will find it advantageous to specialize in auto production

until the two countries' relative prices of autos equalize. Suppose this occurs at production point B, where the U.S. price rises to Canada's price, depicted by line tt. Also suppose that line tt becomes the international terms-of-trade line. Starting at production point B, the United States will export autos and import wheat, trading along line tt. The immediate problem the United States faces is to determine the level of trade that will maximize its welfare.

Suppose that the United States exchanges 6 autos for 50 bushels of wheat at terms of trade tt. This would shift the United States from production point B to posttrade consumption point D. But the United States would be no better off with trade than it was in autarky. This is because in both cases the consumption points are located

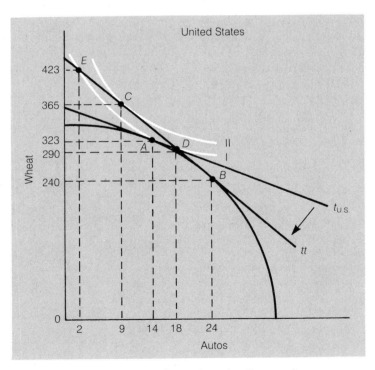

Figure 3.4   Basis for trade, gains from trade.

along indifference curve I. Trade volume 6 autos and 50 bushels of wheat thus represents the minimum acceptable volume of trade for the United States. Any smaller volume would force the United States to locate on a lower indifference curve.

Suppose instead that the United States decides to trade 22 autos for 183 bushels of wheat. The United States would move from production point B to posttrade consumption point E. With trade, the United States would again locate on indifference curve I, resulting in no gains from trade. From the U.S. viewpoint, trade volume 22 autos and 183 bushels of wheat therefore represent the maximum acceptable volume of trade. Any greater volume would find the United States moving to a lower indifference curve.

Trading along terms of trade line tt, the United States can achieve maximum welfare if it exports 15 autos and imports 125 bushels of wheat. The U.S. posttrade consumption location would be at point C along indifference curve II, the highest attainable level of satisfaction. Comparing point A and point C reveals that with trade the United States consumes more wheat, but fewer autos, than it does in the absence of trade. Yet point C is clearly a preferable consumption location. This is because under indifference curve analysis, the gains from trade are measured in terms of total satisfaction rather than in the number of goods consumed.

The Classical Explanation of the Terms of Trade

A major shortcoming of the Ricardian principle of comparative advantage stemmed from its inability to explain fully the distribution of the gains from trade among trading partners.[3] The best explanation of the gains from trade that Ricardo provided was to describe only the outer limits within which the equilibrium terms of trade would fall. Because the Ricardian theory did not recognize the role that demand plays in setting market prices, it could not project how national bargaining strengths could achieve an exact international terms of trade.

To appreciate the limitations that Ricardian theory faced in explaining the distribution of the gains from trade, consider Figure 3.5, which depicts the domestic cost conditions of the United States and Canada. Note that we have translated the domestic cost ratio, given by the negatively sloped transformation curve, into a positively sloped price ratio line. In both diagrams, the relative costs or prices of autos for wheat are the same. As seen in the figure, the relative price of each auto produced equals ½ bushel of wheat for the United States. For Canada the relative price of producing each auto is 2 bushels of wheat. The United States therefore has the comparative advantage in autos, whereas Canada has the comparative advantage in wheat. Figure 3.6 combines the results of Figure 3.5 and illustrates both the U.S. and Canadian domestic price ratios for autos and wheat.

According to Ricardo, the domestic price ratios set the outer limits for the equilibrium terms of trade. If the United States is to export autos, it would not be willing to accept any terms of trade less than a ratio of ½:1, indicated by its domestic price line. Otherwise, the U.S. posttrade consumption point would lie inside its domestic transformation curve. The United States would clearly be better off without trade than with trade. The U.S. domestic price line therefore becomes its no-trade boundary. Similarly, Canada would require a minimum of 1 auto for every 2 bushels of wheat exported, as indicated by its domestic price line. Any terms of trade less than this rate would be totally unacceptable to Canada. The no-trade boundary line for Canada is thus defined by its domestic price ratio line.

Because the Ricardian theory relied only on supply analysis, it could only define the outer limits within which the equilibrium terms of trade must fall. It was recognized that for

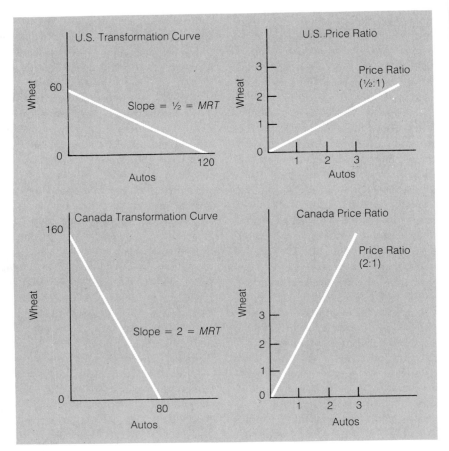

Figure 3.5   Relative prices of autos and wheat: constant cost conditions.

international trade to exist, a nation would have to achieve a posttrade consumption location at least equivalent to its autarky point along its domestic transformation curve. Any acceptable international terms of trade would have to be more favorable than, or equal to, the rate defined by the domestic price line. The region of mutually beneficial trade is thus bounded by the cost ratios of the two countries. But where will the equilibrium terms of trade actually lie? It was not until John Stuart Mill developed his theory of reciprocal demand that this question could be answered.

Law of Reciprocal Demand

By bringing into the picture the relative strengths of the trading partners' demands, John Stuart Mill (1806–1873) was able to formulate the theory of reciprocal demand.[4] According to Mill, if we know the domestic demands expressed by both trading partners for both products, the exact equilibrium terms of trade can be defined. The *theory of reciprocal demand* suggests that the actual price at which trade takes place depends on the trading partners' interacting demands.

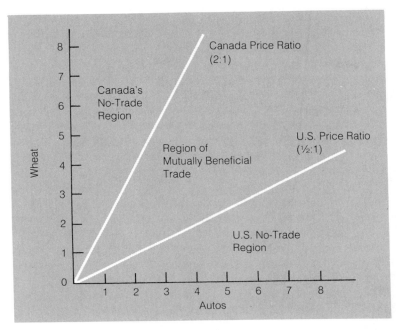

Figure 3.6   Equilibrium terms-of-trade limits.

In Figure 3.7 suppose Canada, which has a comparative advantage in the production of wheat, expresses an enormous demand for autos, both domestically produced and imported. It will be willing to pay a high price in terms of wheat for those autos demanded. The United States would therefore achieve most of the gains from trade, since its terms of trade would improve. Starting at point *A* in the figure, an improving U.S. terms of trade suggests that a given quantity of auto exports buys larger amounts of wheat imports. The United States would achieve a post-trade consumption point farther outside its transformation curve. At the extreme, the Canadian auto demand could be so enormous that the terms of trade would settle along its domestic price ratio line. The United States then would enjoy all of the gains from trade.

Starting at point *A* in Figure 3.7, suppose the United States expresses an enormous de-mand for wheat, both domestically produced and imported. Since the price the United States is willing to pay for wheat would rise, Canada would enjoy most of the gains from trade. As Figure 3.7 illustrates, an improving Canadian terms of trade suggests that a given amount of wheat exports trades for increasing amounts of auto imports. The terms of trade could at the extreme settle at the U.S. domestic price ratio, at which all of the gains from trade would accrue to Canada.

Mill's theory reasons that the equilibrium terms of trade depends on the Canadian demand for autos and wheat, as well as on the U.S. demand for the same products. The stronger the Canadian demand for autos relative to the U.S. demand for wheat, the closer the terms of trade will settle to the Canadian domestic price ratio. The reverse is equally true. The reciprocal de-mand theory thus contends that the equilibrium

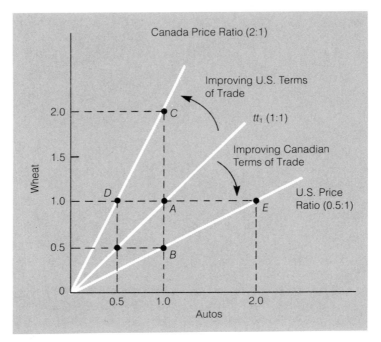

Figure 3.7   Movements in the terms of trade.

terms of trade depends on the relative strength of each country's demand for the other country's product.

Although Mill's theory of reciprocal demand provides a useful explanation of the terms of trade, it explains only a portion of international trade. The reciprocal demand theory applies only when both countries are of equal economic size so that the demand of each country has a noticeable effect on market prices. Given two countries of unequal economic size, it is possible that the relative demand strength of the smaller country will be dwarfed by that of the larger country. In this case, the domestic price ratio of the larger country will prevail. Assuming the absence of monopoly or monopsony elements working in the markets, the small country can export as much of the com-modity as it desires, enjoying large gains from trade.

Consider trade in crude oil and autos between Venezuela and the United States before the rise of the OPEC oil cartel. Venezuela as a small nation accounted for only very small shares of the U.S.–Venezuelan market, whereas the U.S. market shares were overwhelmingly large. Since the Venezuelan consumers and producers had no influence on market price levels, they were in effect price takers. In trading with the United States, no matter what was the Venezuelan demand for crude oil and autos, it was not strong enough to affect U.S. price levels. As a result, Venezuela traded according to the U.S. domestic price ratio, buying and selling autos and crude oil at the price levels existing within the United States.

Measuring the Terms of Trade

The gains a country enjoys from its foreign trade consist of a larger income owing to a wider range of goods available to consumers and the favorable influence trade has on productivity levels. Estimating these gains at a particular point in time would be extremely difficult, for it would require knowledge of what a country's imports would have cost had it produced them itself instead of purchasing them from a less expensive foreign source. Instead, economists have attempted to measure the direction of these gains over time. This is accomplished by calculating changes in the terms of trade.

The commodity terms of trade (also referred to as the barter terms of trade) is the most frequently used measure of the direction of trade gains. It measures the relationship between the prices a country gets for its exports and the prices it pays for its imports over a given time period. This is calculated by dividing the change in a country's export price index by the change in its import price index between two points in time, multiplied by 100 to express the terms of trade in percentages:

$$\text{Terms of Trade} = \frac{\text{Export Price Index}}{\text{Import Price Index}} \times 100.$$

An improvement in a country's terms of trade requires that the price of its exports have risen relative to the prices of its imports over the given time period. A smaller number of export goods sold abroad is required to obtain a given number of imports. On the other hand, a deterioration in a country's terms of trade is due to a rise in its import prices relative to its export prices over the time period. The purchase of a given number of imports would require the sacrifice of a greater number of exports.

Table 3.1 gives the commodity terms of trade for selected countries. With 1980 as the base year (equal to 100), the table shows that by 1983 the U.S. index of export prices had risen to 112, an increase of 12 percent. During the same period, the index of U.S. import prices rose by 1 percent to a level of 101. Using the terms-of-trade formula just described, we find that the U.S. terms of trade improved by 11 percent ($\frac{112}{101} \times 100 = 111$) over the 1980–1983 period. This means that to purchase a given quantity of imports, the United States had to sacrifice 11 percent fewer exports, or that for a given number of exports the United States could obtain 11 percent more imports.

Table 3.2 gives historical movements in the commodity terms of trade for the industrial countries, oil-exporting countries, and nonoil

Table 3.1 Commodity Terms of Trade (1980 = 100)

Country	1983* Export Price Index	1983* Import Price Index	Terms of Trade
United States	112	101	111
Austria	85	86	99
West Germany	86	85	101
Japan	100	95	105
United Kingdom	80	84	95

Source: International Monetary Fund, *IMF Financial Statistics*, June 1983, pp. 56–57.
*First quarter.

Table 3.2   Movements in the Commodity Terms
of Trade (1975 = 100)

Year	Industrial Countries	Oil-Exporting Countries	Nonoil Developing Countries
1955	98.8		121.6
1960	106.2	33.5	109.0
1965	109.0	32.1	109.8
1970	111.5	29.9	116.0
1973	110.6	40.4	116.3
1974	97.7	103.9	110.8
1979	98.0	117.3	105.9
1980	89.8	171.7	95.5
1981	88.5	199.3	90.3

Source: International Monetary Fund, *International Financial Statistics: Supplement on Trade Statistics*, no. 4, 1982, pp. 2–3. See also pp. 158–163.

developing countries. The real-world significance of changes in the terms of trade is especially apparent when considering the experience of the oil-exporting countries (Chapter 8 discusses the terms-of-trade issue for the nonoil developing nations).

Throughout the 1960s, the terms of trade decreased marginally each year for the oil-exporting countries as oil export prices stagnated, whereas import prices rose by less than 2 percent a year. From 1970 to 1973, oil exporters' terms of trade improved, largely owing to moderate increases in petroleum prices. From 1973 to 1974, the oil-exporting countries dramatically increased the price of oil from $3.60 to $11.45 per barrel, leading to a 150 percent improvement in their terms of trade. In effect, these countries realized a 150 percent increase in the amount of imports received for each barrel of oil that was exported. The standard of living of the oil-exporting countries improved at the expense of the oil-importing countries. Another dramatic change in the terms of trade occurred in 1979–1980, when oil prices leaped from $17 to $29 per barrel.

Although changes in the commodity terms of trade indicate the direction of movement of the gains from trade, their implications must be interpreted with caution. Suppose there occurs an increase in the foreign demand for American exports, leading to higher prices and revenues for American exporters. In this case, an improving terms of trade implies that the U.S. gains from trade have increased. However, suppose the cause of the rises in export prices and terms of trade is falling productivity of American workers. If this results in reduced export sales and less revenue earned via exports, we could hardly say the U.S. welfare has improved.[5] Despite its limitations, commodity terms of trade is a useful concept. Over a long period, it illustrates how a country's share of the world gains from trade has changed and gives a rough measure of the fortune of a nation in the world market.[6]

APPENDIX: Offer Curves

The theory of reciprocal demand did consider the significance of demand's influence on the terms of trade. But this theory was somewhat vague and generalized. It was Alfred Marshall who formally demonstrated the usefulness of offer curves as a graphic method of illustrating how the interaction of supply and demand determines the terms of trade.[7]

An offer curve depicts the various amounts of two commodities that a country wishes to trade, given different price ratios. For each price, the offer curve shows how much of one commodity a nation is willing to trade for certain amounts of the other commodity. An offer curve can be thought of as both a supply curve and a demand curve. An offer curve is a supply curve in the sense that it shows the amounts of an export product that will be offered for sale at various terms of trade. Reflecting domestic supply factors—technology, productivity, resource endowments—an offer curve shows that more of an export will be supplied on the market as its relative price increases. This is especially plausible if it is assumed that the nation produces under increasing cost conditions.[8]

In Figure 3.8, as the U.S. terms of trade improve, the United States finds that a given amount of autos trades for larger quantities of the import good. This results in the United States being willing to offer more autos for sale. Similarly, improving terms of trade for Canada results in its being willing to offer additional amounts of its export product for sale.

As a demand curve, an offer curve shows the quantities of imports that will be demanded at various terms of trade. Reflecting domestic taste and preference conditions, the offer curve concept shows that more of the import product will be demanded as its relative price falls. In Figure 3.8, we see that as the terms of trade improve for the United States, the relative price of its import good falls. Because it takes more wheat to purchase a given amount of auto exports, it requires fewer autos to purchase a given quantity of wheat imports—hence the fall in wheat's relative price. The United States moves upward along its

offer curve, demanding larger amounts of wheat. The reverse holds equally true for Canada.

The purpose of offer curve analysis is to determine the relative prices at which trade actually takes place—that is, the *equilibrium terms of trade*. By bringing together the supply characteristics embodied in an economy's transformation curve and the demand preferences depicted in an indifference curve, offer curve analysis exhibits the condition of *general market equilibrium*.

If the existing terms of trade is to be the equilibrium terms of trade, the amount of a commodity that a country wants to export must match the amount demanded as imports by another country. Referring to Figure 3.9, suppose the offer curves of the United States and Canada are denoted as $U.S._0$ and $Canada_0$, respectively. Point E represents the market equilibrium for the United States and Canada. At terms of trade tt_0, the quantity of cotton the United States is willing to export, 11 bales, equals the quantity of natural gas demanded by Canada, 11 units. In like manner, Canada's natural gas exports just match U.S. natural gas imports.

Figure 3.9 also illustrates a case of market disequilibrium. At terms of trade tt_1, the amount

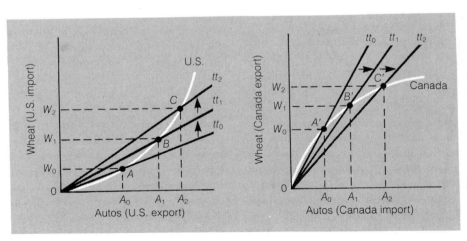

Figure 3.8   Offer curve: demand and supply interpretations.

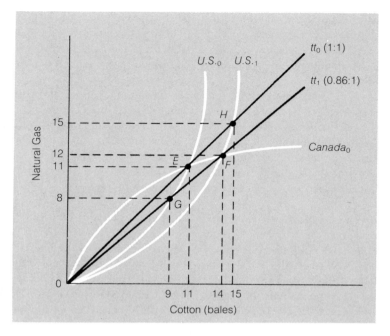

Figure 3.9   Offer curves and the terms of trade.

of cotton that the United States is willing to supply, 9 bales, falls short of the amount of cotton demanded by Canada, 14 bushels. A shortage of cotton thus exists. At terms of trade tt_1, the amount of natural gas that Canada is willing to supply, 12 units, exceeds the amount demanded by the United States, 8 units. The market supply of natural gas is in surplus. The relative price of cotton will rise and the relative price of natural gas will fall until all shortages and surpluses are eliminated. At equilibrium point E, the international supply matches the international demand for both commodities.

Recall that the shape and location of a country's offer curve reflect its domestic supply and demand conditions. Changes in either of these factors will induce shifts in the offer curve as well as changes in the terms of trade and volume of trade. In general, *any occurrence that leads to an increased domestic demand for import products, an increased domestic supply of export products, or a decreased domestic supply of import-competing products will result in a decline in the country's terms of trade but a rise in its volume of trade.* The opposite holds equally true.

Referring to Figure 3.9, let the offer curves of the United States and Canada be given by $U.S._0$ and $Canada_0$. Market equilibrium exists at point E, the terms of trade being one bale of cotton equal to one unit of natural gas. Suppose the United States experiences a large increase in demand for natural gas, its import good, owing to a rise in domestic income. Since the United States has a greater desire for natural gas, it would be willing to offer Canada more cotton for a given amount of natural gas. The U.S. offer curve thus shifts outward from $U.S._0$ to $U.S._1$. At the original terms of trade, tt_0, there now exists an excess demand for natural gas, 4 units, and an excess supply of cotton, 4 bales. The terms of trade therefore moves from tt_0 to tt_1, and market equilibrium is restored at point F. The United States finds that its terms of trade has deteriorated, since a bale of cotton will now trade for only 0.86 units of natural gas (that is, $\frac{12}{14} = 0.86$). However, the volume of U.S. trade with Canada has risen by three bales of cotton and one unit of natural gas.

Starting again at equilibrium point E in Figure 3.9, suppose the United States faces an increase in the supply of cotton, owing to improved farming techniques. With domestic demand remaining constant, efforts to increase exports result in an outward shift of the U.S. offer curve from $U.S._0$ to $U.S._1$. This forces the price of cotton downward. At the new equilibrium point F, the U.S. terms of trade has deteriorated, although the volume of trade has risen due to increased export activity.

Finally, suppose that dwindling reserves lead to decreases in the U.S. supply of natural gas, its import-competing good. The resulting scarcity would cause the United States to import greater quantities of natural gas. Starting at equilibrium point E in Figure 3.9, the U.S. offer curve shifts outward to $U.S._1$. At the new equilibrium point F, the volume of trade has risen as the United States uses more of its cotton to buy additional Canadian natural gas. But the U.S. terms of trade has deteriorated, owing to the upward pressure on Canadian natural gas prices caused by rising U.S. demand.

Summary

1. Demand as well as supply conditions determine the basis for trade and direction of trade. Demand also helps establish the international terms of trade—that is, the relative prices at which commodities are exchanged between nations.

2. A community indifference curve depicts a nation's tastes or preferences. Community indifference curves illustrate the various combinations of two commodities that yield equal satisfaction to a nation. A higher indifference curve indicates more satisfaction. Community indifference curves are analogous to an individual's indifference curve. The slope of a community indifference curve at any point indicates the marginal rate of substitution between two goods in consumption. This shows the amount of one good a nation is willing to sacrifice in order to gain an additional unit of another good, while still remaining on the same indifference curve.

3. The introduction of community indifference curves into the trade model permits a restatement of the basis for trade and the gains from trade.

4. In the absence of trade, a nation achieves equilibrium when its community indifference curve is tangent to its transformation curve. The domestic relative commodity price is denoted by the common slope of these two curves at their point of tangency. When the relative commodity prices of two nations differ, a basis for mutually beneficial trade exists.

5. A nation will benefit from trade when it is able to reach a higher indifference curve (level of satisfaction) than could be achieved without trade. Gains from trade will be maximized when a nation's posttrade consumption point is located where the international terms-of-trade line is tangent to a community indifference curve.

6. Because Ricardian trade theory relied solely on supply analysis, it was not able to determine precisely the equilibrium terms of trade. The solution was first provided by John Stuart Mill in his law of reciprocal demand. This law suggested that before the equilibrium terms of trade can be established, it is necessary to know both countries' demands for both products.

7. The commodity terms of trade is often used to measure the direction of trade gains. It indicates the relationship between the prices a country gets for its exports and the prices it pays for its imports, over a given time period.

Study Questions

1. What advantages are provided by introducing community indifference curves into the trade model?

2. What is the difference between the marginal rate of transformation and the marginal rate of substitution?

3. Even though the production conditions of two nations are identical, gainful trade may still occur if demand conditions are dissimilar. Demonstrate this by using community indifference curves.

4. Why is it that the gains from trade could not be determined precisely under the Ricardian trade model?

5. What is meant by the law of reciprocal demand? How does it provide a meaningful explanation of the international terms of trade?

6. How is the international terms of trade influenced by changing supply and demand conditions?

7. Why is it that in the absence of trade, the cost ratios of two countries provide limits to the equilibrium terms of trade?

8. How does the commodity terms of trade concept attempt to measure the direction of trade gains?

9. What problems do we encounter when attempting to interpret the commodity terms of trade?

10. An offer curve can be interpreted from the perspectives of supply and demand. Explain.

11. What factors underlie the shape and location of a country's offer curve?

12. How does an offer curve illustrate what is meant by the equilibrium terms of trade?

Notes

1. A concise treatment of indifference curves can be found in Richard H. Leftwich, *The Price System and Resource Allocation*, 6th ed. (Hinsdale, Ill.: Dryden Press, 1973), chap. 5.

2. An introduction of community indifference curves into international trade theory can be found in Wassily W. Leontief, "The Use of Indifference Curves in the Analysis of Foreign Trade," *Quarterly Journal of Economics*, 47 (May 1933). For the technique of drawing a community indifference curve see Paul A. Samuelson, "Social Indifference Curves," *Quarterly Journal of Economics*, 70 (February 1956), pp. 1–22.

3. See Gottfried Haberler, *The Theory of International Trade* (London: William Hodge, 1936), chaps. 9–11.

4. John Stuart Mill, *Principles of Political Economy* (New York: Longmans, Green, 1921), pp. 584-585.

5. Other difficulties encountered when interpreting the commodity terms of trade include: (1) allowing for changes in product quality and for new products; (2) determining methods of valuing exports and imports; (3) determining methods to weight the products included in the price indices.

6. Other terms of trade measures include the *income terms of trade*, the *single factorial terms of trade*, and the *double factorial terms of trade*. A fuller discussion of terms-of-trade measurement can be found in J. Viner, *Studies in the Theory of International Trade* (New York: Harper & Brothers, 1937). See also G. Meier, *The International Economics of Development* (New York: Harper & Row, 1968), chap. 3.

7. See Alfred Marshall, *Money, Credit and Commerce* (London, Macmillan, 1923). See also James Meade, *A Geometry of International Trade* (London: Allen & Unwin, 1952), chaps. 2–3.

8. A nation's offer curve is derived from its community indifference curve, transformation curve, and the various relative commodity

prices at which trade may occur. See Imanuel Wexler, *Fundamentals of International Economics* (New York: Random House, 1972), pp. 94-100.

Mill, J. S. *Principles of Political Economy.* New York: Appleton, Century, Crofts, 1902.

Samuelson, P.A. "Social Indifference Curves." *Quarterly Journal of Economics*, February 1956.

Suggestions for Further Reading

Allen, W. R. "The Effects of Trade on Shifting Reciprocal Demand Schedules." *American Economic Review,* March 1952.

Baldwin, R. E. "Secular Movements in the Terms of Trade." *AER Papers and Proceedings*, May 1955.

Dantwala, M. L. "Commodity Terms of Trade of Primary Producing Countries." In E. A. G. Robinson, ed., *Problems of Economic Development*. New York: St. Martins Press, 1965.

Haberler, G. "Survey of International Trade." *Special Finance Papers in International Economics,* no. 1, *International Finance Section,* Princeton University, 1961.

Jones, R. W. "Stability Conditions in International Trade: A General Equilibrium Analysis." *International Economic Review,* May 1961.

Kindleberger, C. P. "The Terms of Trade and Economic Development." *Review of Economics and Statistics,* February 1958.

Leontief, W. "The Use of Indifference Curves in the Analysis of Foreign Trade." *Quarterly Journal of Economics*, May 1933.

Lerner, A. "The Diagrammatical Representation of Demand Conditions in International Trade." *Economica,* August 1934.

Marshall, A. *The Pure Theory of Foreign Trade.* London: London School of Economics and Political Science, 1930.

Meade, J. *The Stationary Economy.* London: Allen & Unwin, 1965.

4

TRADE MODEL
EXTENSIONS
AND APPLICATIONS

In our analysis so far, we have stressed the importance of relative price differentials among trading partners as an immediate basis for trade. Relative prices of goods entering international trade reflect the supply and demand conditions existing in the trading nations. An account should thus be made of supply and demand factors such as resource endowments, technology, tastes and preferences, and income levels among nations. In this chapter, we first consider some leading theories that attempt to explain what creates the immediate basis for trade. We then turn our attention to the role of transportation costs and their impact on trade flows.

It was not until two Swedish economists, Eli Heckscher and Bertil Ohlin, formulated the *factor endowment theory* that an explanation was provided for the differences in comparative costs among trading partners.[1] According to Heckscher-Ohlin, international differences in supply conditions explain much of international trade. Supply conditions include factor productivities as well as factor endowments. Unlike Ricardian trade theory, which places primary reliance on factor productivities as the main determinant of the basis for trade, the Heckscher-Ohlin model delegates primary importance to the factor endowments nations enjoy.

The Heckscher-Ohlin Theory of Factor Endowments

Ricardian trade theory argues that the basis for trade stems from differences in international production characteristics and factor productivities, owing to domestic differences in natural advantages and acquired advantages. But other than offering this general explanation, Ricardian theory does little to explain what causes discrepancies in comparative costs and differences in domestic transformation curves.

Factor Endowment Model

The *factor endowment model* asserts that the pattern of trade is explained primarily by differences in relative national supply conditions. Heckscher-Ohlin attribute relative price differentials to differences in national resource endowments. Heckscher-Ohlin assumed that trading partners have the same tastes and preferences (demand conditions), use factors of production that are of uniform quality, and use the same technology. The productivity or efficiency

47

of a given resource unit is thus identical for both trading nations.

The factor endowment model argues that relative price levels differ among nations because (1) they have different relative endowments of factors of production and (2) different commodities require that the factor inputs be used with differing intensities in their production. Given these circumstances, a nation will export that commodity for which a large amount of the relatively abundant (cheap) input is used. It will import that commodity in the production of which the relatively scarce (expensive) input is used. The principal explanation of the pattern of trade lies in the uneven distribution of world resources among nations, coupled with the fact that commodities require different proportions of the factors of production. When a nation possesses an abundance of the factors of production required in great amounts to produce a commodity, its price for that commodity will be low relative to its price for another commodity requiring great amounts of scarce resources.

Figure 4.1 illustrates the trading position of France and Germany, whose transformation curves are located on the same diagram. Assume that auto production is capital intensive, requiring much capital and little land. Similarly, wheat production is assumed to be land intensive, requiring much land and little capital. Suppose that capital is relatively abundant in Germany. Indicating the suitability of its resources for producing capital-intensive autos, Germany's transformation curve is biased toward the auto axis. The abundance of land in France causes its transformation curve to be biased toward the wheat axis.

According to the factor endowment model, demand conditions are assumed to be identical for each nation. This is illustrated in Figure 4.1 by the community indifference curves (curve I and curve II), which are common for both France and Germany. Referring to the top portion of the figure, the point where community indifference I is tangent to the transformation curves of Germany and France indicates the autarky equilibrium locations for each country. In autarky, Germany locates at point G on its transformation curve, whereas France locates on its transformation curve at point F. The relative price ratios at these points suggest that Germany has the comparative advantage in auto production, and France has the comparative advantage of producing wheat.

The preceding example depicts the Heckscher-Ohlin reasoning that given identical demand conditions and input productivities, the differences in the relative abundance of factors of production determine relative price levels and the pattern of trade. Capital becomes relatively cheaper in the capital-abundant country and land relatively cheaper in the land-abundant country. The capital-abundant country will thus export the capital-intensive product, and the land-abundant country will export the land-intensive product. The factor endowment model concludes that each country exports the commodities that are relatively intensive in the factor with which it is relatively well endowed.

Refer to the lower part of Figure 4.1. With trade, each nation will continue to specialize in the production of the commodity of its comparative advantage until its commodity price equalizes with that of the other country. Specialization in production continues until France reaches point F' and Germany reaches point G', where the transformation curves of each nation are tangent to the common relative price line, t_1. France will exchange 10 bushels of wheat for 12 autos, and will consume at point H located on community indifference curve II. Germany will exchange 12 autos for 10 bushels of wheat, also consuming at point H. With trade, both nations achieve a higher level of satisfaction, community indifference curve II, than that which occurs in the absence of trade, community indifference curve I.

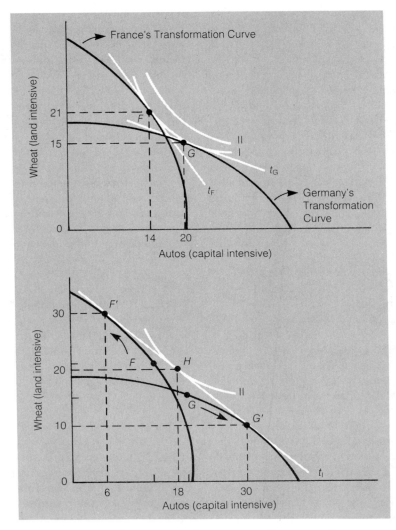

Figure 4.1 Comparative advantage according to the factor endowment theory.

Factor Price Equalization

Free trade tends to result in an equalization of commodity prices among trading partners. Can the same be said for factor input prices?[2] A nation with trade finds output expanding in its comparative advantage industry, which uses a lot of the cheap, abundant factor. The price of the abundant factor increases as the result of the rise in its demand. The expensive, scarce factor is simultaneously being released from the comparative disadvantage industry. To induce producers to employ this factor, its price must decrease. Because this situation occurs at the same time in both trading partners, there will occur in each nation a rise in the price of its abundant factor and a fall in the price of the scarce factor. Trade therefore leads toward an equalization of the relative factor prices in the two trading partners.

In the preceding example, the French demand for inexpensive German autos results in an increased German demand for its abundant factor, capital. The price of capital rises in Germany. As France produces fewer autos, its demand for capital decreases, the result being a fall in the price of capital. The effect of trade is to equalize the price of capital in the two nations. Similarly, the German demand for cheap French wheat leads to France demanding more land, its abundant factor. The French price of land rises. With Germany producing less wheat, its demand for land decreases, and the price of land falls. The price of land with trade tends to equalize in the two trading partners.

By redirecting global demand away from the scarce factor toward the abundant factor in each nation, trade leads toward factor price equalization. In each country, the cheap factor becomes more expensive while the expensive factor becomes cheaper. The factor endowment theory suggests that trade leads toward an equalization of factor prices. But in the real world, actual differences in factor prices do exist. For example, the average salary of unskilled labor in the United States is higher than in Korea. That resource prices may not fully equalize between trading partners can in part be explained by the fact that the assumptions underlying the factor endowment theory are not completely met in the real world. For example, to the extent that different countries use different technologies or that markets are not perfectly competitive in trading nations, factor prices may only partially equalize. The existence of transportation costs and barriers to trade may prevent product prices from becoming equal. Such market imperfections reduce the volume of trade, limiting the extent to which commodity prices as well as factor prices can equalize.

An example of the tendency toward factor price equalization is provided by the American auto industry. By the early 1980s, the compensation of the American autoworker was roughly double that of the Japanese autoworker. In 1981, the average General Motors worker earned hourly wages and benefits of $19.65, as opposed to the $10.70 earned by the average Japanese autoworker. Owing to factors including the domestic recession and high gasoline prices, the demand for American-produced autos deteriorated. However, the American consumer continued to purchase Japanese vehicles up to the limit permissible under the prevailing quota system. According to the factor price equalization theory, falling domestic demand for American-produced autos places downward pressure on the wages of the U.S. autoworker. This was seen in the wage reductions that the United Auto Workers (UAW) union accepted to save the jobs of its members. It is no wonder that the UAW pushed for trade legislation that further restricts foreign autos entering the United States, insulating the wages of domestic autoworkers from the market pressure created by foreign competition.

The Distribution of Income and Trade

It has been shown how free trade can increase the level of world output. Each trading nation can obtain higher combinations of commodities that lie beyond its domestic capacity to produce. A nation's income thus rises with trade. But the prices of the factors of production determine factor incomes. Trade therefore affects not only the national income level but also the internal distribution of income among the factors of production.

The factor endowment theory reasons that the export of commodities embodying large amounts of the relatively cheap, abundant factors makes those factors less abundant in the domestic market. The import of the commodities intensely using the expensive, scarce factor makes those factors less scarce. Exports tend to increase the return going to the cheap, abundant factor, whereas imports lower the return going to the expensive, scarce factor. The relative share of a country's national income going to the abundant factor rises, and that going to the scarce factor falls. The factor endowment theory concludes that with free trade, the abundant factor enjoys a greater portion of the gains from trade than the scarce factor.

Does this set of circumstances mean that the scarce factor is worse off with free trade than it is in the absence of trade? Does the adverse redistribution of income that occurs mean its absolute level of income with trade is actually lower than without trade? Not necessarily! Even though the scarce factor suffers an adverse relative redistribution of income, the country's income will be rising with trade. By accepting free trade, the scarce factor may be able to benefit with a smaller share of a rising income that is superior to the greater share of the smaller income it would have in the absence of trade.

The Leontief Paradox

The first major attempt to investigate the factor endowment theory empirically was undertaken by Wassily Leontief in 1953.[3] Leontief noted that it was widely recognized that in the United States capital was relatively abundant and labor was relatively scarce. Applying the factor endowment theory to the United States, isn't it reasonable that the Unites States would be exporting capital-intensive goods while its import-competing goods would be labor intensive?

Leontief tested this proposition by analyzing the capital/labor ratios for some 200 export industries and import-competing industries in the United States. As indicated in Table 4.1, Leontief found that the capital/labor ratio for U.S. export

Table 4.1   Domestic Capital and Labor Requirements per Million Dollars of U.S. Exports and of Competitive Import Replacements (of average 1947 composition)

	Exports	Import Replacements
Capital (in 1947 dollars)	2,550,780	3,091,339
Labor (person years)	182	170
Capital-labor ratio (capital per person year)	14,015	18,184

Source: Wassily Leontief, "Domestic Production and Foreign Trade: The American Capital Position Reexamined," *Proceedings of the American Philosophical Society*, 97 (September 1953); reprinted in Richard E. Caves and Harry C. Johnson, eds., *Readings in International Economics* (Homewood, Ill.: Richard D. Irwin, 1968), pp. 503–527.

industries was lower than that of its import-competing industries, suggesting that exports were less capital intensive than import-competing goods! But the United States is supposed to be endowed with relatively large amounts of capital compared with the rest of the world. In a later study, Leontief again found that U.S. import goods were more capital intensive relative to U.S. exports. Leontief concluded that contrary to what the factor endowment theory suggests, the *production of U.S. exports is labor intensive compared with import-competing goods, which are capital intensive*. Leontief's paradoxical results motivated similar studies for other countries. Although the Leontief analysis has been questioned on both statistical and methodological grounds, many other studies have challenged the general applicability of the factor endowment theory.

Comparative Labor Costs

Shortcomings of the factor endowment theory prompted efforts to explain international trade patterns in terms of comparative labor costs. At least two factors determine a country's competitive position—labor productivity and wage levels. Together they constitute the unit labor costs involved in producing a commodity. One country may find its labor productivity to be much higher than that of its trading partner, while its average wage rates are also higher. Should the overall difference in productivity more than offset the overall difference in wage rates, the first country may still find itself in a favorable position!

One of the earliest investigations of the theory of comparative costs was made by the British economist G. D. A. MacDougall in 1950.[4] MacDougall compared the export pattern of 25 separate industries for the United States and the United Kingdom. As shown in Table 4.2, in each industry studied, the U.S. labor productivity exceeded that of the United Kingdom. MacDougall also found that on average, American wage rates were twice as high as British wage rates. According to MacDougall, it would follow that the U.S. share of world export markets would exceed the United Kingdom share in those industries where American labor was more than twice as productive as British workers. In those industries where British workers were more than half as productive as their American competitors, Britain would have the cost advantage and would find its share of export markets rising above that of the United States.

Referring to Table 4.2, we note that of the 25 industries studied, 20 fit the predicted pattern. The United States had the largest share of the exports when its labor productivity was at least twice the British productivity. MacDougall's findings appear to have merit in relating export patterns to wage levels and labor productivity. But his test of the theory of comparative costs is not without limitations. Labor is not the only factor input. Allowance should be made where appropriate for production and distribution costs other than direct labor. Differences in product quality also explain trade patterns in industries such as automobiles and footwear.

Table 4.2   United States and United Kingdom Prewar Output per Worker and Quantity of Exports in 1937

United States Output per Worker More than Twice the United Kingdom

Product	U.S. Exports Compared to U.K. Exports (ratio)
Wireless sets and valves	8:1
Pig iron	5:1
Motor cars	4:1
Glass containers	3½:1
Tin cans	3:1
Machinery	1½:1
Paper	1:1

United States Output per Worker 1.4 to 2.0 Times the United Kingdom

Product	U.S. Exports Compared to U.K. Exports (ratio)
Cigarettes	1:2
Linoleum, oilcloth, etc.	1:3
Hosiery	1:3
Leather footwear	1:3
Coke	1:5
Rayon weaving	1:5
Cotton goods	1:9
Rayon making	1:11
Beer	1:18

United States Output per Worker Less than 1.4 Times the United Kingdom

Product	U.S. Exports Compared to U.K. Exports (ratio)
Cement	1:11
Men's/boy's outer wool clothing	1:23
Margarine	1:32
Woolen and worsted	1:250

Exceptions (U.S. output per worker more than twice the United Kingdom, but U.K. exports exceed U.S. exports): electric lamps, rubber tires, soap, biscuits, watches.

Source: G. D. A. MacDougall, "British and American Exports: A Study Suggested by the Theory of Comparative Costs," *Economic Journal*, 61 (1951).

One should therefore proceed with caution in explaining a country's competitive position on the basis of labor productivity and wage levels.

International Labor Comparisons

The previous section illustrates the impact of comparative labor cost on the pattern of trade. This section reviews some recent international labor trends. Table 4.3 displays international comparisons of hourly compensation in manufacturing. In the early 1960s, American labor in manufacturing was compensated at levels significantly above those of most other countries. By the late 1970s, other industrialized countries had eliminated much of the compensation differentials as foreign workers enjoyed larger percent-

age increases in compensation than did American workers. Although labor compensation has been on the upswing in many less-developed countries, on average it still remains quite low.

Another variable behind a country's competitive position is productivity growth. As seen in Table 4.4, throughout the 1970s and early 1980s, the annual productivity gain of the United States has been below that of many other industrial countries. Incorporating the concepts of labor productivity and compensation levels, Table 4.5 summarizes recent trends in unit labor costs in manufacturing or the costs of labor per unit of manufacturing output. It should be emphasized that unit labor costs are not an all-embracing guide to a country's competitive position. They are an important determinant of the prices of manufactured goods, but

Table 4.3   Trends in Hourly Compensation in Manufacturing in U.S. Dollars (annual percentage rate of change)

Year	United States	France	West Germany	Italy	Netherlands	United Kingdom	Japan	Canada
1970s (av.)	8.8	17.7	19.8	16.7	21.1	16.2	21.0	9.6
1980	11.7	17.5	9.6	15.1	6.1	35.4	3.0	9.2
1981	10.2	9.1	−14.5	−7.5	8.4	1.1	11.0	8.3
1982	9.1	−2.6	−1.1	−2.4	—	−5.9	−8.6	7.8

Source: U.S. Department of Commerce, *International Economic Indicators*, various issues.

Table 4.4   Trends in Productivity in Manufacturing: Output per Labor-Hour (annual percentage rate of change)

Year	United States	France	West Germany	Italy	Netherlands	United Kingdom	Japan	Canada
1970s (av.)	2.7	5.2	5.2	4.7	5.7	2.6	6.0	3.6
1980	0.0	1.6	1.4	5.5	1.3	0.1	6.8	−3.3
1981	2.8	1.6	2.7	3.4	3.1	6.0	6.2	1.0
1982	−0.9	6.9	1.7	1.3	—	3.5	1.0	−2.7

Source: U.S. Department of Commerce, *International Economic Indicators*, various issues.

Table 4.5   Trends in Unit Labor Cost in Manufacturing in
U.S. Dollars (annual percentage rate of change)

Year	United States	France	West Germany	Italy	Nether-lands	United Kingdom	Japan	Canada
1970s (av.)	5.5	11.3	14.0	14.1	13.4	12.8	16.3	5.9
1980	11.9	15.7	8.1	8.9	10.6	27.3	−3.5	13.0
1981	7.2	−11.5	−15.7	−10.6	−18.5	−4.6	6.6	8.0
1982	10.0	−1.8	−3.8	−2.6	—	−9.0	−9.5	10.8

Source: U.S. Department of Commerce, *International Economic Indicators*, various issues.

other costs also influence price—notably those of capital, energy, and raw materials. Moreover, a country's competitive position is not solely determined by price. Salesmanship, credit terms, adherence to delivery schedules, and so on also have a bearing on competitiveness.

Economies of Scale

Another explanation of trade patterns involves efficiencies of large-scale production, which reduce a firm's costs. Such *economies of scale* are pronounced in industries, including steel and autos, that use mass production techniques and capital equipment. The economic justification of economies of scale is that a large firm may experience cost reductions through specialization in machinery and labor, assembly-line production operations, utilization of by-products, and quantity discounts obtained on the purchase of inputs.

For example, steel mills generally find that a steel furnace, which can produce twice as much as another furnace, costs less than twice as much to construct. Auto plants are able to take advantage of the assembly line, where each worker (or robot) performs a single operation on a car as it moves by. Multiplant operations, like the McDonald's hamburger chain, also realize eco-

nomies of scale. By operating many restaurants as an integrated system, McDonald's is able to produce food ingredients at centralized kitchens and train its managers at the "Hamburger University." McDonald's also enjoys economies of scale in advertising, marketing, and finance.

How large a production run must a plant realize to exhaust its economies of scale? Table 4.6 furnishes estimates of scale economies for 12 industries. Column 1 gives estimates of the minimum efficient scale of plant for each industry, expressed as a percentage of U.S. consumption. This level corresponds to the plant size where scale economies vanish and unit costs cease to fall. Column 2 shows the percentage increase in unit cost for a plant operating at one-third of its minimum efficient scale. This column suggests the steepness of the downward-sloping portion of the unit cost curve by giving estimates of the cost disadvantage faced by a plant operating at a third of its minimum efficient scale.

How can economies of scale serve as a determinant of comparative advantage? Adam Smith gave the answer in his 1776 classic, *The Wealth of Nations*, which emphasized that the division of labor is limited by the size of the market. International trade, by widening the market's size, can permit longer production runs, which lead to increasing efficiency. An example is Boeing Inc., which has sold about half of its jet planes overseas in recent years. Without exports,

Boeing would have found it difficult to cover the large design and tooling costs of its jumbo jets, and the jets might not have been produced at all.

Referring to Figure 4.2, assume that an American and a Mexican auto company face identical demand conditions for their products, a situation that permits 100,000 autos to be produced. Also assume that identical cost conditions result in the same long-run average cost curve for the two producers, *ATC*. Note that scale economies result in decreasing unit costs over the first 275,000 autos produced. In terms of the trade model discussed in Chapter 2, there would be no basis for gainful trade, since each company realizes a production cost of $10,000 per auto. Now suppose that rising income in the United States results in 200,000 autos being demanded, the demand for Mexican autos remaining constant. The larger market would allow the American manufacturer greater volume and lower unit

cost, now at $8,000. When trade opens up, the cost advantage of American firms will permit their autos to be exported to Mexico. The economies-of-scale hypothesis thus concludes that a large domestic market facilitates exports of goods whose production is subject to decreasing costs as the scale of operation expands.

In recent years, the United Auto Workers (UAW) has pressured the Japanese auto companies to locate assembly plants in the United States to preserve UAW jobs. The UAW has maintained that the American sales of the major Japanese producers more than justify the construction of assembly plants in the United States, where minimum efficient scales are estimated to be approximately 250,000 units annually. Although some Japanese firms have located in the United States (for example, Honda in Ohio and Nissan in Tennessee), the Japanese generally have resisted such pressures. They have maintained that, as the U.S. auto producers shift

Table 4.6   Plant Economies of Scale

Industry	Minimum Efficient Plant Size as a Percentage of U.S. Consumption	Percentage Increase in Unit Cost for a Plant One-Third of Minimum Efficient Scale
Ball and Roller Bearings	1.4	8.0
Beer Brewing	3.4	5.0
Cement	1.7	26.0
Cigarettes	6.6	2.2
Cotton and Synthetic Fabrics	0.2	7.6
Glass Containers	1.5	11.0
Paints	1.4	4.4
Petroleum Refining	1.9	4.8
Refrigerators	14.1	6.5
Shoes	0.2	1.5
Storage Batteries	1.9	4.6
Wide-Strip Steel Works	2.6	11.0

Source: F. M. Scherer, et al., *The Economics of Multi-Plant Operation: An International Comparisons Study* (Cambridge, Mass.: Harvard University Press, 1975), pp. 80, 94.

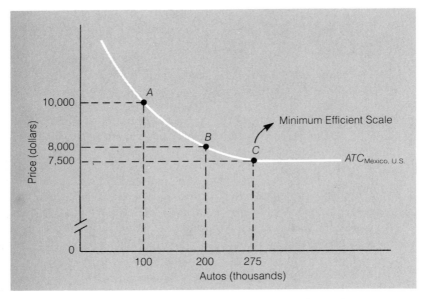

Figure 4.2   Economies of scale as a basis for trade.

their emphasis to small-car production, the small-car market in the United States will become saturated and the Japanese assembly plants no longer will be profitable.

Theory of Overlapping Demands

According to the Heckscher-Ohlin model, international trade is founded upon dissimilar economic structures among trading partners. Applying the factor endowment model to the real world, one would expect that the largest amount of international trade would be between the capital-abundant, industrialized countries and the labor and land-abundant developing countries. It might also be expected that the world trade pattern would involve primarily the exchange of manufactured products for primary commodities. However, post–World War II empirical evidence largely contradicts these extensions of the factor endowment theory. It has been found that international trade primarily has involved manufactured goods for manufactured goods, largely among the industrialized nations. Rather than becoming less similar in economic structure, the industrialized nations have become more similar.

This negative empirical evidence has led to considerable doubt as to how much of international trade can be explained by the factor endowment theory. Dissatisfaction with the factor endowment model has become particularly acute regarding its ability to explain the trade in *manufactured* goods. During the 1960s, a substantial contribution to international trade theory was made by Staffan Linder, a Swedish economist who emphasized the importance that demand plays in explaining the pattern of trade in manufactured goods.[5] Staffan Linder visualizes two explanations of international trade. Linder contends that for trade in *primary* commodities, the factor endowment theory has considerable explanatory value. But for trade in *manufactured* goods, national factor endowment levels hold little explanatory value. This is because the primary force influencing trade in manufactured goods is domestic demand conditions. It follows that because most international trade involves manufactured products, the influence of demand plays the key role in explaining the movement of goods among nations.

Overlapping Demands

According to Linder, the composition of a country's exports in manufactured goods mainly depends on domestic demand conditions. Before products can be sold in competitive international markets, they must first be produced and marketed domestically. A business firm will generally desire to sell its product in familiar domestic markets before undertaking operations in less certain foreign markets. For a business firm to initiate production, there must be favorable domestic conditions. Internal demand not only gives rise to the initial production of a manufactured good, but also it allows the industry to grow large enough to become competitive in foreign markets.

Because an industry initially bases its production decisions on internal demand conditions, it follows that international trade will be most pronounced among countries with similar demand structures for manufactured goods. An industry generally finds that the most favorable foreign market conditions occur when demand patterns abroad are very similar to domestic ones. Linder therefore attributes trade in manufactured goods mainly to the existence of overlapping demands among trading partners.

If two trading partners experience the same demand conditions, they will purchase products characterized by similar degrees of sophistication of quality. But what underlies Linder's concept of demand? Linder contends that tastes and preferences must be supported by purchasing

power to become effective. The demand for manufactured goods becomes an effective demand when it is backed up by income. It follows that if overlapping demand patterns explain international trade in manufactured goods, countries with similar income levels will tend to be trading partners. The *greater the degree of overlap in national demand structures (income levels), the larger will be the potential trade in manufactured goods.*

Overlapping Demand Pattern Model

Figure 4.3 illustrates Linder's concept of overlapping demand structures for manufactured goods.[6] The horizontal axis represents a nation's per capita income, considered to be the best measure of effective demand. The vertical axis depicts the degree of product quality or sophistication of each manufactured good demanded. The theory of overlapping demand asserts that there is a strong relationship between the level of per capita income and the degree of quality of the national demand structure as a whole. A rise in per capita income brings about an increase in the level of product sophistication demanded by the public. This relationship is denoted by the line *OA*.

Most societies generally are characterized by uneven distributions of income. To the extent that various members of a given society earn different income levels, there will be a range in the quality of manufactured goods demanded. Lower income earners tend to demand products of lower quality than do higher income earners. For example, Figure 4.3 suggests that although the U.S. per capita income level is at $12,000, the various manufactured goods demanded by different groups in the United States are in quality range *ab*, with *c* as the average. Lines *OB* and *OC* depict a band whose inner area represents the range of product qualities demanded by countries with different per capita incomes. As

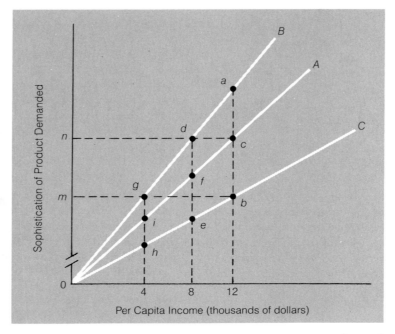

Figure 4.3 Overlapping demands as a determinant of manufactured goods trade.

per capita income rises, the width of the band increases, suggesting that the range of product qualities demanded by a country grows larger as it becomes more affluent.

Consider two industrialized countries, the United States and Canada, whose per capita income levels are respectively denoted by $12,000 and $8,000. Demand structures of the two countries suggest that the United States demands products in the quality range *ab*, with *c* as the average. For Canada, the qualitative range is *de*, with *f* as the average. The qualitative range common to both countries is given by *mn*. Trade in manufactured goods will thus be within this range of product quality. Because the U.S. and Canadian income levels are very similar, the countries have substantial overlap in their demand patterns, and a relatively large potential for trade between the two countries exists.

We would also expect that trade in manufactured goods between an industrialized country like the United States and a relatively poor nation like Hong Kong would be relatively low. Inspection of Figure 4.3 reveals that the low level of Hong Kong per capita income, $4,000, provides little demand overlap with that of the United States. The high-income earners of the poor country are barely able to afford the same manufactured goods purchased by the lower income earners of the wealthy country. There would only exist a minimal amount of trade in manufactured goods between the two countries.

The predictive accuracy of the Linder theory has been empirically tested. To date, the empirical tests offer mixed results of the theory's explanatory power.[7] The Linder theory does present an opposing view to the factor endowment theory regarding the basis for trade.

Rather than emphasizing supply determinants, Linder assigns primary explanatory value to the role of demand. Unlike the factor endowment theory, which suggests that trade is most pronounced when national economic structures differ, Linder concludes that it is the similarity between national economic structures that gives rise to international trade.

Product Cycles

The underlying explanations of international trade presented so far are similar in that they presuppose a given and unchanging state of technology. The basis for trade was ultimately attributed to such factors as differing labor productivities, factor endowments, and national demand structures. In a dynamic world, technological changes occur in different nations at different rates of speed. Technological innovations commonly result in new methods of producing existing commodities, in the production of new commodities, or in commodity improvements, often affecting the direction of comparative advantage and the pattern of trade.

Recognition of the importance of dynamic changes has given rise to another explanation of international trade in manufactured goods, the product life cycle theory. The product life cycle theory is primarily concerned with the role of technological innovation as a key determinant of trade patterns in *manufactured* products. Using a dynamic framework, this theory attempts to show how many manufactured products follow a predictable cycle over time.[8]

The Product Life Cycle Model

According to the *product life cycle* concept, many manufactured goods such as electronic products and office machinery undergo a trade cycle.

During this cycle, the home country is initially an exporter, then loses its competitive advantage vis-à-vis its trading partners, and may eventually become an importer of the commodity. Figure 4.4 illustrates the stages that many manufactured products go through. These stages include the following:

1. Manufactured good is introduced to home market.
2. Domestic industry shows export strength.
3. Foreign production begins.
4. Domestic industry loses competitive advantage.
5. Import competition begins.

The introduction stage of the trade cycle begins when an innovator establishes a technological breakthrough in the production of a manufactured good. The home country initially has an international technological gap in its favor. At the start, the relatively small local market for the product and technological uncertainties imply that mass production is not feasible. The manufacturer will likely operate close to the local market to gain quick feedback on the quality and overall appeal of the product. During the trade cycle's next stage, the domestic manufacturer begins to export its product to foreign markets. Once a new product has been successfully introduced and sold at home, it likely will be exported to foreign nations having similar tastes and income levels. The local manufacturer finds that during this stage of growth and expansion, its market becomes large enough to support mass production operations and the sorting out of inefficient production techniques. The home country manufacturer is therefore able to supply increasing amounts of the world markets.

As time passes, the domestic manufacturer realizes that to protect its export profits, it must locate production operations closer to the foreign markets. The domestic industry enters its

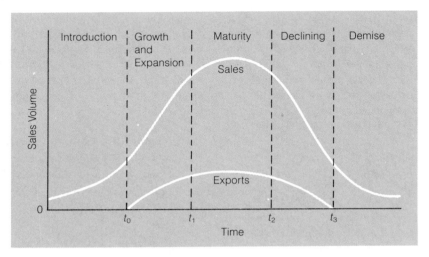

Figure 4.4   Product life cycle.

mature stage as innovating firms establish branches abroad. A major reason for this is that the cost advantage initially enjoyed by an innovator is not likely to last indefinitely. Over time, the innovating country may find that its technology has become more commonplace and that transportation costs and tariffs play an increasingly important role in influencing selling costs. The innovator may also find that the foreign market is large enough to permit mass production operations. The innovating country therefore tends to locate its production facilities abroad to maintain its foreign sales.

Although an innovating country's monopoly position may be prolonged by legal patents, it tends to break down over time. This is because knowledge tends to be a free good in the long run. The benefits an innovating country achieves from its technological gap are short-lived, to the extent that import competition from foreign producers begins. Once the innovative technology becomes fairly commonplace, foreign producers begin to imitate the production process. The innovating country gradually loses its comparative advantage and its export cycle begins to experience a declining phase.

The trade cycle is complete when the production process becomes so standardized that it can be easily utilized by all nations. The technological breakthrough therefore no longer benefits only the innovating country. In fact, the innovating country may finally itself become a net importer of the product as its monopoly position is eliminated by foreign competition. Textiles and paper products are generally considered to have run the full course of the trade cycle, whereas electronic computers are still in the early stage of export strength. The spread of automobile production into many parts of the world implies that its production process is close to becoming standardized.

The experience of American and Japanese radio manufacturers illustrates the product life-cycle model. Following World War II, the radio was a well-established product. American firms dominated the international market for radios, owing to vacuum tubes being initially developed in the United States. But as production technologies spread, Japan used cheaper labor and captured a large share of the world radio market. The transistor was then developed by U.S. companies. For a number of years, American radio manufacturers were able to compete with the Japanese, who continued to use outdated technologies. Again, the Japanese imitated the U.S. technologies and were able to sell radios at more competitive prices. The development of printed circuits in the United States permitted American firms to regain their ability to compete against the Japanese. It is not clear whether printed-circuit technology will result in radios being capital intensive or labor intensive or whether lower wage nations, such as Taiwan, will displace the United States and Japan as radio manufacturers.[9]

Transportation Costs

Because the movement of goods among nations involves the role of economic distance, the effects of transportation costs cannot be ignored. Transportation costs refer to the costs of the movement of goods. Included are freight charges, packing and handling expenses, and insurance premiums. The introduction of transportation costs into the analysis modifies the trade model in two ways. First, the trade effects

of transportation costs result in a lower volume of trade, higher import prices and thus lower gains from trade. Second, transportation costs affect the location of industry and the geographic pattern of trade.

Trade Effects

The trade effects of transportation costs can be illustrated with a conventional supply and demand model based on increasing cost conditions. Figure 4.5 illustrates the demand and supply curves of autos for the United States and Canada. Reflecting the assumption that the United States has the comparative advantage in auto production, the U.S. and Canadian equilibrium autarky locations are respectively at points E and F. In the absence of trade, the U.S. auto price, $4,000, is lower than that of Canada, $8,000.

When trade is allowed, the United States will move toward greater specialization in auto production, whereas Canada will produce fewer autos. Under increasing cost conditions, the U.S. cost and price levels rise and that of Canada falls. The basis for further growth of trade is

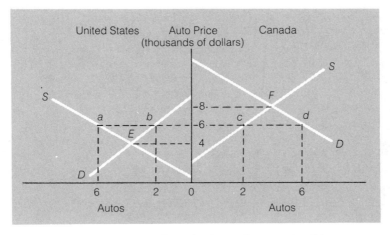

Figure 4.5   Free trade under increasing cost conditions.

eliminated when the two countries' prices equalize at $6,000. At $6,000, the United States produces 6 autos, consumes 2 autos, and exports 4 autos. At $6,000, Canada produces 2 autos, consumes 6 autos, and imports 4 autos. Six thousand dollars becomes the equilibrium price for both countries, since the excess auto supply of the United States just matches the excess auto demand in Canada.

The introduction of transportation costs into the analysis modifies the conclusions of the preceding example. Suppose the per-unit cost of transporting an auto from the United States to Canada is $2,000, as shown in Figure 4.6. The United States would find it advantageous to produce autos and export them to Canada until its relative price advantage is eliminated. But by including transportation costs in the analysis, the U.S. export price reflects domestic production costs plus the cost of transporting autos to Canada. The basis for trade thus stops growing when the U.S. auto price plus the transport cost rises to Canada's auto price level. This occurs when the U.S. auto price rises to $5,000 and Canada's auto price falls to $7,000, the differ-

ence between them being the $2,000 per-unit transport cost. Instead of a single price ruling in both countries, there will be two domestic auto prices differing by the cost of transportation.

Compared with free trade in the absence of transport costs, under transport costs the high-cost importing country will produce more, consume less, and import less! The low-cost exporting country will produce less, consume more, and export less! *Transportation costs therefore tend to reduce the volume of trade, the degree of specialization in production among the nations concerned, and thus the gains from trade.*

The inclusion of transportation costs in the analysis modifies our trade model conclusions. A product will be internationally traded as long as the pretrade price differential between the trading partners is greater than the cost of transporting the product between them. When trade is in equilibrium, the price of the traded product in the exporting nation is less than that of the importing country by the transportation cost.

Transportation costs also have implications for the factor price equalization theorem presented earlier in this chapter. Recall this theorem

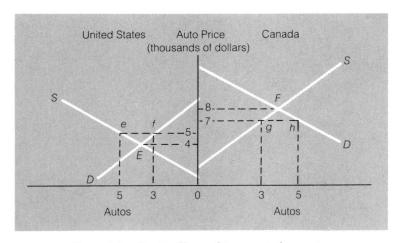

Figure 4.6   Trade effects of transportation costs.

suggests that free trade tends to equalize commodity prices and factor prices so that all workers will earn the same wage rate and all units of capital will earn the same interest income in both countries. Free trade permits factor price equalization to occur because factor inputs that cannot move to another country are implicitly being shipped in the form of commodities. Looking at the real world, however, we see American autoworkers earning more than Japanese autoworkers. One possible reason for this differential is transportation costs. By making low-cost Japanese autos more expensive for American consumers, transportation costs reduce the volume of autos shipped from Japan to the United States. The reduced trade volume stops the process of commodity and factor price equalization before it is complete. In other words, the prices of American automakers and the wages of American autoworkers do not fall to the levels of the Japanese. Transportation costs thus provide some relief to high-cost domestic workers who are producing goods subject to import competition.

Location of Industry

Besides having significant trade effects, transportation costs affect the location of industry. A profit-seeking business firm recognizes the costs of production as well as the costs of transporting raw materials and final products. A firm will achieve its best location when it can minimize its total operating costs, including both production and transportation costs. In terms of location theory, production can be classified into three categories: (1) resource or supply oriented; (2) market or demand oriented; (3) footloose or neutral.

Resource-oriented industries such as steel and lumber are generally considered *weight losing*. Because the final product is so much less weighty or bulky than the materials from which it is made, the industry will find it advantageous to undergo production near the resource supplies.

This is because the cost of transporting finished products is substantially lower than the cost of transporting the inputs used in their manufacture. A firm's transportation costs thus decrease as it locates near the supply of resources. A classic example is the case of the U.S. steel industry, which has tended to undertake steel production closer to the coal supply than to the iron ore supply. This is because, per ton of steel produced, a greater amount of coal than iron ore is used in the production process.

Industrial processes that add weight or bulk to the commodity are likely to be located near the product market to minimize transportation costs. An industry tends to be *market oriented* when its production process is *weight gaining*. This is because the cost of shipping the final product exceeds the cost of transporting the raw materials that go into its production. A firm's transport costs are minimized as it locates close to its product market. A prominent example of weight gaining occurs in the case of Coca-Cola and Pepsi-Cola. These companies transport syrup concentrate to plants all over the world, which add water to the syrup and bottle it. Another example is the U.S. auto industry, which has located assembly plants near regional and even foreign markets. This is because it is cheaper to ship the unassembled auto parts than to ship the finished automobile.

Footloose or *neutral* industries are those that do not find their manufacturing operations pulled close to the resource supplies or the location of market demand. This may occur when (1) a product is extremely valuable, such as electronic products, so that transportation costs are a very small portion of the product's total costs or (2) when the product is neither weight gaining nor weight losing. Given these circumstances, the industry tends to be quite mobile, locating where the availability and cost of factor inputs permit total production costs to be minimized. Because transportation costs are not of particular significance in a footloose industry, production costs count more as a key determinant of industry location.

ry

1. The immediate basis for trade stems from relative commodity price differences among nations. Because relative prices are determined by supply and demand conditions, the role of such factors as resource endowments, technology, and national income are important determinants of the basis for trade.

2. The Heckscher-Ohlin theory suggests that differences in relative factor endowments and factor prices constitute the most important explanation of the basis for trade. According to the Heckscher-Ohlin theory, a nation will export the commodity in the production of which a relatively large amount of its relatively abundant and cheap resource is used. Conversely, it will import commodities in the production of which a relatively large amount of its relatively scarce and expensive resource is used. The Heckscher-Ohlin theory also states that with trade the relative differences in resource prices between nations tend to be eliminated.

3. Contrary to the predictions of the Heckscher-Ohlin model, the empirical tests of Wassily Leontief demonstrated that for the United States exports are labor intensive and import-competing goods are capital intensive. This was exactly the opposite of what the Heckscher-Ohlin model predicted. To the extent that factor intensity reversal does occur, then the Leontief paradox is inconclusive.

4. One of the earliest empirical tests of the comparative advantage theory was carried out by G. MacDougall. Contrasting the export patterns of the United States and Great Britain, MacDougall found that wage levels and labor productivity were important determinants of the basis for trade and the direction of trade.

5. By widening the size of the domestic market, international trade permits larger production runs, which can lead to increasing efficiencies for domestic producers. Such economies of large-scale production can be translated into lower product prices, which improves a firm's competitive position.

6. According to Staffan Linder, two explanations of world trade patterns exist. Trade in primary products conforms well to the factor endowments theory suggested by Heckscher-Ohlin. But the pattern of trade in manufactured goods is best explained by overlapping demands between countries for a commodity. The basis for trade is stronger the more similar the structure of demand for manufactured goods in two countries. Per-capita income constitutes the most important determinant of demand structure.

7. One dynamic explanation of international trade patterns is the product life cycle model. This model views a wide variety of manufactured goods as going through a trade cycle, during which a country is initially an exporter, then loses its export markets, and may finally become an importer of the product. Empirical studies have demonstrated that trade cycles do exist for manufactured goods at some times.

8. Transportation costs tend to reduce the volume of international trade by increasing the prices of traded goods. A product will be traded only if the cost of transporting it between nations is less than the pretrade difference between their relative commodity prices. Transportation costs also help govern the location of industry.

Study Questions

1. What are the effects of transportation costs on the location of industry and on the volume of trade?

2. Explain how the international movement of products and of factor inputs promotes an equalization of the factor prices among nations.

3. How does the Heckscher-Ohlin model differ from the Ricardian model in explaining international trade patterns?

4. The Heckscher-Ohlin model points out how trade affects the distribution of income within trading partners. Explain.

5. How does the Leontief paradox question the overall applicability of the factor endowment model?

6. Why can't we necessarily judge an industry's competitiveness merely by looking at its unit labor costs relative to those of foreign industries?

7. According to Staffan Linder, there are two separate explanations of international trade patterns—for manufacturers and for primary goods. Explain.

8. Do recent world trade statistics support or refute the notion of a product life cycle for manufactured goods?

9. How can economies of large-scale production affect world trade patterns?

Notes

1. Eli Heckscher's explanation of the factor endowment theory was outlined in his article "The Effects of Foreign Trade on the Distribution of Income," *Economisk Tidskrift*, 21 (1919), pp. 497–512. Bertil Ohlin's account is summarized in his *Interregional and International Trade* (Cambridge, Mass.: Harvard University Press, 1933).

2. See Paul A. Samuelson, "International Trade and Equalization of Factor Prices," *Economic Journal* (June 1948), pp. 163–184 and "International Factor-Price Equalization Once Again," *Economic Journal* (June 1949), pp. 181–197.

3. Wassily W. Leontief, "Domestic Production and Foreign Trade: The American Capital Position Reexamined," *Proceedings of the American Philosophical Society*, 97 (September 1953).

4. G. D. A. MacDougall, "British and American Exports: A Study Suggested by the Theory of Comparative Costs," *Economic Journal*, 61 (1951), pp. 697–724.

5. Staffan B. Linder, *An Essay on Trade and Transformation* (New York: John Wiley, 1961), chap. 3.

6. Adapted from Linder, *Essay on Trade*, p. 100.

7. Empirical tests of the theory of overlapping demands can be found in David Greytak and Richard McHugh, "Linder's Trade Thesis: An Empirical Examination," *Southern Economic Journal*, (January 1977), pp. 86–89 and Joel W. Sailors, "Empirical Verification of Linder's Trade Thesis," *Southern Economic Journal*, (October 1973), pp. 262–268.

8. See Raymond Vernon, "International Investment and International Trade in the Product Life Cycle," *Quarterly Journal of Economics*, 80 (May 1966), pp. 190–207 and Louis T. Wells, "A Product Life Cycle For International Trade?" *Journal of Marketing*, 32 (July 1968), pp. 1–6.

9. The semiconductor (chip-making) industry also provides an example of the product life cycle model. See "Chip Wars: The Japanese Threat," *Business Week*, May 23, 1983, pp. 80–96.

Suggestions for Further Reading

Baldwin, R. E. "Determinants of the Commodity Structure of U.S. Trade." *American Economic Review,* March 1971.

Brecher, R. A., and E. U. Choudhri. "The Leontief Paradox, Continued." *Journal of Political Economy,* August 1982.

Das, S. P. "Economies of Scale, Imperfect Competition, and the Pattern of Trade." *Economic Journal*, September 1982.

Deardorff, A. V. "The General Validity of the Heckscher-Ohlin Theorem." *American Economic Review*, September 1982.

Giddy, I. H. "The Demise of the Product Cycle Model in International Business Theory." *Columbia Journal of World Business*, Spring 1978.

Hufbauer, G. C. "The Impact of Natural Characteristics and Technology on the Commodity Composition of Trade in Manufactured Goods." *The Technological Factor in International Trade*. New York: National Bureau of Economic Research, 1970.

Johnson, H. G. "Factor Endowments, International Trade, and Factor Prices." *The Manchester School of Economics and Social Studies*, September 1957.

Kennedy, T. E., and R. McHugh. "An Intemporal Test and Rejection of the Linder Hypothesis." *Southern Economic Journal*, January 1980.

Kurth, J. R. "The Political Consequences of the Product Cycle." *International Organization*, Winter 1979.

Ozawa, T. "The Rybczynski Theorem: A Diagrammatic Note and Corollary Proposition." *Economica*, August 1970.

Samuelson, P. A. "International Trade and the Equalization of Factor Prices." *Economic Journal*, June 1948.

Stern, R. "British and American Productivity and Comparative Costs in International Trade." *Oxford Economic Papers*, October 1962.

Tovias, A. "Testing Factor Price Equalization in the EEC." *Journal of Common Market Studies*, June 1982.

Vernon, R. "The Product Cycle Hypothesis in a New International Environment." *Oxford Bulletin of Economics and Statistics*, November 1979.

Wells, L. T. "The International Product Life Cycle and the Regulation of the Automobile Industry." In D. H. Ginsburg and W. J. Abernathy, eds., *Regulation of American Business and Industry*. New York: McGraw-Hill, 1980.

5

THE THEORY OF TARIFFS

The conclusion of the trade models presented so far is that free trade leads to the most efficient use of world resources. When nations specialize according to the comparative advantage principle, the level of world output is maximized. Not only does free trade enhance world welfare but also it can benefit each participating nation. Every country can overcome the limitations of its own productive capacity to consume a combination of goods that exceeds the best it can produce. In spite of the power of the free trade argument, governments have often interfered with the movement of goods among nations. Virtually every country has adopted trade restrictions such as tariffs, quotas, and subsidies. This chapter considers tariff barriers and their impact on trade.

Tariff Concept

Tariffs are simply taxes levied on products when they cross national boundaries. They may be imposed for purposes of protection or revenue. *Protective tariffs* are designed to insulate domestic producers from foreign competition. Although a protective tariff generally is not intended to totally prohibit imports from entering the country,

it does place foreign producers at a competitive disadvantage when selling in the domestic market. *Revenue tariffs* are imposed by national governments for the purpose of generating tax revenues and may be placed on both exports and imports. During the 1970s, the OPEC nations increased their oil revenues by raising the tariffs imposed on their oil exports. Revenue tariffs are also placed on imported products. The United States, for example, has imposed modest tariffs on commodity imports including bananas, coffee, and tin. Because they are easy to collect, tariffs are an important source of revenue for countries without well-developed tax systems.

Specific and Ad Valorem Tariffs

There are two kinds of tariffs—specific and ad valorem. A *specific* tariff is expressed in terms of a fixed amount of money per physical unit of the imported product, say $100 per imported auto. An *ad valorem* tariff, much like a sales tax, is a fixed percentage of the value of the imported product as it enters the country. Table 5.1 illustrates selected tariffs for the United States in 1981.

What are the relative merits of specific and ad valorem tariffs? As a fixed monetary duty per

Table 5.1   Selected Tariffs of the United States

Product	Rates of Duty
Guitars	13.2% ad val.
Motion picture cameras	9.2% ad val.
Eyeglass frames	12.1% ad val.
Vermouth	21¢ per gal
Cheddar cheese	12% ad val.
Dried apples	0.75¢ per lb
Sheets and pillowcases	32.3% ad val.
Lamb	0.5¢ per lb
Postcards	7.8% ad val.
Steel wire rods	5.4% ad val.
Chinaware	13.9% ad val.
Clothespins	10¢ per gross
Bicycles	15% ad val.
Fish hooks	5% ad val.
Wool gloves	47% ad val.
Cigar holders	0.9¢ each

Source: U.S. International Trade Commission, 1981. *Tariff Schedules of the United States*.

unit of the imported product, a specific tariff is relatively easy to apply and administer, particularly to standardized commodities. But a main disadvantage of a specific tariff is that the degree of protection it affords domestic producers varies inversely with changes in import prices. For example, a specific tariff of $100 on autos will discourage imports priced at $9,000 per auto to a greater degree than those priced at $10,000. During times of inflating import prices, a given specific tariff loses some of its protective effect. On the other hand, a specific tariff has the advantage of providing domestic producers more protection during a business recession, when cheaper products are purchased.

An ad valorem tariff is superior to a specific tariff as it can be applied to products with a wide range of grade variations. As a percentage applied to a product's value, an ad valorem tariff can distinguish among small differentials in product quality to the extent that they are reflected in product price. Under a system of ad valorem tariffs, a person importing a $10,000 Datsun (Nissan) would have to pay a higher tariff duty than a person importing a $9,900 Toyota. The person would likely pay the same duty under a system of specific tariffs. Ad valorem tariffs generally are more satisfactorily applied to manufactured goods with grade variations.

Another advantage of an ad valorem tariff is that it tends to maintain a constant degree of protection for domestic producers during periods of changing prices. If the tariff rate is 20 percent ad valorem and the imported product price is $200, the duty is $40. If the product's price increases, say to $300, the duty collected amounts to $60, whereas if product price falls to $100, the duty drops to $20. An ad valorem tariff yields revenues proportionate to values, maintaining a constant degree of relative protection at all price levels. An ad valorem tariff is similar to a proportional tax as the real proportional tax burden or protection does not change as the tax base changes.

Determination of duties under the ad valorem principle at first appears to be quite simple, but in practice is has suffered from administrative complexities. The main problem has been trying to determine the value of an imported product, a process referred to as *customs valuation*. Import prices are estimated by customs appraisers, who may disagree on product values. What is more, import prices tend to fluctuate over time, which makes the valuation process rather difficult.

Another customs valuation problem stems from the fact that there is currently no universal methodology for determining a commodity's value to which the ad valorem tariffs can be applied. For example, the United States has primarily used the F.O.B. (free on board) valuation concept, whereby the tariff is applied to a product's value as it leaves the exporting country. But the European countries have largely adopted the C.I.F. (cost-insurance-freight) procedure, whereby ad valorem tariffs are levied as a percentage of the imported commodity's total value as it arrives at its final destination. The C.I.F. price thus includes transportation costs such as insurance and freight.

Effective Rate of Protection

A main objective of an import tariff is to protect domestic producers from foreign competition. By increasing the domestic price of an import, a tariff serves to make home-produced goods more attractive to resident consumers. The result is that output in the import-competing industry can expand beyond what would exist in the absence of a tariff. The degree of protection afforded by a tariff reflects the extent to which domestic prices can rise above foreign prices without the home producers being priced out of the market.

The *nominal* tariff rates published in a country's tariff schedule give us a general idea of the level of protection afforded the home industry. But they may not always truly indicate the actual or effective protection given by the nominal tariff. For example, it is not necessarily true that a 25 percent import tariff on an automobile provides the domestic auto industry a protective margin of 25 percent against foreign producers. This is because the nominal tariff rates apply only to the total value of the final import product. But when in the production process the home import-competing industry uses imported material inputs or intermediate products that are subject to a different tariff than that on the final product, then the *effective* tariff rate will differ from the nominal tariff rate.[1]

The effective tariff rate is an indicator of the actual level of protection that a nominal tariff rate provides the domestic import-competing producers. It signifies the total increase in domestic productive activities (value added) that an existing tariff structure makes possible, compared with what would occur under free trade conditions. The effective rate tells us how much more expensive domestic production can be relative to foreign production and still compete in the market.

Assume the domestic stereo industry adds value to imported inputs by assembling component stereo parts imported from abroad. Suppose the imported components can enter the home country on a duty-free basis. Suppose also that 20 percent of a stereo's final value can be attributed to domestic assembly activities (value added), the remaining 80 percent reflecting the value of the imported components. Furthermore, let the cost of the stereo components be the same for both the domestic country and foreign country. Finally, assume the foreign country can produce a stereo for $100.

Referring to Table 5.2, suppose the home country imposes a nominal tariff of 10 percent on finished stereos so that the domestic import price rises from $100 to $110 per unit. Does this mean that home producers are afforded an effective rate of protection equal to 10 percent? Certainly not! Because the imported component parts enter the country duty free (at a nominal tariff rate less than that on the finished import product), the effective rate of protection is 50 percent. Compared with what would exist under free trade, domestic stereo producers can be 50 percent more costly in their assembly activities and still be competitive.

To see this, examine Table 5.2. If free trade were to exist (zero tariff), a foreign stereo could be imported for $100. To meet this price, domestic producers would have to hold their assembly costs down to $20. But under the protective umbrella of the tariff, domestic producers could afford to pay up to $30 for assembly and still meet the $110 domestic price of imported stereos. The result is that domestic assembly costs could rise to a level of 50 percent above what would exist under free trade conditions $(\frac{\$30 - \$20}{\$20} = 0.5)$.

Table 5.2   The Effective Rate of Protection

Foreign Stereo Import		Domestic-Competing Stereo	
Component parts	$ 80	Component parts	$ 80
Assembly activity (value added)	20	Assembly activity (value added)	?(30)
Nominal tariff	10		
Import price	$110	Domestic price	$110

In general, the effective tariff rate is given by the following formula:

$$e = \frac{n - ab}{1 - a}$$

where

e = the effective rate of protection

n = the nominal tariff rate on the final product

a = the ratio of the value of the imported input to the value of the final product

b = the nominal tariff rate on the imported input.

When the values from the above hypothetical example are plugged into the formula, we obtain:

$$e = \frac{0.1 - 0.8 \ (0)}{1 - 0.8}$$

$$e = 0.5.$$

The result is that the nominal tariff rate of 10 percent levied on the final import product affords domestic productive activities an effective degree of protection equal to 50 percent, five times the nominal rate.

Two consequences of the effective rate calculation are worthy of mention. First, the degree of effective protection increases as the value added by domestic producers declines (the ratio of the value of the imported input to the value of the final product increases). In the formula, the higher the value of a, the greater the effective protection rate for any given nominal tariff rate on the final product. Second, a tariff on imports used in the production process reduces the level of effective protection. The higher the value of b, the lower the effective protection rate for any given nominal tariff on the final product. This is because as b rises, the numerator of the formula declines and hence e decreases.

Generalizing from this analysis, when material inputs or intermediate products enter a country at a very low duty while the final imported commodity is protected by a high duty, the result tends to be a high protection rate for the domestic producers. The nominal tariff rate on finished goods thus understates the effective rate of protection. But should a tariff be imposed on imported inputs that exceeds that on the finished good, the nominal tariff rate on the finished product would tend to overstate its protective effect. Such a situation might occur if the home government desired to protect raw material suppliers more than domestic manufacturers.

Tariff Escalation

As illustrated in Table 5.3 and Table 5.4, in many industrialized nations the effective rate of protection is several times the nominal rate.[2] The

Table 5.3   Nominal and Effective Tariff Rates: Selected Products

Product	United States Tariff Rate		Japan Tariff Rate		EEC Tariff Rate	
	Nominal	Effective	Nominal	Effective	Nominal	Effective
Meat and meat products	5.9	10.3	17.9	69.1	19.5	36.6
Preserved fruits and vegetables	14.8	36.8	18.5	49.3	20.5	44.9
Milk, cheese, and butter	10.8	36.9	37.3	248.8	22.0	59.9
Manufactured and processed foods	5.0	1.0	24.0	59.3	14.6	17.7
Flour, cereal, and bakery products	6.9	15.6	22.4	46.4	16.1	24.9
Cocoa products and chocolate	4.2	16.2	22.8	80.7	12.8	34.6
Wood products	10.4	18.3	12.4	22.0	8.2	9.5
Paper products and wood pulp	2.7	5.5	6.6	12.1	7.4	20.1
Rubber products	6.1	12.5	9.3	20.2	8.3	19.0
Yarns and threads	19.5	37.1	9.9	24.2	6.2	19.4
Fabrics and clothing	27.3	40.4	13.0	22.0	14.3	29.1
Plant and vegetable oils	9.4	17.7	10.1	64.9	11.1	138.0
Leather and leather products	7.0	12.8	14.8	22.6	7.8	14.6
Cigars and cigarettes	68.0	113.2	339.5	405.6	87.1	147.3
Soaps and detergents	7.9	19.3	16.6	44.4	7.5	14.4

Source: A. J. Yeats, "Effective Tariff Protection in the United States, the European Economic Community, and Japan," *Quarterly Review of Economics,* 14, no. 2 (1974), p. 45.

apparently low nominal tariffs on the final import products may thus understate the effective rate of protection, which takes into account the effects of tariffs levied on raw materials and intermediate goods. Not only has the effective tariff rate been several times the nominal rate but also the industrialized countries' tariff structures generally have been characterized by an escalation of tariff rates to permit higher degrees of protection on intermediate and finished products than on primary commodities. This is commonly referred to as the *tariff escalation effect*. Although raw materials are often imported at zero or low tariff rates, the nominal and effective protection increases at each stage of production. Many industrialized nations afford a relatively high degree of protection to their manufacturing sector, as suggested in Table 5.5.

The tariff structures of the industrialized nations may indeed discourage the growth of pro-

cessing and manufacturing industries in the less-developed nations. The industrialized nations' low tariffs on primary commodities encourage the developing nations to expand operations in these sectors. But the high protective rates levied by the industrialized nations on their manufacturing industries pose a significant entry barrier for any developing nation wishing to compete in this area. As for the less-developed countries, it

Table 5.4   Overall Tariff Rates: Weighted Averages

Country	Nominal Tariff Average	Effective Tariff Average
United States	8.6	18.0
Japan	16.5	45.4
EEC	12.2	33.1

Source: Yeats, "Effective Tariff Protection," p. 45.

Table 5.5   Escalation of Tariff Protection by Production Stages

Production Stage	United States		Japan		EEC	
	Nominal	Effective	Nominal	Effective	Nominal	Effective
Paper and paper products						
Logs, rough	0.0	—	0.0	—	0.0	—
Wood pulp	0.0	−0.5	5.0	10.7	1.6	2.5
Paper and paper articles	5.3	12.8	5.9	17.6	13.1	30.2
Wood products						
Logs, rough	0.0	—	0.0	—	0.0	—
Sawn wood	0.0	0.0	0.7	2.0	1.9	4.9
Wood manufacturers	7.4	8.4	9.8	15.3	7.4	10.7
Dairy products						
Fresh milk and cream	6.5	—	0.0	—	16.0	—
Condensed and evaporated milk	10.7	30.1	31.7	154.8	21.3	44.3
Cheese	11.5	34.5	35.3	175.6	23.0	58.8
Butter	10.3	46.7	45.0	418.5	21.0	76.6
Wool fabrics						
Raw wool	21.1	—	0.0	—	0.0	—
Wool yarn	30.7	62.2	5.0	9.3	5.4	16.0
Wool fabrics	46.9	90.8	14.7	35.1	14.0	32.9
Cotton fabrics						
Raw cotton	6.1	—	0.0	—	0.0	—
Cotton yarn	8.3	12.0	8.1	25.8	7.0	22.8
Cotton fabrics	15.6	30.7	7.2	34.9	13.6	29.7
Leather products						
Bovine hides	0.0	—	0.0	—	0.0	—
Leather	17.8	57.4	6.2	20.2	7.0	21.4
Leather goods, excluding shoes	22.4	32.5	10.5	15.8	7.1	10.3
Chocolate						
Cocoa beans	0.0	—	—	—	5.4	—
Cocoa powder and butter	2.6	22.0	15.0	125.0	13.6	76.0
Chocolate products	10.3	5.7	30.6	36.3	12.0	−6.8

Source: Yeats, "Effective Tariff Protection," p. 47.

may be in their best interest to discourage disproportionate tariff reductions on primary commodities. This is because the effect of these tariff reductions would be to magnify the discrepancy between the nominal and effective tariffs of the industrialized nations, worsening the potential competitive position of the less-developed nations in the manufacturing and processing sectors.[3]

Tariff Welfare Effects: Small-Country Model

What are the effects of a tariff on a country's national welfare? Consider the case of a country whose imports constitute a very small portion of the world market supply. This small country would be a price taker, facing a constant world price level for its import commodity. This is not a rare case, for it frequently applies to nations that are not important enough to influence the terms at which they trade.

Referring to Figure 5.1, the small country before trade produces at market equilibrium point E, as determined by the intersection of its domestic supply and demand schedules. At equilibrium price $9,500, the quantity supplied is 50 units and the quantity demanded is 50 units. Now suppose the economy is opened to foreign trade and that the world auto price, $8,000, is less than the domestic price. Because the world market will supply an unlimited amount of autos at price $8,000, the world supply curve would appear as a horizontal (perfectly elastic) line. Line S_{d+w} shows the supply of autos available to the small-country consumers from domestic and foreign sources combined. This overall supply curve is the one that would prevail in free trade.

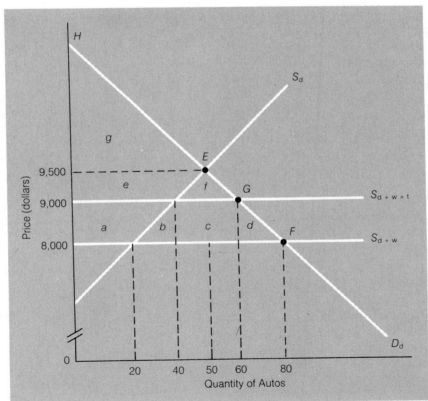

Figure 5.1   Tariff trade and welfare effects: small-country model.

c = revenue effect
a = income redistribution · Income to producers
b = dead weight loss (production efficiency)↓
d = consumption effect ↓

e = producer's surplus.
f = loss or surplus in demand
g = consumer surplus

Free trade equilibrium is located at point F. Here the amount of autos demanded is 80 units, whereas the amount produced domestically is 20 units. The excess domestic auto demand is fulfilled by 60 auto imports. Compared with the situation before trade occurred, free trade results in the domestic auto price falling from $9,500 to $8,000. Consumers are better off as they can import more autos at a lower price. However, domestic producers find they now sell fewer autos at a lower price than they did before trade.

Under free trade, the domestic auto industry is being damaged by foreign competition. Industry sales and profits are falling, while workers are losing their jobs. Suppose management and labor unite and convince the government to levy a protective tariff on auto imports. Assume the small country imposes a tariff of $1,000 on auto imports. Because the small country is not important enough to influence world market conditions, the world supply price of autos remains constant, unaffected by the tariff. This means that the small country's terms of trade remains unchanged. The introduction of the tariff raises the home price of imports by the full amount of the duty, falling entirely on the domestic consumer. The overall supply curve shifts upward from S_{d+w} to S_{d+w+t} by the amount of the tariff.

The protective tariff results in a new equilibrium quantity at point G, the home auto price rising to $9,000. Domestic production increases by 20 units, whereas home consumption falls by 20 units. Imports decrease from their pretrade level of 60 units to 20 units. This reduction can be attributed to falling domestic consumption and rising domestic production. The effects of the tariff are to impede imports and protect home producers. But what are the tariff's effects on the country's national welfare?

Figure 5.1 shows that before the tariff was levied, consumer surplus[4] equaled areas $a + b + c + d + e + f + g$. With the tariff, consumer surplus falls to areas $e + f + g$, an overall loss of consumer surplus equalling areas $a + b + c + d$.

This affects the country's welfare in a number of ways. The welfare effects of a tariff are classified as the revenue effect, redistribution effect, protective effect, and consumption effect. As might be expected, the tariff provides the government with some additional revenue, benefits domestic auto producers, wastes resources, and harms the domestic consumer.

The tariff's *revenue effect* represents the duty collections accruing to the government. Found by multiplying the number of imports, 20 units, times the tariff, $1,000, the government revenue equals area c, or $20,000. This represents the portion of the loss of consumer surplus, in monetary terms, that is transferred to the government. For the country as a whole, the revenue effect does not result in an overall welfare loss, for consumer surplus is merely shifted from the private to the public sector.

The *redistribution effect* is the transfer of consumer surplus, in monetary terms, to the home producers of the import-competing product. This is shown by area a, or $30,000. Under the tariff, home consumers will buy from domestic firms 40 autos at a price of $9,000, total expenditures equaling $360,000. However, that same quantity, 40, would have yielded $320,000 expenditures under a free trade price of $8,000. The imposition of the tariff thus results in home producers receiving additional revenues totaling areas $a+b$, or $40,000, the same as the difference $360,000 minus $320,000. As the tariff encourages home production from 20 to 40 units, producers must pay part of the increased revenue as higher costs of producing the increased output, depicted by area b, or $10,000. The remaining revenue, $30,000, area a, is a net gain in producer income. The redistribution effect therefore is a transfer of income from consumers to producers. Like the revenue effect, it does not result in an overall loss of welfare for the economy.

Area b, totaling $10,000, is referred to as the *protective effect* of the tariff. It illustrates the loss to the domestic economy resulting from wasted resources used to produce additional autos at increasing unit costs. As the tariff-induced domestic output expands, resources that are less adaptable to auto production are eventually utilized, forcing up unit production costs. This means that resources are used less efficiently than they would have been with free trade, whereby autos would be purchased from low-cost foreign producers. A tariff's protective effect thus arises because less efficient home auto production is substituted for more efficient foreign auto production. Referring to Figure 5.1, as domestic output increases from 20 to 40 units, the home cost of producing autos rises, as shown by supply curve S_d. But the same increase in autos could have been obtained at a unit cost of $8,000 before the tariff was levied. The loss to the economy is designated by area b, which represents the protective effect.

Most of the consumer surplus lost because of the tariff has been accounted for: c went to the government as revenue; a was transferred to home suppliers as income; b was lost by the economy owing to inefficient domestic production. The *consumption effect* represented by area d, equaling $10,000, is the residual, not accounted for elsewhere. It arises from the decrease in consumption resulting from the tariff bidding up the import product price to $9,000. The consumption effect is due to the import tariff on autos artificially increasing the price of autos, which denies domestic consumers the opportunity to purchase autos at the lower price, $8,000. A loss of welfare occurs because of the increased price and lower consumption of autos. This loss of consumer surplus represents a real cost to society. The *protective effect and the consumption effect combined* result in a loss of welfare for society. This is because they represent a loss of consumer surplus that is not transferred to other sectors of the economy. Together these effects sum to equal the *deadweight loss* of a tariff.

As long as it is assumed that a country accounts for a negligible portion of international trade, its levying an import tariff necessarily lowers its national welfare. This is because there is no favorable welfare effect resulting from the tariff that would offset the deadweight loss of consumer surplus. If a country could impose a tariff that would improve its terms of trade vis-à-vis its trading partners, it would enjoy a larger share of the gains from trade. This would tend to increase its national welfare, offsetting the deadweight loss of consumer surplus. Because it is so insignificant relative to the world market, the country is unable to influence the terms of trade. Levying an import tariff therefore reduces a small country's national welfare.

Tariff Welfare Effects: Large-Country Model

Consider the case in which an importing nation accounts for a significant portion of the world market. A large country, as a major consumer, is important enough to affect the terms at which it trades. Changes in a large country's domestic economic conditions or trade policies can therefore influence the distribution of the gains from trade that affects its national welfare.

One of the justifications for an import tariff is that it may enable a country to extract larger gains from trade. A tariff-levying nation is similar to a monopsonist who restricts the level of purchases to reduce the price of inputs. By reducing the volume of imports with a tariff, a nation hopes to force down the prices it pays to foreign producers. This would improve the importing nation's terms of trade and result in larger gains from trade.[5] But an importing nation would face a decline in its national welfare if the negative effects of a reduced volume of trade outweighed the positive effects of a favorable change in the terms of trade. This is like a monopolist who cuts back output too far and finds that price gains are more than offset by losses in volume.

Figure 5.2 illustrates the trade position of an importing country. Line S_d represents the home supply curve and line D_d depicts the home demand curve. Autarky equilibrium is achieved at point E. With free trade, the importing nation faces an overall supply curve of S_{d+w}. This curve shows the number of autos that both domestic and foreign producers together offer home consumers. Notice that the overall supply curve is upward sloping rather than horizontal. This is because the foreign supply price is not a fixed constant. The price depends on the quantity

purchased by an importing country when it is a large buyer of the product. With free trade, our country achieves market equilibrium at point F. The price of autos falls to $8,000, domestic consumption rises to 110 units, and domestic production falls to 30 units. Auto imports totaling 80 units satisfy the excess home demand.

Suppose that the importing country imposes a specific tariff of $1,000 on imported autos. By increasing the selling cost, the tariff results in a shift in the overall supply curve from S_{d+w} to S_{d+w+t}. Market equilibrium moves from point F to point G, while product price rises from $8,000 to $8,800. The tariff-levying nation's

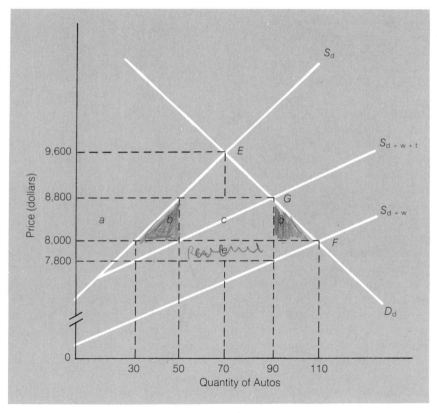

Figure 5.2   Tariff trade and welfare effects: large-country model.

$e > b + d \Rightarrow$ welfare has increased

$e < b + d \Rightarrow$ welfare has decreased

consumer surplus falls by an amount equal to areas $a + b + c + d$. Area a, totaling $32,000, represents the redistribution effect, whereby income is transferred from home consumers to home producers. Areas $d + b$ depict the tariff's deadweight loss, in which national welfare deteriorates because of reduced consumption (consumption effect = $8,000) and an inefficient use of resources (protective effect = $8,000).

As in the small-country example, a tariff's revenue effect is determined by multiplying the import tariff times the number of auto imports. This yields areas $c + e$, or $40,000. Notice that the tariff revenue accruing to the government now comes from foreign producers as well as domestic consumers. This is unlike the small-country case, where the supply curve is horizontal and where the tariff's burden fell entirely on domestic consumers.

To the free trade import price, $8,000, the tariff of $1,000 is added. Although the price in the protected market will exceed the foreign supply price by the amount of the duty, it will not be higher than the free trade foreign supply price by this amount. Compared with the free trade foreign supply price, $8,000, with the tariff home consumers must pay an additional price of $800 per auto import. This magnitude is the amount of the tariff shifted forward to the consumer. On the other hand, the foreign supply price of autos falls by $200. This means that foreign producers earn smaller revenues, $7,800, for each auto exported. Since foreign production takes place under increasing cost conditions, the reduction of imports from abroad triggers a decline in foreign production and thus unit costs decline. The reduction in the foreign supply price, $200, represents that portion of the tariff borne by the foreign producer. The levying of the tariff raises the home price of the import by less than the amount of the duty as foreign producers lower their prices in an attempt to maintain sales in the tariff-levying country. The importing country hence finds that its terms of trade has improved if the price it pays foreign producers for auto imports decreases while the price it charges foreigners for its exports remains the same.

The revenue effect of the import tariff can now be fully identified. The first component is the amount of tariff revenue shifted from home consumers to the tariff-levying government, determined in Figure 5.2 by multiplying the level of imports, 40 units, by the portion of the import tariff borne by domestic consumers, $800. The domestic revenue effect is depicted by area c which equals $32,000. Next is the tariff revenue extracted from foreign producers in the form of a lower supply price. Found by multiplying the auto imports, 40 units, by the portion of the tariff falling on foreign producers, $200, the terms-of-trade effect is shown as area e which equals $8,000. Note that the terms-of-trade effect represents a redistribution of income from the foreign country to the tariff-levying country as the result of the new terms of trade. Together the domestic revenue effect and the terms-of-trade effect sum to equal the total revenue effect of the tariff.

A country that is a major importer of a product is in a favorable trade situation. It may be able to use its tariff policy to improve the terms at which it trades and hence its national welfare. But remember that the negative welfare effect of a tariff is the deadweight loss of consumer surplus that results from the protection and consumption effects. Referring to Figure 5.2, to determine if a tariff-levying country can improve its national welfare, the overall impact of the deadweight loss of consumer surplus (areas b plus d) must be compared with the benefits of a favorable terms of trade (area e). The conclusions about the welfare effects of a tariff are as follows:

1. If $e > (b + d)$, national welfare is increased.
2. If $e = (b + d)$, national welfare remains constant.
3. If $e < (b + d)$, national welfare is diminished.

In the preceding example, the domestic economy's welfare would have declined by an amount equal to $8,000. This is because the deadweight welfare losses, totaling $16,000, more than offset the $8,000 gain in welfare due to the terms-of-trade effect.

Tariff Welfare Effects: Examples

The previous section analyzed the welfare effects of import tariffs from a theoretical perspective. Now let us turn to some examples of import tariffs and examine estimates of their costs and benefits to the nation.[6]

Citizen Band Radios

In 1978, President Carter extended temporary relief to American products of citizen band (CB) radio transceivers when he raised import tariffs from 6 percent to 21 percent. Over the following three years, the tariffs were phased down annually—from 21 to 18 to 15 percent—until final termination. The president's action was taken in response to the government's finding that imports of CB radios were seriously hurting the domestic industry.

Over the period 1972–1976, American demand for CB radios increased twentyfold to a level valued at $940 million. However, imports as a share of the U.S. market also were rising, from 78 percent to 90 percent. By 1977, the sales of U.S. producers had fallen by almost 40 percent, and domestic employment in the manufacture of CB radios was down considerably. These circumstances led to the president's decision to provide additional protection for American producers.

As estimated by the Federal Trade Commission (FTC), the first-year welfare effects of the tariffs are summarized in Table 5.6. An increase in the tariff from 6 percent to 21 percent would be expected to result in an $8 increase in the price of CB radios, from $54 to $62 per unit. Domestic consumption would fall by 1.53 million units, whereas domestic production would expand by 221,000 units. The total reduction in consumer surplus, resulting from the losses of those consumers who now have to pay a higher price plus the losses of those forced out of the market owing to the higher price, amounts to $48.8 million. Of this sum, tariff revenues would rise by $33.6 million, and profits to U.S. producers would increase by $3 million. The deadweight losses to the U.S. economy would stem from a $1.5 million loss due to production inefficiencies and a $10.7 million loss due to consumption inefficiencies. Approximately 587 jobs would be created for American workers, but at a cost to the U.S. consumer of some $83,000 per job created.

Based on these estimates, the FTC concluded that the tariff would yield only modest benefits to the domestic industry. What is more, the American consumer and the economy at large would face considerable costs, whereas employment and sales of companies distributing imported CB radios would drop.

Oil

The U.S. oil industry is another example of a sector of the economy traditionally subjected to import restrictions. During the 1950s, American

Table 5.6   Estimated Costs and Benefits of an Increased Tariff on CB Radios

Welfare Effect	Cost/Benefit (millions of dollars)
Losses to domestic consumers	48.8
Deadweight losses	
Consumption	10.7
Production	1.5
Increase in tariff revenues	33.6
Gains to domestic producers	3.0

Source: Morris E. Morkre and David G. Tarr, *Effects of Restrictions on U.S. Imports*, Federal Trade Commission, 1980, p. 71.

oil companies were able to convince President Eisenhower that cheap foreign oil was placing domestic producers at a competitive disadvantage. Viewing the health of the domestic oil industry as vital to the nation's security, in 1954 the President introduced quota restrictions on imported oil to reduce U.S. dependence on foreign producers. However, by 1970, foreign oil prices began to rise under the stimulus of OPEC, the result being less pressure to insulate American prices from those of cheap foreign oil. This led to the suspension of import restrictions in 1973.

Throughout the seventies and early eighties, OPEC was able to use its dominance of the world oil market as a lever in bidding up oil prices. However, by 1982, OPEC prices were plummeting as the demand for oil in the industrial countries collapsed under the impact of economic recession, surprisingly high levels of conservation, expanded use of alternate energy sources, and rising oil production in Mexico, the North Sea, and Alaska. It was feared that a collapse in oil prices might reverse U.S. efforts to conserve

and to invest in energy production. The question arose whether the United States should again adopt restrictions on oil imports.

Although no restrictions have been implemented to date, one proposal called for the imposition of an oil import tariff of $3 or $4 per barrel. The purpose of the tariff would be to support the U.S. price of oil above that of OPEC. This would encourage investment in energy-efficient products, including autos and capital equipment, which might be imperiled by an oil price collapse. The tariff would also encourage production of oil in the United States, limiting its dependence on imported oil. Furthermore, the federal government's budget deficit would be lessened by the additional tax revenues generated by the tariff.

On the other hand, supporting the price of oil in the United States via an import tariff would contribute to price inflation as well as dampen economic growth. Energy-intensive industries such as steel, in which energy comprises 15 percent to 20 percent of final costs, would also be adversely affected by high oil prices.

Table 5.7   How an Oil Import Fee Would Hit the U.S.

	Effect on U.S. Economy if a Fee Were Imposed on January 1, 1983	
	At $4 per bbl	*At $3 per bbl*
Gasoline, heating oil price	Up 8¢ per gal	Up 6¢ per gal
Crude oil imports	Down by 200,000 bbl per day in 1983, as much as 260,000 per day in 1986–1987	Down by 150,000 bbl per day in 1983, as much as 200,000 per day in 1986–1987
Oil production	Up slightly after 3 to 4 years	Up slightly after 3 to 4 years
Reduction of federal deficit 1983–1985	$8.5 billion annually	$6.2 billion annually
Inflation rate, 1983	Add 1 point	Add 0.8 point
Gross national product	Real growth cut 1 point in 1983, recovering in 1984	Real growth cut 0.7 point in 1983, recovering in 1984

Reprinted from the April 5, 1982 issue of *Business Week* by special permission, © 1982 by McGraw-Hill, Inc.
Data: Wharton Econometrics Long-Term U.S. Forecast Service.

By subjecting U.S. industries to higher energy costs than their foreign competitors, a tariff might reduce their competitiveness in world markets. Table 5.7 furnishes estimates of the economic effects of an oil import tariff.

Evaluation of Tariff Welfare Effects

In the previous sections, we have seen that a tariff affects a country's welfare in two opposing ways: (1) a terms-of-trade effect and (2) a volume-of-trade effect.

Imposition of a tariff may result in an improvement in a country's terms of trade (that is, the rate at which products are exchanged in international trade). Because a tariff makes imports more expensive for, say, American consumers, the number of imports demanded tends to decline. This makes it more difficult for foreigners to generate the revenues necessary to finance purchases from the United States. Foreigners may reduce their export prices in an attempt to enhance their capacity to finance purchases. So the tariff improves the U.S. terms of trade by lowering the prices the nation must pay for its imports. However, a reduced volume of imports due to the tariff results in a negative welfare effect for the United States in the form of a deadweight loss in consumer surplus. U.S. welfare thus improves if the favorable terms-of-trade effect outweighs the adverse trade volume effect.

By modifying the relative prices at which nations exchange goods and services, a tariff results in a redistribution of the gains from trade among nations. A favorable terms of trade, yielding a larger share of the gains from trade for one country, means the opposite for the other country. The welfare gains for the tariff-levying country come at the expense of its trading partner. Because tariffs are unable to increase the world gains from trade, they have no positive effect on global welfare. Tariffs do produce a negative welfare effect, a reduction in the volume of world trade. The net result is that for the world as a whole, tariffs reduce the level of welfare. A single country that is dissatisfied with the distribution of the world gains from trade may consider whether it should initiate a tariff on imports. But in an interdependent world, the country realizes that this act would not be welcomed by its trading partners. The possibility of foreign tariff retaliation may be a sufficient deterrent for any country considering whether to impose higher tariffs.

A classic case of a tariff-induced trade war was the implementation of the Smoot-Hawley tariff by the U.S. government in 1930. The tariff initially was intended to provide relief to American farmers. However, senators and members of Congress from industrial states used the technique of vote trading to obtain increased tariffs on manufactured goods. The result was a policy that increased tariffs on more than 1,000 products, the average nominal duty on protected goods being 53 percent! Viewing the Smoot-Hawley tariff as an attempt to force unemployment on its workers, 12 nations promptly increased their duties against the United States. American farm exports fell to one-third of their former level, and between 1930 and 1933, total American exports fell by almost 60 percent. Although the Great Depression contributed to much of that decline, the adverse psychological impacts of the Smoot-Hawley tariff on business activity cannot be ignored.

Tariff Quotas

Another restriction used to insulate a home industry from foreign competition is the *tariff quota*. Although not widely used as a trade restriction, the tariff quota has been levied by the U.S. government to protect industries, including milk, cattle, fish, brooms, tobacco products, and coconut oil.

As its name suggests, a tariff quota displays both tarifflike and quotalike characteristics. This device allows a specified number of goods to be imported at one tariff rate (the *within-quota rate*), whereas any imports above this level face a higher tariff rate (the *over-quota rate*). For example, during the early seventies, the U.S. tariff quota on fluid milk was set at 3 million gallons per year. Milk imports within this limit faced a duty of 2 cents per gallon, and a duty of 6.5 cents per gallon was applied to any imports over this limit.

The tariff quota generally is viewed as a compromise between the interests of the consumer, who desires low-cost imports, and the domestic producer, who desires protectionism. This is because the tariff quota attempts to minimize the adverse costs for the consumer by a modest within-quota rate, while still shielding home producers from severe import competition by a stiffer over-quota rate.

Welfare Effects

Figure 5.3 illustrates the hypothetical case of welfare effects of tariff quotas on trade in steel. Assume the U.S. demand and supply curves for steel are given by $D_{U.S.}$ and $S_{U.S.}$, the equilibrium price of steel being $540 per ton. Assuming free trade, suppose the United States faces a constant world price of steel equal to $400 per ton. At the

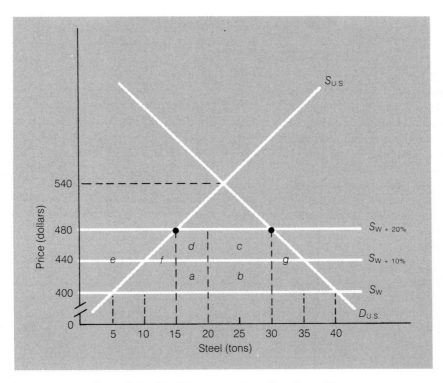

Figure 5.3   Tariff quota trade and welfare effects.

free trade price, U.S. production equals 5 tons, U.S. consumption equals 40 tons, and imports equal 35 tons.

To protect its producers from foreign competition, suppose the United States enacts a steel quota of 5 tons. Imports within this limit face a 10 percent tariff, while a 20 percent tariff is applied to imports in excess of the limit.

Since the United States initially is importing an amount exceeding the limit as defined by the tariff quota, both the within-quota rate and the over-quota rate would apply. This two-tier tariff results in a rise in the price of steel sold in the United States from $400 to $480 per ton. Domestic production increases to 15 tons, domestic consumption falls to 30 tons, and imports fall to 15 tons. Increased sales would permit the profits of U.S. steel producers to rise by an amount equal to area e. The deadweight losses to the American economy, in terms of production and consumption inefficiencies, would equal areas $f + g$, respectively.

The interesting feature of the tariff quota is the revenue it generates, some of which accrues to the domestic government as *tariff revenue*, the remainder being captured by business as *windfall profits*. In the preceding example, 15 tons of steel are imported after the enactment of the tariff quota. The U.S. government collects area a, found by multiplying the within-quota duty of $40 times 5 tons. Area $b + c$ also accrues to the government, ascertained by multiplying the remaining 10 tons of imported steel times the over-quota duty of $80.

It is area d in the figure that represents windfall profits, a gain to business resulting from sudden or unexpected governmental policy. Under the tariff quota, the domestic price of the first 5 tons of steel imported is $440, reflecting the foreign supply price of $400 plus the import duty of $40. Suppose U.S. import companies are able to obtain foreign steel at $440. By reselling the 5 tons to American consumers at $480 per ton, the price that over-quota steel would be

going for, U.S. importers would capture area d as windfall profits. But this opportunity will not last long, since foreign steelmakers will want to capture the windfall gain. To the extent they can restrict steel exports to the United States in a monopolistic fashion, foreign firms could force up that price of steel and expropriate profits from U.S. importers. Foreign firms conceivably could capture the entire area d by raising their supply price to $440 per ton. The portion of the windfall profits captured by foreign steelmakers represents an overall welfare loss to the U.S. economy.

Stainless Steel Flatware

The stainless steel flatware (knives, forks, spoons) industry provides another example of a tariff quota's welfare effects.

Between 1953 and 1958, the American consumption of stainless steel flatware increased from 11.6 million dozen pieces (mdp) to almost 23 mdp. Although American producers' sales of flatware increased from 1953 to 1955, their sales stagnated from 1956 to 1958. A major reason for this stagnation was rising imports from Japan, which were able to capture 40 percent of the U.S. market by 1958.

To minimize the adverse impact of trade restrictions on consumers while still protecting manufacturers, in 1959 President Eisenhower levied a tariff quota on imports of stainless steel flatware. The initial import quota was set at 5.75 mdp on a global basis. The within-quota rates on the various types of flatware ranged from approximately 12.5 percent ad valorem to 17.5 percent ad valorem, whereas the over-quota rates were in the 60 percent to 115 percent range. In subsequent years, the sales of American manufacturers increased so that by 1967 their share of the domestic market was 75 percent.

In 1967, the tariff quota expired. As a result, the share of the U.S. market captured by imports rose to 60 percent. In 1971, the president reimposed the tariff quota, which then remained in effect until 1975. The new tariff quota set the import limit at 16.2 mdp, allowing for 6 percent growth annually. The average within-quota rate for flatware was approximately 23 percent ad valorem, whereas the over-quota rate averaged 62 percent. But under the second tariff quota, American producers' sales continued to deteriorate with the weakening U.S. economy and the rise of new foreign competition from Korea and Taiwan.

Table 5.8 summarizes one estimate of the economic effects of the second tariff quota on flatware for the year 1974. Compared with free trade, the tariff quota resulted in increased expenditures to consumers of $45.7 million. Of this sum, $10.8 million was captured by domestic manufacturers as profits, $13.9 million went to the government as tariff revenue, $6.5 million accrued to importers and foreign exporters as windfall profits, and $14.5 million was lost by the economy as deadweight inefficiencies. Domestic output increased by 12.06 mdp. In addition, the tariff quota generated 1,357 jobs for American workers. The annual cost to the consumer per job protected was $33,667 and the deadweight inefficiency was $10,685 per job.

Arguments for Trade Restrictions

The *free trade argument* is in principle persuasive. It states that if each nation produces what it does best and permits trade, over the long run all will enjoy lower prices and higher levels of output, income, and consumption than could be achieved in isolation. In a dynamic world, comparative advantage is constantly changing owing to shifts in technologies, input productivities, and wages, as well as tastes and preferences. A free market compels adjustment to take place. Either the efficiency of an industry must improve or else resources will flow from low productivity uses to those with high productivity. Tariffs and other trade barriers are viewed as tools that prevent the economy from undergoing adjustment, the result being economic stagnation. To a free trade advocate, exports are the cost of trade and imports are the returns from trade, not the other way around.

Although the free trade argument tends to dominate in the classroom, virtually all nations have imposed *restrictions* on the international flow of goods, services, and capital. This is often because proponents of protectionism say, "Free trade is fine in theory, but it does not apply in the real world." Modern trade theory assumes perfectly competitive markets whose characteristics tend to depart from real-world market conditions. Moreover, even though protectionists may concede that economic losses occur with tariffs and other restrictions, they often argue that noneconomic benefits such as national security may be achieved to more than offset the economic losses. In seeking protection from imports, domestic industries and labor unions attempt to better their economic welfare. Over the years, a number of arguments have been

Table 5.8.   Tariff Quota Welfare Effects: Stainless Steel Flatware

Effect	Millions of Dollars
Consumer expenditure increase	45.7
Producer profit (surplus)	10.8
Deadweight welfare losses (protection and consumption effects)	14.5
Tariff revenue for the government	13.9
Windfall profits to domestic importer/foreign exporter	6.5
Increase in domestic output	12.06 mdp

Source: Charles Pearson, "Protection by Tariff Quota: Case Study of Stainless Steel Flatware," *Journal of World Trade Law*, 13 (July–August, 1979), p. 318.

advanced to pressure the president and Congress to enact restrictive measures.

Job Protection

The issue of jobs has been a dominant factor in motivating government officials to levy trade restrictions on imported goods. During periods of economic recession, workers are especially anxious to point out that cheap foreign goods undercut domestic production, the result being a loss of home jobs to foreign labor. Alleged job losses to foreign competition appear to have been a major force behind the desire of most U.S. labor leaders to reject free trade policies.

U.S. labor leaders are quick to refer to statistics of the type illustrated on the left-hand side of Table 5.9, which estimates the number of American jobs lost due to import competition in the period 1975-1976. Such job losses are readily observed by workers, labor union officials, and government policy makers. This data indeed may lead us to conclude that trade liberalization policies may contribute to a decline in total domestic employment and therefore are not in the best interest of domestic labor.

This view, however, has a serious omission— it fails to acknowledge the dual nature of international trade, which recognizes that changes in a country's imports of goods and services are closely related to changes in its exports. Countries export goods because they desire to import products from other countries. When the United States imports goods from abroad, foreigners gain purchasing power that eventually will be spent on U.S. goods, services, or financial assets. American export industries then enjoy gains in sales and employment, whereas the opposite occurs in American import-competing industries. Rather than promoting overall unemployment, imports tend to generate job opportunities in some industries as part of the process by which they decrease employment in other industries. The result is a tendency in the long run for a country's exports and imports to have a neutral impact on overall employment; that

Table 5.9.   Estimated Effects of Imports and Exports on U.S. Labor Markets
(1975–1976)

Industry	Jobs Lost to Imports	Industry	Jobs Gained from Exports
Radio and TV equipment	14,300	Transportation equipment	44,000
Automobiles	67,000	Nonelectrical machinery	58,100
Steel	17,000	Chemicals	6,800
Iron and steel foundries	6,900	Agricultural	235,900
Clothing	39,700	Scientific equipment	4,300
Footwear	19,700	Textiles	20,400
Mining	85,500		
Total	250,100	Total	369,500

Source: Clifton B. Luttrell, "Imports and Jobs: The Observed and the Unobserved," *Review*, Federal Reserve Bank of St. Louis (June 1978), pp. 4, 8. See also Clifton B. Luttrell, "The Voluntary Automobile Import Agreement with Japan—More Protectionism," *Review*, Federal Reserve Bank of St. Louis (November 1981), pp. 25–30.

is, employment losses in some industries will be offset by employment gains in others.

As seen in Table 5.9, there have been significant increases in employment in American export industries, which have offset employment losses in import-competing industries. Major gains have occurred in machinery, transportation equipment, and agriculture. However, these gains tend to be less visible to the public than the readily observable losses in jobs stemming from foreign competition. This has often led many of our nation's business and labor leaders to combine forces in their opposition to free trade.

Protection Against Cheap Foreign Labor

One of the most common arguments used to justify the protectionist umbrella of trade restrictions is that tariffs are needed to defend domestic jobs against cheap foreign labor. As indicated in Table 5.10, production workers in the United States have been paid much higher wages, in

Table 5.10.   Estimated Hourly Compensation in U.S. Dollars per Hour Worked for Production Workers in Manufacturing, 1982

Country	Hourly Compensation (dollars per hour)
United States	11.79
Canada	10.77
West Germany	10.43
Japan	5.82
United Kingdom	6.67
South Korea	1.22
Mexico	1.97
Taiwan	1.57
Ireland	5.29
Hong Kong	1.55

Source: U.S. Department of Labor, Bureau of Labor Statistics, "Hourly Compensation Costs for Production Wokers in Manufacturing" (unpublished data), April 1983. See also Handbook of Labor Statistics, U.S. Department of Labor, 1983.

terms of the U.S. dollar, than workers in countries like Japan and the United Kingdom. So it could be argued that low wages abroad make it difficult for American producers to compete with producers using cheap foreign labor and that unless American producers are protected from imports, domestic production and employment levels will decrease. Although this viewpoint may have widespread appeal, it fails to recognize the links among efficiency, wages, and production costs.

Even if domestic wages are higher than those abroad, if home labor is more productive than foreign labor, domestic labor costs still may be competitive. Total labor costs reflect the wage rate as well as the output per labor hour. If the productive superiority of home labor more than offsets the higher domestic wage rates when compared with other nations, the home country's labor costs will be less than they are abroad.

Another limitation of the cheap foreign labor argument is that low-wage countries tend to have a competitive advantage only in the production of goods requiring much labor and little of the other factor inputs. This means that the wage bill is the largest component of the total costs of production, which include payments to all factor inputs. It is true that a high-wage country may have a relative cost disadvantage compared with its low-wage trading partner in the production of labor-intensive commodities. But this does not mean that foreign producers can undersell the home country across the board in all lines of production, causing the overall domestic standard of living to decline. Foreign nations should use the revenues from their export sales to purchase the products in which the home country has a competitive advantage—that is, in products requiring a large share of the factors of production that are abundant domestically.

Contemporary international trade theory suggests that as economies become integrated through trade, there is a tendency for resource payments to become equalized in different nations, given competitive markets. A nation with expensive labor will tend to import products embodying large amounts of labor. As imports rise and domestic output falls, the resulting decrease in demand for domestic labor will cause home wages to fall to the foreign level.

In automobile manufacturing, for example, there is sufficient international competition to warrant such a process. This was seen in 1982 when high unemployment in the American auto industry permitted General Motors and Ford to scale down the compensation levels of their employees as a means of offsetting their cost disadvantages against the Japanese. The adverse implications that resource price equalization would have for the wages of autoworkers is an apparent motivation of the UAW's support for protectionism. By shielding American wage levels from market pressures created by foreign competition, protectionism would result in the U.S. government validating high wages and benefits of UAW members, more than $8 per hour above the levels earned by the Japanese autoworker as of 1982. International price equity is thus negated by trade restrictions.

Maintenance of Domestic Standard of Living

Advocates of trade barriers often contend that tariffs are useful in maintaining a high level of income and employment for the home country. It is argued that by reducing the level of imports, tariffs encourage home spending, which stimulates domestic economic activity. As a result, the home country's level of employment and income is enhanced.

Although this argument appears appealing on the surface, it merits several qualifications. It is apparent that all nations together cannot levy tariffs to bolster domestic living standards. This is because tariffs result in a redistribution of the gains from trade among nations. To the degree that one nation imposes a tariff that improves its income and employment, it occurs at the expense of its trading partner's living standard. Nations adversely affected by trade barriers are likely to impose retaliatory tariffs, resulting in a lower level of welfare for all countries. It is little wonder that tariff restrictions designed to enhance a country's standard of living at the expense of its trading partner are referred to as *beggar-thy-neighbor* policies.

Equalization of Production Costs

Proponents of this argument, sometimes called the *scientific tariff,* desire to eliminate what they consider to be unfair competition from abroad. Owing to such factors as lower wage costs, tax concessions, or governmental subsidies, foreign sellers may enjoy cost advantages over domestic firms. To offset any such advantage, tariffs equivalent to the cost differential should be imposed. Such tariff provisions were actually part of the U.S. Tariff Acts of 1922 and 1930.

In practice, the scientific tariff suffers from a number of problems. How can costs actually be compared, since within a given industry costs differ from firm to firm? Suppose that all American steel firms were extended protection from all foreign steel producers. This would require the costs of the most efficient foreign firm to be set equal to the highest costs of the least efficient American company. Given today's cost conditions, prices would certainly rise in the United States. But this would benefit the more efficient American firms who would enjoy economic profits, whereas the American consumer would be subsidizing inefficient production. Because the scientific tariff approximates a prohibitive tariff, it completely contradicts the notion of comparative advantage and wipes out the basis for trade and gains from trade.

Infant Industry Argument

One of the more commonly accepted cases for tariff protection is the infant industry argument. This argument does not deny the validity of the case for free trade, but is does contend that for free trade to be meaningful, trading nations should temporarily shield their newly developing industries from foreign competition. Otherwise, the mature foreign firms, who are at the time more efficient, can drive the young domestic firms out of the market. Only after the young firms have had time to become efficient producers should the tariff barriers be lifted and free trade take place.

Figure 5.4 illustrates the logic of the infant industry argument. During its infant stage, shown as time period t_0-t_1, a new industry will not likely be able to compete against mature foreign firms. Not only are its operations too small to realize economies-of-scale efficiencies but also its production methods may be untested and need further improvements. Only after these long-run adjustments are made can the

young industry prosper and become an efficient producer. This occurs during time period t_1-t_2 in Figure 5.4. Eventually the infant industry will mature and achieve its competitive advantage.

Although there is some truth in the infant industry argument, it must be qualified in several respects. First, once a protective tariff is initiated, it is very difficult to remove, even after industrial maturity has occurred. Special-interest groups can often convince policy makers that further protection is justified. Second, it is very difficult to determine which industries will be capable of realizing comparative advantage potential and thus merit protection. Third, the infant industry argument generally is not valid for the mature industrialized nations such as the United States, West Germany, and Japan. Last, it is often contended that there are other ways of insulating a developing industry from cutthroat competition. Rather than adopting a protective tariff, a subsidy could be granted to the industry. Although subsidy has the advantage of not distorting domestic consumption and relative prices, its drawback is that rather than

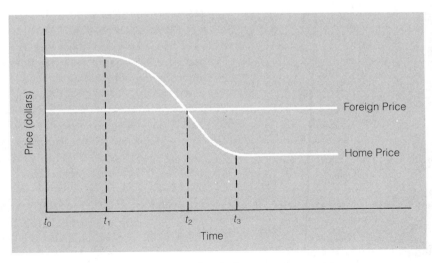

Figure 5.4   Infant industry argument.

1g revenue as an import tariff does, a subsidy spends revenue.

Noneconomic Arguments

One can also argue that there are noneconomic considerations that must be dealt with in addition to economic factors when assessing the merits of protectionism. One consideration is the question of *national security*. The national security argument contends that a country may be put in jeopardy in the event of an international crisis or war if it is heavily dependent on foreign suppliers. Even though domestic producers are not as efficient, tariff protection should be granted to ensure their continued existence. A good application of this argument involves the major oil-importing countries, which saw several Arab nations impose oil boycotts on the West to win support for the Arab position against Israel during the 1973 Middle East conflict. However, the problem of the national security argument is stipulating what constitutes an essential industry. If the term is broadly defined, many industries may be able to win protection from import competition and the argument loses its meaning.

Another noneconomic argument is based on cultural and sociological considerations. New England may desire to preserve small-scale fishing or West Virginia may argue for tariffs on hand-blown glassware on the grounds that these occupations enrich the fabric of life, or certain products such as narcotics may be considered socially undesirable and restrictions or prohibitions placed on their importation. These arguments constitute legitimate reasons and cannot be ignored. All the economist can do is to point out the economic consequences and costs of protection and identify alternative ways of accomplishing the same objective.

It is important to note that most of the arguments justifying tariffs are based on the assumption that the national welfare will be enhanced as well as the individual's welfare. The strategic importance of tariffs for the welfare of import-competing producers is one of the main reasons why reciprocal tariff liberalization has been so gradual. It is no wonder that import-competing producers make such strong and politically effective arguments that increased foreign competition will undermine their welfare as well as that of the nation as a whole. Although a liberalization of tariff barriers may be detrimental to a particular group, one must be careful to differentiate between the individual's welfare and the national welfare. If tariff reductions result in greater welfare gains from trade, and if the adversely affected party can be compensated for the loss it has faced, the overall national welfare will increase. However, proving that the gains more than offset the losses in practice is very difficult.

Summary

1. Even though the free trade argument has strong theoretical justifications, trade restrictions are widespread throughout the world. Trade barriers consist of (1) tariff restrictions and (2) nontariff trade barriers.

2. There are two types of tariffs. An ad valorem tariff is stated as a percentage of an imported commodity's value. Specific tariffs represent fixed monetary duties per unit of the imported commodity.

3. Concerning ad valorem tariffs, several procedures exist for the valuation of imports. The free-on-board measure indicates a commodity's price as it leaves the exporting country. The cost-insurance-freight measure shows the product's value as it arrives at the port of entry.

4. The effective rate of protection tends to differ from the nominal tariff rate when the domestic import-competing industry uses imported resources whose tariffs differ from those

on the final commodity. Developing countries have traditionally argued that the tariff structures of many advanced countries on industrial commodities are escalated to yield an effective rate of protection several times the nominal rate.

5. The welfare effects of a tariff can be measured by the following: (1) protective effect, (2) consumption effect, (3) redistribution effect, (4) revenue effect, and (5) terms-of-trade effect.

6. If a home country is small compared with the rest of the world, its welfare necessarily falls by the amount indicated by the protective effect plus consumption effect if it levies a tariff on imports. But should the importing country be large relative to the world, the imposition of an import tariff may improve its international terms of trade by an amount that more than offsets the welfare losses associated with the consumption effect and protective effect.

7. Although tariffs may improve one country's economic position, they generally come at the expense of other countries. Should tariff retaliations occur, the volume of international trade would decrease and world welfare would suffer. Tariff liberalization is intended to promote freer markets so that the world can benefit from expanded trade volumes and international specialization of inputs.

8. Although not widely used as a trade restriction, tariff quotas have been used to protect certain industries. A tariff quota permits a limited number of goods to be imported at a lower tariff rate, while any imports beyond this limit face higher tariffs. An interesting feature of the tariff quota is the revenue it generates, some of which accrues to the domestic government as tariff revenue, the remainder being captured by producers as windfall profits.

9. Tariffs are sometimes justified on the grounds that they (1) protect domestic employment, (2) equate the cost of imported products with the cost of domestic import-competing products, (3) protect industries necessary for national security, or (4) allow domestic industries to be insulated temporarily from foreign competition until they can grow and develop.

Study Questions

1. Distinguish between a specific tariff and an ad valorem tariff. What are the advantages and disadvantages of each?

2. What are the major methods that customs appraisers use to determine the values of commodity imports?

3. Under what conditions does a nominal tariff applied to a product import overstate or understate the actual or effective protection afforded by the nominal tariff?

4. How is it that less-developed countries sometimes argue that the industrialized nations' tariff structures discourage the less-developed countries from undergoing industrialization?

5. Distinguish between consumer surplus and producer surplus. How do these concepts relate to a country's economic welfare?

6. When a nation imposes a tariff on the importation of a commodity, economic inefficiencies that detract from the national welfare tend to develop. Explain.

7. What factors influence the size of the revenue, protective, consumption, and redistribution effects of a tariff?

8. A country that imposes tariffs on imported goods may find its welfare improving should the tariff result in a favorable shift in the terms of trade. Explain.

9. Which of the arguments for tariffs do you feel are most relevant in today's world?

10. Although tariffs may improve the welfare of a single country, the world's welfare may decline. Under what conditions would this be true?

11. What impact does the imposition of a tariff normally have on a nation's terms of trade and volume of trade?

12. In 1978, President Carter extended relief to the U.S. CB radio industry when he increased import duties for a three-year period. What would be the likely effects of this policy for the U.S. economy if it were continued?

13. Would a tariff imposed on U.S. oil imports promote energy development and conservation for the United States?

14. A tariff quota is often viewed as a compromise between the interests of the domestic consumer and those of the domestic producer. Explain.

15. How does the revenue effect of a tariff quota differ from that of an import tariff?

Notes

1. See Harry G. Johnson, "The Theory of Tariff Structure With Special Reference to World Trade and Development," in Harry G. Johnson and Peter B. Kenen, *Trade and Development* (Geneva: Libraire Droz, 1965).

2. Other estimates of the effective rate of protection can be found in M. K. Loken, "The Effective Protection of the Canadian Exporting Industry," *Quarterly Review of Economics and Business* (Spring 1975), pp. 65–76 and G. Motha and H. Plunkett, "The Effective Rate of Protection," *Quarterly Review of Agricultural Economics* (July 1974), pp. 125–141.

3. See Bela A. Balassa, *The Structure of Protection in Developing Countries* (Baltimore: Johns Hopkins Press, 1971).

4. *Consumer surplus* can be thought of as the difference between any payment made by a

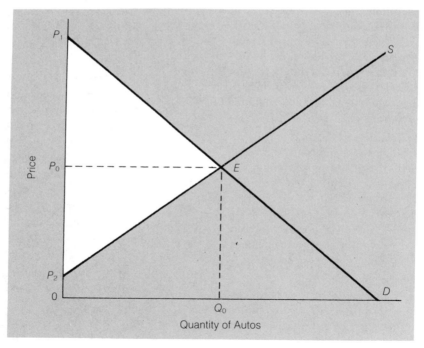

Figure 5.5   Consumer Surplus and Producer Surplus.

buyer and the maximum she would have been willing to pay for a given commodity. In Figure 5.5, each point along the demand curve shows the maximum price a buyer would pay for individual units of autos. Assuming the market price to be P_0, one could buy OQ_0 autos for OP_0EQ_0 dollars. For this quantity, consumer surplus is the area between the market price line (P_0E) and the demand curve and equals the triangle P_0EP_1. *Producer surplus* represents the difference between the actual market price and the minimum price a firm would be willing to accept rather than not producing the good at all. In the diagram, the supply schedule shows the minimum price necessary to call forth various levels of output. If the market price is P_0, then the value of quantity OQ_0 equals OP_0EQ_0 dollars. The difference is the triangle P_0EP_2, which is the amount of producer surplus.

5. See Lloyd Metzler, "Tariffs, the Terms of Trade, and the Distribution of National Incomes," *Journal of Political Economy,* 57 (February 1949), pp. 1–29 and Tibor Scitovsky, " A Reconsideration of the Theory of Tariffs," *Review of Economics and Statistics* (Summer 1942).

6. This section assumes the U.S. elasticity of supply of imports (CB radios and oil) is infinite and increasing cost conditions prevail in the U.S. market. Since the United States can import as much of the product as it desires without affecting import price, it is considered a small country. Although this assumption does not reflect the reality of the CB radio and oil markets for the United States, it does correspond to the assumptions underlying the empirical estimates of the welfare costs of tariff restrictions presented in this section. Because the precise character of real-world demand and supply curves is unknown, the statements of the welfare effects of tariffs are at best merely estimates, and often very rough estimates. This also applies to the welfare estimates of nontariff trade barriers that are presented in subsequent chapters.

Suggestions for Further Reading

Adams, W. et al. *Tariffs, Quotas, and Trade: The Politics of Protectionism*. San Francisco, Institute for Contemporary Studies, 1979.

Aho, C. M., and Orr, J. A. "Trade-Sensitive Employment: Who Are the Affected Workers?" *Monthly Labor Review*, February 1981.

Baldwin, R. E. "The Case Against Import-Industry Protection." *Journal of Political Economy*, May/June 1969.

Black, J. "Arguments for Tariffs." *Oxford Economic Papers*, June 1959.

Corden, W. M. "The Structure of a Tariff System and the Effective Protective Rate." *Journal of Political Economy*, June 1966.

Evans, J. W. *The Kennedy Round in American Trade Policy: The Twilight of GATT*? Cambridge, Mass.: Harvard University Press, 1971.

Grubel, H. G. "Effective Tariff Protection: A Nonspecialist Guide to the Theory, Policy Implications and Controversies." In H. G. Grubel and H. G. Johnson, eds., *Effective Tariff Protection*. Geneva: General Agreement on Tariffs and Trade, 1971.

Hervey, J. L. "Economic Stagnation and the Resurgence of Trade Restrictions." *Economic Perspectives*, Federal Reserve Bank of Chicago, Winter 1982.

Kravis, I. "The Current Case for Import Limitations." In Bela Balassa, ed., *Changing Patterns in Foreign Trade and Payments*, 3rd ed. New York: W.W. Norton, 1978.

Rom, M. *The Role of Tariff Quotas in Commercial Policy*. New York: Holmes & Meier, 1979.

6

NONTARIFF TRADE BARRIERS

A major development in international trade policy in recent years has involved the substitution of nontariff trade barriers for explicit tariffs. Sometimes referred to as the *new mercantilism* or the *new protectionism*, nontariff barriers constituted the most widely discussed topic at recent multilateral trade negotiations. Nontariff trade barriers include such diverse measures as orderly marketing agreements, import quotas, employment and industrial subsidies, safety standards, voluntary export quotas, discriminatory government procurement practices, trigger prices, and dumping. This chapter investigates the operation and economic effects of some major nontariff trade barriers.[1]

Quotas

Although the tariff has traditionally been an important instrument of protection, it certainly is not the only means. There also exist other nontariff restrictions on the flow of trade, an important one being the quota. The quota has several effects similar to that of a tariff, but the quota is a more restrictive, selective instrument.

An *import quota* is a quantitative measure of protection designed to curtail a nation's imports, presumably below the level existing under free trade conditions. For example, the 1964 Meat Import Law requires the president to impose quotas on frozen, chilled, or fresh veal, mutton, beef, and goat meat when the secretary of agriculture determines that imports during a year will exceed 110 percent of an adjusted base quota. The adjusted base quota maintains imports at about 7 percent of domestic production. Although import quotas primarily have been used to afford protection to home producers, they have also been intended to help reverse balance-of-payments deficits as well as to stimulate domestic employment. The administration of import quotas involves the government issuing import licenses to domestic importing firms.

Owing to international accords like the historic General Agreement on Tariffs and Trade (GATT), quotas cannot be used by a country as a means of regulating international trade. Quotas have been considered appropriate for meeting balance-of-payments crises, assuring the effectiveness of agriculture price-support programs, and safeguarding the national security. Trade in manufactured goods for the industrial nations has been relatively free from quantitative restrictions throughout the 1960s and 1970s, the main exception being textile products. However, quotas have traditionally distorted trade in coal, petroleum, and agricultural products.

Trade and Welfare Effects

Like a tariff, an import quota affects an economy's welfare. Figure 6.1 represents the case in autos of the United States in trade with Japan and West Germany. Assume that $S_{U.S.}$ and $D_{U.S.}$ denote the supply and demand curves of autos for the United States. S_J denotes the supply curve of Japan, assumed to be the world's low-cost producer, whereas S_{WG} denotes the supply curve of West Germany. Under free trade, the price of autos to the American consumer would equal $6,000 per unit. At this price, U.S. firms would produce 1 million autos and U.S. consumers would purchase 7 million autos. Imports from Japan would total 6 million autos, whereas West German autos would be too costly to be exported to the United States at the free trade price. (The role of West Germany in Figure 6.1 is emphasized later in this chapter when voluntary export restraints are discussed.)

Suppose the United States decides to limit its imports to 2 million units by levying an import quota. By reducing available supplies, the quota would force up the price of autos to $7,000. This leads to a fall in domestic consumption to 5 million units and a rise in domestic production to 3 million units, which together represent the quota's trade effect.

Import quotas also can be analyzed in terms of the welfare effects identified for tariffs in the preceding chapter. Since the quota in our example results in the price of auto imports rising to $7,000, U.S. consumer surplus falls by an amount equal to area $a + b + c + d + e + f + g + h + i + j + k + l$. Area $a + h$ represents the redistribution effect, area $b + c + i$ represents the protective effect, and area $f + g + l$ represents the consumption effect.

The deadweight loss of welfare to the economy resulting from the quota is depicted by the protective effect plus the consumption effect.

But what about the quota's revenue effect? The revenue effect, denoted by area $d + e + j + k$, arises from the fact that American consumers must pay an additional $1,000 for each of the 2 million units imported under the quota, as a result of the quota-induced scarcity of autos. Where does this revenue go?

One outcome occurs when American importing companies organize as buyers. Such importers might bargain favorably with foreign exporters and purchase autos at the prevailing world price of $6,000, reselling the autos to American consumers at a price of $7,000. The quota's revenue would thus accrue to the import companies as profits. Another instance is when foreign exporters organize as sellers and drive up the delivered price of autos to $7,000, thereby capturing the quota's revenues. Still another outcome results if the U.S. government auctions off import licenses to domestic importers according to the highest bidder. Such auctions are intended to permit the government to recoup the quota revenue that would have accrued to importers in the form of monopoly profits. This technique is seldom used.

Auto Import Quotas

The U.S. auto industry provides an example of the welfare effects of an import quota. Historically, American auto producers have been prosperous. American firms, most notably General Motors, often have enjoyed profits above the average for all manufacturers. However, by 1980, domestic auto sales were more than 40 percent below the level of 1978, and autoworker employment fell to 804,000, down from the 1975–1979 average of 922,000. Among the factors leading to falling sales were the doubling of gasoline prices in 1979–1980, the weakening

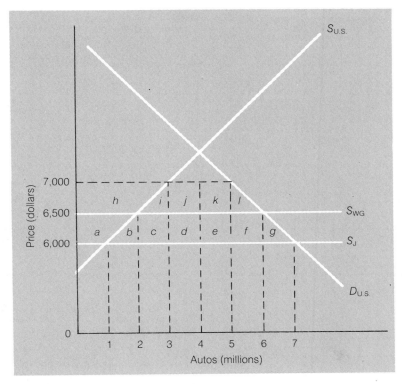

Figure 6.1   Quota trade and welfare effects.

U.S. economy, and a production cost disadvantage faced by U.S. firms against the Japanese amounting to $1,000–$1,500 per auto.

Triggered by skyrocketing oil prices, small-car imports surged as American consumers rejected large gas guzzlers produced by domestic firms. In 1980, imports as a share of the U.S. market jumped to more than 26 percent, up from the 22 percent level of 1979. In particular, it was the Japanese auto companies (Toyota, Datsun, Honda) that accounted for 18 percent of U.S. car sales in 1980.

As the growth in Japanese auto sales gained momentum in the early months of 1980, American labor and industry leaders filed petitions with the U.S. government. The first petition called for a quota on imported autos equal to 1.7 million units, compared with actual imports of 2.3 million autos in 1979. The other petition requested an increase in the duty on auto imports from the existing 2.9 percent to 20 percent. Both the proposed quota and the tariff were to last for a period of five years to allow U.S. companies time to retool and invest in small-car production facilities. In the end, the government ruled that imports of passenger cars were not the substantial cause of the American auto industry's problems, and protectionist relief was denied.

Whether to protect the U.S. auto industry from foreign competition was a most controversial issue, for it put the interests of the consumer and the country at large against those of the auto company owners and workers. Table 6.1 summarizes the welfare effects of the import quota and tariff proposals for the small-car segment of the market (compacts and subcompacts), as estimated by the Federal Trade Commission (FTC).

The FTC's estimates suggest that restricting auto imports via a quota would yield gains for domestic producers and workers. But the quota's cost to the American consumer would be sizable. Not only would the buying public be limited in its choice of models but also the resulting average price increase of $527 per auto would lead to rising consumer expenditures of $2.85 billion. As for the proposal for a 20 percent import duty, the costs to the nation would be even higher. The FTC's conclusion was that there may be more efficient methods of providing additional capital and maintaining employment in the auto industry. One such method would be government subsidies granted to the domestic industry, a topic that we consider later in this chapter.

Sugar Import Quotas

The U.S. sugar industry furnishes another example of the impact of an import quota on a nation's welfare. Traditionally, American sugar growers have received subsidies from the government in the form of price supports. Under this system, the government supplements the income of growers by guaranteeing a price for sugar sufficient to provide a fair rate of return. In maintaining its support price, the government purchases from growers through its Commodity Credit Corporation any excess supplies of sugar that exist at the support price.

The price support program ran into trouble when a glut of sugar in the world market led to the commercial price of sugar plunging to 6 cents per pound in 1982, compared with 41 cents per pound in 1980. This price was well below the 17 cents-per-pound support price of the federal government. It was estimated that unless the government took action to prop up the commercial price paid to American growers, the cost to the government of maintaining the support price through governmental purchases of sugar would amount to an extra $800 million. What is more, because the Congress had failed to appropriate funds for the price-support program in the 1982 federal budget, the government directed the Commodity Credit Corporation not to purchase surplus sugar. This left the price of American-produced sugar to be determined in the world market.

Table 6.1   Effects of UAW-Ford Trade Restraint Proposals: Small-Car Market

Effect	*20 Percent Duty*	*Quota of 1.7 Million Imported Autos*
Auto price increase	$1,162	$527
Import sale decrease	1,540,000 units	700,000 units
Domestic sales increase	570,000 units	260,000 units
Producer profit increase	$4.34 billion	$1.89 billion
Domestic employment increase	47,200 jobs	21,700 jobs
Consumer expenditure increase	$5.64 billion	$2.85 billion
Cost to consumer per job	$118,126	$126,641

Source: Michael Lynch, et al., *Certain Motor Vehicles and Certain Chassis and Bodies Therefor,* Federal Trade Commission, October 1980.

One way of shoring up the American commercial price of sugar would be to boost the tariff on sugar imports. But according to U.S. tariff codes, import duties could not exceed 50 percent of the world price of sugar. Although import duties were raised to their legal maximum, the import duty system was deemed inadequate to protect American growers from cheap foreign sugar as world prices fell throughout 1982.

Given a tight budget, the federal government chose not to channel additional revenues to the Commodity Credit Corporation to finance the purchases of U.S.-produced sugar. However, the government did impose quotas on imported sugar as a means of boosting domestic prices. In 1982, a quota system was announced that restricted imports on a country-by-country basis. Each country's quota was based on its average exports to the United States between 1975 and 1981, excluding the highest and lowest years. The total amount any country could export to the United States was to be adjusted on a quarterly basis in light of changing market conditions. By reducing sugar supplies, the quota would have the effect of forcing up the commercial price of sugar in the United States. The quota program thus transferred the cost of the sugar-support program from the American taxpayer to the American sugar consumer.

Early estimates by the U.S. Department of Agriculture indicated that the sugar quotas would increase the price of sugar by 2 to 4 cents per pound, an additional cost to consumers amounting to $400 million to $800 million per year. In addition to higher sugar prices, the prices of nonsugar sweeteners were expected to increase, further adding to consumer costs. The U.S. industrial sugar users, including the soft drink companies and candy makers, were among the first to complain about the adverse consequences of higher sugar prices.

In addition to the consequences for domestic consumers, the imposition of sugar quotas had international repercussions. About half of the U.S. sugar requirements are fulfilled with imported sugar, much of which comes from poorer developing countries. The restricted market created financial problems for countries like the Dominican Republic, where sugar accounted for almost 40 percent of its exports to the United States.

By 1983, the U.S. domestic price of sugar, as supported by the import quotas, stood at 22 cents a pound compared with the world price of 7 cents a pound. However, like most regulations, the sugar quotas had loopholes waiting to be discovered. It turns out that when sugar comes into the United States blended with at least 6 percent of another sweetener, flavoring, or food, the government does not consider it sugar. Thus the sugar quotas do not apply.

In 1981, the year before the implementation of the sugar quota program, only 300 tons of "blended sugar" were imported by the United States. In 1982, however, the amount rose to 13,000 tons, and industry sources estimated that in 1983, some 75,000 tons would find its way into U.S. soft drinks, ice cream, and candy bars. The majority of blended sugar imports came from Canada. This was because Canadian refiners could import sugar at low world prices and despite U.S. tariffs, export to the United States at roughly 8 cents below the U.S. domestic refined price. Located adjacent to the United States, Canada also enjoyed the advantage of lower transportation costs compared with most other sugar-exporting countries.

Quotas Versus Tariffs

Previous analysis suggests that the revenue effect of import quotas differs from that of tariffs. These two commercial policies can also differ in the impact they have on the volume of trade. The following example illustrates how during periods of growing demand, an import quota restricts the volume of imports by a *greater* amount than does an equivalent import tariff.[2]

Figure 6.2 represents the trade situation of the United States in autos. The U.S. supply and demand schedules for autos are given by $S_{U.S._0}$ and $D_{U.S._0}$, and S_{J_0} represents the Japanese auto supply schedule. Suppose the U.S. government has the option of levying a tariff or quota on auto imports to protect American companies from foreign competition.

In Figure 6.2(a), a tariff of $1,000 would raise the price of Japanese autos from $6,000 to $7,000. Auto imports would fall from 7 million units to 3 million units. In Figure 6.2(b), an import quota of 3 million units would put the United States in a trade position identical to that which occurs under the tariff. So far it appears that the tariff and quota are equivalent with respect to their restrictive impact on the volume of trade.

Now suppose the American demand for autos rises from $D_{U.S._0}$ to $D_{U.S._1}$. Figure 6.2(a) shows that in spite of the increased demand, the price of auto imports remains at $7,000. This is because the U.S. price cannot differ from the Japanese price by an amount exceeding the tariff duty. Auto imports rise from 3 million units to 5 million units. The fundamental point is that under an import tariff, domestic adjustment takes the form of an increase in the number of autos imported rather than a rise in auto prices.

In Figure 6.2(b), an identical increase in demand induces a rise in domestic auto prices. Under the quota, there is no limit on the extent to which the U.S. price can rise above the Japanese price. Given an increase in domestic auto prices, American companies are able to expand production. *The domestic price will rise until the increased production plus the fixed level of imports are commensurate with the domestic*

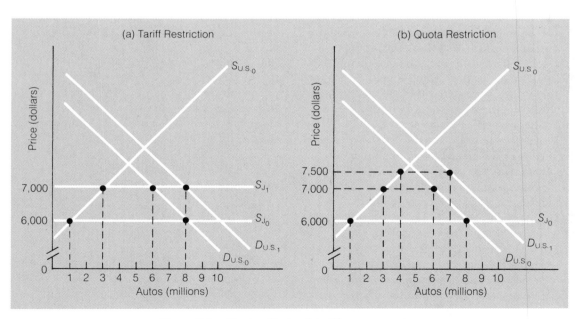

Figure 6.2   Trade effects of tariffs versus quotas.

demand. Figure 6.2(b) shows that an increase in demand from $D_{U.S._0}$ to $D_{U.S._1}$ forces auto prices up from $7,000 to $7,500. At the new price, domestic production equals 4 million units and domestic consumption equals 7 million units. So imports total 3 million units, the same amount that occurred under the quota just before the increase in domestic demand. Adjustment therefore occurs in domestic import prices rather than in the quantity of autos imported.

This analysis concludes that during periods of growing demand, an import quota is a more restrictive trade barrier than an equivalent import tariff. Under a quota, the government arbitrarily limits the quantity of imports. As for a tariff, the domestic price can rise above the world price only by an amount up to the tariff duty. Home consumers can still buy unlimited quantities of the import if they are willing and able to pay the tariff duty. The reader might test his or her understanding of the approach used here by working out the details of other hypothetical situations: (1) a reduction in the domestic supply of autos caused by rising production costs and (2) a reduction in domestic demand due to economic recession.

Besides differing in their revenue effects and restrictive impacts on the volume of trade, tariffs and quotas have several other notable differences. Quotas are administratively easier to manage than tariffs, but they normally do not provide government tax revenues. Quotas are relatively easy to enact for emergency purposes, whereas enactment of tariffs is a time-consuming process requiring statutory legislation.

Orderly Marketing Agreements

Throughout the 1970s and 1980s, trading nations have witnessed an emerging form of protectionism that has moved alongside tariffs and quotas as a major restrictive device. This new measure of protectionism is the so-called *orderly marketing agreement* (OMA), which essentially is a market-sharing pact negotiated by trading partners. Its main purpose is to moderate the intensity of international competition, allowing less efficient domestic producers to participate in markets that would have been lost to foreign producers that sell a superior product or price on a more competitive basis. Orderly marketing agreements involve trade negotiations between importing and exporting countries, generally for a variety of labor-intensive manufactured goods. A typical pact consists of *voluntary controls* (quotas) applied to exports. Such export controls may be supplemented by backup import controls to ensure that the restraints are effective. For example, Japan may impose limits on steel exports to Europe, or Taiwan may agree to cutbacks on shoe exports to the United States. Voluntary export restraints are intended to prevent home producers from being driven out of the market.

Because orderly marketing agreements are reached through negotiations, on the surface they appear to be less one-sided than unilateral protectionist devices such as tariffs and quotas. But in practice, the distinction between negotiated versus unilateral trade curbs becomes blurred. This is because trade negotiations are often carried out with the realization that the importing countries may adopt more stringent protectionist devices should the negotiators be unable to reach an acceptable settlement. An exporting country's motivation to negotiate orderly marketing pacts may thus stem from its desire to avoid a more costly alternative—that is, full-fledged trade wars.

Throughout the 1970s, the world has seen an upsurge in the number of market-sharing accords reached by trading partners. Table 6.2 outlines several major accords. Market-sharing pacts generally have been based on export quotas, import quotas, controls placed on annual growth rates of output, and curbs on price

Table 6.2   Recent Orderly Marketing Agreements

Manufactured Good	Principal Countries	Accord Provisions
Specialty steel	U.S., Common Market, Sweden, Japan, Canada	Japan negotiates export quota in U.S. market, U.S. imposes import quota on others
Carbon steel	Japan, South Africa, Spain, Common Market, South Korea	Japan voluntarily restrains exports to Common Market, Common Market requests export restraints by others
Television sets	Japan, Benelux, Britain	Japan voluntarily limits exports to Britain and Benelux
Ships	Japan, European Countries	Japan enters into agreement with European countries to curb price competition
Garments and textiles	41 exporting and importing countries	Export and import quotas, annual growth rates
Autos	Japan, U.S.	Japan voluntarily restrains exports to the U.S.
Carbon steel, pipe, tube	Common Market, U.S.	Common Market voluntarily limits exports to the U.S.

Source: *Annual Report of the President of the United States on the Trade Agreements Program* (Washington, D.C.: U.S. Government Printing Office, various issues).

competition. By 1978, orderly marketing agreements covered trade in such commodities as television sets, steel, shoes, textiles, calculators, radios, and ships.

As for the United States, the 1974 Trade Act gives the president the option of negotiating market-sharing agreements with other nations. Partly owing to the mid-1970's recession, the United States witnessed its labor and business community as well as Congress becoming more protectionist minded. The result has been an aggressive pursuit by the United States of orderly marketing agreements. Orderly marketing pacts are viewed by their proponents as an escape valve for rising protectionist pressures by labor and business and are considered much less disruptive to international transactions than the unilaterally imposed tariffs and quotas. Moreover, they avert the dangers of a 1930s-style trade war. Free trade advocates oppose such accords, however, on the grounds that they create a misallocation of world resources. Because resources are being prevented from flowing to their most productive usage, product prices are forced upward while world output levels are reduced.

Voluntary Export Restraints and Import Quotas

A typical orderly marketing agreement involves limitations on export sales administered by one or more exporting nations or industries. What are the trade and welfare effects of such voluntary export restraints?[3]

Like import quotas, voluntary export restraints can be analyzed by using the automobile trading example illustrated in Figure 6.1. Suppose that Japan, responding to protectionist sentiment in the U.S. Congress, decides to restrain auto shipments to the United States rather than face the possibility of mandatory restrictions being placed on its exports. Assume that the Japanese government levies an export quota on its auto firms equal to 2 million units, down from the free trade level of 6 million units. With the volume of imports constrained, U.S. consumers find the price of Japanese autos rising from $6,000 to $7,000. Consumer surplus falls by area $a + b + c + d + e + f + g + h + i + j + k + l$. Area $a + h$ represents the transfer to American auto companies as profits. The export quota results in a deadweight welfare loss for the U.S. economy equal to the protection effect, denoted by area $b + c + i$, and the consumption effect, denoted by area $f + g + l$. The export quota's revenue effect equals area $d + e + j + k$, found by multiplying the quota-induced increase in the Japanese price times the volume of autos shipped to the United States.

Remember that under an import quota, the disposition of the revenue effect is indeterminate. It will be shared between foreign exporters and domestic importers, depending on the relative concentration of bargaining power. But under a voluntary export quota, it is the foreign exporter who is able to capture the largest share of the quota revenue. In our example of the auto export quota, the Japanese exporters, in compliance with their government, self-regulate shipments to the United States. This supply-side restriction, resulting from Japanese firms behaving like a monopoly, leads to a scarcity of autos in the United States. Japanese auto firms then are able to raise the price of their exports, capturing the quota revenue. For this reason, it is not surprising that exporters might prefer to negotiate a voluntary restraint pact in lieu of facing other protectionist measures levied by the importing country. As for the export quota's impact on the U.S. economy, the expropriation of revenue by the Japanese represents a welfare loss in addition to the deadweight losses of production and consumption.

Another characteristic of a voluntary export agreement is that it typically applies to the most important exporting country or countries. This is in contrast to a tariff or import quota, the coverage of which generally applies to imports from all sources. When voluntary limits are imposed on shipments of the chief exporter, the exports of

the nonrestrained suppliers may be stimulated. This may be due to a desire to increase profits by making up part of the cutback in the restrained country's shipments. Nonrestrained suppliers also might want to achieve the maximum level of shipments against which to base export quotas they fear may be imposed on them in the future. For example, Japan was singled out by the United States for restrictions in textiles during the 1950s and in color TVs in the 1970s. Other nations quickly increased shipments to the United States to fill in the gaps created by the Japanese restraints. Hong Kong textiles replaced most Japanese textiles, and TVs from Taiwan and Korea supplanted Japanese TVs.

Referring to Figure 6.1, let us start again at the free trade price of $6,000, with U.S. imports from Japan totaling 6 million autos. Assume that Japan agrees to reduce its shipments to 2 million units. However, suppose West Germany, a nonrestrained supplier, exports autos to the United States in response to the Japanese cutback. Given an auto supply curve of S_{WG}, assume that West Germany ships 2 million autos to the United States. With combined shipments totaling 4 million units, auto prices to American consumers rise to $6,500. The resulting deadweight losses of production and consumption inefficiencies equal area $b + g$, less than the deadweight losses under Japan's export quota in the absence of nonrestrained supply. Assuming that Japan administers the export restraint program, Japanese companies would be able to raise the price of their auto exports from $6,000 to $6,500 and earn profits equal to area $c + d$. Area $e + f$ represents a *trade diversion effect*, which reflects inefficiency losses due to the shifting of 2 million units from Japan, the world's low-cost producer, to West Germany, a higher cost source. Such trade diversion results in a loss of welfare to the world, since resources are not being used in their most productive manner.

When increases in the nonrestrained supply offset part of the cutback in shipments that occur under an export quota, the overall inefficiency loss for the importing country (deadweight losses plus revenue expropriated by foreign producers) is less than that which would have occurred in the absence of nonrestrained exports. In the preceding example, this amounts to area $i + j + k + l$.

Japanese Auto Restraint

As previously discussed, the U.S. government in 1980 turned down the requests of the auto industry for additional protectionism in response to rising imports. However, by 1981, protectionist sentiment was gaining momentum in Congress as domestic auto sales plummeted, and legislation was introduced calling for import quotas. This momentum was a major factor in the administration's desire to negotiate a voluntary restraint pact with the Japanese. Japan's acceptance of this agreement apparently was based on its view that by voluntarily limiting its auto shipments, any protectionist momentum in Congress for more stringent measures would be derailed.

The restraint program called for self-imposed export quotas applied to Japanese auto shipments to the United States for three years, beginning in 1981. First-year shipments were to be held to 1.68 million units, 7.7 percent below the 1.82 million units exported in 1980. In subsequent years, auto shipments were to be held to the same number plus 16.5 percent of any increase in domestic U.S. auto sales recorded in 1981. As it turned out, falling U.S. sales resulted in Japanese auto exports being limited to 1.68 million units in 1982 and 1983. Still facing a weak auto industry, the United States was able to negotiate an export restraint pact with Japan for 1984, during which Japanese firms would limit auto shipments to the United States to 1.85 million units.

The purpose of the export agreement was to help American automakers by diverting to domestic showrooms those customers who could not buy Japanese imports. The pact was intended to increase domestic autoworker employment, whereas funds would be generated to finance the industry's revitalization. It was assumed that Japan's export quota would assist the U.S. auto industry as it went through a transition period of reallocating production toward smaller, fuel-efficient autos and adjusting production to become more cost competitive. The restraint program would provide U.S. auto companies temporary relief from foreign competition so they could restore profitability and reduce unemployment. Estimates suggested that U.S. auto firms would experience a $1.9 billion increase in revenues, while unemployment among U.S. autoworkers would fall by about 30,000 workers. However, the scarcity of autos resulting from the export quota would lead to higher prices for American consumers as well as a limited choice of available models. Moreover, Japanese producers would have the incentive to enrich their product mix by concentrating their shipments to the United States in the higher-priced models at the expense of low-cost models.

The available statistics are consistent with these predictions. During the first year of the export quota, Japanese auto companies sold 1.81 million units in the United States. The excess above the 1.68 million limit mainly reflected a reduction in inventories built up in anticipation of the imposition of restrictions. Throughout 1982, Japanese sales ran only marginally above the export quota limit.

Japanese manufacturers did attempt to increase revenues by increasing auto prices. The average price of Japanese autos at American ports of entry rose from $4,700 in 1980 to $5,600 by 1982. The Japanese also enriched their product mix, which added to consumer costs. In 1982, the number of autos sold in the United States by the two largest Japanese companies, at a price of $6,500 or less, declined by 30 percent from that of 1981. In 1982, the number of cars priced between $6,500 and $11,000 increased 15 percent, whereas sales of cars at more than $11,000 rose by 60 percent.

European Steel Restraint

In 1982, officials of the European Economic Community (EEC) and the United States reached an agreement to limit EEC shipments of steel to the U.S. market. The Europeans agreed to hold down shipments of carbon and alloy steel products to 5.46 percent, on average, of the projected U.S. market. Steel pipe and tube product shipments would be held to 5.9 percent of the projected U.S. market. Plans called for the restrictions to be enforced by an export-licensing scheme in which the United States would require imports from the EEC to be accompanied by government-issued export certificates. Export licenses would be issued to EEC exporters in quantities no greater than the percentages of projected U.S. consumption, as summarized in Table 6.3. The agreement covers about 99 percent of total U.S. imports of basic steel mill products from the EEC and runs from 1982 through 1985.

Foreign competition for U.S. steelmakers has been a sensitive issue. During the late sixties, the domestic steel industry pressed the U.S. government to recognize that steel was traded unfairly by companies that are government owned, controlled, and subsidized. The result was a wave of steel import quota bills introduced in the House of Representatives. These congressional initiatives apparently motivated the U.S. government to negotiate voluntary export restraint programs with the Japanese and Europeans in the early seventies. However, when world steel demand skyrocketed in the mid-seventies, the agreements were allowed to terminate as foreign companies

Table 6.3   Restrictions on EEC Steel Shipments to the United States

Product	Percentage
Hot-rolled sheet and strip	6.81
Cold-rolled sheet	5.11
Plate	5.36
Structurals	9.91
Wire rods	4.29
Hot-rolled bars	2.38
Coated sheets	3.27
Tin plate	2.20
Rails	8.90
Sheet piling	21.85
Pipe and tube	5.90

Source: U.S. Department of Commerce, "U.S.-E.C. Steel Arrangements: Fact Sheet," *News*, October 21, 1982.

satisfied their domestic markets first, shipping only limited quantities of steel to the United States and only at premium prices.

World demand for steel slowed in the late seventies and again in the early eighties, and steel shipments to the United States increased as foreign producers viewed exports as a way of maintaining acceptable levels of plant utilization. By 1981, U.S. steel companies were complaining that foreign governments were subsidizing steel produced for sale in the United States. The U.S. government did find that European steel was being subsidized and that such shipments to the United States were causing substantial injury to American firms. The EEC agreed to a voluntary export restraint program rather than suffer the consequences of penalty tariffs being applied to their steel shipments to the United States.

The export restrictions placed on EEC steel shipments would reduce the supply of steel in the United States and lead to upward pressure on prices paid by U.S. steel consumers. This would be distributed as increased revenues to steel producers in the United States and Europe.

American manufacturers, such as the auto companies, would find their competitive position adversely affected by higher steel prices. Restricting EEC steel shipments would have a mixed effect on the U.S. balance of payments. The restrictions would reduce outflows of dollars to Europe, strengthening the dollar. However, Europeans would now have fewer dollars to spend on U.S. goods and services, the result being a decline in export sales.

Multifiber Arrangement

Ever since the early 1950s, U.S. textile producers have sought protectionist relief from the federal government. Cotton textiles from Japan accounted for over 60 percent of the U.S. textile imports during the 1950s. In spite of domestic producers pressing for import quotas, the United States opposed such restrictive measures, given its commitment to trade liberalization under the General Agreement on Tariffs and Trade. Relief was finally granted U.S. producers in 1957 when Japan agreed to place voluntary export controls on textiles to the United States. This assistance, however, was short-lived because other suppliers such as Hong Kong were gaining stronger footholds in U.S. markets. By 1959, Hong Kong was supplying the United States in excess of 28 percent of its imports of cotton textiles.

To broaden the scope of the orderly marketing arrangements, the United States in 1962 entered into the so-called *Long-Term Arrangements* (LTA). By 1973, some 82 countries were participating in this multilateral market-sharing pact. Although the LTA encouraged countries to adopt restraint in their export policies to avoid disruptive effects on import markets, the LTA's flaw was that it applied only to cotton textiles. The result was that there were incentives for foreign producers to switch operations over to artificial fiber textiles. By 1970, U.S. imports of artificial fiber textiles were at 329 million pounds, up from the 31

million pounds of 1961. What was needed was an arrangement that included trade in artificial fiber textiles as well as cotton textiles.

In 1974, some 50 countries signed the *Multifiber Arrangement* (MFA). This orderly marketing pact applied to trade in textile products manufactured from cotton, wool, and artificial fibers. The basic objective of the MFA is to promote trade in textiles, while at the same time avoiding market disruptions on export and import sectors by having participating countries enter into export and import quota agreements. Under the general terms of the MFA, the United States has entered into bilateral orderly marketing pacts with 18 major textile-exporting countries. In 1982, the MFA was extended for another four years.

Local Content Requirements

Although voluntary export restraints may help insulate domestic companies from sales of competitors abroad, they do not help with the problem of *foreign sourcing*. In terms of the American auto industry, foreign sourcing refers to the purchase of foreign components by an American company for use in its domestic vehicle production. For example, General Motors has obtained engines from its subsidiaries in Mexico and Brazil, Chrysler has purchased ball joints from Japanese producers, and Ford has purchased cylinder heads from European companies. Foreign sourcing commitments often reflect a desire to take advantage of lower costs overseas, including lower wage rates. They have also permitted American automakers a rapid means of building up their capacity for small cars and trucks. Furthermore, a variety of foreign rules have required American auto firms with overseas assembly plants to use locally produced components for vehicles assembled overseas.

To limit the practice of foreign sourcing and to encourage the development of domestic industry, countries have sometimes adopted *local content requirements*. Such requirements typically stipulate the percentage of a product's total value that must be produced domestically for that product to be sold domestically. As seen in Table 6.4, content requirements have been widely used by many auto-producing nations.

For autos, domestic content requirements have traditionally been used by developing nations who are attempting to establish domestic automobile industries. These countries are often committed to the industrialization strategy of *import substitution*, in which domestic industrial production gradually replaces imports. Import substitution in autos has the objective of initially establishing final assembly operations, which necessitates minimal design and engineering techniques, and then expanding into component production farther backstream. Virtually all of the auto companies located in the countries of Table 6.4 are American, Japanese, or European firms.

Figure 6.3 illustrates the welfare effects for the United States of a local content requirement on autos. Assume that $D_{U.S._0}$ represents the auto demand schedule in the United States, whereas S_{J_0} represents the auto supply schedule of the Japanese, assumed to be the world's most efficient producer. Under free trade, the United States would import 4 million units at a price of $7,000 each.

Now suppose that a content requirement initiated by the U.S. government forces Japan to locate manufacturing facilities in the United States. Assume that higher resource costs in the United States bid the Japanese supply curve up to S_{J_1}. The additional production costs would result in auto prices in the United States rising to $8,000 and consumption falling to 3 million units. Consumer surplus therefore would fall by area $a + b$. Area b denotes the consumption effect resulting from a smaller quantity being bought at a higher price. Area a depicts the welfare loss resulting from the excess cost to the

Table 6.4   Local Content Laws Regarding Auto Trade

Country	Content Requirement (percent)
Algeria	25–40
Argentina	90
Australia	85
Brazil	85–100
Chile	15–30
Colombia	30–45
Egypt	Announced goal of 100
Greece	25
India	40–45
Indonesia	25
Kenya	45
Malaysia	8–17
Mexico	70–80
New Zealand	30–40
Nigeria	15
Peru	30
Philippines	30–62.5
Portugal	25
Singapore	13
South Africa	66
Spain	50
Taiwan	32–60
Thailand	40
Tunisia	20–44
Turkey	65–80
Uruguay	5–25
Venezuela	70–75
Yugoslavia	50

Source: *Auto Situation, Autumn 1980*, Hearing Before the Subcommittee on Trade of the Committee on Ways and Means, U.S. House of Representatives, 96th Cong., 2nd Sess. (Washington, D.C.: U.S. Government Printing Office, 1980), p. 15.

Japanese producers on their U.S. sales under the content program. Both of these effects represent an overall welfare loss for the U.S. economy.

Throughout the early 1980s, the UAW pressured the U.S. government for protection against foreign-produced autos as unemployment increased among American autoworkers.

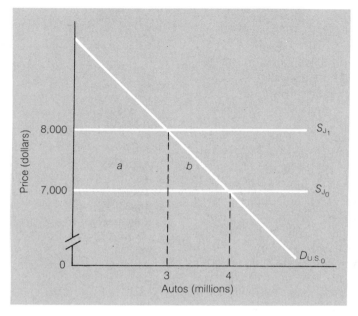

Figure 6.3   Costs of content protection.

Defending the interests of its members, the UAW maintained that domestic content legislation was needed to ensure that all companies that sell autos in the United States build a portion of each vehicle with American parts and assembly. In December 1982, the U.S. House of Representatives passed a domestic content bill entitled the Fair Practices in Automotive Products Act.

As summarized in Table 6.5, the content bill would ensure that beginning with model year 1984, all domestic and foreign manufacturers producing more than 100,000 vehicles (cars and light trucks) for sale in the U.S. market would have to achieve minimal domestic content requirements. The domestic content requirement was calculated as the U.S. added domestic value as a percentage of wholesale price. Increasingly stringent requirements would be imposed until 1986 when the schedule would be complete. Table 6.6 illustrates how the content requirements of the completed schedule would apply to

manufacturers producing vehicles for sale in the United States, based on 1981 sales figures. The penalty for violating the minimum domestic content requirement is an import quota. This quota would equal the number of vehicles imported during the model year in which the violation occurred cut back by the same percentage as the violator fell short of the minimum content requirement.

Domestic content requirements would tend to raise auto prices for American consumers. Auto manufacturers would be forced to accept the relatively high production costs in the United States, which resulted in American firms obtaining components from foreign sources in the first place and which discouraged foreign manufacturers from locating production facilities in the United States. By restricting the ability of foreign auto companies to sell their autos in the United States, content requirements would likely result in fewer choices for American consumers.

Table 6.5 Proposed Content Ratios for Model Year
1984 and Thereafter

Number of Motor Vehicles Produced by the Manufacturer and Sold in the United States During Such Year	Minimum Domestic Content Ratio
Model year 1984:	
Not over 100,000	0%
Over 100,000 but not over 900,000	The number, expressed as a percentage, determined by dividing the number of vehicles sold by 30,000
Over 900,000	30%
Model year 1985:	
Not over 100,000	0%
Over 100,000 but not over 900,000	The number, expressed as a percentage, determined by dividing the number of vehicles sold by 15,000
Over 900,000	60%
Each model year after model year 1985:	
Not over 100,000	0%
Over 100,000 but not over 900,000	The number, expressed as a percentage, determined by dividing the number of vehicles sold by 10,000
Over 900,000	90%

Source: U.S. Congress, House of Representatives, Committee on Energy and Commerce, *Fair Practices in Automotive Products Act* (HR 5133), as amended, 97th Cong., 2nd Sess. (Washington, D.C.: U.S. Government Printing Office, September 21, 1982), pp. 2–3.

Estimates suggested that the proposed content legislation for autos would generate some 100,000 new jobs for American workers in the auto and auto-related industries. However, the prices of cars and light trucks sold in the United States would increase by $333 on average. This would result in cost increases amounting to $4.9 billion for consumers, or $49,000 per job created.

Subsidies

National governments also may grant *subsidies* to domestic producers to help improve their trade position. Such devices are an indirect form of protection provided to home business firms, whether they be import-competing producers or exporters. A main purpose of a subsidy is to permit less efficient domestic producers to be more competitive against the more efficient foreign producers. Subsidies allow home business firms to market their products at prices lower than the firms' actual cost or profit considerations would normally warrant. Governments wanting to see certain domestic industries expand may pay them subsidies to encourage their development.

Governmental subsidies may assume a variety of forms. The simplest method is where a government makes an outright cash disbursement to a domestic exporter after the sale has been completed. The payment may be according to the

Table 6.6   Proposed Content Requirements:
Impact on Auto Manufacturers

Manufacturer	Number of Vehicles* Sold in the United States in 1981 (thousands)	Minimum U.S. Content Requirement (percent)
General Motors	4,582	90
Ford	2,034	90
Chrysler	883	88
Toyota	714	71
Datsun (Nissan)	580	58
Honda	371	37
VW of America	341	34
Toyo Kogyo-Mazda	247	25
American Motor-Renault	231	23
Subaru	152	15
Mitsubishi	145	14
VW-Porsche-Audi	144	14
Isuzu	89	0
Mercedes Benz	67	0
Volvo	65	0
BMW	42	0
Fiat	33	0
Fiesta (Ford, Germany)	33	0
Jaguar-Rover-Triumph	19	0
Peugeot	17	0
Saab	15	0
DeLorean	3	0
Alfa Romeo	2	0

Source: *Automotive News*, January 11, 1982, p. 45 and January 18, 1982, p. 48.
*Vehicles include cars and light trucks.

discrepancy between the exporter's actual costs and the price received or on the basis of a fixed amount for each unit of a product sold. The overall result is to permit the producer a cost advantage that would not otherwise exist. Such direct export subsidies when applied to manufactured goods have been prohibited by the General Agreement on Tariffs and Trade. Industrialized nations have thus sometimes resorted to various indirect subsidies to achieve the same general result.

Governments, for example, may give their exporters special privileges, including tax concessions, insurance arrangements, and loans at below-market interest rates. Governments may also sell surplus materials such as ships to home exporters at favorable prices. The government may purchase a firm's product at a relatively high price and then dump it in foreign markets at lower prices. This has traditionally been the technique used by the U.S. government in conjunction with its farm-support programs. Similar to the direct cash disbursements applied to home producers, indirect subsidies are intended to encourage the expansion of a country's exports by permitting them to be sold abroad at lower prices. The Export-Import Bank of the United States encourages American firms to sell overseas by providing direct loans and guaranteed/insured loans to foreign purchasers of American goods and services. U.S. exporters can also set up "paper" corporations called Domestic International Sales Corporations (DISC), through which they can funnel their export activities and receive a 50 percent tax deferral of their export income.[4]

For purposes of our discussion, two types of subsidies can be distinguished: *domestic subsidies*, which are sometimes granted to producers of import-competing goods, and *export subsidies*, which are made to producers of goods that are to be sold overseas. In both cases, the recipient producer views the subsidy as tantamount to a negative tax. This is because the government adds an amount to the price the purchaser pays rather than subtracting from it. The net price actually received by the producer equals the price paid by the purchaser plus the subsidy. Because the subsidy offers a cost advantage to the producer, she is able to supply a greater quantity at each consumer's price.[5]

Domestic Subsidy

The trade and welfare effects of a subsidy granted to domestic producers of an import-competing good is illustrated in Figure 6.4. Assume that the initial supply and demand curves of the United States for steel are depicted by curves $S_{U.S._0}$ and $D_{U.S._0}$, the market equilibrium price being $430 per ton. Assume also that since the United States is a small buyer of steel, changes in its purchases do not affect the world price of $400 per ton. Given a free trade price of $400 per ton, the United States consumes 14 tons of steel, producing 2 tons and importing 12 tons.

To partially insulate domestic production from foreign production, suppose the U.S. government grants a subsidy of $25 per ton for steel produced by its import-competing steelmakers. The cost advantage made possible by the subsidy results in the U.S. supply curve shifting right from $S_{U.S._0}$ to $S_{U.S._1}$. Domestic production expands from 2 to 7 million tons, while imports fall from 12 to 7 million tons. This represents the subsidy's trade effect.

The subsidy to import-competing firms also affects the national welfare of the United States. According to Figure 6.4, the subsidy permits U.S. output to rise to 7 million tons. Note that at this output, the net price of the steelmaker equals $425, the sum of the price paid by the consumer ($400) plus the subsidy ($25). To the U.S. government, the total cost of protecting its steelmakers equals the amount of the subsidy ($25) times the amount of output to which it is applied (7 million tons), an amount equal to $175 million.

Where does this subsidy revenue go? Part of it is redistributed to the more efficient U.S. producers in the form of producer surplus. This amount is denoted by area *a* in the figure. There is also a protective effect, whereby more costly domestic output is allowed to be sold in the market as a result of the subsidy. This is denoted by area *b* in the figure. To the United States as a whole, the protective effect represents a deadweight loss of welfare.

A government attempting to encourage production by its import-competing producers might levy tariffs or quotas on domestic imports. But tariffs and quotas involve larger sacrifices in national welfare than would occur under an equivalent subsidy. Unlike subsidies, tariffs and quotas distort choices for domestic consumers (resulting in a decrease in the domestic demand for imports), in addition to permitting less efficient home production to occur. The result is the familiar consumption effect of protection, whereby a deadweight loss of consumer surplus

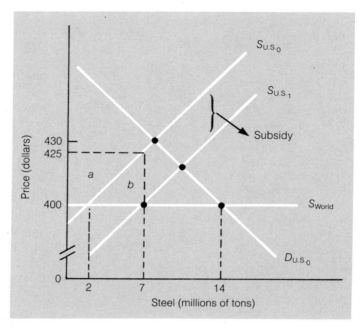

Figure 6.4   Economic effects of a domestic subsidy.

is borne by the home country. This welfare loss is absent in the subsidy case. A subsidy tends to yield the same result for home producers as does an equivalent tariff or quota, but at lower cost in terms of national welfare.

Subsidies are not free goods, however, for they must be financed by someone. The direct cost of the subsidy is a burden that must be financed out of tax revenues paid by the public. Moreover, when a subsidy is given to an industry, it often is in return for accepting governmental conditions on key matters (for example, employee compensation levels). The superiority of a subsidy over other types of commercial policies may thus be less than the preceding analysis suggests.

Export Subsidy

Besides attempting to protect import-competing industries, many national governments grant subsidies, including special tax exemptions and the provision of capital at favored rates, to increase the volume of exports.[6] By providing a cost advantage to home producers, such subsidies are intended to encourage a country's exports by reducing the price paid by foreigners. The result is that foreign consumers are favored over domestic consumers to the extent that the foreign price of a subsidized export is less than the product's domestic price.

Imposition of an export subsidy yields two direct effects for the home economy: (1) a terms-of-trade effect and (2) an export revenue effect. Because subsidies tend to reduce the foreign price of home country exports, the home country's terms of trade are worsened. But lower foreign prices generally stimulate export volume. Should the foreign demand for exports be relatively elastic, so that a given percentage drop in foreign price is more than offset by the rise in export volume, the home country's export revenues would increase.

Figure 6.5 illustrates the case of an export subsidy applied to TV sets in trade between Japan and the United States. Under free trade, market equilibrium exists at point E, where Japan exports one million TVs to the United States at a price of $100 per unit. Suppose the Japanese government, to encourage export sales, grants to its exporters a subsidy of $50 per TV. The Japanese supply curve shifts from S_{Japan_0} to S_{Japan_1}, with market equilibrium moving to point F. The terms of trade thus turns against Japan because its export price falls from $100 to $75 per TV exported. Whether Japan's export revenue rises depends on how Americans in their purchasing decisions respond to the price decrease. If the percentage increase in the number of TVs sold to Americans more than offsets the percentage decrease in price, Japan's export revenue will rise. This is the case in Figure 6.5, for Japan's export revenue rises from $100 million to $112.5 million as the result of the decline in the price of its export good.

Although export subsidies may benefit firms and workers in a subsidized industry by increasing sales and employment, the benefits may be offset by certain costs falling upon the society as a whole. Consumers in the export country suffer as the international terms of trade moves against them. This is because, given a fall in export prices, a greater number of exports must be made for a given dollar amount in imports. Domestic consumers also find they must pay higher prices than foreigners for the goods they help subsidize. Furthermore, to the extent that taxes are required to finance the export subsidy, domestic consumers find themselves poorer. In the previous example, the cost of the subsidy to the Japanese taxpayers totals $75 million ($50 subsidy times 1.5 million TVs).

One type of export subsidy that has become increasingly controversial in recent years is the *export credit subsidy*. To encourage exporting by domestic firms, governments frequently extend loans to foreign customers. These loans often are awarded when private banks are unwilling to grant credit to importing firms viewed as high risk. The interest rates charged on export credits traditionally have been less than those demanded by private banks on similar loans. Export credit subsidies transfer money from the domestic taxpayer to the subsidized export industry, the foreign purchaser, or both. In 1980, export credit subsidies exceeded $7 billion. The nations granting the largest amount of export credits were France ($3.1 billion), United Kingdom ($1.1 billion), Japan ($0.7 billion), United States ($0.7 billion), and West Germany ($0.4 billion).

Export subsidies have been justified on a number of grounds. To the extent that credit subsidies lead to increased exports, the home country's balance of trade is strengthened. Rising exports also result in higher levels of domestic employment. Credit subsidies thus are often viewed as a relatively cheap alternative to unemployment and welfare payments. Credit subsidies have helped industries increase their scales of production and overcome inefficiencies or other presumed disadvantages. They have been used to encourage industrial sectors favored by the government. Finally, credit subsidies have been viewed as a kind of foreign aid, as they help ease the debt burdens of the recipient developing countries.

To prevent nations from attaining unfair competitive advantage through export subsidies, guidelines have been maintained by the industrial countries; the interest rate, term, and down payment for credit programs are stipulated. However, by 1981, market interest rates had risen significantly above the minimum permissible interest rates on export credits, which had not been altered since 1975. Over this period, therefore, the extent of credit subsidization was rising. In 1981, 22 industrial countries agreed to raise the minimum export credit rate from an average of 7.75 percent to 10 percent. This represented the principle that export credit interest rates should relate to the interest rates

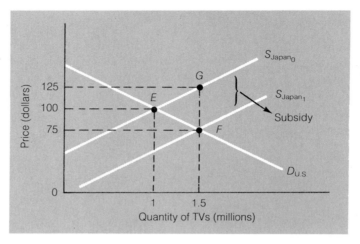

Figure 6.5   Economic effects of an export subsidy.

established by the private market in each country. The result was a reduction in subsidies by almost 30 percent.

Dumping

The case for protecting import-competing producers from foreign competition is bolstered by the popular antidumping argument. *Dumping* is recognized as a form of international price discrimination. It occurs when foreign buyers are charged lower prices than domestic buyers for an identical product, after allowing for transportation costs and tariff duties. In practice, dumping is often considered as selling in foreign markets below costs of production.[7]

Forms of Dumping

Why would a business firm practice dumping? Commercial dumping is generally viewed as either sporadic, predatory, or persistent in nature. *Sporadic* or distress dumping occurs when a firm with excess inventories disposes of them on foreign markets by selling abroad at lower prices than at home. This form of dumping may be the result of misfortune or poor planning by foreign producers. Unforseen changes in supply and demand conditions can result in excess inventories and thus in dumping. Although sporadic dumping might be beneficial to importing consumers, it may be quite disruptive to import-competing producers who face falling sales and short-run losses. Temporary tariff duties might be levied to protect home firms, but because it is often recognized that sporadic dumping has minor effects on international trade, governments are reluctant to grant tariff protection under these circumstances.

Predatory dumping occurs when a firm temporarily reduces the prices charged abroad to drive foreign competitors out of business. When the firm succeeds in acquiring a monopoly position, prices are then raised commensurate with its market power. The new price level must be sufficiently high to offset any losses that occurred during the period of cutthroat pricing. The firm would presumably be confident in its ability to prevent the entry of potential competitors long enough for it to enjoy economic profits. To be successful, predatory dumping would have to be practiced on a massive basis to provide home consumers with sufficient opportunity for bargain shopping. Home governments generally are concerned about predatory pricing for monopolizing purposes and may retaliate with antidumping tariff duties that eliminate the price differential.

Persistent dumping, as its name suggests, goes on indefinitely. In an effort to maximize economic profits, a producer may consistently sell abroad at lower prices than at home. The rationale underlying persistent dumping is explained in the next section.

International Price Discrimination

Consider the case of a domestic seller who enjoys market power resulting from barriers restricting competition at home. Suppose this firm sells in foreign markets that are highly competitive. This means that the domestic consumer response to a change in price is less than that abroad (the

home demand is more inelastic than the foreign demand). A profit-maximizing firm would benefit by charging a higher price at home, where competition is weak, while charging a lower price in foreign markets to meet competition.

During the 1970s, U.S. steel manufacturers complained that the European Economic Community was selling sheet steel in the United States for \$240 per ton while selling the identical sheet steel in the community for \$318 per ton. Such international price discrimination can be analyzed in the framework of Figure 6.6.

Let D_C be the community steel demand and $D_{U.S.}$ be the U.S. steel demand, with the corresponding marginal revenue curves represented by MR_C and $MR_{U.S.}$. $MR_{C+U.S.}$ denotes the total marginal revenue curve, found by adding horizontally the marginal revenue curves of each submarket. The firm's marginal cost curve is given by MC. The profit-maximizing output would be at $Q_{C+U.S.}$ at which marginal revenue equals marginal cost. A profit-maximizing firm faces the problem of how to distribute total output $Q_{C+U.S.}$, and thus set price, in the two submarkets in which it sells. To accomplish this,

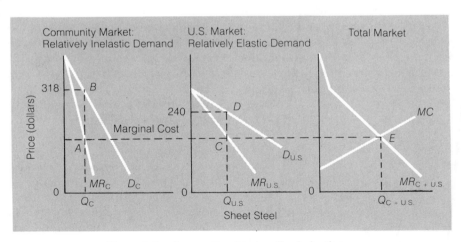

Figure 6.6   International price discrimination.

the firm follows the familiar $MR = MC$ principle, whereby the marginal revenue of each submarket equals the marginal cost at the profit-maximizing value. This can be shown in Figure 6.6 by first constructing a horizontal line from the point where $MC = MR_{C+U.S.}$. The optimal output in each market is then found where this horizontal line intersects the MR curves of the two submarkets. The firm will therefore sell Q_C output in the domestic market at the price \$318. It will sell the remaining $Q_{U.S.}$ units in the foreign market at the price \$240. International price discrimination results in the higher price, \$318, charged in the more inelastic (domestic) market and the lower price, \$240, in the more elastic (foreign) market.

For international price discrimination to be successful, certain conditions must hold. First, to ensure that at any price the demand curves in the two markets have different demand elasticities, the markets' demand conditions must differ. Domestic buyers may, for example, have income levels or tastes and preferences that differ from those of buyers abroad. Second, the monopolist must be able to separate the two markets, preventing any significant resale of commodities from the lower-priced to the higher-priced market. This is because any resale by consumers will tend to neutralize the effect of differential prices and narrow the discriminatory price structure to the point where it approaches a uniform price to all consumers. Because of high transportation costs and governmental trade restrictions, markets are often easier to separate internationally than nationally.

Excess Capacity

One of the major reasons behind sporadic or distress dumping is that producers sometimes face reductions in demand that leave them with idle productive capacity. The *excess capacity* threat is of particular concern to a country like Japan, which has guaranteed lifetime employment to much of its industrial labor force. For such Japanese companies, labor comes close to being a fixed cost, since wages must be paid regardless of the company's production, sales, or profitability. Management thus has the incentive to compete vigorously for sales and to keep output high to generate revenues.

Should a firm find that its productive capacity exceeds the requirements of the home market, it may consider it more profitable to use the capacity to fulfill export orders at low prices rather than allow the capacity to go idle. To keep exports high, a firm may be willing to sell abroad at a loss if necessary. Any profits generated by the higher-priced domestic sales would in part be intended to subsidize the goods that are dumped in foreign markets.

Consider the case of a stereo producer under the following assumptions: (1) The producer's physical capacity is 150 units of output over the given time period; (2) the domestic market's demand for stereos is price inelastic, while foreign demand is price elastic. Referring to Table 6.7, suppose that the home producer charges a uniform price (no dumping) of \$300 per unit to both domestic and foreign consumers. With home demand being inelastic, say the firm finds domestic sales totaling 100 units. But with elastic demand conditions abroad, suppose the firm is unable to market any stereos at the prevailing price. Sales revenues would equal \$30,000, with variable costs plus overhead costs totaling \$30,000. The conclusion is that by not practicing dumping, the firm would find itself with excess plant capacity of 50 stereos. What is more, the firm would just be breaking even on its domestic market operations.

Suppose our producer decides to dump stereos abroad at lower prices than at home. The general rule is that as long as all variable costs are covered, a price that contributes to overhead costs would permit larger profits (smaller losses) than those realized with idle plant capacity at

Table 6.7   Dumping and Excess Capacity

	No Dumping	Dumping
Home sales	100 units @ $300	100 units @ $300
Export sales	0 units @ $300	50 units @ $250
Sales revenue	$30,000	$42,500
Less variable costs of $200 per unit	−$20,000	−$30,000
	$10,000	$12,500
Less overhead costs of $10,000	−$10,000	−$10,000
Profit	$0	$2,500

hand. According to Table 6.7, by charging $300 to home consumers, the firm can sell 100 units. To fully utilize its capacity, suppose the firm is able to sell an additional 50 units abroad by charging a price of $250 per unit. The sales revenue of $42,500 would not only cover variable costs as well as overhead costs but also would permit a profit of $2,500.[8] With dumping, the company is able to increase profits even though it is selling abroad at a price less than full cost (full cost $= \frac{\$40,000}{150} = \$267$). Companies facing excess productive capacity may have the incentive to stimulate sales by cutting prices charged to foreigners, perhaps to levels that just cover variable production costs. Of course, home prices must be sufficiently high to keep the firm operating in the black over the relevant time period.

Antidumping Regulations

In spite of the benefits that dumping may offer importing consumers, governments have often levied stiff penalty duties against commodities they believe are being dumped into their markets from abroad. For the United States, the popularity of antidumping complaints on the part of domestic producers stems from a provision of the 1974 Trade Reform Act that defines dump-

ing as the sale of a product in the United States at less than its full production cost (average total cost). Dumping traditionally had been defined as selling in the United States at less than the sales price in the home market to gain an advantage in competition with foreign suppliers. The new, broader definition triggered off a rash of antidumping complaints, notably by U.S. steelworkers, during the mid-1970s. This was because it was easier to estimate the full production costs of foreign producers than to determine home market prices of steel products. What is more, home market prices might at times be below full production costs.

Upon receiving a dumping complaint, the U.S. Department of Commerce must first decide if dumping did occur within the meaning of the 1974 Trade Reform Act. Because cost data of foreign producers are not always available, the Commerce Department is permitted to reconstruct foreign costs and assign its own fair market value to the foreign goods. A decision that dumping did take place results in the case being sent to the International Trade Commission, which decides whether home producers were injured by foreign dumped goods. An affirmative decision by the International Trade Commission is forwarded to the president, who decides whether to levy tariff duties on foreign imports equal to the margin of dumping—the difference between the U.S. sales price and the home market sales price abroad. In this manner, the assigned fair market value of the dumped goods is brought into alignment with the sales prices of domestic-produced goods. Table 6.8 gives examples of instances where dumping did occur under the provisions of the 1974 Trade Reform Act.

Steel Subsidies and Dumping

In 1982, the American steel industry was handed an affirmative decision by the Commerce Department on its antidumping complaint against seven European producers and Brazil and South Africa. The action was based in part on U.S. trade law, which permits protection from imports if they are sold at prices below the exporter's costs of production and if they materially injure domes-

tic producers or their employees. The dumping charges were initiated because U.S. Steel Co. contended it was not getting sufficient protection against foreign imports under the trigger price program, which is discussed later in this chapter. Table 6.9 summarizes U.S. Steel's antidumping complaint against West Germany, one of the nations accused of unfair trade practices.

In its filings, U.S. Steel maintained that foreign governments were illegally subsidizing exports of steel to the United States. Some practices cited included the following: The United Kingdom, which owns British Steel Co., reimbursed the company for losses; South Africa provided its firms interest-free loans; West Germany extended research and development grants of 50 percent to 100 percent for the cost of new plant and equipment. U.S. Steel's allegations were supported by a Commerce Department

Table 6.8　Selected Findings of Dumping Under the
1974 Trade Reform Act, 1978–1980

Country	Product	Trade (million of dollars)
Japan	Melamine	1.0
Japan	Swimming pools	4.5
Canada	Parts for paving equipment	2.0
Italy	Plastic tape	2.5
Yugoslavia	Inedible gelatin	0.6
West Germany	Inedible gelatin	0.7
Sweden	Inedible gelatin	0.5
Netherlands	Inedible gelatin	1.0
Japan	Impression fabric	3.6
Taiwan	Polyvinyl chloride sheet and film	8.6
Japan	Carbon steel plate	173.8
Japan	Steel wire strand	19.6
Austria	Railway track maintenance equipment	1.3
Belgium	Viscose rayon staple fiber	2.0
Canada	Sugar and syrups	28.4
Italy	Spun yarn	3.9
Japan	Electric motors	1.5

Source: *Annual Report of the President of the United States on the Trade Agreements Program* (Washington, D.C.: U.S. Government Printing Office, 1977, 1978, 1980).

Table 6.9   U.S. Steel Co.'s Antidumping Petition Against West Germany

Product	Constructed Cost, West Germany (dollars per ton)	Export Price to the United States (dollars per ton)	Margin of Dumping (dollars per ton)
Structurals	419	401	18
Plate	412	351	61
Hot-rolled sheets	402	310	92
Cold-rolled sheets	506	390	116
Galvanized sheets	617	437	180

Source: U.S. Steel Co., *Petition for Relief Under the U.S. Antidumping Statute from Certain Steel Products Imported from West Germany*, 1982.

investigation in 1982, which concluded that producers in six countries were benefiting from subsidies. Table 6.10 furnishes estimates of steel subsidies for selected products.

Responding to the antidumping complaint of U.S. Steel, the Commerce Department ruled that European steel was being "dumped" in the U.S. market. Subsequently, the International Trade Commission ruled that subsidies to foreign steelmakers caused "material injury" to the U.S. steel industry. The U.S. government prepared to levy countervailing duties against European steel that was shipped to the United States. It was at this point that the European Economic Community agreed to limit steel shipments to the United States, as discussed earlier in this chapter. Accepting the voluntary export restraint program, U.S. Steel withdrew its complaint and the countervailing duties were not levied.

In 1982, the Federal Trade Commission estimated the welfare effects for the United States of the imposition of countervailing tariffs on

Table 6.10   Estimated Subsidies to Some Major Producers of Steel

Company (country)	Product	Rate of Subsidy, as percentage of F.O.B. value
Cockerill-Sambre (Belgium)	Structurals	13.2
Fabrique de Fer de Charleroi (Belgium)	Plate	2.2
Siderurgie Maritime (Belgium)	Hot-rolled sheet	4.6
Stahlwerke (Germany)	Structurals	1.1
Dilling (France)	Cold-rolled sheet	3.7
Sacilor (France)	Structurals	14.2
Usinor (France)	Hot-rolled sheet	18.0
Italsider (Italy)	Cold-rolled sheet	26.1
Arbed (Luxembourg)	Structurals	0.5

Source: U.S. Department of Commerce, "Commerce Makes Final Determinations in Steel Subsidy Investigations," *News*, August 25, 1982.

steel imports had they been provided in response to U.S. Steel's antidumping petition. A countervailing duty would be expected to result in higher prices of steel imports for the United States. This would lead to a fall in domestic consumption, a rise in domestic production, and a fall in the volume of imports. These estimates are summarized in Table 6.11.

Trigger Price Mechanism

In early 1974, the demand for steel was at record levels in the United States and the rest of the world. American producers enjoyed strong markets and steelmakers everywhere were drafting plans for expanding plant capacity in anticipation of a global steel shortage in the 1980s. But the world steel market is subject to strong cyclical fluctuations. With demand falling in response to the 1975 world recession, the boom went bust. Governments increasingly began to consider proposals to restrict international trade in steel with producers operating well below capacity.

In 1977, a Treasury Department task force concluded that the U.S. steel industry had faced a deterioration in its competitive position with respect to overseas producers. From 1972 to 1977, U.S. production costs rose by some 89 percent, in part attributable to increasing costs of labor, energy, raw materials, and pollution abatement. By 1977, the share of the American market supplied by foreign steelmakers ran at 20 percent, compared with a 13 percent average over the period 1973 to 1976. Lagging sales led to American steel firms operating at only 80 percent utilization of capacity and to the closing of several older steel plants in Ohio, Pennsylvania, and New York.

Many hard-pressed American steel producers viewed their dwindling market shares as primarily the result of foreign firms dumping their products in the United States at prices below full cost of production. According to the U.S. antidumping laws, the fair value of steel exports to America must be calculated as the sum of direct

Table 6.11   Annual Welfare Effects of the Imposition of Countervailing Duties on Steel Products

Welfare Effect	Tariff = 10%	Tariff = 15%
Deadweight losses (consumption effect and protective effect)	$148.5–184.8 million	$237.7–257.3 million
Consumers' losses (consumer surplus)	350.7 million	480.9 million
Producers' gains	165.9 million	223.6 million
Additional tariff revenue	0–36.3 million	0–19.6 million
Jobs created	5,357 jobs	8,278 jobs
Cost to consumer per job created	$65,446	$58,094
Cost to the economy per job created	$27,720–34,497	$28,715–31,082

Source: Robert Tollison et al., *In the Matter of Certain Steel Products from Belgium, Brazil, the Federal Republic of Germany, France, Italy, Luxembourg, the Netherlands, Romania, South Africa, Spain, and the United Kingdom*, Federal Trade Commission, 1982, Appendix, pp. 1–5.

production costs, 10 percent overhead, and a profit equal to 8 percent of total costs. By practicing dumping, it was alleged that countries like Japan could keep their plants running and their people employed, while exporting unemployment to the United States.

Under the U.S. antidumping law, foreign firms could be penalized for dumping their products in American markets at prices lower than fair value. For action to be taken against dumping, an injured U.S. firm would have to file a complaint with the Commerce Department documenting home market prices, foreign costs, and delivery prices on shipments to the United States. But obtaining this data is most difficult, since they generally are not directly available to U.S. producers. Major antidumping complaints tend to be very time-consuming and expensive and in many cases are not feasible. Another problem with the antidumping laws is that enforcement may be too slow to be effective. It takes in the neighborhood of one year for the Commerce Department to decide if dumping did actually occur, for the International Trade Commission to determine if dumping resulted in injury to the American firm, and for countervailing duties to be levied. According to U.S. steelmakers, speedier action was needed to make the antidumping codes more effective.

Responding to protectionist demands, in 1978, the president agreed to extend additional relief to American steelmakers against unfair import competition. But instead of relying on tariffs or import quotas, protection assumed the form of *trigger prices* applied to steel imports. Under this trigger price system, the Commerce Department could self-initiate antidumping investigations whenever imported steel is sold in the United States below the trigger price level for that product. The result would be a more efficient way of determining the existence of sales at less than fair value. Such sales would be subject to countervailing duties imposed by the U.S. government.

Trigger prices are applied to foreign steel entering the United States. In 1978, it was announced that the price of the most efficient foreign steel producers would on average be raised to about 5 percent below U.S. levels. Prevailing estimates indicated that Japanese steelmakers, the most efficient in the world, were able to hold their costs some 15 percent to 20 percent below the U.S. average. This permitted the Japanese to market steel in U.S. markets at discounts below U.S. list prices. The raising of Japanese prices was intended to ensure that the price would cover "full cost" plus a reasonable rate of profit. Japan could thus no longer be accused of dumping steel in the United States. To reflect changing market conditions, the steel benchmarks were to be revised quarterly.

Note that the trigger price mechanism is not a minimum price system that sets a price floor for foreign steel sold in the United States. For example, some Canadian exports to the United States have been reported at full costs below the trigger price as a result of lower transportation costs than those indicated in the Commerce Department basing point schedule. The thinking behind the trigger price program was to provide American steel firms "temporary" relief from sales at prices less than fair value by foreign producers. As the world economy expands and the excess supply of steel is eliminated, steel-pricing behavior would return to more normal patterns. The need for trigger prices would be eliminated at this time and the program could be terminated by the president.

Trade and Welfare Effects

For the United States, the trade and welfare effects of a trigger price applied to steel imports are analyzed in Figure 6.7.[8] Assume the foreign supply curve of carbon steel, S_f, to be perfectly elastic at the price of $300 per ton. Let the U.S. supply and demand schedules be designated $S_{U.S.}$

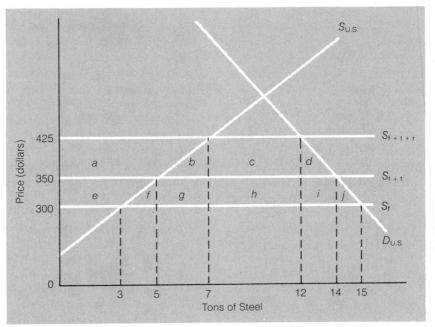

Figure 6.7   Trigger prices: trade and welfare effects.

and $D_{U.S.}$. Under conditions of free trade, the United States would produce 3 tons of steel and consume 15 tons, with imports totaling 12 tons. As was the case before the initiation of the trigger price program, suppose the United States grants partial protection against foreign steel to its domestic producers by levying a tariff on imports equal to $50 per ton. With the import price now at $350, the United States would find its production rising to 5 tons, its consumption falling to 14 tons, and its imports dropping to 9 tons. U.S. consumer surplus would fall by an amount equal to area $e + f + g + h + i + j$. Of this sum, area e represents the redistribution effect where income is transferred from home consumers to home producers, areas $g + h + i$ represent the tariff revenue collected by the home government, and the deadweight welfare loss is measured by f (the protective effect) $+ j$ (the consumption effect).

Pressured by U.S. steelmaker complaints of

dumping on the part of foreign producers, the president may decide to extend additional relief to domestic firms by placing a trigger price on steel imports at $425 per ton. Foreigners must therefore increase the price of their steel to American bel to its domestic producers by levying a tariff on imports equal to $50 per ton. the import price now at $350, the United States s would find its production rising to 5 tons, its consumption falling to 14 tons, and its imports imports totaling 5 tons. As for the welfare effects, the increase in price would result in a fall in U.S. consumer surplus by areas $a + b + c + d$. But where does this surplus wind up? Similar to our tariff analysis, area a goes to American steelmakers as producer surplus, whereas areas $b + d$ represent deadweight welfare losses in the forms of the protective and consumption effects. But it is the revenue effect of trigger prices that differs from that of import tariffs. Because foreigners are forced to sell 5 tons of steel at the floor price of $425 instead of $350, area *c* represents *foreign exporter profits*. As for the U.S. government, its tariff revenue falls by areas *g* + *i* as the result of trigger prices (the government is still able to collect area *h* as tariff revenue). The welfare losses of trigger prices to the U.S. economy thus consists of the consumption and protective effects, the loss of tariff revenue to the government, and the transfer of revenue to foreign firms as profits!

A recent Federal Trade Commission study looked at the welfare costs of protecting U.S. steel-makers from foreign competition. As summarized in Table 6.12, a trigger price mechanism that raised the average price of steel products by $11 above the levels set by the existing tariff structure (that is, from $311 to $322 per ton) would impose an annual cost on American consumers of $1,003.9 million. It was also estimated that domestic producers would enjoy gains of $868.5 million, whereas the consumption and protective effects combined would result in welfare losses of $56 million. Furthermore, foreign steel firms would expropriate $121 million as monopoly profit.

Finally, the U.S. Treasury would lose $41.6 million in tariff revenue. Table 6.12 also summarizes the welfare effects of protecting U.S. steelmakers by an increase in tariff rates by 3.5 percent or the establishment of a 12 percent import quota (orderly marketing agreement) with the existing tariff structure.

The trigger price mechanism was intended as an alternative to antidumping suits being filed by U.S. steel companies. However, in 1982, the U.S. steel industry filed antidumping complaints against nine foreign nations. The Commerce Department thus suspended the trigger price mechanism on the affected products.

Other Nontariff Trade Barriers

There are other nontariff trade barriers, which take the form of governmental codes of conduct applied to imports. Even though such provisions are often well disguised, they remain important sources of commercial policy.

Table 6.12 Summary of the Estimated Annual Effects of an Orderly Marketing Agreement, Trigger Prices, and an Equivalent Tariff

Welfare Effects	Impact of 12 Percent Quota (OMA) with Existing Tariff	Impact of a $322 Trigger Price with Existing Tariff	Impact of a 3.5 Percent Increase in Tariffs
Cost to consumers (millions of dollars)	1,003.9	1,003.9	1,003.9
Inefficiency costs due to resource misallocation (millions of dollars)	177.0	177.0	56.0
Gains to domestic producers (millions of dollars)	868.5	868.5	868.5
Monopoly profits accruing to foreign exporters (millions of dollars)	121.0	121.0	0.0
Changes in tariff revenue (millions of dollars)	−41.6	−41.6	79.4
Increase in the price of steel (dollars per net ton)	11.0	11.0	11.0

Source: Richard Duke et al., *The U.S. Steel Industry and Its International Rivals*, Federal Trade Commission, Bureau of Economics, 1978, p. 557. See also Robert W. Crandall, *The U.S. Steel Industry in Recurrent Crisis* (Washington, D.C.: The Brookings Institution, 1981), pp. 129–139.

Government Procurement Policies

If governments purchased goods and services only from the least-cost producers, the pattern of trade would not differ significantly from what occurs in a competitive market. Government purchases have in practice tended to favor home producers over foreign producers. According to the Buy American Act of 1933, the U.S. government gives preferences to domestic suppliers, ranging from 6 percent to 50 percent on federal contracts in bidding with foreign firms. Several state and local governments have also initiated policies that favor local suppliers. As is discussed in Chapter 7, the role of buy-national policies was reduced with the completion of the Tokyo Round of Multilateral Trade Negotiations in 1979.

Technical and Administrative Regulations

Today, a large variety of technical and administrative regulations are imposed by national governments on imports. Even though not all such codes are intended to restrict international trade, they have the effect of doing so. Several examples are discussed here.

Marketing and packaging standards may be used to limit imports. For instance, a few countries refuse to allow a product to be marketed as "beer" unless it contains specified types and amounts of certain key ingredients. In Canada, the government stipulates container sizes for canned goods being imported.

Governmental health and safety standards also may modify international trade patterns. In the 1970s, the United States made efforts to restrict imports that did not meet U.S. pollution control standards. Such was the issue in granting landing rights at Kennedy Airport to the Concorde supersonic plane produced by the French and British. Many New Yorkers contended that the noise level of the plane made it environmentally unsound. Mandatory antipollution control devices on automobiles have also discouraged the sale of foreign automobiles in the United States. In short, government codes of conduct have often placed effective import barriers against foreign commodities, whether they are intended to do so or not.

Summary

1.   With the decline in the relative importance of import tariffs in recent years, nontariff trade barriers have gained in importance as a measure of protection. Nontariff trade barriers include such practices as (1) trigger prices, (2) import quotas, (3) antidumping regulations, (4) subsidies, (5) orderly marketing agreements, (6) voluntary export quotas, (7) safety standards, (8) discriminatory government procurement practices, and (9) content requirements.

2.   The import quota has been a primary nontariff trade restriction. A quota refers to a governmentally imposed limit on the quantity of a product permitted to cross national borders. Although quotas are characterized by many of the same economic effects as tariffs, they tend to be more restrictive.

3.   Orderly marketing agreements refer to market-sharing pacts negotiated by trading nations and generally involve quotas being applied to exports and imports. Proponents of orderly marketing agreements contend they are less disruptive on international trade than unilaterally determined tariffs and quotas. The Multifiber Arrangement has been the world's oldest and most extensive market-sharing accord.

4.   Local content requirements try to limit the practice of foreign sourcing and encourage the development of domestic industry. They typically provide that a significant portion of a product's value must be produced in the home country for that product to be sold there. Content

protection tends to adversely affect the home economy by imposing welfare losses owing to high production costs and high-priced goods.

5.   Governmental subsidies are often granted as a form of protection to domestic exporters and import-competing firms. They may take the form of direct cash bounties, tax concessions, credit extended at low interest rates, and special insurance arrangements. Direct production subsidies for import-competing producers tend to involve a smaller loss in economic welfare than do equivalent tariffs and quotas. The imposition of export subsidies results in a terms-of-trade effect and an export-revenue effect for the home economy.

6.   Commercial dumping is a recognized form of international price discrimination. Dumping is widely understood as selling in foreign markets at prices below costs of production. Dumping can be sporadic, predatory, or persistent in nature. Idle productive capacity may be a reason behind dumping. Governments often have imposed stiff penalties against commodities that are believed to be dumped in the home economy.

7.   In 1978, the president enacted a trigger price mechanism to help insulate the U.S. steel industry from foreign competition. A trigger price is a price floor applied to imports coming into a country. It is primarily the revenue effect of trigger prices that best distinguishes this form of protectionism from tariffs and quotas.

8.   Governmental rules and regulations in areas such as safety and technical standards and marketing requirements can have significant impacts on world trade patterns.

Study Questions

1.   In recent years, nontariff trade barriers have gained in importance as a protectionist device. What are the major nontariff trade barriers?

2.   How does the revenue effect of a quota differ from that of a tariff?

3.   What are the major forms of subsidies that governments grant to domestic producers?

4.   What is meant by voluntary export restraints and how do they differ from other protective barriers?

5.   Should U.S. antidumping laws be stated in terms of full production costs or marginal costs?

6.   Which is a more restrictive trade barrier— a tariff or an equivalent quota?

7.   Why would one favor trigger prices over other trade barriers as a means of protecting home producers?

8.   Differentiate among sporadic, persistent, and predatory dumping.

9.   Why is it that an import subsidy may provide home producers the same degree of protection as tariffs or quotas but at a lower cost in terms of national welfare?

10.   Rather than generating revenue as do tariffs, subsidies require revenues. They thus are not an effective protective device for the home economy. Do you agree?

11.   In 1980, the U.S. auto industry proposed that import quotas be imposed on foreign-produced cars sold in the United States. What would be the likely benefits versus costs of such a policy?

12.   Why did the U.S. government in 1982 provide aid to domestic sugar producers in the form of import quotas?

13.   Which tends to result in a greater welfare loss for the home economy: (1) an import quota levied by the home government or (2) a voluntary export quota imposed by the foreign government?

14.   For the United States, what would be the likely economic effects of the voluntary export restraint programs agreed to with other nations for autos and steel in 1981 and 1982?

15.   Why have the United Auto Workers been a strong advocate of domestic content protection for autos? What would be the likely impact of content protection for domestic companies, workers, and consumers? How about the impact on foreign companies?

Notes

1.   See Franklyn D. Holzman, "Comparison of Different Forms of Trade Barriers." *Review of Economics and Statistics* (May 1969) and Robert M. Stern, "Tariffs and Other Measures of Trade Control: A Survey of Recent Developments," *Journal of Economic Literature* (September 1973), pp. 857–888.

2.   See Jagdish N. Bhagwati, "On the Equivalence of Tariffs and Quotas," *Trade, Tariffs and Growth* (London: Weidenfeld & Nicholson, 1969).

3.   See C. Fred Bergsten, "On the Nonequivalence of Import Quotas and Voluntary Export Restraints," in *Toward a New International Economic Order* (Lexington, Mass.: D. C. Heath, 1975), pp. 157–189.

4.   An excellent study of the nature and scope of subsidies can be found in U.S. Joint Economic Committee, *The Economics of Federal Subsidy Programs*, 92nd Cong., 1st Sess. (Washington D.C.: U.S. Government Printing Office, 1974).

5.   See W. M. Corden, "Tariffs, Subsidies, and the Terms of Trade," *Economica* (August 1957), pp. 235–242 and Trent J. Bertrand and Jaroslav Vanek, "The Theory of Tariffs, Taxes, and Subsidies: Some Aspects of the Second Best," *American Economic Review* (December 1971), pp. 925–931.

6.   See Gottfried Haberler, "Import Taxes and Export Subsidies: A Substitute for Realignment of Exchange Rates?" *Kyklos* (1967) and Jagdish N. Bhagwati and V.K. Ramaswami, "Domestic Distortions, Tariffs, and the Theory of the Optimum Subsidy," *Journal of Political Economy* (February 1963), pp. 44–50.

7.   See Jacob Viner, *Dumping: A Problem in International Trade* (Chicago: University of Chicago Press, 1923) and William A. Wares, *The Theory of Dumping and American Commercial Policy* (Lexington, Mass.: D.C. Heath, 1977).

8.   Barbara Epstein, "The Illusory Conflict Between Antidumping and Antitrust," *Antitrust Bulletin* (Fall 1973), pp. 3–4.

Suggestions for Further Reading

Baldwin, R. E. *Nontariff Distortions of International Trade*. Washington, D.C.: Brookings Institution, 1970.

Bergsten, F., ed. *Toward a New World Trade Policy: The Maidenhead Papers*. Lexington, Mass.: D.C. Heath, 1975.

Bertrand, T. J., and J. Vanek. "The Theory of Tariffs, Taxes, and Subsidies: Some Aspects of the Second Best." *American Economic Review*, December 1971.

Chambers, R. G., et al. "Estimating the Impact of Beef Import Restrictions in the U.S. Import Market." *Australian Journal of Agricultural Economics*, August 1981.

Ethier, W. J. "Dumping." *Journal of Political Economy*, June 1982.

Gomez-Ibanez, J. A., and D. Harrison. "Imports and the Future of the U.S. Automobile Industry." *American Economic Review*, May 1982.

Grossman, G. "The Theory of Domestic Content Protection and Content Preference." *Quarterly Journal of Economics*, November 1981.

Kawahito, K. "Steel and U.S. Antidumping Statutes." *Journal of World Trade Law*. March–April 1982.

Morkre, M. E., and D. Tarr. *Effects of Restrictions on U.S. Imports: Five Case Studies and Theory*. Washington, D. C.: Federal Trade Commission, 1980.

Wares, W. A. *The Theory of Dumping and American Commercial Policy*. Lexington, Mass.: D. C. Heath, 1977.

7

COMMERCIAL POLICIES OF
THE UNITED STATES

The commercial policy of the United States is influenced by the political as well as economic motivations of government officials, business and labor leaders, and consumers. For example, the U.S. government may impose trade embargoes on exports to South Africa or Chile in response to the human rights movement; or the military policy of the United States may result in it prohibiting exports with potential military use to communist countries. Our commercial policy is therefore but one aspect of the government's overall foreign policy. This chapter provides an overview of the major developments in the history of American commerical policy. It should be emphasized that sociological, political, and other factors have played a role in the shaping of all economic policies, including commercial policies. Although it is impossible to trace the entire development of U.S. commercial policy in only one chapter, we present a brief sketch of the major events.

U.S. Commercial Policies Before 1934

As Table 7.1 makes clear, U.S. tariff history has been marked by fluctuations. This was especially true until the Reciprocal Trade Agreements Act of 1934, after which the overall trend of U.S.

tariffs has been downward. The dominant motive behind the early tariff laws of the United States was to provide our government an important source of tax revenue. This *revenue* objective was historically the main reason Congress passed the first tariff law in 1789 and followed it up with 12 more tariff laws by 1812. But as the U.S. economy diversified and developed alternate sources of tax revenue, justification for the revenue argument was weakened. The tariffs collected by the federal government today are less than 1 percent of total federal revenues, a negligible amount.

As the revenue argument weakened, the *protective* argument for tariffs in the United States was developing strength. In 1791, Alexander Hamilton presented to Congress his famous "Report on Manufacturers," which proposed that the young industries of the United States be granted import protection until they could grow and prosper—the *infant industry* argument. Although Hamilton's writings did not initially have a legislative impact, by the 1820s protectionist sentiments in the United States were well established. In 1816, the average level of tariffs on U.S. imports was some three to four times the 8 percent levels of 1789.

The surging protectionist movement reached its high point in 1828 with the passage of the

Table 7.1   United States Tariff History:
Average Tariff Rates

Tariff Laws and Dates	Average Tariff Rate* (percent)
McKinley Law, effective Oct. 6, 1890	48.4
Wilson Law, effective Aug. 28, 1894	41.3
Dingley Law, effective July 24, 1897	46.5
Payne-Aldrich Law, effective Aug. 6, 1909	40.8
Underwood Law, effective Oct. 4, 1913	27.0
Fordney-McCumber Law, effective Sept. 22, 1922	38.5
Smoot-Hawley Law, effective June 18, 1930	53.0
1930–1939	43.6
1940–1949	24.1
1950–1959	12.0
1960–1969	11.8
1970–1979	7.4
1980	5.5

Source: *Twenty-Fifth Annual Report of the President of the United States on the Trade Agreements Program*, 1980–1981 (Washington, D.C.: U.S. Government Printing Office, 1982), p. 149.
*Ratio of duties collected to F.O.B. value on dutiable imports.

so-called Tariff of Abominations. This measure increased duties to an average level of 45 percent, the highest in the years before the Civil War, and provoked the South, which wanted low duties for its imported manufactured goods. The South's opposition to this tariff led to the passage of the Compromise Tariff of 1833, providing for a general liberalization of the tariff protection afforded U.S. manufacturers. During the 1840s and 1850s the U.S. government was finding that it faced an excess of tax receipts over expenditures. Although such a development would be considered earthshaking today, in 1846 the government passed the Walker tariffs, which cut duties to an average level of 23 percent to eliminate the budget surplus! Further tariff cuts took place in 1857, bringing the average tariff

levels to their lowest level since 1816, around 16 percent.

During the Civil War era, tariffs were again raised with the passage of the Morrill tariffs of 1861, 1862, and 1864. These measures were primarily intended as a means of paying for the Civil War. By 1870, protection climbed back to the heights of the 1840s: however, this time the tariff levels would not be reduced. During the latter part of the nineteenth century, U.S. policy makers were impressed by the arguments of American labor and businessmen who complained that cheap foreign labor was causing goods to flow into the United States. The enactment of the McKinley and Dingley tariffs largely rested upon this argument. By 1897, tariffs on protected imports averaged some 46 percent.

Although the Payne-Aldrich tariff of 1909 marked the turning point against rising protectionism, it was enactment of the Underwood tariff of 1913 that reduced duties to 27 percent on average. Trade liberalization might have remained on a more permanent basis had it not been for the outbreak of World War I. Protectionist pressures built up during the war years and maintained momentum after the war's conclusion. During the early 1920s, the *scientific tariff* concept was influential, and in 1922, the Fordney-McCumber tariff contained, among other provisions, one that allowed the president to increase tariff levels if foreign production costs were below those of the United States. Average tariff rates climbed to 38 percent under the Fordney-McCumber Law.

The high point of U.S. protectionism culminated with the Smoot-Hawley Act of 1930. Originally the bill was intended to give moderate protection to U.S. farmers who faced stiff import competition. But following the stock market crash of 1929, protectionist pressures were so strong and widespread that average tariffs were raised to some 53 percent on protected imports. The Smoot-Hawley Act was viewed by other countries as a beggar-thy-neighbor attempt by the United States to export its depression abroad. Retaliatory trade restrictions followed, resulting in a decline in the volume of trade. By 1933, the level of world trade was only a third of what it was back in 1929. Between 1930 and 1933, the volume of U.S. exports witnessed a greater deterioration than that of any of the other industrialized countries. During the early thirties, the U.S. share of world trade fell from 16 percent to about 11 percent.

The Reciprocal Trade Agreements Act of 1934

The combined impact on American exports of the Great Depression and the foreign retaliatory tariffs imposed in reaction to the Smoot-Hawley Act resulted in a major reversal of U.S. trade policy. In 1934, Congress passed the Reciprocal Trade Agreements Act, which set the stage for a wave of trade liberalism. Specifically aimed at tariff reduction, the act contained two major features: (1) negotiating authority and (2) generalized reductions. Under this law the president was given the unprecedented authority to negotiate tariff agreements with foreign governments without the necessity of approval by Congress. The president could lower tariffs by an amount up to 50 percent of the existing level. Enactment of any tariff reductions was dependent on the willingness of other countries to reciprocally lower their tariffs against American goods. The Reciprocal Trade Agreements Act thus transferred the authority to grant tariff changes from the legislative to the executive branch of the government. From 1934 to 1947, the United States entered into 32 reciprocal tariff agreements, and over this period the average level of tariffs on protected products fell to about half of the 1934 levels.

The Reciprocal Trade Agreements Act also provided for generalized tariff reductions

through its *most-favored-nation clause,* whereby tariff reductions would apply, not only to any given country entering into an agreement with the United States, but also to all nations. Such a tariff policy is intended to be nondiscriminatory in nature: Inclusion of the most-favored-nation principle into tariff treaties results in a more uniform tariff pattern as the treaties account for increasingly larger portions of world trade.

The General Agreement on Tariffs and Trade

Partly in response to the disruptions to international trade during the Great Depression era, the United States and some of its trading partners sought to impose order on the flow of goods among nations after World War II. Plans called for the establishment of a *multilateral* system of world trade. Under the Reciprocal Trade Agreements Act, only bilateral negotiations could take place among trading nations. The first major postwar step toward liberalization of world trade was the General Agreement on Tariffs and Trade (GATT) signed in 1947 by 23 countries including the United States. Today GATT's more than 80 members account for some 85 percent of world trade. There is widespread agreement that GATT has constituted a vital element in the liberalization of trade, especially in the industrial countries. GATT's purpose has been to stipulate a basic set of rules under which trade negotiations can occur. Participating countries agree to three basic principles: (1) nondiscrimination in trade through unconditional most-favored-nation treatment; (2) the reduction of tariffs by multilateral negotiations; and (3) elimination of most import quotas, with exceptions such as protection of domestic agriculture or safeguarding of a country's balance-of-payments position.

An important function of GATT is to furnish member countries a mechanism whereby disputes concerning trade policy can be settled. Suppose, for example, that Canada finds it necessary to raise tariffs on imported autos to protect its home industry, which harms West Germany. West Germany can issue a complaint, which is sent to member countries for review, discussion, and possibly the attainment of a settlement. If an agreement cannot be reached, GATT will provide a conciliation panel to review the complaints and make recommendations. Canada, for example, may be encouraged to moderate its tariff barriers. Should this recommendation not be acknowledged, GATT has the authority to warrant West Germany's enactment of retaliatory tariffs.

One of the most hotly contested trade disputes involving GATT was the so-called chicken war of 1963. During 1962, members of the European Common Market (comprising countries of the European Economic Community) increased their import tariffs on poultry, triggering a decline in U.S. exports to Europe of more than 60 percent. After many rounds of accusations, the GATT conciliation panel ruled that the U.S. exporters suffered losses of more than $25 million. Although the ruling was accepted by both parties, the question of settlement was not resolved. In 1965, the United States levied retaliatory tariffs on selected imports from the Common Market. Although the GATT forum did not completely settle the conflict, it was widely felt that it helped limit the possibilities of a major trade war.

In spite of GATT's success in liberalizing world trade relations, its operation has remained somewhat controversial. Many developing countries have refused to join GATT on the grounds that it is a rich nations' club. Their concern is that when wealthy industrial countries bargain with poor developing countries on a multilateral, nondiscriminatory basis, the latter will remain as producers of primary commodities instead of being able to undergo industrialization. Developing countries sometimes also argue that strict trade controls over imports for nonessential pur-

poses are necessary if foreign currencies are to be available to finance domestic developmental programs. Another general area of concern is that GATT has been unable to establish procedures for phasing out nontariff trade measures, nor has it significantly liberalized trade in agricultural commodities. GATT's future is directly tied to its finding solutions for these problems.

Trade Liberalization Modifications

The movement toward free trade occasioned by the Reciprocal Trade Agreements Act and the formation of GATT was weakened by several pieces of legislation during the 1940s and 1950s. Partly because of the uncertain attitudes our government held regarding trade liberalization versus protectionism, three devices were introduced to nullify major tariff concessions by our government: (1) the peril-point clause, (2) the escape clause, and (3) the national security clause.

From 1948 to 1962, protectionist safeguards were enacted that called for the president to negotiate tariff concessions under a *peril-point clause*. This provision required the U.S. Tariff Commission to determine in advance of any treaty to what extent tariffs could be lowered before serious injury would be inflicted on home producers. The president was not bound to keep tariff levels above the peril point, but he could not enter into tariff concessions below that level without a congressional review of the reductions. The operation of the peril-point policy suffered from a flaw of interpretation. Because *serious* and *injury* were not precisely defined in economic terms, any estimate of the peril-point level involved an educated guess.

Another safeguard has been the *escape clause*,[1] which initially gained prominence during the 1950s. Under this provision, if the president extends tariff concessions to other countries, a domestic producer might apply for temporary relief (for example, import quotas) on the grounds that such trade liberalization resulted in its being seriously injured by foreign competition.

An escape clause action is usually initiated by a petition from an American industry to the U.S. International Trade Commission (USITC), which investigates and recommends to the president. All of the following conditions must be met for USITC to recommend that import relief be extended: (1) Imports are increasing, either actually or relative to domestic production. (2) A domestic industry producing an article like or directly competitive with the imported article is being seriously injured or threatened with such injury. (3) The increased imports are a substantial cause of serious injury or threat to the domestic industry producing a like or directly competitive article. An affirmative decision by USITC is reported to the president who determines what remedy, if any, is in the national interest. Table 7.2 supplies examples of relief granted to American firms under the escape clause.

An example of relief granted under the escape clause occurred in 1983 when the president increased tariffs and set import quotas on a variety of foreign-made steel products. The ruling was made following a recommendation by USITC that American producers of stainless steel products were being seriously injured by foreign competition. Under the program, tariffs of 8 percent to 10 percent were placed on stainless sheet, strip, and plate imports. After a period of four years, the tariffs would decrease to 4 percent. The program also set global tonnage quotas for bar, rod, and alloy tool steel. The purpose of the restrictions was to give American steel firms temporary relief from import competition while they modernize and regain profitability.

The final area in which tariff relief was provided came under the *national security clause*. In 1955, legislation was passed allowing the imposition of trade barriers on imports that threatened the security of the United States. Although many industries such as textiles and electrical equipment have attempted to convince the government that the nation's security is at stake if foreign producers gain control of our markets, few have been successful in establishing an argu-

Table 7.2   Escape Clause Relief: Selected Examples

Product	Type of Relief
Porcelain on steel cooking ware	Additional duties imposed for 4 years are 20, 20, 15, and 10 cents per pound in the first, second, third, and fourth years, respectively
Prepared or preserved mushrooms	Additional duties imposed for 3 years are 20%, 15%, and 10% ad valorem in the first, second, and third years, respectively
Clothespins	Temporary global quota
Bolts, nuts, and large screws	Temporary duty increase
High-carbon ferrochromium	Temporary duty increase
Color television receivers	Orderly marketing agreements with Taiwan and Korea
Footwear	Orderly marketing agreements with Taiwan and Korea

Source: *Twenty-Fifth Annual Report of the President of the United States on the Trade Agreements Program, 1980–1981* (Washington, D.C.: U.S. Government Printing Office, 1982), p. 180.

ment that wins governmental approval. The main exception has been the U.S. oil companies, which historically have enjoyed barriers applied to crude oil imports. This is due to the threat that such imports pose for domestic exploration, which is required to assure a long-run supply in case of a national crisis.

Countervailing Duties

The previous chapter discussed how subsidies have been used to help firms become more competitive. As American consumers, we might appreciate purchasing subsidized British steel at artificially low prices. But American firms, such as U.S. Steel Co., do not appreciate competing against foreign firms subsidized by their governments.

According to U.S. commercial policy, whenever a bounty or grant is paid or bestowed in a foreign country upon the manufacture or production or export of any good produced in that country, a countervailing duty equal to the amount of the subsidy is to be levied upon import of such goods into the United States. Countervailing duties are intended to affect any unfair competitive advantage that foreign manufacturers of exports might gain over American producers because of foreign subsidies.

Upon the receipt of a petition by an American industry, the U.S. Commerce Department and the U.S. International Trade Commission determine whether subsidized goods threaten or cause substantial injury to American producers. If the determinations are affirmative, a countervailing duty order is issued by the Commerce Department directing the assessment of duties on goods from the country under investigation equal to the amount of the subsidy. Table 7.3 summarizes countervailing duties in effect as of 1981.

It can be argued, however, that preventing foreign subsidized goods from entering the domestic economy is not in the best interest of

Table 7.3　Selected Countervailing Duty Orders as of January 1, 1981

Country	Product	Rate of Duty
Argentina	Woolen garments	3.23%
Australia	Butter	3 pence per lb
Belgium	Float glass	2.0%
Brazil	Footwear	1.0%
Canada	Radial tires	1.5%
India	Metal castings	13.3%
Israel	Fresh-cut roses	2.0%
Japan	Industrial fasteners	4.0%
Sweden	Rayon fiber	8.9%

Source: *Twenty-Fifth Annual Report of the President of the United States on the Trade Agreements Program, 1980–1981* (Washington, D.C.: U.S. Government Printing Office, 1982), p. 174.

society. Economic theory suggests that if a nation is a net importer of a product subsidized by foreigners, the nation as a whole gains from the foreign subsidy. This is because the gains to domestic consumers of the subsidized good more than offset the losses to domestic producers of the import-competing goods.[2]

Consider the trade situation illustrated in Figure 7.1. Let the price of steel produced by both American and Japanese steelmakers be $400 per ton. Assume that owing to a successful "Buy American" campaign initiated by the U.S. government, American consumers purchase from American producers all of their requirements, 9 million tons. U.S. consumer surplus is given by area a, whereas the producer surplus accruing to U.S. firms equals areas $b + e$. Suppose the Japanese government, to penetrate the U.S. market, provides its steelmakers a subsidy of $50 per ton of steel produced. This cost advantage permits Japan's supply curve to shift from S_{Japan_0} to S_{Japan_1}. The resulting decrease in Japanese steel prices triggers a rise in American consumption to 12 million tons and a fall in American production to 6 million tons, with imports totaling

6 million tons. The subsidy has hurt American steel firms, for their producer surplus has decreased by area b. However, American buyers find their consumer surplus rises by areas $b + c + d$. The United States as a whole benefits from the foreign subsidy, since the benefits to its consumers exceed the losses to its producers by areas $c + d$.

The Trade Expansion Act of 1962

The Trade Expansion Act of 1962 was enacted in response to two major factors. First was the challenge posed by the birth of the European Economic Community in 1960. Europe was a key market for U.S. exporters, and the possibility that it might be reduced by trade restrictions was sufficient concern for the president to negotiate a new trade pact. Second, increasingly restrictive provisions (the escape and peril-point clauses) were being applied to renewals of the reciprocal

trade agreements program, which greatly limited the president's authority to lower tariffs. Rather than pressing for another renewal of the reciprocal trade agreements program, in 1962 President Kennedy won congressional approval of the Trade Expansion Act. Under this act, the former peril-point clause was eliminated, while the eligibility provisions of the escape clause were tightened up. The president could continue entering into tariff pacts without congressional approval. He could now cut tariffs across the board by up to 50 percent of their July 1962 level instead of cutting tariffs on a product-by-product basis. On certain industrial goods, tariff reductions could be even greater. Also subject to removal were tariffs on agricultural products in the tropical and temperate zones.

Under the authority of the Trade Expansion Act, the United States entered into tariff negotiations with other industrial countries from 1964 to 1967 in what was referred to as the Kennedy Round of negotiations. The negotiations did not

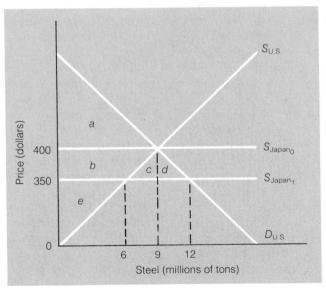

Figure 7.1   Impact of Japanese export subsidy on U.S. welfare.

achieve the 50 percent tariff reductions that were permitted by Congress, but they did yield an average reduction in tariffs of 35 percent on 60,000 industrial products valued at some $40 billion. The Kennedy Round also established the precedent that negotiations would include non-tariff trade barriers as well as tariffs on agricultural commodities. All in all, the Kennedy Round resulted in the most sweeping tariff reductions since GATT went into effect.

Adjustment Assistance

According to the free trade argument, in a dynamic economy where trade proceeds according to the comparative advantage principle, resources flow from uses with low productivity to those with higher productivity. The result is a more efficient allocation of the world's resources over time. But in the short run, painful adjustments may occur as less efficient firms go out of business and workers lose their jobs. These displacement costs can be quite severe to affected parties. Many industrial countries in recent years have enacted programs for giving adjustment assistance to those who incur short-run hardships owing to displaced domestic production. The underlying rationale comes from the notion that if society in general enjoys welfare gains from the increased efficiency stemming from trade liberalization, some sort of compensation should be provided for those who are temporarily injured by import competition. As long as free trade generates significant gains to the country, the winners can compensate the losers and still enjoy some of the gains of free trade.

Trade adjustment assistance was initially afforded U.S. workers and firms with the passage of the 1962 Trade Expansion Act. Whenever the U.S. Tariff Commission found that tariff concessions were resulting in severe import competition, it could recommend adjustment assistance. Injured workers were entitled to job-training

programs, cash payments, and relocation allowances. To firms, the program offered technical aid in moving into new lines of production, market research assistance, and low-interest loans. The adjustment assistance program, however, did not live up to full expectations during the 1960s. This is because eligibility requirements were very strict, with the result that labor and business became frustrated in not being able to obtain relief. In the 1970s the eligibility requirements were loosened with the passage of the 1974 Trade Act. Either the secretary of labor or the secretary of commerce could determine whether aid should be extended to workers, firms, and communities affected by increased imports. With the eligibility criteria liberalized, the number of grants has shot up. In 1977, for example, relief was extended to displaced workers of such firms as Zenith, RCA, Youngstown Steel, General Motors, and U.S. Steel. Table 7.4 summarizes the financial adjustment assistance provided by the U.S. government to firms in 1980.

Enactment of adjustment assistance programs is widely considered a significant innovation of commercial policy. Although it is often recognized that such programs are a political necessity in today's world, not all interested parties are enthusiastic about implementation of these programs. Adjustment assistance is intended to help domestic firms become more competitive by switching to superior technologies and developing new products. But in practice, it is alleged that such programs can be manipulated to financially sustain a losing concern rather than help it become competitive. A study by the Organization for Economic Cooperation and Development (OECD) points out how this has sometimes been the case in the European programs.[3] Proponents of adjustment assistance argue that it is preferable to help domestic labor and business become more productive or to move into new occupations or product lines than to curb import competition via tariffs and quotas. In

Table 7.4   Adjustment Assistance Authorized in 1980 for U.S. Firms

Industry	Number of Firms	Financial Assistance Authorized (millions of dollars)
Apparel	30	29.4
Footwear	8	10.4
Textiles	4	3.5
Machinery and equipment	3	4.9
Electronic components	2	2.4
Toys	2	1.1
Handbags	2	0.5
All other	12	9.6
	63	61.8

Source: *Twenty-Fifth Annual Report of the President of the United States on the Trade Agreements Program, 1980–1981* (Washington, D.C.: U.S. Government Printing Office, 1982), p. 197.

this manner, the societal welfare gains arising from a competitive market are still attainable.

The Trade Act of 1974

Inmediately following the successful conclusion of the Kennedy Round in 1967, a revival of protectionism in the United States began to unfold. In 1968, the president provided relief for our textile industry from foreign competition when he entered into voluntary export agreements with Japan and other textile-producing nations. Pressures were also mounting to liberalize trade adjustment assistance. The framers of the Burke-Hartke bill, which called for significant restrictions on imports and limits on foreign investment by U.S. corporations, had widespread support, although the bill failed to win congressional approval. In retrospect, it appears that with the conclusion of the Kennedy Round, the thrust of trade liberalization reached its postwar high point.

Fearful of backsliding into protectionism, the U.S. Congress passed the Trade Act of 1974, an act intended to be flexible in nature, with both liberal and restrictive features. Essentially the act endorsed liberalized trade in both industrial products and agricultural commodities. The president was authorized to reduce or eliminate various tariff and nontariff trade barriers. It also recognized the superiority of adjustment assistance over other restrictive trade practices. The act furthermore contained safeguard provisions that permit relief from severe import competition and unfair trade practices such as foreign export subsidies, dumping, and predatory conduct by foreign sellers. The passage of the 1974 Trade Act was quite controversial, with liberal trade proponents viewing the act as having a dangerous potential for further trade curbs and protectionists considering it overly permissive in allowing for import competition.

The Tokyo Round

The Tokyo Round of Multilateral Trade Negotiations came to a conclusion in April 1979, following five years of intensive bargaining among 99 nations. Earlier rounds of trade negotiations were concerned only, or primarily, with reductions in tariffs. As average tariff rates in industrial countries became progressively lower during the postwar period, the importance of nontariff trade barriers increased. In response to these changes, negotiators shifted emphasis to the issue of nontariff distortions in international trade. The Tokyo Round was directed mainly at reducing or eliminating certain nontariff trade barriers, although additional tariff cutting was also desired.

Tariff Reductions

Under the Tokyo Round, the major industrial countries were able to achieve significant reductions in tariffs. As seen in Table 7.5, the average reductions for industrial products amounted to 31 percent for the United States, 27 percent for the European Economic Community, 28 percent for Japan, and 34 percent for Canada. The most important tariff cuts came in nonelectrical machinery, wood products, chemicals, and transportation equipment. For agricultural products, the average tariff cut was 17 percent for the United States, 30 percent for the EEC, 4 percent

for Japan, and 20 percent for Canada. Although the tariff reductions were substantial in percentage terms, they were not large in absolute terms since most tariffs were already fairly low.

Agreements on Nontariff Trade Barriers

A second accomplishment of the Tokyo Round was the agreement to remove or lessen the restrictive impact of a number of nontariff barriers to trade. Rules and guidelines were established that prevented otherwise reasonable domestic policies (for example, environmental controls, promotion of domestic employment) from becoming hidden restraints on international trade. The rules and guidelines were specified in the form of several codes of conduct, the most important of which are discussed here.

Customs Valuation.   The customs valuation code is an agreement on how to value imported goods for the purpose of levying ad valorem duties. It is intended to promote a uniform standard

Table 7.5   Tariff Reductions Agreed to in the Tokyo Round

Country (Sector)	Pre-Tokyo Round Average Tariff Level (percent)	Post-Tokyo Round Average Tariff Level (percent)	Degree of Tariff Cut (percent)
United States			
Industrial goods	8.2	5.7	31
Agricultural goods	8.7	7.2	17
European Economic Community			
Industrial goods	9.8	7.2	27
Agricultural goods	7.0	4.9	30
Japan			
Industrial goods	6.9	4.6	28
Agricultural goods	14.0	13.5	4
Canada			
Industrial goods	13.1	8.7	34
Agricultural goods	6.5	5.2	20

Source: Office of the Special Representative for Trade Negotiations.

whereby goods are neither undervalued nor overvalued for ad valorem duties. Exporters thus are able to accurately predict the valuation of their products and the import duties attached to them. The customs valuation code was seen as a way of preventing product values from being substantially inflated by arbitrary valuation methods, resulting in higher duty payments.

Government procurement. In most countries, the government and its agencies are the largest purchasers of goods. However, discrimination in favor of domestic suppliers has resulted in trade barriers in products subject to government purchasing. The government procurement code prevents a government from discriminating against the products of foreign suppliers. The agreement's coverage extends to purchases of goods by central governments on contracts valued at approximately $200,000 and over. The code does not apply to purchases by state and local governments, national security items, construction contracts, or purchases from small and minority businesses. By limiting favoritism to domestic suppliers, the agreement is intended to promote competition in the government procurement market.

Technical trade barriers (standards). In the postwar period, the number of product standards has grown as governments have become increasingly involved in the protection of public health, the environment, and consumer welfare. Besides meeting these objectives, however, product standards have been structured to interfere with international trade. Product certification systems have been manipulated to limit access of imports or deny the right of a certification mark to imported goods. Product testing also has been conducted, increasing expenses for importers. The agreement on technical trade barriers outlaws discriminatory manipulations of product standards, product testing, and product certification systems. The code is intended to ensure access to markets to both domestic and foreign suppliers.

Subsidies and countervailing duties. Recognizing that subsidies may have harmful effects on competitive forces at work in international trade, the subsidies code attempts to control the impact of subsidies on international trade flows. The use of export subsidies on manufactured goods and minerals is flatly prohibited, whereas greater discipline is encouraged in the use of export subsidies for agricultural, fishery, and forest products. Although the code acknowledges that domestic subsidies can be useful in promoting objectives of national policy (such as employment, research and development, or farm income security), they are not to be used in ways that would injure the industries of other countries. Also specified are procedures in which countervailing duties can be used to defend home producers from injurious, subsidized import competition in their domestic market.

Licensing. Governments issue import licenses to gather statistical information about imports and to administer certain import restrictions such as quotas. Internationally traded products often have been subject to needless bureaucratic delays as a result of import licensing systems. Red tape involved in obtaining licenses can be expensive for importers. The import license code requires that the procedures importers must follow in obtaining a license be simplified and harmonized to the greatest extent possible. Governments must publish rules governing procedures for applying for import licenses and must permit any firm, person, or institution to apply for a license. The code encourages governments to administer import licenses in a fair and neutral manner to prevent any distortions of international trade.

Welfare Effects of Trade Liberalization

Presumably a country would desire to participate in the Tokyo Round if the liberalization of trade barriers would lead to an increase in its national welfare. This would occur if the gains stemming from freer trade (for example, higher domestic income and employment, lower cost products, or wider selection of goods) more than offset the disadvantages associated with expanding import competition (such as displacement of home producers and workers).

Table 7.6 gives estimates of the effects of the reductions in tariffs and certain nontariff trade barriers negotiated at the Tokyo Round. The estimates suggest that the Tokyo Round would have small but beneficial overall effects on trade, prices, employment, and economic welfare for virtually all industrialized countries. There would also be small gains for some, but not all, developing countries. For some developing countries, such as Singapore or South Korea, the Tokyo Round would have adverse welfare effects.

As the result of the Tokyo Round, it was estimated that the United States would see an increase in domestic employment equal to 0.14

percent of its labor force. The strongest gains would accrue to the U.S. agriculture sector and to those industries that employ sophisticated technologies and skilled workers, such as aircraft, electrical machinery, and chemicals. Output and employment might fall in industries that are labor intensive and employ older, well-known technologies—industries like apparel, plastic products, and china. As for the probable impact on domestic prices, the Tokyo Round agreement was expected to reduce U.S. consumer prices by only 0.07 percent from what would have occurred in the absence of trade liberalization. Concerning the impact of lower trade barriers on domestic consumers and producers, the overall economic welfare of the United States (as measured by changes in consumer surplus and producer surplus) was expected to rise by 0.03 percent of gross domestic product.

For the participating countries as a group, the Tokyo Round will probably yield only minor welfare gains. This is partly explained by the cuts in tariffs, which are small in absolute terms and also relative to the size of the participating countries' economies, and are of limited scope. What is more, the implementation of the agreements

Table 7.6   Economic Effects of the Reductions in Trade Barriers Negotiated at the Tokyo Round of Multilateral Trade Negotiations

Country/Area	Percentage Change in Employment	Percentage Change in Price Index	Change in Welfare as a Percentage of Gross Domestic Product
All countries	0.13	−0.11	0.10
Industrial countries	0.24	−0.25	0.11
Developing countries	0.04	−0.70	0.04
United States	0.14	−0.07	0.03
European Economic Community	0.37	−0.50	0.11
West Germany	0.42	−0.59	0.10
Japan	0.06	−0.10	0.08
Canada	0.26	−0.25	0.21
Sweden	0.55	−0.44	0.98

Source: Alan V. Deardoff and Robert M. Stern, "Economic Effects of the Tokyo Round," *Southern Economic Journal*, 49, no. 3, January 1983, pp. 612–613.

reached at the Tokyo Round will be phased in over a number of years, diluting the impact on output, employment, and prices in any single year. Perhaps the major benefit of the Tokyo Round is that it resulted in an agreement to lower trade barriers during an era in which protectionism was reemerging as a major force.

Export Policies of the United States

Although the United States has remained the world's largest exporter during the 1970s, it also has been an enormous importer. Throughout this period, Americans again and again have found imports exceeding exports, resulting in alarming U.S. trade deficits. Meanwhile, West Germany and Japan were piling up huge trade surpluses. The erosion of a country's ability to compete in world markets is traditionally explained by business factors such as the cost of labor and capital as well as productivity. We must also look at a country's official policies and regulations, which promote or hinder exports.

Export Promotion and Market Development

The U.S. government maintains a variety of export programs to encourage firms to expand their overseas sales. A primary objective behind U.S. export promotion programs is to offset or minimize deficiencies in the market system. Because of high costs of obtaining information, for example, many foreign buyers might remain unaware of prospective American sellers were it not for U.S. promotion programs. American exporters might likewise remain ignorant of foreign sales possibilities as a result of lack of knowledge about foreign markets and exporting procedures. The U.S. government furnishes exporters with marketing information and technical assistance, in addition to trade missions that

help expose new exporters to foreign customers. The government also promotes exports by sponsoring exhibits of U.S. goods in international trade fairs and establishing overseas trade centers that enable U.S. firms to exhibit and sell machinery and equipment.

In most countries, export promotion programs include market information, government trade missions, export subsidies, tax incentives, and export financing. The U.S. government is generally cautious about interfering with competitive markets and so refrains from enacting export subsidies and other policies that distort trade flows. The United States does encourage firms to export by making sure that our exporters have access to competitive credit terms to finance export transactions and that sufficient tax incentives exist so American exporters can survive in world markets.

The maintenance of competitive credit terms for American exporters is a function of the U.S. Export-Import Bank and the Commodity Credit Corporation. The Export-Import Bank (Eximbank) is an independent agency of the U.S. government designed to finance U.S. exports. Direct loans are generally made to foreign buyers of American high-technology products or capital equipment. The Eximbank may even guarantee loans and provide insurance for loans made by private-sector commercial banks. The Eximbank normally extends its financial assistance in cases where the risks, maturity, and amounts involved are beyond the lending scope of the private sector. In offering competitive interest rates in financing exports, the Eximbank has sometimes been criticized because part of its funds are borrowed from the U.S. Treasury. The question has been asked whether American tax revenues should subsidize exports to countries like the Soviet Union at interest rates lower than could be obtained by private institutions. To this extent, it is true that tax funds distort trade and redistribute income toward exporters.

Officially supported lending for American exports is also provided by the Commodity Credit Corporation (CCC), a government-owned corporation administered by the U.S. Department of Agriculture. The CCC makes available export credit financing for eligible agricultural commodities. The interest rates charged by the CCC are usually slightly below prevailing rates charged by private financial institutions.

The formation of the Domestic International Sales Corporation (DISC) in 1972 was intended to offset the competitive disadvantage of American export firms because of both foreign and U.S. tax regulations. The effect of these regulations was to encourage U.S. companies to produce overseas by establishing foreign subsidiaries rather than exporting from the United States. Under U.S. tax law, profits of foreign subsidiaries were not subject to U.S. income taxes until repatriated to the parent firm. When foreign tax rates were below that of the United States, overseas production was favored. The 1972 provisions eliminate the bias in the U.S. tax code by allowing American export companies to defer U.S. income taxes on half of their export income. Separate export sales corporations (DISCs) are set up by the parent firm, whose profits are not directly subject to U.S. income tax regulations. The parent firm (shareholder of DISC) is taxed on half of the DISC profits, and taxes on the remaining profits are deferred indefinitely. Such reduction on export income taxes gives firms an incentive to remain as exporters instead of locating production facilities abroad. DISC has proved to be of major significance for U.S. exports.

Other U.S. agencies active in overseas sales financing include the Agency for International Development, which makes available loans and grants to developing nations. A significant portion of each loan or grant is used to finance American exports. The U.S. Overseas Private Investment Corporation encourages American direct investments (for example, factories) in developing countries through the provision of political risk insurance and financing services. Many of these investment projects require the export of U.S. capital equipment and other products. For example, a flour mill may require continuing exports of American wheat. The U.S. Trade and Development Program finances planning services for major development projects. The program supports only those projects that offer a strong likelihood of future American exports. The U.S. Small Business Administration encourages export expansion by providing credit to American firms for the purpose of export market development and the purpose of financing labor and materials for preexport production.

Trade Regulation and Restraint

Besides promoting foreign sales, the U.S. government currently exercises control over exports. According to the Export Administration Act of 1969, export controls can be used for reasons of *national security, foreign policy,* and *short supply.* They also can be used to require domestic firms to obtain authorization to participate in restrictive practices or boycotts against countries friendly to the United States. For national security reasons, the United States has stipulated a list of commodities that normally would be prevented from being exported to countries like the Soviet Union, People's Republic of China, and communist countries of Eastern Europe. The list of embargoed products pertains to nuclear weapons, explosive devices, and high-technology goods of strategic importance. For foreign policy reasons, the United States has placed curbs on exports headed for North Vietnam and Cambodia, Cuba, North Korea, and Zimbabwe. As for products in short supply, the United States has monitored foreign sales of crude oil, fertilizers, natural gas, and other energy-related products. The underlying reason has been to protect the American economy from excessive outflows of commodities in tight supply and to offset the impact of foreign demand on the U.S. inflation rate.

An example of commercial sanctions imposed by the United States occurred in 1980 when the president levied an embargo on exports to the Soviet Union following the Soviet invasion of Afghanistan. Characterizing the invasion as a threat to peace, the president apparently initiated the sanctions to show the Soviets in tangible ways that aggression is costly and would be met with firmness. The embargo resulted in the termination of major sales of U.S. agricultural products and tighter restrictions on sales of U.S. high technology and phosphates. However, the embargo did not exert as much economic pressure as desired. Grain shipments by Australia, Canada, and the European Economic Community immediately rose following the U.S. boycott, resulting in a shortfall of only 2 percent to 3 percent of total Soviet requirements. The grain embargo noticeably affected Soviet livestock and poultry production, which declined dramatically following the sanctions.

Besides initiating export restrictions on products headed abroad, American commercial policy has also dealt with boycotts and restrictive practices imposed by other countries against countries friendly to the United States. During the 1970s, the Arab nations attempted to interfere with U.S. trade with Israel by blacklisting those American manufacturers and exporters who were doing business with importers from Israel. Not only did the Arab states boycott these firms' goods but also they requested that American vessels and aircraft transport only nonblacklisted goods. Subcontracts were not to be awarded to any blacklisted firm. In opposing the Arab boycott, the U.S. government in 1976 began to step up its campaign against firms complying with the boycott. The Justice Department filed antitrust suits against such firms on the grounds that they were part of a conspiracy to refuse to conduct business with blacklisted persons or entities.

Concerted Action in Export Trade

U.S. business often has complained that other countries do not hesitate to make the benefits of joint exporting available to their companies. For the sole purpose of increasing exports, foreign companies have been permitted to combine to bid large projects and to form sales organizations that sell a variety of products overseas. U.S. businesses have been handicapped in establishing joint-exporting organizations by inadequate funding, fears of antitrust prosecution, and legislation prohibiting the exports of the services of engineers, architects, accountants, and other professionals. However, the U.S. government does provide *limited exemptions* from antitrust laws for associations of U.S. exporters as well as export trading companies.

Export Trade Associations

In the early 1900s, various exporters of the United States, led by the copper producers, urged the passage of legislation allowing firms in a given industry to export through a single sales agency. The justification for such legislation was the existence of many selling and buying cartels in countries such as Germany and the United Kingdom. The American exporters maintained they should be allowed to combine in selling to match the market power of foreign cartels. However, export trade associations are an exception to U.S. antitrust laws, which normally prevent competitors from behaving collusively. Pressured by the efforts of organized exporters, in 1918 Congress passed the Export Trade Act, also called the Webb-Pomerene Act.

As a way of helping U.S. firms trade in the world market on more equal terms with their organized competitors and buyers, the Export Trade Act of 1918 provides an exemption from the antitrust laws for horizontal combinations of U.S. firms, particularly small businesses, engaged solely in export trade. Firms have been permitted to form marketing associations that operate as individual sales agencies. Small firms thus gain through combination the advantages large firms enjoy when they sell abroad. The antitrust exemption has resulted in U.S. firms' fixing prices and allocating customers in foreign markets. Associations also have attempted to reduce the costs of exporting by spreading overhead, eliminating duplicate sales organizations, and obtaining lower rates on shipping and insurance. However, the antitrust exemption is limited in that export associations are prohibited from restraining trade within the United States, nor can they restrain exports of any U.S. firm competing with the association.

There are some 30 export associations in the United States that market chemicals, dried fruit, motion pictures, wood chips, tire equipment, soybean oil, rice, and other commodities. At the peak of their popularity during the 1930s, American export trade associations numbered 57 and accounted for 19 percent of U.S. exports. Today, the export trade associations have a minimal impact on U.S. overseas sales, accounting for less than 2 percent of U.S. exports.

One reason for this modest impact is that small firms often have been reluctant to enter international trade. Beyond this, it is not clear that export associations offer significant advantages over selling abroad through brokers and export merchants. Business people also have questioned the certainty of the antitrust exemption, hesitating to become members of an association that, if challenged on legal grounds, would become involved in an expensive and long-term court case. Moreover, the antitrust exemption has not included service industries (for example, management consulting and architecture), which have become important contributors to U.S. exports.

Export Trading Companies

Most American producers traditionally have devoted minimal effort to export promotion. Throughout the 1970s, the U.S. share of world exports decreased, whereas many foreign competitors maintained or increased their market share. Apparently there was little need for a strong export orientation by U.S. firms, since the U.S. market offered sufficient opportunities for the sale of American-produced goods and services. What is more, many small and medium-sized American firms have not exported, owing to lack of knowledge about foreign selling, difficulties of financing foreign sales, and the belief that exporting is too risky. As of 1982, only 10 percent of U.S. manufacturing firms exported, and less than 1 percent of U.S. firms accounted for 80 percent of U.S. exports. However, pressured by organized business, the U.S. government signed into law the Export Trading Company Act in 1982, aimed at giving American firms new tools to penetrate and expand overseas markets.

The Export Trading Company (ETC) legislation encourages small and medium-sized companies to enter foreign markets for the first time. It permits producers of goods and services, banks, export marketing companies, and others to combine their resources into a joint effort to export their own products or to act as an export service for other producers. Export trading companies are used widely by other industrial nations. Two-thirds of Japan's exports are handled by export trading companies. Several Western European countries, Korea, and Hong Kong also use them.

The legislation permits American business firms to organize an export trading company (ETC), which exports the goods and services of its members or provides facilitating export services for nonmember companies. Banks also are permitted to loan money to, and invest in, an ETC. The ETC is given immunity from ·U.S. antitrust laws.

Exporting through an ETC allows U.S. companies to enjoy various economies of scale associated with exporting. An ETC might pool the shipments of several American companies, taking advantage of lower transportation costs. Exporting a large volume of products also permits lower per-unit costs of establishing overseas offices, insurance, and warehousing. ETCs also are intended to offer a wider range of products and services and be equipped to better recognize potential overseas opportunities than individual exporters.

A number of ETCs have been established in the United States. The General Electric Trading Company serves GE business as well as external clients. Stressing industrial and technical goods, this trading company exports primarily to the high-growth developing countries. The Sears Roebuck Trading Company has emphasized the sale of technology and management services to more than 30 countries. Other major U.S. corporations having ETCs include Rockwell, Control Data, and General Motors.

International Services

Besides the exchange of tangible goods such as autos and oil, international trade increasingly has involved an exchange of services. Exports of services such as banking, transportation, motion pictures, tourism, insurance, advertising, engineering, construction, and computer services are gaining recognition as significant contributors to the foreign sales of many countries.

The rise of the service sector, now the dominant part of the U.S. economy, has become a global phenomenon. Most other industrial nations have experienced a pattern similar to that of the United States—the goods-producing sector (manufacturing, mining, agriculture) continues to grow, but while doing so becomes a smaller portion of an expanding economy.

Moreover, this trend has not escaped the developing countries. Singapore, for example, has a leading international airline, and South Korea is a major exporter of engineering and construction services.

The services sector has replaced the production of goods as the dominant element in the gross national product of the United States. By the 1980s, services accounted for more than three-fifths of the U.S. gross national product, compared with a 32 percent level in 1949. What is more, almost 7 out of every 10 Americans work in service industries. As recently as 1950, services accounted for less than half of overall U.S. employment.

The growth in the service sectors of the United States and other countries conforms to recent economic theory, which suggests that the evolution of industrial nations typically occurs through three developmental cycles. The initial era is one of capital accumulation via savings generated from mineral extraction or agriculture. Next occurs a period of industrialization during which the production of manufactured goods replaces agriculture and mining as the main source of domestic output. Finally, as the economy expands and income increases, services account for ever-increasing shares of national output, encroaching on the primacy of the manufacturing sector. It often is maintained that the United States has entered this third stage of development. Statistics showing services as a percentage of U.S. output tend to agree with this theory.

As seen in Table 7.7, service exports generate significant revenues for the United States. The importance of services lies not only in their growing volume but also in the role they play in support of exported American goods. Growth of trade in services can promote growth of trade in goods. Service exports in such industries as construction and telecommunications have become a crucial factor in increasing American exports of capital goods by generating additional

Table 7.7   Estimated Foreign Business of U.S.
Service Industries: Exports from the U.S.
and Income of Overseas Affiliates, 1981
(millions of dollars)

Receipts for exports, total	40,520
Travel	12,168
Passenger fares	2,991
Other transportation	12,168
Fees and royalties	
from affiliated foreigners	5,867
from unaffiliated foreigners	1,386
Other private services	5,940
Income of foreign affiliates	99,953
Oil and gas field services	6,454
Petroleum tanker operations	9,576
Pipeline transmission, oil and gas	1,823
Finance (except banking), insurance and real estate	20,703
Banking	4,290
Construction	20,889
Wholesale and retail trade	5,196
Transportation and communication	15,570
Hotels and lodging	1,799
Advertising	1,583
Motion pictures and TV tape and film	1,234
Engineering, architecture, surveying	4,695
Accounting	503
Other personal and business services	5,638
Total, exports plus affiliates' income	140,473

Source: "The Importance of Services," *Business America*, November 1, 1982, p. 5.

demand for American products. A strong link thus exists between goods and services trade.

The U.S. services sector has consistently been a *net exporter* (that is, the value of exports exceeds the value of imports). It may come as a surprise that West Germany and Japan, two of the biggest foreign competitors of the United States in manufactured goods, have consistently been net importers of services!

How did the United States develop a competitive edge in service exports? As personal income increases, people tend to devote larger shares of income to services. The U.S. demand for services has been strong in the postwar era, given the high, and rising, incomes of Americans. This demand led to specialization in the domestic services sector and greater efficiencies in production and delivery of services. The postwar era also saw rising income and increasing demand for services in other countries, providing the United States strong export markets. However, service industry techniques and management practices can be learned and copied, just as in manufacturing. American service firms have witnessed increasing competition from foreign companies.

Although the dollar value of U.S. service exports has risen over the years, it has remained about 30 percent of the value of total exports. One reason for the apparent lagging performance of the services element within total U.S. exports is that most services are intrinsically nonexportable. For example, services such as auto repair and hairdressing have become sizable contributors to the nation's gross national product but are not important among American exported services. Furthermore, American exporters of services complain that U.S. government policies are formidable barriers to exports. These policies include taxation of Americans working overseas and the Foreign Corrupt Practices Act, which limits corporate payment of fees to obtain contracts abroad.

American service exporters have also complained of foreign trade restrictions. As seen in Table 7.8, foreign barriers to service trade are numerous, ranging from government procurement problems to discriminatory tax policies.

The motion picture industry offers an illustration of some of the barriers levied by governments to service imports. The United States is the world's leading producer and exporter of motion picture films. The U.S. motion picture industry greatly relies on overseas markets, which generate about half of the industry's

Table 7.8   Examples of Foreign Discrimination Against U.S. Service Industries

Service, Country	Trade Restriction
Accounting, Brazil	All accountants must possess the requisite professional degree from a Brazilian University
Advertising, Australia	Radio and TV commercials produced outside of the country are forbidden
Air transport, Chile	National carriers are given preferential user (landing and other) rates, whereas foreign carriers are not
Banking, Nigeria	Local incorporation of existing and new branches are mandatory
Hotel, Switzerland	Work permits for foreign employees are difficult to obtain, extend, or renew
Modeling, West Germany	All models must be hired only through German agencies
Motion pictures, Egypt	Imports must be made through state-owned commercial companies; no foreign films may be shown if Egyptian films are available
Telecommunication, West Germany	International leased lines are prohibited from being connected to German public networks unless the connection is made via a computer in Germany that carries out at least some processing

Source: Office of the Special Representative for Trade Negotiations, *Selected Impediments to Trade in Services*, October 5, 1981.

revenues through fees for rentals. In an attempt to protect their domestic motion picture markets, foreign governments have imposed screen-time quotas requiring theaters and television stations to devote specified amounts of time to showing domestic films. Import quotas also are set to restrict the number of films that can enter a country. Local work requirements reserve to domestic laboratories the manufacture of film prints. Discriminatory admissions taxes require local patrons to pay a premium to see foreign films.

Summary

1.   The commercial policies of the United States have reflected the motivations of many groups, including government officials, labor leaders, and business management.

2.   U.S. tariff history has been marked by ups and downs. Many of the traditional arguments for tariffs (revenue, jobs and employment, infant industry) have been incorporated into U.S. tariff legislation.

3.   The Smoot-Hawley Act of 1930 resulted in U.S. tariffs reaching an all-time high. The passage of the Reciprocal Trade Act of 1934 resulted in generalized tariff reductions by the United States, as well as the enactment of most-favored-nation provisions.

4.   The purpose of the General Agreement on Tariffs and Trade has been to establish a set of rules under which trade negotiations can take place. In spite of GATT's efforts in promoting trade liberalization, developing nations often have maintained that lowering tariffs on a multilateral, nondiscriminatory basis has favored the advanced countries.

5.   Several devices have served to neutralize trade liberalization efforts during the post–World War II era. These include the peril-point clause, the escape clause, and the national security clause.

6.   Countervailing duties are intended to offset any unfair competitive advantage that foreign

producers might gain over domestic producers because of foreign subsidies.

7.   Economic theory suggests that if a nation is a net importer of a product subsidized by foreigners, the nation as a whole gains from the foreign subsidy. This is because the gains to domestic consumers of the subsidized good more than offset the losses to domestic producers of the import-competing goods.

8.   The Trade Expansion Act of 1962 laid the legislative groundwork for the Kennedy Round of tariff negotiations held under the auspices of GATT and completed in 1967. The Kennedy Round succeeded in cutting the average level of tariffs by some 35 percent and applied to $40 billion worth of goods.

9.   Because foreign competition may displace import-competing firms and workers, the United States and other countries have initiated programs of adjustment assistance involving government aid to adversely affected firms, workers, and communities.

10.   The Trade Reform Act of 1974 and the most recent round of GATT negotiations in Tokyo and Geneva emphasized reductions in nontariff barriers to trade. Given the existing world environment of recession, inflation, and balance-of-payments problems, achieving lasting trade agreements has been difficult.

11.   The United States maintains a host of policies on export promotion and market development. The Export-Import Bank and the Commodity Credit Corporation provide competitive credit terms for American exporters. Domestic International Sales Corporations have also been influential in encouraging exports by U.S. companies.

12.   The U.S. government exercises control over exports for reasons of national security, foreign policy, and short supply.

13.   Concerted action in export trade is permitted by the U.S. government. American firms can join export trade associations or form export trading companies so as to expand overseas sales.

14.   Trade in services has become increasingly important in the post–World War II era. However, restrictions to service trade are employed by many nations.

Study Questions

1.   To what extent have the traditional arguments that justify protectionist barriers actually been incorporated into pieces of U.S. trade legislation?

2.   At what stage in U.S. trade history did protectionism reach its high point?

3.   What is meant by the most-favored-nation clause and how does it relate to the tariff policies of the United States?

4.   The General Agreement on Tariffs and Trade is intended to establish a basic set of rules for the commercial conduct of trading nations. Explain.

5.   What has been the purpose of the peril-point clause, the escape clause, and the national security clause as part of U.S. tariff legislation?

6.   What was the Kennedy Round? Why was it so important from the perspective of trade liberalization?

7.   What is meant by adjustment assistance? Does the existence of such a program justify the imposition of trade barriers on imports?

8.   Under the recent Tokyo Round of trade negotiations, what were the major policies adopted concerning nontariff trade barriers?

9.   In what ways has the U.S. government attempted to promote exports by American firms?

10.   Why are countervailing duties considered to be a defensive instrument of commercial policy?

11. If the United States is a net importer of a product that is being subsidized by Japan, not only do American consumers gain but they also gain more than American producers lose from the Japanese subsidies. Explain why this statement is true.

12. How do export trade associations and export trading companies promote U.S. exports?

13. Why has trade in services become increasingly important in the post–World War II era? Why is the United States a major exporter of services?

Notes

1. Today the escape clause is commonly referred to as the *safeguard provision*, whose purpose is to allow governments to take temporary action to restrict imports to give home firms time to adjust to injurious competition.
2. Melvyn B. Krauss, *The New Protectionism* (New York: New York University Press, 1978), p. 79.
3. Organization for Economic Cooperation and Development, *Adjustment for Trade* (Paris: Organization for Economic Cooperation and Development, 1975).

Suggestions for Further Reading

Baldwin, R. E., J. Mutti, and J. D. Richardson. "Welfare Effects on the United States of a Significant Multilateral Tariff Reduction." *Journal of International Economics*, August 1980.

Bale, M. D. "Estimates of the Trade Displacement Costs for U.S. Workers." *Journal of International Economics*, August 1976.

Chen, J. H. "U.S. Concessions in the Kennedy Round and Short-Run Labor Adjustment Costs." *Journal of International Economics*, November 1974.

General Agreement on Tariffs and Trade. *The Activities of GATT*. Geneva, annual.

Hartigan, J. C., and E. Tower. "Trade Policy and American Income Distribution." *Review of Economics and Statistics*, May 1982.

Levy, R. "The Applicability of the Antitrust Laws to International Cartels Involving Foreign Governments." *Yale Law Journal*, March 1982.

Luttrell, C. B. "The Russian Grain Embargo: Dubious Success." *Review*, Federal Reserve Bank of St. Louis, August–September 1980.

Pincus, J. "Pressure Groups and the Pattern of Tariffs." *Journal of Political Economy*, July 1975.

Preeg, E. H. *Traders and Diplomats*. Washington, D.C.: The Brookings Institution, 1970.

Shelp, R. K. *Beyond Industrialization: Ascendancy of the Global Service Economy*. New York: Praeger, 1981.

Stein, L. "Trade Adjustment Assistance as a Means of Achieving Improved Resource Allocation Through Freer Trade." *American Journal of Economics and Sociology*, July 1982.

Yeats, A. J. *Trade Barriers Facing Developing Countries*. New York: St. Martins Press, 1979.

8

TRADE POLICIES FOR THE
DEVELOPING COUNTRIES

It is a commonly accepted practice to array all countries according to real income and then draw a dividing line between the advanced and the developing ones. Included in the category of the advanced countries are those of North America and Western Europe, plus Australia, New Zealand, and Japan. However, most nations of the world are classified as developing countries, or less-developed countries. The developing countries are most of the countries in Africa, Asia, Latin America, and the Middle East.

Compared with advanced countries, developing countries are characterized by low per-capita income, a large fraction of the labor force in agriculture or primary activities (for example, copper mining), high rates of population growth, and high levels of illiteracy. As of 1981, more than 2 billion people lived in countries where per-capita income was barely $300 per year! Another 500 million people lived in countries with a per-capita income between $700 and $1,000 per year. In international trade, developing countries mainly export agricultural products and raw materials, while importing manufactured goods from the industrial nations.

Although international trade can provide benefits to domestic producers and consumers, some economists maintain that the current international trading system hinders economic development in the developing nations. They believe that conventional international trade theory based on the principle of comparative advantage is irrelevant for these countries.

This chapter examines the reasons some economists advance to explain their misgivings about the current international trading system. The chapter also considers policies aimed at improving the economic conditions of the developing countries.

Trade Problems of the Developing Countries

The theory of comparative advantage, as described in Chapter 2, is presumably relevant for nations in all stages of development. The theory maintains that all countries can enjoy the benefits of free trade if they specialize in production of those goods in which they have a comparative advantage and exchange some of these goods for goods produced by other countries. Free trade serves the best interests of advanced countries as well as developing countries.

The United States and many other developed countries (the North) maintain that the market-oriented structure of the international trading system, as formulated by the General Agreement on Tariffs and Trade, furnishes a setting in which the benefits of comparative advantage can materialize. The advanced countries claim that the existing international trading system has provided widespread benefits and that trading interests of all countries are best served by pragmatic, incremental changes in the existing system. Advanced countries also maintain that to achieve trading success, they must administer their own domestic and international economic policies.

On the basis of their trading experience with the advanced countries, the developing countries (the South) are dubious of any benefits of trade with the advanced countries. The developing countries insist that the structure of the international trading system and the practices of the advanced countries are major impediments to faster growth in the developing countries. It is maintained that the pattern of specialization, in which advanced nations specialize in manufactured goods and the developing countries specialize in primary products, leaves developing countries poor, underdeveloped, and dependent. What is more, the protectionist trading policies of the advanced nations (such as tariff escalation) hinders industrialization of the developing countries.

Accordingly, developing countries have sought a new international trading order with improved developing-country access to advanced countries' markets and preferential treatment. Developing nations want redeployment of labor-intensive industrial production from advanced countries to developing countries and international commodity agreements to bolster developing-country export earnings from primary commodities.

Developing countries maintain that the existing pattern of trade and specialization will make them even more dependent on primary products. Among the key reasons for this fear are *unstable export markets* and *secularly declining terms of trade*.

Unstable Export Markets

It is often argued that commodity-producing nations are subject to sudden price changes that result in erratic swings in export receipts. A poor harvest or a decrease in market demand, for example, can induce a large decline in export receipts. As seen in Table 8.1, many of the developing countries' economies are heavily dependent upon commodity exports. Unpredictable export earnings can thus exert a disruptive influence on national income and domestic development programs.

Perhaps the key factor underlying the instability of primary product prices and export receipts is the low elasticity of the demand and supply schedules for such products as tin, copper, coffee, and sugar. Recall that the elasticity of demand (elasticity of supply) refers to the percentage change in quantity demanded (quantity supplied) resulting from a 1 percent change in price. To the extent that commodity demand and supply schedules are relatively inelastic, suggesting that the percentage change in price exceeds the percentage change in quantity, a small shift in either schedule may be expected to induce a

Table 8.1   Developing Countries' Dependence on Primary Products, 1981

Country	Major Export Product	Major Export Product as a Percentage of Total Exports
Zambia	Copper	89
Liberia	Iron ore	62
Saudi Arabia	Oil	100
Bolivia	Tin	40
Suriname	Alumina	54
Guatemala	Coffee	24
Mauritania	Iron ore	65

Source: International Monetary Fund, *International Financial Statistics*, June 1983.

large change in price export receipts. Table 8.2 summarizes estimates of the supply elasticities and demand elasticities for selected primary products.

Figures 8.1(a) and 8.1(b) illustrate the supply and demand schedules for a primary product, bauxite, confronting a single producer and the entire market. Assume the relevant time to be the very short run, whereby the single producer's supply remains fixed at all price levels. Also assume the producer accounts for only a small portion of the market supply so that the single producer's price is determined by the market supply and demand curves.

Referring to Figure 8.1(a), suppose a technological improvement in bauxite mining induces a shift in the market supply curve from MS_0 to MS_1. Given a relatively inelastic market demand curve, a modest increase in supply induces a substantial decline in the market price as well as that of the individual producer—that is, by amount P_0P_1. This situation results in two opposing forces for the producer's earnings. First, the reduction in market price induces a drop in the producer's receipts by the amount P_0P_1FE in the diagram. Second, participating in the overall

increase in the market supply, the producer finds that his supply schedule shifts from S_0 to S_1. The increase in supply yields an additional amount of sales revenue by the amount Q_0Q_1GF, given market price P_1. Depending on the exact nature of the schedules' elasticities, the net effect of these opposing forces may or may not provide expanding sales receipts for the producer.

The individual producer also finds that his prices can be significantly affected by changes in market demand, given inelastic supply conditions. In Figure 8.1(b), suppose economic recession in the importing countries touches off a decrease in the market demand from MD_0 to MD_1. A modest decrease in market demand would induce a large decrease in price from P_0 to P_1. The producer's earnings thus fall by area P_0P_1FE. Should the prices of the country's imports remain unchanged, it would find itself in a still worse position when facing a fall in the demand for its export.[1]

Table 8.3 illustrates fluctuations in price and export receipts for 13 primary commodities for the period 1953–1972. These fluctuations seem quite large, especially when it is remembered

Table 8.2   Long-Run Price Elasticities of Supply and Demand for Selected Commodities

Commodity	Supply Elasticity (Developing Countries)	Demand Elasticity (Advanced Countries)
Coffee	0.3	0.2
Cocoa	0.3	0.3
Tea	0.2	0.1
Sugar	0.2	0.1
Wheat	0.6	0.5
Copper	0.1	0.4
Rubber	0.4	0.5
Bauxite	0.4	1.3
Iron ore	0.3	0.7

Source: Jere R. Behrman, "International Commodity Agreements: An Evaluation of the UNCTAD Integrated Commodity Program," in William R. Cline, ed., *Policy Alternatives for a New International Economic Order* (New York: Praeger, 1979), pp. 118–121.

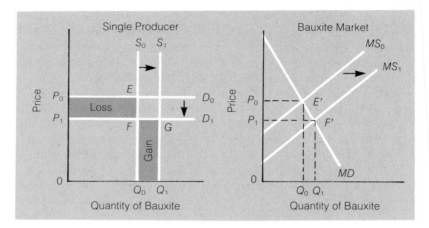

Figure 8.1(a)   Unstable commodity market: increase in supply.

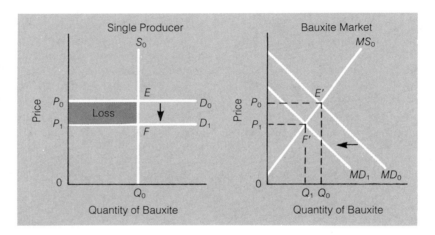

Figure 8.1(b)   Decrease in demand.

that the time period includes the 1960s, when commodity prices were relatively stable. Since 1973, commodity prices have fluctuated even more widely.

Worsening Terms of Trade

How the gains from free international trade are distributed among trading partners has been a controversial issue, especially among the devel-

oping countries. These countries generally have maintained that the benefits of free trade have accrued disproportionately to the industrial countries. One of the main reasons given for this inequitable distribution is the persistent, long-run tendency of the developing countries' commodity terms of trade[2] to deteriorate. Worsening terms of trade has been used to justify the refusal of developing countries to participate in trade liberalization efforts such as the Tokyo

Table 8.3   Fluctuations in Price and Export Value
of Selected Commodities, 1953–1972

Commodity	Average Annual Percentage Change from Trend*	
	Market Price (percent)	Value of Exports (percent)
Sugar	33.4	9.2
Cocoa	23.0	13.4
Copper	21.5	17.1
Beef and veal	20.8	15.4
Sisal	18.0	26.3
Coffee	17.0	11.1
Rubber	13.2	14.7
Jute	11.9	12.2
Wool	11.4	10.2
Rice	11.3	12.9
Iron ore	8.3	10.8
Cotton	8.2	9.1
Tin	7.9	18.8

Source: Jere Behrman, *Development, The International Economic Order and Commodity Agreements* (Reading, Mass.: Addison-Wesley, 1978), p. 49.

*Average over the period of differences between annual observations and calculated trend values (absolute value) expressed as percentages of the trend value.

Round of multilateral trade negotiations. It also has been behind the developing countries' demands for preferential treatment in trade relations with the industrial countries.

The exports of the developing countries consist mainly of primary products, including raw materials and agricultural goods, whereas industrial countries emphasize manufactured goods. According to the developing countries, the monopoly power of manufacturers in the industrial countries results in prices continually rising. Gains in productivity accrue to manufacturers in the form of higher earnings rather than price reductions. The developing countries further contend that the export prices of their primary products are determined in competitive markets. These prices fluctuate downward as well as up-

ward. Gains in productivity are shared with foreign consumers in the form of lower prices. The developing countries maintain that market forces cause the prices they pay for imports to rise faster than the prices commanded by their exports, the result being a deterioration in their commodity terms of trade.[3]

The developing countries' assertion of worsening commodity terms of trade was supported by a United Nations study in 1949.[4] The study concluded that from the period 1876–1880 to 1946–1947, the prices of primary products compared with those of manufactured goods fell from 100 to 68. This means that exporters of primary products received only 68 percent of the amount of manufactured goods they received during the late 1870s. The commodity terms of trade worsened for the producers of primary products.

Owing to data inadequacies and the problems of constructing export (import) price indices, the 1949 UN study was hardly conclusive evidence of the tendency for the terms of trade to worsen for developing countries. Other studies led to opposite conclusions about terms-of-trade movements. For example, a 1963 study found that the developing countries' commodity terms of trade, compared with those of the United States, did not suffer continual downward movement from 1880 to 1960.[5]

Since many empirical studies have yielded conflicting conclusions, the evidence of deterioration in the developing countries' terms of trade appears to be mixed and does not substantiate the deterioration hypothesis. Developing countries generally compare terms-of-trade movements against a base period such as 1953, when commodity prices were high. This allows them to show that their terms of trade worsened over time. However, if we use as a base period the year 1962, when commodity prices were low, the opposite tendency occurs.

Note that movements in alternative terms-of-trade measures may lead to implications opposite those of the commodity terms-of-trade movements. Consider the income terms of trade, which indicates a country's capacity to import. This measure is especially important for developing countries that rely on capital-good imports. For the income terms of trade, we multiply the change in the commodity terms of trade (that is, Export Price Index divided by Import Price Index) by the quantity of exports, measuring export receipts compared with import prices. A 1969 study concluded that higher export volumes led to improving income terms of trade for developing countries from 1950 to 1965. Although the developing countries' commodity terms of trade declined 9 percent over this period, rising export volume led to a 56 percent improvement in the income terms of trade. This improvement meant that developing countries enjoyed increasing export receipts, which could be used to finance increasing import purchases.[6]

Stabilizing Commodity Prices

In an attempt to attain export market stability, developing nations have pressed for the formation of international commodity agreements (ICAs). ICAs typically consist of agreements between leading producing and consuming countries about matters such as stabilizing commodity prices, assuring adequate supplies to consumers, and promoting the economic development of producers.

Both producers and consumers desire stable commodity markets. For producers, volatile commodity prices may disrupt the flow of export earnings, which are necessary to pay for imported goods, as well as create an unfavorable climate for investment in additional productive facilities. Consumers have also been motivated to form ICAs. During the 1970s, consuming countries were concerned by the sharp rise in commodity prices and by the questions raised about the longer-term availability of commodities. Consumers were also alarmed about the example of OPEC—that is, by the possibility that commodity supplies might be restricted by the collusion of producing countries.

Table 8.4 summarizes recent ICAs for producing and consuming countries. To promote stability in commodity markets, ICAs have relied on production and export controls, buffer stocks, and multilateral contracts.

Table 8.4   International Commodity Agreements

Agreement	Membership	Principal Stabilization Tools
International Cocoa Organization	26 consuming countries 18 producing countries	Buffer stock, Export quota
International Tin Agreement	16 consuming countries 4 producing countries	Buffer stock, Export controls
International Coffee Organization	24 consuming countries 43 producing countries	Export quota
International Sugar Organization	8 consuming countries 26 producing countries	Export quota, Buffer stock
International Wheat Agreement	41 consuming countries 10 producing countries	Multilateral contract up to 1981

Source: *Annual Report of the President of the United States on the Trade Agreements Program*, 1979 (Washington, D.C.: U.S. Government Printing Office), pp. 95–99 and "The Sixth International Tin Agreement," *IMF Survey*, July 5, 1982, p. 207.

Production and Export Controls

If an ICA accounts for a large share of total world output (or exports) of a commodity, its members may agree on *export restriction* measures to stabilize export revenues. The idea behind such schemes is to offset a decrease in the market demand for the primary commodity by assigning cutbacks in the market supply. If successful, the rise in price due to the supply curtailment would be sufficient to compensate for the reduction in demand, so that total export earnings would remain at the original level.

The process by which export receipts can be maintained at target levels is illustrated in Figure 8.2, which hypothetically represents the market situation facing the International Coffee Agreement. Assume market equilibrium initially to be located at point E. With the equilibrium price at

$1 per pound and 60 million pounds being sold, the association's export receipts total $60 million. Let this figure be the target receipts that the association wishes to maintain. Suppose now that due to a global recession the market demand for coffee decreases from D_0 to D_1. The association's export revenues would thus fall below the target level. To prevent this from occurring, the coffee producers could artificially hold back the supply of coffee to S_1. Market equilibrium would be at point F, where 40 million pounds of coffee would be sold at a price of $1.50 per pound. Total export receipts would again be at $60 million, the association's target figure. This stabilization technique may be contrary to what we might expect, since it is based on efforts to increase prices during eras of worsening demand conditions.

In their efforts to stabilize export receipts, producers' associations like the International

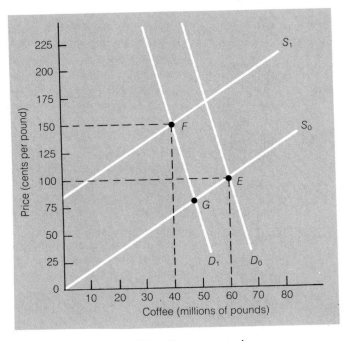

Figure 8.2   Export controls.

Tin Agreement have adopted export quotas to regulate market supply. Over the not-so-long run, however, export quotas must be accompanied by production controls to be effective. Should this not occur, expanding surpluses of the member countries would lead to a greater likelihood of price cutting and the eventual downfall of the association.

Buffer Stocks

Another technique for limiting commodity price swings is the buffer stock, in which a producers' association (or international agency) is prepared to buy and sell a commodity in large amounts. The *buffer stock* consists of supplies of a commodity financed and held by the producers' association, a scheme that permits the buffer stock manager to buy from the market when supplies are abundant and prices are falling below acceptable levels and to sell from the buffer stock when supplies are tight and prices are high.

Perhaps the best-known case where buffer stocks have been used to moderate commodity price fluctuations is the case of the International Tin Agreement. Assume the association sets a price range with floor ($3.27 per pound) and ceiling ($4.02 per pound) levels to guide the stabilization operations of the buffer stock manager. Starting at equilibrium point A in Figure 8.3, suppose the buffer stock manager sees the demand for tin rising from D_0 to D_1. To defend the ceiling price of $4.02, the manager must be prepared to sell 20,000 pounds of tin to offset the excess demand for tin at the ceiling price. Conversely, starting at equilibrium point E in Figure 8.4, suppose the supply of tin rises from S_0 to S_1. To defend the floor price at $3.27, the buffer stock manager must purchase the 20,000-pound excess supply that exists at that price.

Proponents of buffer stocks contend that the scheme offers the primary producing nations several advantages. A well-run buffer stock can

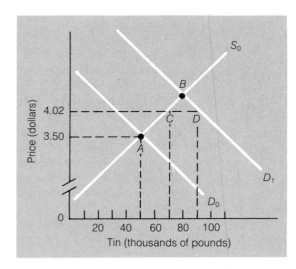

Figure 8.3   Buffer stock: price ceiling in face of rising demand.

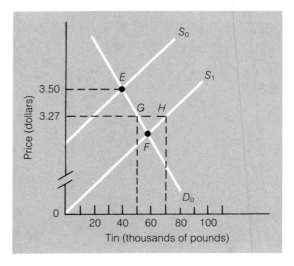

Figure 8.4   Buffer stock: price support in face of abundant supplies.

promote economic efficiency, as primary producers would be able to plan investment and expansion if they knew that prices would not gyrate. It is also argued that soaring commodity prices invariably ratchet industrial prices upward, whereas commodity price decreases exert no comparable downward pressure. By stabilizing commodity prices, buffer stocks can moderate the price inflation of the industrialized countries. Buffer stocks in this context are viewed as a means of providing primary producers more stability than is provided by the free market.

But setting up and administering a buffer stock program is not without costs and problems. The basic difficulty in stabilizing prices with buffer stocks is agreeing on a target price that reflects long-term market trends. If the target price is set too low, the buffer stocks will become depleted as the stock manager sells the commodity on the open market in an attempt to hold market prices in line with the target price. If the target price is set too high, the stock manager must purchase large quantities of the commodity in an effort to support market prices. The costs of holding the stocks tend to be quite high, for they include transportation expenses, insurance, and labor costs. In their choice of price targets, buffer stock officials have often made poor decisions. Rather than conduct massive stabilization operations, buffer stock officials will periodically revise target prices should they fall out of line with long-term trend prices.

Multilateral Contracts

Another method of stabilizing commodity prices is the long-term contract that determines price and/or quantity. Such pacts generally stipulate a minimum price at which importers will purchase guaranteed quantities from the producing countries and a maximum price at which producing nations will sell guaranteed amounts to the importers. Such purchases and sales are designed to hold prices within a target range. Trading on a *multilateral contract* basis has often occurred between several exporters and several importing nations, as in the case of the Interna-

tional Sugar Agreement and the International Wheat Agreement.

One possible advantage of the multilateral contract as a price stabilization device is that in comparison with buffer stocks or export controls, it tends to distort less the operation of the market mechanism and the allocation of resources. This is because the typical multilateral contract does not involve output restraints and thus does not check the development of more efficient low-cost producers. But if target prices are not set near the long-term equilibrium price, discrepancies will occur between supply and demand. Excess demand would indicate a ceiling too low, whereas excess supply would suggest a floor too high. Multilateral contracts also tend to furnish only limited market stability, given the relative ease of withdrawal and entry by participating members.

Commodity Agreement Experience

Commodity-producing nations have faced the fact that imbalances between demand and supply on the commodity markets tend to trigger large fluctuations in prices. This is true for agricultural commodities as well as for metals and other raw materials. The desire to achieve orderly marketing during the 1920s and 1930s led to the establishment of producers' associations for tin, sugar, rubber, tea, and wheat. But it was not until after World War II that an international mechanism was formally initiated by the United Nations in which commodity agreements, among both producers and consumers, could be implemented under the auspices of a world body.

Efforts to enact commodity agreements gained momentum following the stunning success of the Organization of Petroleum Exporting Countries, which was able to raise prices fourfold in 1973–1974. The goals of the various commodity agreements generally have involved at least one of the following: (1) guarding against gyrating commodity prices, (2) stabilizing incomes or export revenues rather than prices, or (3) bidding prices significantly above their long-term trend. Part of the problem facing commodity agreements is that these objectives sometimes conflict with one another. The goal of stabilizing income, for example, may conflict with the goal of moderating price fluctuations for the pact countries. If a drought were to destroy part of the sugar crop, sales from a buffer stockpile might cushion price increases, but that suggests falling revenues for sugar exporters.

The International Tin Agreement generally is regarded as the commodity agreement with the best track record. Started in 1956, the International Tin Agreement has used buffer stocks and export controls to limit price swings. The Tin Council periodically determines upper and lower price limits to guide the activities of the buffer stock manager. When the buffer stock operations are unable to moderate price decreases, they are sometimes supplemented by export controls.

When the International Tin Agreement went into operation in 1956, prices remained within the target limits set by the Tin Council. Strong demand conditions resulted in the manager of the buffer stock being forced to sell tin, and by 1961 the stocks were exhausted and prices pushed above the ceiling. In the face of strong demand, the upper and lower price limits were raised several times during the 1960s to keep pace with current market conditions. During the commodity boom of the 1970s, tin prices shot through the ceiling. However, during the early 1980s, the weakening of demand caused by recession led to a progressively lower price. In 1981, the price fell to the bottom of the target limit, triggering price support actions by the buffer stock.

In 1982, the International Tin Agreement was extended for a five-year period. Consuming and producing countries agreed to set the target

price range of tin equal to $5.67 per pound at the lower limit and $6.81 per pound at the upper limit. Defense of price floors and ceilings would be facilitated by export controls and a buffer stock. The participating countries of the pact account for 79 percent of world tin output and 50 percent of tin consumption. The United States, however, chose not to sign the 1982 agreement, mainly because it contended that the target price range benefited inefficient producers. Moreover, the U.S. government had a tin stockpile of 200,000 tons, equal to four years of domestic use.

Other Trade Strategies

Besides attempting to stabilize commodity prices and export earnings through international commodity agreements, developing countries have pursued trade strategies of import substitution and export promotion. They also have attempted to win from the advanced countries trade concessions known as the generalized system of preferences.

Import Substitution Versus Export Promotion

Developing countries realize that the most prosperous nations are industrial countries, with the exception of the wealthy oil-exporting countries. Distrust of the claims about gains from trade involving exports of primary products and imports of manufactured goods has led many developing countries to pursue domestic industrialization. Industrialization has been viewed as yielding widespread benefits, including economic growth, creation of employment, and self-reliance.

During the 1950s and 1960s, the trade strategy of import substitution became popular among developing countries such as Argentina,

Brazil, and Mexico. Import substitution was seen as a way of promoting domestic industrialization, particularly in consumer goods (for example, shoes, clothing, and household articles). *Import substitution* schemes restrict imports of manufactured goods so that the domestic market is preserved for domestic producers who thus can take over markets already established in the country. During the 1950s and 1960s, import substitution appears to have been beneficial for several countries such as Argentina and Brazil, which found that their ratios of imports to total output decreased.[7]

However, import substitution is no easy road to self-reliance. A developing country's dependence on foreign manufacturers can increase for some time, since reliance on foreign inputs (for example, machinery and spare parts) often increases with the domestic production of finished manufactures. Also, the costs of import substitution become apparent when developing countries protect industries with no potential comparative advantage. In Chile, Peru, and Colombia, where local content laws require that a high percentage of an auto's value be produced domestically, the cost of autos has run two to three times higher than the cost of similar autos produced abroad.[8] Although many developing countries moved toward export-oriented strategies by the 1970s, import substitution continues to be popular among developing countries.

Pessimistic about the merits of import substitution strategies and disenchanted about exporting primary products, developing countries have pursued export promotion (export-led growth) as an industrialization strategy. *Export promotion* replaces commodity exports with nontraditional exports such as processed primary products, semimanufactures, and manufactures. Export promotion often results from multinational corporations subcontracting the production of parts and components to developing countries to take advantage of favorable labor costs. Hong Kong, South Korea, and Singapore are examples of developing countries that have pursued export-led industrialization. Their major exports consist of footwear, textiles, clothing, and consumer goods; these exports are directed primarily to a few markets, including the United States, Japan, West Germany, and the United Kingdom.

Compared with import-substitution policies, export promotion is market oriented, placing greater emphasis on pricing incentives and on the comparative advantage principle as a guide to resource allocation. Developing nations attempt to identify industries that have a potential comparative advantage. Although subsidies and other devices may be used to encourage development of these industries, it is expected that the industries eventually will produce and sell their goods at prices competitive with foreign producers.

South Korea is an example of a developing country that has utilized export promotion policies. During the 1960s, South Korea initiated measures encouraging exports of manufactures. Tariffs and quotas were eliminated on inputs imported for use in exported goods. Tax laws were modified to encourage foreign investment and to favor production that earned a profit on exports. The South Korean *won* was devalued. Furthermore, the labor market was unregulated, having no labor unions and no minimum wage laws. From 1963 to 1975, manufacturing employment in South Korea grew 10.7 percent per year. Exports as a percentage of South Korean gross national product rose from 3 percent in 1960 to 36 percent in 1977. Export growth accounted for 10 percent of South Korea's overall growth during 1955–1963; the figure was 22 percent in 1963–1970 and 56 percent in 1970–1973.[9]

Not everyone agrees with the implications of the South Korean example. Some maintain that import-substitution policies are necessary to lay the groundwork for export expansion. Others argue that although some developing countries have been able to penetrate the world market for manufactured goods, not all developing countries have the capability of doing so. Moreover, widespread penetration would trigger complaints of market disruption by importing countries and possibly protectionism by advanced countries.

Table 8.5 summarizes the effects of alternative trade strategies on growth rates in 10 countries. For most countries, the results suggest a strong relationship between export growth and the overall growth rate of the economy (as measured by real gross domestic product). Moreover, shifting from import substitution to export promotion generally resulted in improved per-

formance in the economy's earnings, as seen in the cases of Brazil, Colombia, and South Korea.

Generalized System of Preferences

Gaining access to world markets is a problem that has plagued many developing countries. These countries have often found it difficult to become cost efficient enough to compete in a wide range of products in world markets. It has also been contended that developed countries have typically levied low tariffs on raw materials and high tariffs on manufactured goods, discouraging industrial growth in developing countries.

Table 8.5   Trade Strategy, Export Growth, and Gross Domestic Product (GDP) Growth in 10 Countries

Country	Period	Trade Strategy*	Average Annual Rate of Growth (percent)	
			Export Earnings	Real GDP
Brazil	1955–1960	IS	−2.3	6.9
	1960–1965	IS	4.6	4.2
	1965–1970	EP	28.2	7.6
	1970–1976	EP	24.3	10.6
Chile	1960–1970	IS	9.7	4.2
Colombia	1955–1960	IS	−0.8	4.6
	1960–1965	IS	−1.9	1.9
	1970–1976	EP	16.9	6.5
Indonesia	1965–1973	MIS	18.9	6.8
Ivory Coast	1960–1972	EP	11.2	7.8
South Korea	1953–1960	IS	−6.1	5.2
	1960–1970	EP	40.2	8.5
	1970–1976	EP	43.9	10.3
Pakistan	1953–1960	IS	−1.5	3.5
	1960–1970	IS	6.2	6.8
Thailand	1960–1970	MIS	5.5	8.2
	1970–1976	MIS	26.6	6.5
Tunisia	1960–1970	IS	6.8	4.6
	1970–1976	MIS	23.4	9.4
Uruguay	1955–1970	IS	1.6	0.7

Source: Anne O. Krueger, "The Effects of Trade Strategies on Growth," *Finance and Development*, June 1983, p. 7.
*EP = Export Promotion, IS = Import Substitution, MIS = Moderate Import Substitution.

To help developing countries strengthen their international competitiveness and expand their industrial base, many developed countries since the early 1970s have extended nonreciprocal tariff preferences to exports of developing countries. Under the *Generalized System of Preferences* (GSP) program, 18 developed market-economy countries have temporarily reduced tariffs on designated imports from developing countries below the levels applied to developed-country exports. The GSP does not constitute a uniform system, however, since it consists of many individual schemes that differ from one another in terms of types of products covered and extent of tariff reduction.

Having its origins in 1976, the U.S. GSP program is scheduled to run 10 years. Under the program, the United States has extended duty-free treatment to about 2,800 items, accounting for duty-free imports of more than $6 billion in 1980. Beneficiaries of the U.S. program include some 137 developing countries and their dependent territories. Like the GSP programs of other developed countries, the U.S. program excludes certain import-sensitive products from preferential tariff treatment. These products include electronics items, glass, certain steel and iron products, watches, and some articles of footwear. Limits also exist on the amount of a particular product each beneficiary can export to the United States.

To date, the GSP program has had only a modest expansionary influence on the trade of developing countries. One problem is that GSP programs apply to tariff preferences rather than to nontariff trade barriers, which have grown in importance in recent years. Also, developed countries sometimes have to extend preferential treatment in the trade of products in which the developed countries are cost efficient (such as footwear, watches, and electronics items), since these items are viewed as import sensitive. Furthermore, the unilateral and nonbinding nature of the GSP program makes future tariff preferences highly uncertain, tending to limit the beneficial effect the program might have on industrial development.

The OPEC Oil Cartel

The Organization of Petroleum Exporting Countries (OPEC) is a group of 13 oil-producing nations that sells petroleum on the world market. The OPEC nations have attempted to support prices higher than would exist under more competitive conditions to maximize member-country profits. After operating in obscurity throughout the 1960s, OPEC was able to capture control of petroleum pricing in 1973–1974, when the price of oil rose from approximately $3 to $12 per barrel. Oil prices were increased another 10 percent in 1975 and almost 15 percent from 1976 to early 1979. Triggered by the Iranian revolution in 1979, oil prices doubled from early 1979 to early 1980. By December 1980, the price of oil averaged almost $36 per barrel. Largely owing to world recession and falling demand, oil prices fell to $29 per barrel in 1983.

Rationale for Cartelization

Before the formation of OPEC, the world oil market was dominated by the major petroleum-importing countries and several international companies that produced, refined, and marketed the world's oil. The major oil companies— Exxon, British Petroleum, Shell, Gulf, Texaco, Mobil, and Standard of California—had become so powerful, with so many mutual interests alongside their inevitable rivalries, that they came to be known as the Seven Sisters. During the early 1950s, the Seven Sisters accounted for 88 percent of all production outside the United States, and a web of joint ventures bound them together.

Although many independent companies entered the oil market during the fifties, the Seven Sisters were able to control crude prices and output in the producing countries. Each individual oil-producing country was essentially a price taker that accepted the price dictated by the major oil companies. By the late 1950s, however, world oil prices were declining in response to excess oil supplies. In 1959, the Seven Sisters reduced the selling price of oil, without consulting the governments of the producing nations. Discounts off the official price of $2.08 per barrel reached 40 cents. The oil-producing countries immediately protested these discounts, since they received a percentage of the selling price as export revenue. The offspring of this shock was the formation of OPEC in 1960.

Before the formation of OPEC, oil-producing nations behaved as individual competitive sellers. Each nation by itself was so unimportant relative to the overall market that changes in its export levels were unable to significantly affect international prices over a sustained period of time. By agreeing to restrict competition among themselves to exploit their joint market power, the oil-exporting nations found they could exercise considerable control over world oil prices.

Maximization of Cartel Profits

If a group of producers were to combine and form a cartel, as did the OPEC nations, how would they go about maximizing their collective profits? The answer is, by behaving as would an individual profit-maximizing monopolist.

Figure 8.5 illustrates a cartel (that is, a monopoly) that has succeeded in maximizing its profits. Demand curve D_0 indicates varying amounts of oil that the rest of the world will buy from the cartel at each price. Marginal cost curve MC_0 indicates varying amounts of oil the cartel will export at each price.

If perfect competition prevailed in the world oil market, international equilibrium would occur at the point where the marginal cost curve and the demand curve for oil intersect. This occurs at point A, where competitive producers will supply the amount of oil consumers wish to purchase, 60 million barrels, at a price of $25 per barrel. Any producer that attempts to increase its price by restricting output will lose sales to other producers in the industry. However, point A is not ideal in terms of profitability for the producers as a group, as we explain.

Suppose the oil producers form a cartel and behave as a single monopolist. Because they can influence market price in their favor by restricting output, the profit-maximizing level of output will be less, and the price higher, than would occur in a competitive industry. In the figure, the cartel's marginal revenue curve is indicated by MR_0. To maximize profits, the cartel must restrict exports to 50 million barrels and raise the price to $35. Remember that a monopoly maximizes profits by producing at the output where marginal revenue equals marginal cost, point C, and the monopoly price is read from the demand curve at that output, point D.

Shaded area ABC represents the increase in cartel total profits (total revenue minus total cost), compared with what would have occurred under perfect competition. By restricting output below the competitive level of 60 million barrels, the cartel loses the marginal revenue (the change in total revenue) on each successive unit. But the cartel saves the marginal cost (the change in total cost) on each successive unit held back. Between output levels of 50 and 60 million barrels, marginal cost exceeds marginal revenue on all units produced. Reducing output over this range subtracts more from total cost than from total revenue. The cartel's total profits thus increase until output has been cut back to 50 million barrels. The increase in cartel profits represents a redistribution of income from the oil-consuming nations to the cartel.

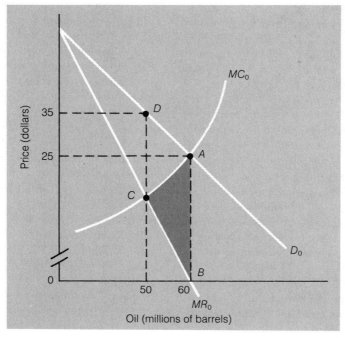

Figure 8.5   Maximization of cartel profits.

As a cartel, the OPEC countries have possessed a considerable degree of market power. The method OPEC has used to boost world oil prices is an excise (export) tax of so many cents per barrel of oil exported. These taxes are treated as a cost of production by the international oil companies. Rising excise taxes increase the world price, since no company can afford to market OPEC oil for less than its production cost plus the tax. How far might OPEC desire to increase oil prices? In terms of the cartel model just discussed, OPEC likely would want to force the price of oil up to the monopoly level. The experience of the 1970s indicated that OPEC achieved a high degree of success in increasing world oil prices. By the 1980s, however, OPEC was forced to cut the price of oil as market demand declined and substitute energies from non-OPEC sources competed against the OPEC producers.

The Evolution of OPEC

The Organization of Petroleum Exporting Countries was founded in 1960 as a protest against unilateral cuts in crude oil prices by the international oil companies. The original objectives of OPEC were to ensure the stabilization of oil prices and the unification of petroleum policies for member countries. Charter members included Venezuela, Iran, Iraq, Kuwait, and Saudi Arabia. OPEC expanded during the 1960s and 1970s, bringing the total membership to 13 nations. After uniting in OPEC, the member countries were able to negotiate on posted prices. They made no attempt, however, to raise posted prices unilaterally until October 1973. Perhaps the most important reason behind this was that during the 1960s, the world enjoyed abundant supplies of crude oil. The OPEC nations lacked influence over oil supply and demand.

Despite OPEC's slow beginnings, it was able to win some concessions from the international oil companies. In 1965, for example, OPEC agreed to tax oil companies on the full posted price of oil even if it was marketed at substantial discounts. In the Teheran Agreement of 1971, OPEC nations won concessions whereby they would have a say in setting posted petroleum prices. OPEC was also becoming more optimistic in its stated goals, as set forth by a 1968 document that identified two important objectives for its members: (1) gaining unilateral control of the determination of the posted price of crude oil and (2) controlling oil production through takeovers and nationalization of production facilities within OPEC borders, leaving the companies as service and technical contractors to the OPEC governments.

By the early 1970s, the world no longer faced a glut of oil, given the strong demand conditions of Japan, Europe, and the United States. Immediately following the October 1973 Yom Kippur War in the Middle East, the OPEC cartel dramatically increased the tax imposed by its members on oil produced in their countries. By October 1973, the export tax was set at $3.50 per barrel, up from the $1.77 level of the previous year. In October 1974, the export tax was raised to $9.75 per barrel. To these costs must be added the costs of extraction and transportation as well as company profits—roughly $2 per barrel. The result was that the price of crude oil shot up from the 1973 level of $3 per barrel to about $12 per barrel in 1974.

Through the 1970s, OPEC publically disavowed the term *cartel*. But its organization is composed of a secretariat, a conference of ministers, a board of governors, and an economic commission. OPEC has repeatedly attempted to formulate plans for systematic production control among its members. Control of production can be used during periods of slack demand as a way of firming up prices. However, the agreements generally have failed because too many member countries broke the ranks, as the international oil companies played OPEC countries against each other to get price discounts.

The burden of production cutbacks has not been shared equally among OPEC countries. Saudi Arabia has served as the dominant evener and adjuster in OPEC. Its eligibility for this role has been based on its large oil reserves, small population, and limited need for oil revenues. That is not to say that OPEC has remained free from internal conflicts. For example, Saudi Arabia increased output considerably to prevent other OPEC countries from achieving their goal of higher prices. During the world oil glut of 1982, Saudi Arabia was pressured by other OPEC countries to stop flooding the market with more oil than the market could absorb. Both Iran and Libya openly threatened to destroy the Saudis' oil fields or their government to force the Saudis to lower production.

Most of the world's cartels have been short-lived. This is because the success of a cartel depends upon several factors that often are difficult to achieve. Cartel members must control a very large share of the world market for their product and should agree to a common set of price and output policies. The length of time a cartel survives depends in part upon the elasticity of supply of noncartel countries. If the noncartel supply is inelastic over the relevant price range, so that a significant increase in the cartel price calls forth only a small increase in output by noncartel countries, there will be only minor competitive pressures facing the cartel. Similarly, the less elastic the demand for the cartel's product, the higher the cartel price can be raised without significantly reducing the amount demanded.

During the 1970s, OPEC was quite successful in increasing the revenues of its members. One reason is that the long-run price elasticity of oil supply in non-OPEC countries is inelastic. Estimates in the 1970s put the non-OPEC supply elasticity between 0.33 and 0.67, suggesting that a 1 percent increase in the OPEC price will induce only a 0.5 percent increase in non-OPEC output. The demand for gasoline in the United States was also estimated to be inelastic, having a long-run price elasticity coefficient of 0.8. What is more, OPEC was able to dominate the world oil market, accounting for more than two-fifths of world production, two-thirds of world reserves, and more than four-fifths of world exports.

However, by the beginning of the 1980s, OPEC increasingly faced the pressures that often lead to the demise of cartels. The OPEC price hikes induced non-OPEC countries to develop new production techniques and initiate new discoveries. The result was a fall in the OPEC share of the world market from 56 percent in 1973 to 32 percent in 1983, as illustrated in Table 8.6. The OPEC price hikes also led to decreases in demand owing to increased usage of smaller autos and insulation and the switch to substitute energy sources, including coal and nuclear power plants. Furthermore, the recession of 1981–1983 led to weakening demand and a glut of oil on the world market. These factors led

many observers to question the future success of OPEC.

Recycling Oil Payments

Table 8.7 illustrates the position of the oil-exporting countries' monetary reserves before and after the 1973–1974 price hikes. With their rising cash reserves, the OPEC nations found themselves facing the problem of what to do with all this money. They began saving most of their oil export revenues rather than spending them on imports of goods and services, because their economies were not geared to absorb all the imports their revenues could buy. In 1974, for example, the OPEC nations were able to spend only about $50 billion on imports of goods and services, leaving roughly $55 billion of the return flow of oil dollars to be invested in the real assets and financial assets of the oil-importing countries.

Financial experts began to question whether the international monetary system could accommodate such large transfers of OPEC investment funds. It was predicted that the investment of OPEC funds might benefit some oil-importing countries at the expense of others. Because credit-worthy countries like the United States

Table 8.6   Crude Oil Production of OPEC Countries

Year	Million of Barrels Per Day	Share of World Production (percent)
1973	31.0	56.0
1974	30.7	54.9
1975	27.1	51.2
1976	30.7	53.4
1977	31.3	52.4
1978	29.8	49.6
1979	30.9	49.4
1980	26.9	45.3
1981	22.6	40.5
1982	18.8	35.3
1983 (Jan.)	16.7	32.2

Source: U.S. Department of Energy, *Monthly Energy Review*, May 1983, p. 97.

Table 8.7   International Reserves of Major Oil-Exporting Countries

Year	Total Reserve Holdings (billions of dollars)
1952	1.7
1962	2.0
1970	5.3
1974	46.1
1978	57.8
1982	87.9
1983 (March)	77.1

Source: International Monetary Fund, *International Financial Statistics*, various issues.

were in a good position to borrow from OPEC, they could attract many of the dollars lost through their oil imports. These countries would find it relatively easy to finance their oil deficits. The less credit-worthy countries like India or Bangladesh were unable to borrow to finance their oil imports and would thus have to curtail their imports of oil or other products. In response to this recycling problem, the International Monetary Fund in 1974 established a lending arrangement whereby the fund borrows from OPEC and relends the monies to its poorer members so they can pay their oil import bills. With the fund providing attractive guarantees, the OPEC nations have been happy to support such a credit facility.

Cartels for Other Commodities?

Stimulated by the success of OPEC and reacting against deteriorating balance-of-payments positions, many developing countries have been inspired to form export cartels in other commodities. Not only did OPEC demonstrate that a group of producing nations could gain control of the oil-pricing mechanism, but the absence of retaliation by the industrialized nations against OPEC convinced other developing nations that a cartel formed by the oil producers was only the first in a new era of commodity power. But the successful formation and operation of export cartels is difficult to achieve in practice. Past concerted attempts by commodity producers to restrict output and increase prices have not been successful for a prolonged period of time.

To maintain prices at levels higher than those existing under more competitive conditions, a cartel must possess several features on both the supply and demand sides. A cartel should control a significant portion of world output of the product in question. The market should be char-

acterized by high entry barriers that prevent new producers from entering. This means that the commodity's supply should be price inelastic. To facilitate strong cohesion, it is best that only a small number of producers belong to the pact. Members must refrain from any temptation to lower prices to increase export earnings. For an artificially high price to pay off, a product should have few substitutes so that its demand is price inelastic. Market demand should also be stable or even growing, regardless of business conditions, permitting the cartel to avoid the uncertainty surrounding production cutbacks that might tempt them to break the cartel agreement.

Table 8.8 indicates the share of the market held by the top four producers of various minerals. Although the production of some minerals is dominated by a handful of countries, the long-run prospects for cartelization do not appear to be favorable. In general, producers of other minerals have faced problems of substitute products, uncertain entry barriers, lack of cohesion among producers, and unstable market demand.

APPENDIX: Commodity Price Stabilization Welfare Effects

Successful stabilization of commodity prices may provide benefits to producers and consumers, as discussed in the preceding sections of Chapter 8. This appendix to the chapter illustrates the welfare effects of commodity price stabilization for producers and consumers.

The welfare effects of stabilizing commodity prices can be measured in terms of *producer surplus* on commodity exports and *consumer surplus* on commodity imports. There are two cases where commodity price stabilization is often used: (1) in markets dominated by demand-side disturbances, such as the markets for tin, bauxite, and most other metals, and (2) in agricultural markets, such as sugar and coffee, where the

Table 8.8 Leading World Producers of Selected Minerals, 1981

Mineral	Top Four Producers	Share of World Production (percent)
Bauxite	Australia, Guinea, Jamaica, U.S.S.R.	63.3
Tin	Malaysia, U.S.S.R., Indonesia, Thailand	64.5
Zinc	Canada, U.S.S.R., Australia, Peru	49.5
Manganese	U.S.S.R., South Africa, Brazil, China	76.0
Chromite	South Africa, U.S.S.R., Albania, Zimbabwe	74.7
Lead	U.S., U.S.S.R., Australia, Canada	47.1

Source: U.S. Department of the Interior, Bureau of Mines, *Minerals Yearbook: Area Reports, International*, 1981, pp. 22–29.

main source of instability comes from the supply side. The welfare implications of price stabilization under each of these circumstances is analyzed in the following sections. The conclusion is that *stabilizing commodity prices around long-term trends tends to benefit consumers (importers) at the expense of producers (exporters) in markets characterized by demand-side disturbances, while the opposite tendency occurs in markets characterized by supply-side disturbances!*

Demand-Side Disturbance

Let Figure 8.6 represent the world tin market, where the supply schedule reflects the tin producers' exports and the demand schedules are based on the consuming nations' imports. The demand schedules in the diagram assume two distinct time periods: (1) the first time period (D_0), where the importing nations' business cycle is in its trough and the demand for tin is low, and (2) the second time period (D_1), where business activity in the importing nations is brisk and the

demand for tin is at peak levels. Suppose that the tin producers adopt a buffer stock facility to moderate the price gyrations that would occur in the trough or peak periods. Assume that the target price of tin is set at $3.50 per pound. The buffer stock manager could stabilize the price of tin at $3.50 in each period by purchasing (selling) 40,000 pounds of tin when the demand is located at its trough (D_0) or peak (D_1) level. The important point is that the price of tin remains at $3.50 during each period rather than falling to $3 when demand is low and jumping up to $4 in times of peak demand.

What are the likely welfare effects of the price stabilization scheme on the tin producers? A stabilized price over the course of two periods would generate producer surplus of areas $2a + 2b + 2c$ ($a + b + c$ in each separate period). This is in contrast to what would take place in the absence of stabilization measures. During the first period (D_0), producer surplus would equal area a, whereas the second period (D_1) would find producer surplus totaling areas $a + b + c + d + e$. Stabilizing prices at $3.50 over the

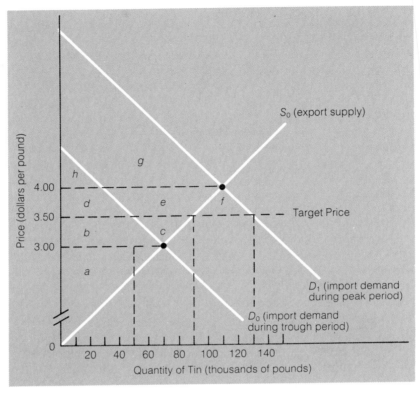

Figure 8.6   Demand-side disturbance: welfare effects of price stabilization.

course of the two periods tends to lower producer surplus by the areas $d + e$ minus $b + c$, compared with the levels that would have existed had prices not been stabilized.

As for the tin importers, consumer surplus in the absence of price stabilization equals area $b + d + h$ when price falls to \$3 (D_0). A price of \$4 (D_1) would result in consumer surplus totaling areas $g + h$. With buffer stock stabilization maintaining prices at \$3.50 for the two periods, the effect on consumer surplus is as follows: (1) By preventing prices from decreasing to \$3 during the trough demand periods, there is a consumer surplus loss of area b; (2) holding prices below \$4 during the peak demand period yields consumer surplus gains of areas $d + e + f$. The

net gain in consumer surplus for the two periods thus amounts to areas $d + e + f$ minus area b. In short, in markets where the main source of instability comes from fluctuations in demand, efforts to stabilize commodity prices may result in welfare gains for importers at the expense of exporters!

Supply-Side Disturbance

Our two-period analysis will now be used in Figure 8.7 to show the welfare effects of price stabilization resulting from supply-based disturbances. Consider the world coffee market, where coffee production largely depends on the

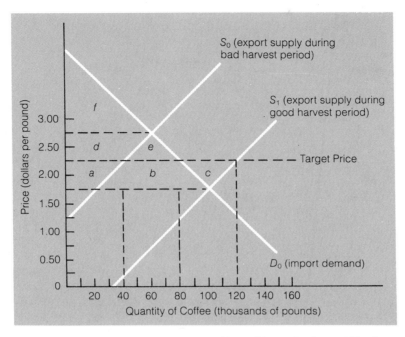

Figure 8.7   Supply-side disturbance: welfare effects of price stabilization.

weather. Assume the first time period (S_0) represents bad harvest years, whereas abundant harvests occur in the second time period (S_1). Suppose the coffee producers enact a buffer stock scheme to stabilize the price of coffee at $2.25 per pound. This could be accomplished by having the buffer stock manager sell (purchase) 40,000 pounds of coffee during years when supply was at S_0 (S_1).

Because this supply disturbance example is parallel to the demand disturbance case already discussed, only the welfare effect results are summarized. For the exporting countries, two-period price stabilization tends to increase producer surplus by an amount equal to areas $a + b + c$ minus area d. Conversely, the importing countries find their consumer surplus falling by area $a + b$ minus $d + e$.

These conclusions have been evaluated empirically in a study conducted by the World Bank for 17 primary commodities. The findings are consistent with the notion that the source of commodity price instability is a crucial element in determining whether importers or exporters gain from price stabilization in terms of welfare (consumer surplus and producer surplus). If the price instability is due to shifts in supply, then stabilization of the long-run price trend would enhance the welfare of the developing countries when they are dominant exporters. Of the 17 commodities studied, developing nations as dominant importers would benefit from price stabilization schemes only in wheat, as seen in Table 8.9. But as dominant exporters, price stabilization would benefit developing countries in sugar, coffee, cocoa, cotton, and jute. Price stabilization schemes would likely detract from the developing countries' welfare in the remaining commodities in the table.

Table 8.9   Source of Price Fluctuations and Potential Benefits to Developing
Countries from World Trade

	Source of Export Price Fluctuations		Developing Countries' Exports Larger than Imports	Developing Countries' Imports Larger than Exports	Potential Benefit from Stabilizing Export Prices
	Demand	Supply			
Wheat	X			X	+
Maize	X		X		−
Rice		X		X	−
Sugar		X	X		+
Coffee		X	X		+
Cocoa		X	X		+
Tea	X		X		−
Cotton		X	X		+
Jute		X	X		+
Wool	X		X		−
Sisal	X		X		−
Rubber	X		X		−
Copper	X		X		−
Lead	X		X		−
Zinc	X		X		−
Tin		X	X		−
Bauxite	X		X		−

Source: Ezriel M. Brook and Euzo R. Grilli, "Commodity Price Stabilization and the Developing
World," *Finance and Development* (March 1977), p. 11.

Summary

1.   Developing countries have attempted to enact trade policies such as cartels and commodity agreements to increase their level of income and standard of living.

2.   Among the alleged problems facing the developing countries are (1) unstable export markets and (2) worsening terms of trade.

3.   International commodity agreements have been formed by producers and consumers of primary products to stabilize export receipts, production, and prices. The methods used to attain these objectives are buffer stocks, export controls, and multilateral contracts.

4.   Past efforts to form viable international commodity agreements have suffered from a number of limitations. Since production is labor intensive, output cutbacks are often socially unacceptable to workers. Agreeing on a target price that reflects existing economic conditions is also troublesome. Agricultural products often face high storage costs and are perishable. Stockpiles of commodities in importing countries can be used to offset production and export controls. Substitute products exist for many commodities.

5. Besides attempting to stabilize commodity prices, developing countries have promoted internal industrialization through import substitution and export promotion policies.

6. To help developing countries gain access to world markets, many industrial countries offer assistance known as a generalized system of preferences.

7. The OPEC oil cartel was established in 1960 in reaction to the control that the major international oil companies exercised over the posted price of oil. OPEC has used export taxes, participation agreements, and to a lesser extent, nationalization schemes to support prices and earnings above what could be achieved in more competitive conditions. The recycling problem has been of major concern to bankers and financial ministers throughout the world.

8. Compared with other commodities, oil enjoyed successful cartelization efforts, largely owing to the structural features of both the supply and demand sides of world oil markets.

Study Questions

1. What are the major reasons for the skepticism of many of the less-developed countries regarding the comparative advantage principle and free trade?

2. Stabilizing commodity prices has been a major objective of many primary product nations. What are the major methods used to achieve price stabilization?

3. What are some current examples of international commodity agreements? Why have many of them broken down over time?

4. Why are the less-developed nations so concerned with commodity price stabilization?

5. How do import substitution and export promotion policies attempt to aid the industrialization of developing countries?

6. The generalized system of preferences is intended to help developing countries gain access to world markets. Explain.

7. The average person probably never heard of the Organization of Petroleum Exporting Countries until 1973 or 1974, when oil prices skyrocketed. In fact, OPEC was founded in 1960. Why is it that OPEC did not achieve worldwide prominence until the 1970s?

8. What is meant by the "recycling problem"?

Notes

1. See Ingo Walter, *International Economics* (New York: Ronald Press, 1975), pp. 254–255.

2. Recall from Chapter 3 that the commodity terms of trade refers to the ratio of an index in export prices divided by an index of import prices, expressed in percentages. Since the commodity terms of trade is the easiest to measure of the various terms-of-trade concepts, most discussion of terms-of-trade movements has been expressed in terms of the commodity terms of trade.

3. Raul Prebisch, "Commercial Policy in the Underdeveloped Countries," *American Economic Review, Papers and Proceedings* (May 1959), pp. 251–273.

4. United Nations Commission for Latin America, *The Economic Development of Latin America and its Principal Problems*, 1950.

5. R. E. Lipsey, *Price and Quantity Trends in the Foreign Trade of the United States* (Princeton, N.J.: Princeton University Press, 1963).

6. T. Wilson et al., "The Income Terms of Trade of Developed and Developing Nations," *Economic Journal* (December 1969), pp. 813–832.

7. Ian Little, T. Scitovsky, and M. Scott, *Industry and Trade in Some Developing Countries* (Oxford: Oxford University Press, 1970), p. 63.

8. See Bernard Munk, "The Colombian Auto-
    mobile Industry: The Welfare Consequences
    of Import Substitution," *Economic and Busi-
    ness Bulletin* (Fall 1970), pp. 6–22. See also
    Bernard Munk, "The Welfare Cost of Con-
    tent Protection: The Automotive Industry in
    Latin America," *Journal of Political Economy*
    (January–February 1969), pp. 85–98.
9. Joel Bergsman, "Growth: A Tale of Two Na-
    tions—Korea and Argentina," *Report: News
    and Views from the World Bank* (May–June
    1980), p. 2. See also Charles R. Frank, et al.,
    *Foreign Trade Regimes and Economic Develop-
    ment: South Korea* (New York: Columbia Uni-
    versity Press, 1975).

Suggestions for Further Reading

Balassa, B. *Policy Reform in Developing Countries*.
    New York: Pergamon Press, 1977.

Baldwin, R. E. "Secular Movements in the Terms
    of Trade." *American Economic Review*, May
    1955.

Bergsten, C. F., ed. *The Future of the International
    Economic Order*. Lexington, Mass.: D. C.
    Heath, 1973.

Berhman, J. R. *International Economic Order and
    Commodity Agreements*. Reading, Mass.: Ad-
    dison-Wesley, 1978.

Dick, H., et al. "Indexation of UNCTAD Core
    Commodity Prices by Buffer Stocks of Ex-
    port Quotas" *Journal of Development Stud-
    ies*, December 1982.

Doran, C. *Myth, Oil, and Politics*. New York: The
    Free Press, 1977.

Gemmell, N. "Economic Development and
    Structural Change: The Role of the Service
    Sector." *Journal of Development Studies*, Oc-
    tober 1982.

International Monetary Fund and the World
    Bank. *Finance and Development*. Washing-
    ton, D.C., quarterly.

Johnson, H. *Economic Policies Toward Less Devel-
    oped Countries*. New York: Praeger, 1967.

Law, A. D. *International Commodity Agreements*.
    Lexington, Mass.: D. C. Heath, 1975.

Lawrence, C., and V. Levy. "On Sharing the
    Gains from International Trade: The Polit-
    ical Economy of Oil Consuming Nations
    and Oil Producing Nations." *International
    Economic Review*, October 1982.

Mikesell, R. "More Third World Cartels Ahead?"
    Challenge, November–December 1974.

Morton, K., and P. Tulloch. *Trade and Developing
    Countries*. New York: Halsted Press, 1977.

Rustow, D., and J. Mugno. *OPEC: Success and
    Prospects*. New York: New York University
    Press, 1977.

Sauvant, K., and H. Hasenpflug, eds. *The New
    International Economic Order*. Boulder,
    Colo.: Westview, 1977.

9

PREFERENTIAL TRADING ARRANGEMENTS

A major ambivalence exists in the economic and political motivations of today's nations. Government leaders are often frustrated in their attempts to achieve national independence and self-reliance while at the same time striving to become more interdependent with the rest of the world. The movement toward integrated national economies has become more pronounced in the modern world. Finding a way to harmonize these two goals has been a major concern of government leaders.

In the post–World War II era, advanced countries have significantly lowered their tariff barriers, most notably on manufactured goods. Such trade liberalization has stemmed from two approaches. The first is a reciprocal reduction of trade barriers on a nondiscriminatory basis. Under the General Agreement on Tariffs and Trade, for example, member nations acknowledge that tariff reductions agreed upon by any two nations will be extended to all other members. Such an international approach encourages a gradual relaxation of tariffs throughout the world. A second approach toward trade liberalization occurs when a small group of nations, typically on a regional basis, forms a *preferential trading arrangement* whereby tariff reductions are limited to participating members only. Organizing a preferential trad-

ing arrangement that discriminates against outsiders involves what is commonly referred to as *economic integration*.

In the post–World War II era, several preferential trade arrangements have been formed. Among the chief trade blocs are the European Economic Community, the European Free Trade Association, and the Soviet–East European group. Trade areas also exist in the developing countries.[1] This chapter investigates some of the theoretical and empirical aspects of preferential trading arrangements.

Nature of Economic Integration

Even though nations have constructed trade barriers, the underlying desire for free trade has been persistent. Since the mid-1950s, the term *economic integration* has become part of the vocabulary of economists. Economic integration is a process of eliminating restrictions on international trade, payments, and factor mobility. Economic integration thus results in the uniting of two or more national economies in a "preferential trade area." Before proceeding, let us delineate the various forms of regional economic integration.

A *free trade area* is an association of trading nations whose members agree to remove all restrictive barriers among themselves. Each member, however, maintains its own set of trade restrictions against outsiders. A good example of this stage of integration is the European Free Trade Association (EFTA), established in 1960. Among its members have been Switzerland, Norway, Austria, Portugal, the United Kingdom, and Sweden. Similar free trade areas have been established by Latin American, African, and Asian countries.

Like a free trade association, a *customs union* is an agreement among two or more trading partners to remove all tariff and nontariff trade barriers among themselves. But each member country imposes identical trade restrictions against nonparticipants rather than different barriers. The effect of the common external policy of trade is to permit free trade within the customs union, while all trade restrictions imposed against outsiders are equalized. A well-known example is Benelux (Belgium, the Netherlands, and Luxembourg), formed in 1948.

A *common market* is a group of trading nations that permits the following: (1) the free movement of goods and services among member nations, (2) the initiation of common external trade restrictions against nonmembers, and (3) the free movement of factors of production across national borders within the economic bloc. The common market represents the most complete stage of integration among the three. The most influential example has been the European Economic Community (EEC), established in 1958. Its members have included Belgium, Denmark, France, Great Britain, West Germany, Ireland, Italy, Luxembourg, the Netherlands, and Greece.

In addition to these stages, economic integration could evolve a step further to the stage of *economic union,* whereby national, social, taxation, and fiscal policies are harmonized and administered by a supranational institu-

tion. Belgium and Luxembourg formed an economic union during the 1920s. The task of forming an economic union is much more ambitious than the other forms of integration. This is because a free trade area, customs union, or common market primarily result from the abolition of existing trade barriers, but an economic union requires the agreement to transfer economic sovereignty to a supranational authority. The ultimate degree of economic union would be the unification of national monetary policies and the acceptance of a common currency administered by a supranational monetary authority. The economic union would thus include the dimension of a *monetary union.*

Preferential Trading Arrangement Effects

What are the possible welfare implications of preferential trading arrangements? We can delineate the theoretical benefits and costs of such devices from two perspectives. First are the *static* or once-and-for-all impacts of integration on productive efficiency and consumer welfare. Second are the *dynamic* effects of integration, which relate to member countries' long-run rates of growth. Combined, these static and dynamic effects determine the overall welfare gains or losses associated with the formation of a preferential trading arrangement.[2]

Static Effects

The static welfare effects of lowering tariff barriers among members of a trade area are illustrated in the following example. Assume a world composed of three countries—Luxembourg, West Germany, and the United States. Suppose Luxembourg and West Germany decide to form a customs union and the United States is a nonmember. The decision to form a customs union requires that Luxembourg and West Germany abolish all tariff restrictions between themselves, while maintaining a common tariff policy against the United States.

Referring to Figure 9.1, assume the supply and demand curves of Luxembourg to be S_L and D_L. Assume also that Luxembourg is very small relative to West Germany and to the United States. This means that Luxembourg cannot influence foreign prices, so that foreign supply curves of grain are perfectly elastic. Let West Germany's supply price be $3.25 per bushel and that of the United States equal $3 per bushel. Note that the United States is assumed to be the most efficient supplier. Before the formation of the customs union, Luxembourg finds that under conditions of free trade,

it purchases all of its import requirements from the United States. West Germany does not participate in the market because its supply price exceeds that of the United States. In free trade equilibrium, Luxembourg's home production equals 1 bushel and home consumption equals 23 bushels, with imports totaling 22 bushels. Suppose that Luxembourg levies a tariff equal to 50 cents on each bushel imported from the United States (or West Germany). Luxembourg then finds its imports falling from 22 bushels to 10 bushels.

As part of a trade liberalization agreement, assume Luxembourg and West Germany form a customs union. Luxembourg's import tariff is dropped against West Germany, but it is still maintained on imports from nonmember United States. This means that West Germany now

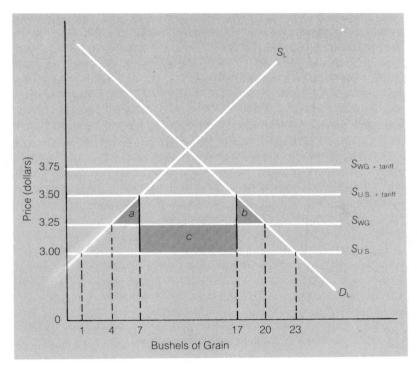

Figure 9.1   Static welfare effects of a customs union.

becomes the low-price supplier. Luxembourg now purchases all of its imports, totaling 16 bushels, from West Germany at $3.25 per bushel, while importing nothing from the United States.

The movement toward freer trade under a customs union affects world welfare in two opposing ways. Included is a welfare-increasing *trade creation effect* and a welfare-reducing *trade diversion effect*. The overall consequence of a customs union on the welfare of its members, as well as on the world as a whole, depends on the relative strength of these two opposing forces. The favorable trade creation effect consists of a consumption effect and a production effect. Before the formation of the customs union and under its tariff umbrella, Luxembourg imports from the United States at a price of $3.50 per bushel. Luxembourg's entry into the economic union results in its dropping all tariffs levied against West Germany. Facing lower import prices, $3.25, Luxembourg increases its purchases from West Germany by the amount of 3 bushels. The welfare gain associated with the increase in consumption resulting from freer trade equals triangle b.

The formation of the customs union also yields a production effect that results in a more efficient use of world resources. This occurs when freer trade results in domestic production being replaced by a lower cost and more efficient producer within the customs union. The effect of Luxembourg eliminating its tariff barriers against West Germany is that the producers of Luxembourg must now compete against more efficient foreign producers. The inefficient domestic producers drop out of the market, resulting in a decline in home output of 3 bushels. The reduction in cost of obtaining this output equals triangle a in the figure. This represents the favorable production effect. From the figure, the overall trade creation effect is given by the sum of triangles a plus b.

Although a customs union may add to world welfare by way of trade creation, its trade diversion effect generally implies a welfare loss. Trade diversion occurs when imports from a low-cost supplier outside the union are replaced by a higher-cost supplier from within. This suggests that world production is reorganized less efficiently. In the figure, although the total volume of trade increases under the customs union, part of this trade (10 bushels) has been diverted from low-cost supplier, United States, to a high-cost source, West Germany. The increase in cost of obtaining 10 bushels of imported grain equals area c. This is the welfare loss to Luxembourg, as well as to the world as a whole. Our static analysis concludes that the formation of a *customs union will increase the welfare of its members as well as the rest of the world if the positive trade creation effect more than offsets the negative trade diversion effect*. Referring to the figure, this occurs if $a + b$ exceeds c. The opposite also holds true.

This analysis illustrates that the success of a customs union depends on the factors contributing to trade creation and diversion. Several factors that bear on the relative size of these effects can be identified. One factor is the kinds of countries that tend to benefit from a customs union. Countries whose preunion economies are quite competitive are likely to benefit from trade creation. This is because the formation of the union offers greater opportunity for specialization in production. Also, the larger the size and the greater the number of countries in the union, the greater the gains are likely to be, since there is a greater possibility that the world's low-cost producers will be union members. In the extreme case where the union consists of the entire world, there can exist only trade creation, not trade diversion. In addition, the scope for trade diversion is smaller when the customs union's common external tariff is lower rather than higher. Because a lower tariff allows greater trade to take place with nonmember countries, there will be less replacement of cheaper imports from nonmember countries by relatively high-cost imports from partner countries.

Dynamic Effects

Not all welfare consequences of customs unions are static in nature. There may also be *dynamic gains* that influence member nation growth rates. These dynamic gains stem from the creation of larger markets by the movement to freer trade under customs unions. The benefits associated with a customs union's dynamic gains may more than offset any unfavorable static effects. Dynamic gains include *economies of scale, greater competition,* and the *stimulus of investment.*

Perhaps the most noticeable result of a customs union is market enlargement. Being able to penetrate freely the domestic markets of other member countries, firms can take advantage of economies of scale that would not have occurred in smaller markets limited by trade restrictions. Larger markets may permit efficiencies attributable to greater specialization of workers and machinery, the use of the most efficient equipment, and the more complete use of byproducts. There is evidence that significant scale economies have been achieved by the European Economic Community in such products as steel, automobiles, footwear, and copper refining.

Broader markets may also promote greater competition among firms within a customs union. It is often felt that trade restrictions promote monopoly power, whereby a small number of firms dominate a domestic market. Such firms may prefer to lead a *quiet life,* forming agreements not to compete on the basis of price. But with the movement to more open markets under a customs union, the potential for successful collusion is lessened as the number of competitors expands. With freer trade, domestic firms must compete or face the possibility of financial bankruptcy. To survive in expanded and more competitive markets, firms must undertake investments in new equipment, technologies, and product lines. This will have the effect of holding costs down and permitting expanded levels of output. Capital investment may also rise if nonmember nations decide to establish subsidiary operations inside the customs unions to avoid external tariff barriers.

European Economic Community

In the years immediately following World War II, the countries of Western Europe suffered balance-of-payments disturbances in response to reconstruction efforts. To deal with these problems, they initiated an elaborate network of tariff and exchange restrictions, quantitative controls, and state trading. In the 1950s, Western Europe began to dismantle its trade barriers in response to successful tariff negotiations under the auspices of the General Agreement on Tariffs and Trade. Trade liberalization efforts within Western Europe were also aided by the establishment of the Organization of Economic Cooperation and Development and the European Payments Union. Convertibility for most European currencies had taken place by 1958 and most quantitative restrictions on trade within Western Europe had been eliminated.

It was against this background of trade liberalization that the European Economic Community (EEC) was created in 1957.[3] The EEC originally consisted of six countries: Belgium, France, Italy, Luxembourg, the Netherlands, and West Germany. EEC membership by 1973 had expanded to nine countries when the United Kingdom, Ireland, and Denmark joined the community. In 1981, Greece became the tenth member of the EEC. An economic profile of the community members is given in Table 9.1.

The primary objective of the EEC has been to create an economic union in which trade and other transactions would be free to move among member countries. According to the 1957 Treaty of Rome, member countries have agreed in principle to the following provisions:

Table 9.1   European Economic Community: Economic Profile, 1980

Country	Area (sq mi)	Population (millions)	Gross National Product (billions of U.S. dollars)	Per-Capita Gross National Product (U.S. dollars)
Belgium	11,781	9.8	119.8	12,180
Denmark	16,629	5.1	66.4	12,950
France	211,208	53.5	627.7	11,730
Greece	50,944	9.3	42.2	4,5210
Ireland	27,136	3.3	16.1	4,880
Italy	116,314	56.9	368.9	6,480
Luxembourg	998	0.4	5.2	14,510
Netherlands	15,892	14.1	161.4	11,470
United Kingdom	94,226	55.9	442.8	7,920
West Germany	95,934	60.9	827.8	13,590
Total	641,062	269.2	2,678.3	

Source: *World Bank Atlas*, 1981, p. 18.

1. Abolition of tariffs, quotas, and other trade restrictions among member countries
2. Imposition of a uniform external tariff on commodities coming from nonmember nations
3. Free movement within the community of capital, labor, and enterprise
4. Establishment of a common transport policy, a common agriculture policy, and a common policy toward competition and business conduct
5. Coordination and synchronization of member nation monetary and fiscal policies

According to community timetable, member countries were to establish a common market over a 12-year period. This was accomplished in 1968 when trade restrictions on manufactured goods were eliminated. During the 1958–1968 period, liberalization of trade within the community was accompanied by a nearly fivefold increase in the value of industrial trade, higher than that of world trade in general. By 1970, the EEC became a full-fledged customs union when a common external tariff system was levied against outsiders.

As for empirical evidence of the overall impact of the EEC on its members' welfare, several studies have been conducted. In terms of static welfare benefits, one study concluded that trade creation was pronounced in machinery, transportation equipment, chemicals, and fuels; trade diversion was apparent in agricultural commodities and raw materials.[4] Another study concluded that from 1965 to 1967, the trade creation effect of the EEC for industrial products totaled $6.2 billion, whereas the trade diversion effect amounted to $2.2 billion.[5] In addition, it is widely presumed that the EEC has enjoyed dynamic benefits from integration. This was particularly the case in the 1960s when its rate of growth surpassed that of the United States.

The EEC today has a combined market large enough to permit possible economies of large-scale production. When the EEC was formed in 1958, the original six members had a combined GNP about one-third that of the United States.

By 1983, the combined GNPs of the original six members were more than four-fifths as large as the U.S. GNP, and the GNP of the 10-member EEC exceeded that of the United States.

EEC manufacturers have also benefited from the stimulus of investment. Before the EEC, manufacturers in the United States were much larger than those in Europe. But by the 1980s, European manufacturers in many industries attained sizes comparable to American competitors. In automobiles, in 1982, Renault (France) had sales of $15.5 billion, and Daimler-Benz (West Germany) had sales of $16.3 billion. These sales exceeded the $10.0 billion sales of America's Chrysler Co. However, General Motors' sales of $60 billion surpassed those of the largest European auto firms.

Agricultural Policy

Besides providing for the free trade of industrial goods among its members, the EEC has abolished restrictions on agricultural products traded internally. A *common agricultural policy* (CAP) has also replaced the agricultural policies of individual member countries, who adopted different practices in their agricultural stabilization policies before the formation of the EEC. A substantial element of CAP has been the support of prices received by farmers for their produce. Schemes involving deficiency payments, output controls, and direct income payments have been used for this purpose. In addition, CAP has supported EEC farm prices through a system of *variable levies*, which applies tariffs to agricultural imports entering the EEC. Exports of any surplus quantities of EEC produce have been assured through the adoption of *export subsidies*.

One problem confronting the EEC's price-support programs is that agricultural efficiencies differ among EEC members. Consider the case of grains. West German farmers, being high-cost producers, have desired high support prices to

maintain themselves as going concerns. But the more efficient French farmers have contested for lower price supports to enable them to undersell their German competitors. In recent years, high price supports have been applied to products such as beef, grains, and butter. CAP has suffered in encouraging inefficient farm production among EEC farmers and by restricting food imports from more efficient nonmember producers.

Figure 9.2 illustrates the operation of a system of variable levies and export subsidies. Assume that S_{EEC_0} and D_{EEC_0} represent the EEC's supply and demand schedules for wheat, while the world price of wheat equals $3.50 per bushel. Suppose the EEC wishes to guarantee its high-cost farmers a price of $4.50 per bushel. This price, however, could not be sustained as long as imported wheat is allowed to enter the EEC at the free market price of $3.50 per bushel. To validate the support price, suppose the EEC initiates a variable levy. Given an import levy of $1 per bushel, EEC farmers are permitted to produce 5 million bushels of wheat, as opposed to the 3 million bushels that would be produced under free trade. Likewise, EEC imports would total 2 million bushels instead of 6 million bushels.

Owing to increased productivity overseas, suppose the world price of wheat falls to $2.50 per bushel. Under a variable levy system, the levy is determined daily and equals the difference between the lowest price on the world market and the support price. The sliding-scale nature of the variable levy results in the EEC increasing the import tariff to $2 per bushel. The support price of wheat is sustained at $4.50, while EEC production and imports remain unchanged. EEC farmers are thus insulated from the consequences of variations in foreign supply. Should EEC wheat production decrease, the import levy could be reduced to encourage imports. EEC consumers would be protected against rising wheat prices.

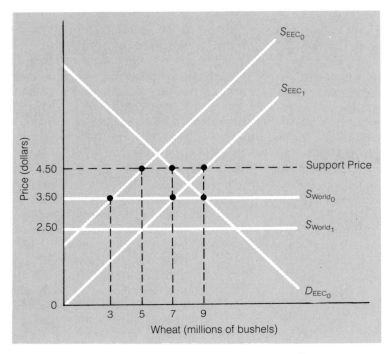

Figure 9.2   Variable levies and export subsidies.

The variable import levy tends to be more restrictive than a fixed tariff. It discourages foreign products from absorbing part of the tariff, and from cutting price, to maintain export sales. This would only trigger higher variable levies. For the same reason, variable levies discourage foreign producers from subsidizing their exports so they may penetrate domestic markets.

The EEC has also used a system of export subsidies to ensure that any surplus agricultural output will be sold overseas. The high price supports of CAP have given EEC farmers the incentive to increase production, often in surplus quantities. But the world price of agricultural commodities has generally been below the EEC price. The EEC pays its producers export subsidies so they can sell surplus produce abroad at the low world price but still receive the higher, internal support price.

In Figure 9.2, let the world price of wheat be $3.50 per bushel. Suppose that improving technologies result in the EEC's supply curve shifting from S_{EEC_0} to S_{EEC_1}. At the internal support price, $4.50, EEC production exceeds EEC consumption by 2 million bushels. To facilitate the export of this surplus output, suppose the EEC provides its producers an export subsidy of $1 per bushel. EEC wheat would be exported at a price of $3.50, and EEC producers would receive a price (including the subsidy) of $4.50. The export subsidies of the EEC are also characterized by a sliding scale. Should the world price of wheat fall to $2.50, the $4.50 support price would be made effective through the imposition of a $2 export subsidy.

The EEC's policy of assuring a high level of income for its politically important farmers has been costly. High support prices for products including milk, butter, cheese, and meat have led to high internal production and low consumption. The result has often been huge surpluses (such as "milk lakes" and "butter mountains"), which must be purchased by the EEC to defend the support price. In recent years, the cost of the farm program has run in excess of $14 billion annually.

To reduce these costs, the EEC has been selling surplus produce in world markets at prices well below the cost of acquisition, subsidizing the sales. Such sales, however, have met resistance from competing farmers. For example, in response to American farmer complaints of EEC agricultural export subsidy programs, in 1983, the U.S. government retaliated by subsidizing exports of wheat flour to Egypt. The subsidy, amounting to $100 per ton, enabled Egyptians to buy U.S. flour through commercial outlets at $155 per ton, well below the EEC subsidized sales price of $175 per ton. The Europeans defended their subsidies by pointing out how the United States uses subsidies to promote its agricultural sector. For example, in 1982, the United States subsidized the sale of 100,000 tons of butter to

New Zealand to reduce the large U.S. dairy product surplus. Also, U.S. import restrictions on sugar and beef help support domestic farm prices without requiring governmental expenditures.

European Free Trade Association

The European Free Trade Association (EFTA) is essentially a free trade area in industrial goods. Founded in 1960, the original intent of EFTA was to take part in a Western European free trade area that would have included the six original members of the EEC as participants. But when negotiations broke down, EFTA nations decided to establish their own free trade area. EFTA today consists of seven member countries: Austria, Finland, Iceland, Norway, Portugal, Sweden, and Switzerland. Table 9.2 summarizes their economic profile. According to the original EFTA agreements, internal trade restrictions on imports in industrial goods were to be eliminated gradually. By the end of 1966, all tariffs were phased out, whereas the abolition of quantitative

Table 9.2 European Free Trade Association: Economic Profile, 1980

Country	Area (sq mi)	Population (millions)	Gross National Product (billions of U.S. dollars)	Per-Capita Gross National Product (U.S. dollars)
Austria	32,274	7.5	76.5	10,230
Finland	130,120	4.9	47.3	9,720
Iceland	39,769	0.2	2.6	11,330
Norway	125,182	4.1	51.6	12,650
Portugal	34,340	9.8	23.1	2,350
Sweden	173,732	8.3	111.9	13,520
Switzerland	15,941	6.5	106.3	16,440
Total	551,458	41.3	419.3	

Source: *World Bank Atlas*, 1981, p. 18.

restrictions on industrial product imports took place in 1975. During this period, EFTA was also negotiating preferential trading arrangements with the EEC countries. The world's largest free trade area was established in 1977 when tariffs were abolished on industrial products traded between members of EFTA and the EEC. This amounted to approximately 22 percent of global trade.

EFTA is a less comprehensive trade scheme than the EEC. Being only a free trade area in industrial goods, EFTA does not provide for common economic policies such as an agriculture program or tariff system levied against outsiders. Nor does EFTA have plans for full integration of member nations' economies. Rather than a permanent entity, EFTA has widely been viewed as a bargaining agent whose purpose is to establish preferential trading arrangements and possibly merger with the EEC.

Trading Arrangements Within the Soviet Bloc

The concept of trade preferences also can be extended to the commercial practices of the Soviet Union and its Eastern European allies. Largely owing to East-West ideological differences and the operational problems of carrying out trade between market-oriented economies and centrally planned economies, the Soviet Union and Eastern Europe have conducted trade among themselves for the most part. This practice has been facilitated by the formation of the *Council for Mutual Economic Assistance* (CMEA), whose declared objectives have been the promotion of economic cooperation and integration among the East European countries. Before discussing CMEA, let us consider the major features of market economies and nonmarket economies.

Market Systems and Nonmarket Systems

The industrialized Western nations, and particularly the United States, are recognized as *market economies*. In such systems, the commercial decisions of independent buyers and sellers acting in their own interest govern both domestic and international trade. Market-determined prices are used for valuing alternatives and allocating scarce resources. This means that prices play rationing and signaling roles so that the availability of goods is made consistent with buyer preferences and purchasing power.

The communist countries and some less-developed countries are essentially centrally planned or *nonmarket economies*. With less regard to market considerations, foreign and sometimes domestic trade is governed by state planning and control. Often the plan controls the prices and output of goods bought and sold, with minimal recognition given to considerations of cost and efficiency. The state fixes prices to ration arbitrary quantities among buyers, and these domestic prices are largely insulated from foreign trade influences. Given these different pricing mechanisms, trade between market economies and centrally planned economies is generally difficult.

· As for the role of foreign trade, nonmarket systems largely rely on state planning and control. The Soviet Union's State Planning Commission and Ministry of Foreign Trade, for example, determines the volume and commodity composition of its trade. The Ministry of Foreign Trade also grants authorization to state trade corporations engaging in international commerce. It is with these organizations that Western exporters and importers must deal when conducting business.

Council for Mutual Economic Assistance

CMEA has been in existence since 1949, when several Eastern European countries formed a preferential trading arrangement. CMEA member countries are: Bulgaria, Cuba, Czechoslovakia, East Germany, Hungary, Mongolia, Poland, Romania, and the Soviet Union. Table 9.3 gives an economic profile of these countries. CMEA's objectives are best summarized in its charter:

> The purpose of the Council for Mutual Economic Assistance is to promote, by uniting and coordinating the efforts of the member countries of the Council, the planned development of the national economy, the acceleration of economic and technical progress in these countries, the rising of industrialization in the industrially less developed countries, a steady increase in the productivity of labour, and a constant improvement in the welfare of the peoples of the member countries of the Council.

For the Soviet Union, economic integration is often a way by which it can exercise economic and political control over other CMEA members. For the more developed member states, CMEA is a means of achieving further industrialization and enjoying the economic gains from trade and cooperation.

Trade among CMEA members is governed by bilateral trading agreements that stem from bargaining between pairs of CMEA member states over what is to be exchanged, in what amounts, and at what prices. World prices provide guidelines and are used as bargaining tools by CMEA nations when negotiating trade prices with each other. Over 90 percent of CMEA trade today is conducted on a bilateral basis, with member countries attempting to keep their trade positions in approximate balance with each other. Such bilateralism reflects the stringent controls that CMEA states exercise over foreign trade. To a minor extent, some CMEA trade is conducted multilaterally.

As for CMEA trade outside its bloc, member countries generally view it as a residual. Trade with nonmembers may occur when intrabloc trade cannot generate sufficient output requirements to meet the needs of consumers. Rather than viewing international trade as a means of achieving economic gains through specialization,

Table 9.3   Council for Mutual Economic Assistance: Economic Profile, 1980

Country	Area (sq mi)	Population (millions)	Gross National Product (billions of U.S. dollars)	Per-Capita Gross National Product (U.S. dollars)
Bulgaria	42,823	9.0	37.4	4,150
Cuba	44,218	9.9	13.9	1,410
Czechoslovakia	49,371	15.3	89.3	5,820
East Germany	41,768	16.9	120.9	7,180
Hungary	35,919	10.8	45.0	4,180
Mongolia	604,250	1.6	1.3	780
Poland	120,725	35.8	139.8	3,900
Romania	91,699	22.3	52.0	2,340
Soviet Union	8,649,500	266.7	1,212.0	4,550
Total	9,680,273	388.3	1,711.6	

Source: *World Bank Atlas*, 1981, pp. 14, 18, 20.

CMEA has considered internal self-sufficiency an objective. Exports are deemed a necessary cost of obtaining imports. Much of CMEA trade, like the Soviet grain deals with the West, has been induced by events that disrupt domestic production operations or by the lack of technological solutions for problem areas such as electronics, automobiles, and machine tool production.

The economic integration efforts of CMEA have affected member country welfare in the areas of trade creation and trade diversion. One study indicates that for the 1965–1970 period, significant trade creation occurred in chemicals, iron, steel, and certain machinery.[6] CMEA countries appear to have diverted trade away from nonmembers and toward each other. When CMEA was first established in 1949, member states had fairly weak economic ties, conducting less than 30 percent of their transactions with each other. This figure currently exceeds 60 percent for most members, suggesting less trade with the outside world. Such trade diversion can be explained in part by the fact that CMEA views international trade as a source of possible instability to its production allocation programs. International trade also is made difficult by the domestic prices set by economic planners, which fail to reflect the supply and demand forces that are characteristic of market economies.

Current Patterns of East-West Trade

The centrally planned communist countries in Eastern Europe and Asia historically have experienced only modest trade flows with the Western world. As recently as 1970, the two-way volume of East-West trade was small, amounting to slightly less than $16 billion. But in the early 1970s, the communist countries were increasingly looking to Western markets. Increased trade with the West may indicate a recognition

that the communist countries have not been satisfied with existing trade patterns.

In terms of the volume and composition of East-West trade, Western Europe accounts for the largest share, whereas the United States accounts for only a minor portion of the total. As of 1982, only 3 percent of U.S. exports went to the communist countries, whereas purchases from communist countries accounted for 1 percent of U.S. imports. Political considerations largely explain the relatively small amount of U.S. trade with the East. The United States and its Western allies historically have placed controls on exchanges of technology and goods of strategic importance to communist countries, and also have initiated restrictions on the credit terms extended to those countries. Although the trade barriers of Western Europe have been reduced over the years, the United States has maintained tight trade controls against the East. Beginning in the early 1970s, the United States began to liberalize trade relations with the communist nations, and U.S. trade with these countries consequently began to increase.

What are some of the major issues that currently affect East-West trade? Among the most important ones are financing limitations and industrial cooperation.

Financing Limitations

The Soviet Union and Eastern Europe throughout the 1970s and 1980s have run up significant trade deficits with the West. The basic problem has been that the communist countries have not been able to increase their exports commensurate with the rise of their imports. Communist country imports must be paid for either with hard currency generated from the exports of goods and services or by the accumulation of debt. Virtually all communist country deficits in practice have been financed by borrowing from Western banks and governments.

One major impediment that communist countries face in obtaining financing for imports from the United States is the absence of U.S. government credit. Most lending has come from our commercial banks instead of the government's export institutions—the Export-Import Bank and the Commodity Credit Corporation. Legal lending restrictions on the amount of commercial bank funds that can be used to finance exports also limits East-West trade. Another check is the Johnson Debt Default Act of 1934, which prevents additional loans from being made by U.S. parties to foreign governments that are in default on debt obligations to the U.S. government. Finally, those communist countries that have not been granted most-favored-nation status cannot receive credit from the U.S. government so long as they put restrictions on immigration, as provided by the Trade Act of 1974.

Industrial Cooperation

East-West trade until recently was carried out on a relatively simple basis. Exports to and imports from communist countries were settled in hard currency or credit. But with the expansion of East-West trade has come countertrade, which establishes a greater degree of interdependence between the private corporations of Western economies and the state enterprises of the communist countries.

Countertrade refers to all international trade in which goods are swapped for goods—a kind of barter. If swapping goods for goods sounds less efficient than using cash or credit, that's because it is. During tough economic times, however, shortages of hard currency and tight credit can hinder East-West trade. Instead of facing the possibility of reduced foreign sales, Western firms have viewed countertrade as the next best alternative.

Many Western nations conduct countertrade with the communist countries, as seen in Table 9.4. For the United States, General Motors, Sears, and General Electric have established trading companies that conduct countertrade. A simple form of countertrade occurs when a communist country agrees to pay for the delivery of plant, machinery, or equipment with the goods produced by the plant. For example, West Germany has sold the Soviet Union steel pipe in exchange for deliveries of natural gas, while Austria has supplied Poland with technological expertise and equipment in exchange for diesel engines and truck components.

Industrial cooperation has also resulted in *coproduction agreements*, whereby Western firms establish production facilities in a communist country. Because most communist countries do not permit foreign ownership of such operations, an agreement is made whereby ownership is held by the communist country. Coproduction agreements are used widely in the areas of machine building, chemical products, electrical and electronic devices, and pharmaceutical goods.

Industrial cooperation may assume a number of other forms. Western nations have often made *joint research and development agreements* with the Soviet Union, particularly in industrial processes and technical areas. The findings of such activities are jointly patented and license royalties are shared between the partners. *Contract manufacturing agreements* are also popular, whereby Western nations supply material inputs and design specifications to communist enterprises, which produce the goods and ship them back to the Western nations.

The motivations for industrial cooperation are varied. For a Western company, such agreements get around the hard currency scarcities of the communist countries and permit them access to the markets of East Europe and the Soviet Union. Western firms may also be able to tap additional supplies of raw materials and intermediate goods or possibly maximize revenues by selling obsolete equipment. The communist partner typically views industrial cooperation as a

Table 9.4   Examples of Soviet Union Countertrade
Agreements with the West

Western Country (supplier)	Type of Soviet Import	Type of Soviet Export
West Germany	Polyethylene plant	Polyethylene
West Germany	Chemical plant	Methanol
Italy	Detergent Plant	Organic chemicals
United States	Fertilizer plant	Ammonia
Japan	Car body stamping assembly lines	Chemicals
Japan	Forestry handling equipment	Timber products
United Kingdom	Methanol plant	Methanol
France	Pulp paper plant	Wood pulp
Austria	Large diameter pipe	Natural gas

Source: U.S. Department of Commerce, International Trade Administration, *Countertrade Practices in East Europe, the Soviet Union, and China*, April 1980, pp. 91–94.

means of obtaining new technologies and expanding industrial capacity with minimal sacrifices of hard currency.

Summary

1. Trade liberalization has assumed a number of forms. One involves the reciprocal reduction in trade barriers on a nondiscriminatory basis, as seen in the operation of the General Agreement on Tariffs and Trade. The other approach is that used by the European Economic Community, whereby a group of nations on a regional basis establishes preferential trading arrangements with each other.

2. A number of preferential trade blocs currently exist. Among the major ones are the following: European Economic Community, European Free Trade Association, Central American Common Market, Latin American Economic System, Council for Mutual Economic Assistance.

3. The term *economic integration* refers to the process of eliminating restrictions to international trade, payments, and factor input mobility. The stages that economic integration may assume are (1) free trade area, (2) customs union, (3) common market, (4) economic union, or (5) monetary union.

4. The welfare implications of economic integration can be analyzed from two perspectives. First are the static welfare effects, reflected in trade creation and trade diversion. Second are the dynamic welfare effects that stem from greater competition, economies of scale, and the stimulus to investment spending that economic integration makes possible.

5. From a static perspective, the formation of a customs union yields net welfare gains if the consumption and production benefits of trade creation more than offset the loss in world efficiency owing to trade diversion.

6. Several factors influence the extent of trade creation and trade diversion: (1) the degree of competitiveness that member nation economies have prior to the customs union's formation, (2) the number and size of the customs union's members, and (3) the size of the customs union's external tariff against nonmembers.

7. The European Economic Community was originally founded in 1957 by the Treaty of Rome. Today it consists of 10 members with a combined population approximately equal to that of the United States and a production output over half as large. By the early 1970s, the community had reached the "customs union" stage of integration. Empirical evidence suggests that the community has enjoyed welfare benefits in trade creation that have outweighed the losses from trade diversion. One of the major stumbling blocks confronting the community has been its common agricultural policy.

8. Established in 1960 by several Western European countries, the European Free Trade Association has gradually reduced tariffs and quotas among its members and fostered economic cooperation among them.

9. CMEA is a preferential trade bloc among the Soviet Union and its Eastern European allies. CMEA countries are generally characterized by nonmarket economies in which domestic and foreign trade are governed by state planning and control. Trade among CMEA members is governed largely by bilateral trading arrangements. Member countries of CMEA generally view trade with outsiders as a residual.

10. Two important issues that affect East-West trade are financing limitations and industrial cooperation.

11. Countertrade is a form of barter that results in goods being exchanged for goods between trading nations. It generally occurs during eras of hard currency shortages and tight credit.

Study Questions

1. How can trade liberalization exist on a nondiscriminatory basis versus a discriminatory basis? What are some actual examples of each?

2. What is meant by the term *economic integration?* What are the various stages that economic integration can take?

3. How do the static welfare effects of trade creation and trade diversion relate to a country's decision to form a customs union? Of what importance are the dynamic welfare effects to this decision?

4. Why has the so-called common agricultural policy been a controversial issue for the European Economic Community?

5. What are the welfare effects of trade creation and trade diversion for the European Economic Community, determined by empirical studies?

6. Distinguish between market economies and nonmarket economies. What significance do these systems have for East-West trade?

7. Compare the objectives and operation of the Council for Mutual Economic Assistance with those of the European Economic Community.

8. Financing East-West trade has created problems for exporters and importers. Explain.

9. What is meant by countertrade? Why does it occur?

Notes

1. Examples of trade areas among developing countries have included the Latin American Integration Association, the Andean Group, and the Caribbean Community.

2. The pioneer work in this area is Jacob Viner, *The Customs Union Issue* (New York: Carnegie Endowment for International Peace, 1950), chap. 4. See also Harry G. Johnson, *Money, Trade, and Economic Growth* (London: Allen & Unwin, 1962), chap. 3.

3. See Anthony Kerr, *The Common Market and How It Works* (New York: Pergamon Press, 1977) and D. Swann, *The Economics of the Common Market* (Baltimore: Penguin Books, 1970).

4. Mordechai E. Kreinin, *Trade Relations of the EEC: An Empirical Approach* (New York: Praeger, 1974), chap. 3.

5. "EEC Effects on the Foreign Trade of EEC Member Countries," *EFTA Bulletin* (June 1972), pp. 14–21.

6. Joseph Pelzman, "Trade Creation and Trade Diversion in the Council of Mutual Economic Assistance: 1954–1970," *American Economic Review* (September 1977), pp. 713–720.

Meier, G. M. *Problems of Trade Policy.* New York: Oxford University Press, 1973.

Swann, D. *The Economics of the Common Market.* Harmondsworth, England: Penguin Books, 1970.

Tinbergen, J. *International Economic Integration.* Amsterdam: Elsevier, 1965.

Viner, J. *The Customs Union Issue.* New York: Carnegie Endowment for International Peace, 1950.

Suggestions for Further Reading

Balassa, B. *The Theory of Economic Integration.* Homewood, Ill.: Richard D. Irwin, 1961.

Catrivesis, B., and T. Hitiris. "The Impact on Greek Agriculture from Membership in the EEC." *European Economic Review*, March 1982.

Commission of the European Communities. *European File*, monthly.

Dizard, J. "The Explosion of International Barter." *Fortune*, February 7, 1983.

Eastman, B. "Split on Farm Trade." *Europe*, January–February 1983.

Hojman, D. "The Andean Pact: Failure of a Model of Economic Integration?" *Journal of Common Market Studies*, December 1981.

Kerr, A. *The Common Market and How It Works.* New York: Pergamon Press, 1977.

Kreinin, M. *EEC Trade Relations: An Empirical Investigation.* New York: Praeger, 1974.

Lipsey, R. G. "The Theory of Customs Unions: Trade Diversion and Welfare." *Economica*, February 1957.

Meade, J. E. *The Theory of Customs Unions.* Amsterdam: North-Holland, 1955.

10

INTERNATIONAL
INVESTMENT
AND MULTINATIONAL
ENTERPRISE

When observing the real world, we see the international movement of factor inputs occurring on a widespread basis. Responding to higher wages in West Germany, Italian workers may move across West German borders, whereas West German factories and machinery may flow into Italy in pursuit of high returns. The *multinational corporation* (MNC) has come to play a decisive role in world trade and investment patterns. The enormous flows of investment capital by the MNCs have pronounced effects on domestic output and employment levels, in addition to international trade flows and the balance of payments. To the extent that MNCs contribute to the international movement of factor inputs, they may lessen the need to move goods among nations. This chapter deals with the MNC and its role as a source of direct foreign investments in such operations as manufacturing facilities as well as mining and petroleum extraction and processing.

The Multinational Corporation

Although the term *corporation* can be precisely defined, there is no universal agreement on the exact definition of an MNC. But a close look at some of the representative MNCs suggests that these firms have a number of identifiable features. Operating in many host countries, the MNC often conducts research and development activities in addition to manufacturing, mining, and extraction operations. The MNC cuts across national borders, and is often directed from a corporate planning center that is distant from the host country where a particular operation occurs. Both stock ownership and corporate management are typically multinational in character. A typical MNC has a high ratio of foreign sales to total sales, often 25 percent or more. Regardless of the lack of agreement as to what constitutes an MNC, there is no doubt that the multinational phenomenon is massive in size.

Table 10.1 gives us a glimpse of the 12 largest industrial corporations of the United States and the rest of the world. Virtually all of these firms are considered MNCs. The major types of multimarket operations in which MNCs may become involved are illustrated in Figure 10.1. MNCs may diversify their operations along vertical, horizontal, and conglomerate lines within the host and source countries.[1]

Vertical integration often occurs where the parent MNC decides to establish foreign subsidiaries to produce the intermediate goods or inputs going into the production of the finished good. For industries such as oil refining and steel, such

187

Table 10.1   Leading Industrial Companies in the World, 1982

Company	Headquarters	Industry	Sales (billions of dollars)
Exxon	United States	Petroleum	97.1
Royal Dutch/Shell	Netherlands, Britain	Petroleum	83.8
General Motors	United States	Motor vehicles	60.0
IBM	United States	Office equipment	33.4
DuPont	United States	Chemicals	33.3
ENI	Italy	Petroleum	27.5
IRI	Italy	Metal manufacturing	24.8
Unilever	Britain, Netherlands	Food products	23.1
Nissan Motor	Japan	Motor vehicles	16.5
Daimler-Benz	West Germany	Motor vehicles	16.0
BAT Industries	Britain	Tobacco	15.5
Nippon Steel	Japan	Metal manufacturing	14.4

Source: *Fortune*, August 22, 1983.

backward integration may include the extraction and processing of raw materials. Most manufacturers, such as producers of television sets or stereos, tend to extend operations backward only to the production of component parts. The major international oil companies represent a classic case of backward vertical integration on a worldwide basis. Oil production subsidiaries are located in areas such as the Middle East, whereas the refining and marketing operations occur in the industrial countries of the West. MNCs may also integrate *forward* in the direction of the final consumer market. Automobile manufacturers, for example, may establish foreign subsidiaries to market the finished goods of the parent firm. Most vertical foreign investment in practice is backward. MNCs often wish to integrate their operations vertically to benefit from economies of scale and international specialization.

Another type of MNC is the *horizontally integrated* company. This occurs where a parent firm producing a commodity in the source country sets up a subsidiary to produce the identical product in the host country. These subsidiaries are independent units in productive capacity and are established to produce and market the parent firm's product in overseas markets. Coca-Cola and Pepsi-Cola, for example, are bottled not only in the United States but also throughout much of the world. MNCs sometimes locate production facilities overseas to avoid stiff foreign tariff barriers, which would place their products at a competitive disadvantage. Parent companies also like to locate close to their customers because differences in national preferences may require special designs for their products.

Besides making horizontal and vertical direct foreign investments, MNCs may diversify along *conglomerate* lines into nonrelated markets. For example, in recent years, the U.S. oil companies have stepped up their nonenergy acquisitions in response to anticipated declines of future investment opportunities in oil and gas. Exxon acquired a foreign copper-mining subsidiary in Chile, and Tenneco bought a French firm producing automotive exhaust systems. But the practice of making direct foreign investment to manufacture products not manufactured by the

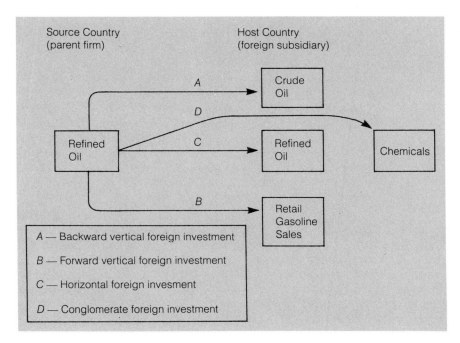

Figure 10.1 International operations of a multinational oil company.

parent company is generally rare, especially when compared with vertical investment, which is by far the most widespread form of direct investment.

A company becomes a multinational enterprise when its management organizes its production and sales operations on a global basis. The process by which this occurs is usually gradual. The firm initially sets up a full export division consistent with its domestic sales division, marketing its products through overseas distributors. This is followed by the establishment of foreign-based subsidiaries to carry out the marketing process. The export manufacturer then undergoes a foreign production stage by way of direct investment in overseas manufacturing facilities. The internationalization process is complete when the parent firm assumes the responsibilities of planning and coordination, while its foreign subsidiary is given full operating authority.

Direct Foreign Investment Statistics

Table 10.2 summarizes the direct investment position (for example, manufacturing facilities, petroleum and mining extraction and processing) of the United States for the year 1982. The table looks at the book value of U.S. direct investment abroad and foreign direct investment in the United States. *Book value* refers to the historical value of an investment in which valuation is based on the time the investment occurred, with no adjustments for price changes. During periods of price inflation, the book value of direct investment understates the replacement value.

Table 10.2 shows that as of 1982, 20 percent of U.S. direct foreign investment was in Canada, 45.1 percent in Europe, 3.1 percent in Japan, and the rest was spread throughout the rest of the world. As for foreign direct investment in the

Table 10.2   Direct Investment by Countries, 1982 (book value, billions of dollars)

| Countries | U.S. Direct Investment Abroad | | Foreign Direct Investment in U.S. | |
	Amount (billions of dollars)	Percent	Amount (billions of dollars)	Percent
Canada	44.5	20.0	9.8	9.6
Europe	99.9	45.1	68.5	67.3
Japan	6.9	3.1	8.7	8.6
Other	70.0	31.8	13.0	14.5
Total	221.3	100.0	101.8	100.0

Source: U.S. Department of Commerce, *Survey of Current Business*, August 1983.

United States, 9.6 percent was from Canada, 67.3 percent was from Europe, 8.6 percent was from Japan, the remainder coming from the rest of the world. The table also suggests that for 1982, the total U.S. direct investment abroad was more than two times larger than the amount of foreign direct investment in the United States.

Table 10.3 contains information on direct investment by industry. In 1982, manufacturing was the most important area in which direct investment occurred for U.S. residents abroad as well as for foreigners in the United States. Americans also invested a lot in petroleum. Foreign direct investments in U.S. trade and petroleum sectors also reached considerable levels in 1982.

Given the assumption that investors attempt to maximize the rate of return on their wealth, we would expect investment to flow from sectors of low return to sectors of high return. Table 10.4 shows the rates of return on U.S. direct investment abroad for 1982. The fact that rates of return on investments in developing countries exceed those on investments in industrial countries in part reflects the political risks and fears of expropriation often associated with the developing countries. U.S. direct investment in "other industries" has yielded higher rates of return

than for manufacturing investments, largely because this category includes extractive industries, which have traditionally been quite profitable.

Table 10.3   Direct Investment by Industries, 1982 (book value, billions of dollars)

	Amount	Percent
U.S. direct investment abroad		
Petroleum	55.7	25.2
Manufacturing	90.7	41.0
Other*	74.9	33.8
All industries	221.3	100.0
Foreign direct investment in U.S.		
Petroleum	20.5	20.1
Manufacturing	32.2	31.6
Trade	20.6	20.2
Insurance	6.5	6.4
Other	22.0	21.7
All industries	101.8	100.0

Source: U.S. Department of Commerce, *Survey of Current Business*, August 1983.
*Includes such industries as mining and smelting, transportation, communications, public utilities, trade, finance, and insurance.

Table 10.4   Percentage Rates of Return on U.S. Direct
Investment Abroad, 1982*

	Developed Countries (percent)	Developing Countries (percent)	All Countries (percent)
Petroleum	14.0	32.7	19.3
Manufacturing	6.0	4.5	5.7
Other industries	7.4	14.7	9.3
All industries	8.2	15.8	10.2

Source: U.S. Department of Commerce, *Survey of Current Business*, August 1983.
*The rate of return equals earnings divided by the average of the beginning-of-year and end-of-year
investment positions at book value.

Motives for Direct Foreign Investment

New MNCs do not just haphazardly pop up in foreign nations. With the exception of the extractive industries, MNCs develop because of conscious planning by corporate managers. Both economic theory and empirical studies support the notion that direct foreign investment is conducted in terms of anticipated future profits. It is generally assumed that investment flows from regions of low anticipated profit to high anticipated profit, after allowing for risk. Although expected profits may ultimately explain the process of direct foreign investment, corporate management may emphasize a variety of other factors when asked about their investment motives. These factors include market demand conditions, trade restrictions, investment regulations, and labor cost advantages. All of these factors have a bearing on cost and revenue conditions and hence on the level of profit.[2]

Demand Factors

Perhaps the most important motive for investing abroad is the search for new sources of profit. Some MNCs set up overseas subsidiaries to tap foreign markets that cannot be maintained adequately by export products. This sometimes occurs in response to dissatisfaction over distribution techniques abroad. Consequently, a firm may set up a foreign marketing division, and later, manufacturing facilities. This incentive may be particularly strong when it is realized that local taste and design differences exist. A close familiarity with local conditions is of utmost importance to a successful marketing program.

The location of foreign manufacturing facilities may also be influenced by the fact that some parent firms find their productive capacity already sufficient to meet domestic demands. If they wish to enjoy growth rates that exceed the expansion of domestic demand, they must either export or establish foreign production operations. General Motors, for example, has felt that the markets of such countries as Britain, France, and Brazil are strong enough to permit the survival of GM manufacturing subsidiaries. But Boeing Aircraft has centralized its manufacturing operations in the United States and exports abroad, because an efficient production plant for jet planes is a large investment relative to the size of most foreign markets.

Market competition also may influence a firm's decision to set up foreign facilities. Corporate strategies may be defensive in nature, as they are directed at preserving market shares from actual or potential competition. The most certain method of preventing foreign competition from becoming a strong force is to acquire foreign business firms. For the United States, the 1960s and early 1970s witnessed a tremendous surge of acquisition of foreign firms. Approximately half of the foreign subsidiaries operated by U.S. multinational firms were originally acquired by the purchase of already existing concerns during this erea. Once again, General Motors exemplifies this practice, purchasing and setting up auto producers around the globe. General Motors has been quite successful in gaining control of many larger foreign-made models, including Monarch (GM Canada) and Opel (GM West Germany). It did not acquire smaller-model firms such as Toyota, Datsun, Fiat, and Volkswagen, all of which have become significant competitors for General Motors.

Cost Factors

MNCs are also influenced by the desire to increase profit levels through reductions in production costs. Such cost-reducing direct foreign investments may take a number of forms. The pursuit of essential raw materials may underlie a firm's intent to go multinational. This is particularly true of the extractive industries and certain agricultural commodities. United Fruit, for example, has established banana-producing facilities in the Honduras to take advantage of the natural trade advantages afforded by the weather and growing conditions. Similar types of natural trade advantages explain why Anaconda has set up mining operations in Bolivia and why Shell produces and refines oil in Indonesia. Natural supply advantages such as resource endowments or climatic conditions may indeed influence a firm's decision to invest abroad.

Another factor explaining multinational investment involves costs other than material inputs, notably labor. Labor costs as well as other production costs tend to differ among national economies. International corporations may be able to hold costs down by locating part or all of their productive facilities abroad. Many American electronic firms, for instance, have had their products either completely produced or at least assembled abroad to take advantage of cheap foreign labor. Remember, however, the mere fact that the United States may pay higher wage rates than those prevailing abroad does not necessarily indicate higher costs. High wages may be due to the fact that American workers are more productive than their foreign counterparts. Only when high U.S. wages are not offset by superior U.S. labor productivity will foreign labor become relatively more attractive.

Government policies may also lead to direct foreign investment. Some nations attempting to lure foreign manufacturers to set up employment generating facilities in their countries might grant subsidies such as preferential tax treatment or free factory buildings to the MNCs. More commonly, the desire to circumvent import tariff barriers may have an impact on direct investment. The very high tariffs that Brazil levies on auto imports means that foreign auto producers wishing to sell in the Brazilian market must locate production facilities in that country. Another example is the response of U.S. business to the formation of the EEC, which placed common external tariffs against outsiders, whereas trade barriers among member countries were reduced. U.S. companies were induced to circumvent these barriers by setting up subsidiaries in the member countries. Another example is Japanese firms that apparently located additional auto assembly plants in the United States in the early 1980s to diffuse mounting protectionist pressures.

Direct Investment Versus Licensing

If a firm is to engage successfully in international business, it must enjoy a cost advantage over competitors. The source of this advantage may be access to superior factor inputs, more capable management, or superior production techniques. Even if a firm does have a competitive advantage over foreign producers, it faces the question of whether production should occur at home for export abroad or whether foreign manufacturing facilities should be set up. The most important factors that underlie this decision are the following: (1) import tariff structures, (2) the size of the foreign market in relation to the firm's most efficient plant size, (3) comparative labor productivities and wage levels, and (4) the amount of capital used in the production process.

Should the firm wish to enter overseas markets by way of foreign production, it must decide whether it is best to set up the overseas operations through direct foreign investment (where the parent organization builds a new foreign subsidiary or purchases a substantial interest in a local producer) or by extending licenses or franchises to local firms to produce its goods. In Great Britain, there are Kentucky Fried Chicken establishments that are owned and run by local residents. The parent organization merely provides its name and operating procedures in return for royalties or fees paid by the local establishments. Although licensing is widely used in practice, it presupposes that local firms are capable of adapting their operations to the producion process or technology of the parent organization.

The decision to set up foreign operations through direct investment or licensing hinges on several determinants: (1) the extent to which the production process uses capital, (2) the size of the foreign market, and (3) the fixed costs that the parent organization must bear when establishing a foreign subsidiary. Figure 10.2 portrays the hypothetical cost schedules of General Motors, which is assumed to face the choice of establishing an overseas automobile manufacturing subsidiary versus extending a franchise to a local producer.[3] Curve AVC_{GM} represents the average variable (production) costs that General

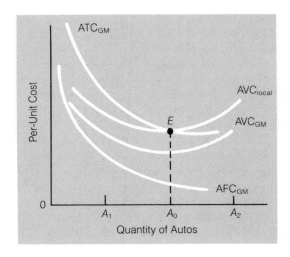

Figure 10.2   The choice between direct investment and licensing.

Motors would face by manufacturing automobiles overseas, and AVC_{local} represents the average variable costs of a local producer. Besides facing variable costs, any GM decision to establish a foreign manufacturing subsidiary would entail additional fixed costs. These would include expenses of coordinating the subsidiary with the parent organization and the sunk costs of assessing the market potential of the foreign country. Curve AFC_{GM} depicts GM's fixed costs per unit of output. The total unit costs that General Motors faces when establishing a foreign subsidiary is given by ATC_{GM}.

Even though General Motors is assumed to have lower variable costs than the local producer at each output level, General Motors must absorb the additional fixed costs of doing business overseas. Comparing ATC_{GM} with AVC_{local}, for small foreign markets (output less than A_0), the local firm has an absolute cost advantage over General Motors. Licensing foreign producers to manufacture autos in this case might be a viable alternative for General Motors. But if the foreign market were quite large (greater than A_0),

General Motors would have an absolute cost advantage and would likely invest in overseas manufacturing plants.

The precise location of the minimum output level where General Motors begins to enjoy an absolute cost advantage over foreign competition (A_0 in the figure) is influenced by several factors. One determinant is the degree to which capital is used in the production process. To the extent that production is capital intensive and General Motors can acquire capital at a lower cost than that paid by foreign auto producers, the variable cost advantage of General Motors would be greater. This would neutralize the influence of GM's fixed cost disadvantage at a lower level of output. The amount of GM's fixed costs also has a bearing on this minimum output level. Smaller fixed costs would lower GM's average total costs, again resulting in a smaller output where General Motors would first begin to have an absolute cost advantage.

International business decisions are influenced by such factors as production costs, fixed costs of locating overseas, the importance of labor and capital in the production process, and the size of the foreign market. Another factor that determines international business decisions is the element of risk and uncertainty. Management is constantly concerned with possible reactions to competitors' currency devaluations, changes of relative prices, and expropriation possibilities. Because these factors may affect the profitability of conducting business overseas, they also must be incorporated into international business decisions.

MNCs as a Source of Conflict

The advocates of MNCs often point out the benefits these corporations can provide for the countries they affect, including both the source country where the parent organization is located and the host country where subsidiary firms are established. Benefits allegedly exist in the forms of additional levels of investment and capital, creation of new jobs, and development of technologies and production processes. But critics contend that MNCs often create restraints of trade and conflict with national economic and political objectives and have adverse effects on a country's balance of payments. The differences between these arguments perhaps explain why some countries frown on direct investment, while others welcome it. This section examines some of the more controversial issues involving the multinationals. The frame of reference is the American MNC, although the same issues apply no matter where the parent organization is based.[4]

Employment

One of the most hotly debated issues surrounding the MNC is its effects on employment in both the host and source countries. MNCs often contend that their direct foreign investment yields favorable benefits to the labor force of the recipient country. Setting up a new multinational automobile manufacturing plant in Canada creates more jobs for Canadian workers. But the MNCs' effect on jobs varies from firm to firm. One source of controversy arises when the direct investment spending of foreign-based MNCs is used to purchase already existing local firms rather than to establish new firms. In this case, the investment spending may not result in additional production capacity, nor may it have noticeable effects on employment in the host country. Another problem arises when MNCs bring in foreign managers and other top executives to run the subsidiary in the host country. The U.S. oil firms locating in Saudi Arabia have found the Saudis increasingly demanding that their own people be employed in higher-level positions.

As for the source country, the issues of runaway jobs and cheap foreign labor are of vital concern to home workers. Although American tourists in Canada, Great Britain, and West Germany might appreciate the large number of U.S. MNCs located there, American labor unions visualize this as lost jobs for their workers. Because labor unions are confined to individual countries, the multinational nature of these firms permits them to escape much of the collective bargaining influence of domestic unions. It is also pointed out that MNCs can seek out those countries where unions have minimal market power. However, MNC proponents challenge these arguments on several grounds. Consistent with the statistics of Table 10.2, they argue that most U.S. direct investment has occurred in Western Europe and Canada where wages have been relatively high.

The ultimate impact that MNCs have on employment in the host and source countries in part seems to depend on the time scale. In the short run, the source country will likely experience an employment decline when production is shifted overseas. But other industries in the source country may over time find foreign sales rising. This is because foreign labor is a consumer in addition to a producer, and tends to purchase more as employment and income increase owing to increasing investment levels. Perhaps the main source of controversy stems from the fact that the MNCs are involved in rapid changes in technology and in the transmission of productive enterprise to host countries. Although such efforts may in the long run promote the global welfare, the potential short-run adjustment problems facing source-country labor cannot be ignored.

National Sovereignty

Another controversial issue on the conduct of MNCs is their effect on the economic and political policies of their host and source governments. There is a suspicion in many nations that the presence of MNCs in a given country results in a loss of its national sovereignty. For example, MNCs may resist government attempts to redistribute national income throughout its society through taxation. By using accounting techniques that shift profits overseas, an MNC might evade taxes of a host country. An MNC could accomplish this by pricing its goods from its subsidiaries in nations with modest tax rates to reduce profits on its operations in a high-tax country where most of its business actually takes place.

The political influence of MNCs is also questioned by many, as illustrated by the case of Chile. For years, American business firms had pursued direct investments in Chile, largely in copper mining. When Salvador Allende, an avowed Marxist, was in the process of winning the presidency, he was opposed by American business firms who feared their Chilean operations would be expropriated by the host government. International Telephone and Telegraph tried to prevent the election of Allende and attempted to promote civil disturbances that would lead to Allende's loss of power. Another case of MNCs meddling in host country affairs is that of United Brands, the multinational firm engaged in food product sales. In 1974, the company paid a $1.25 million bribe to the president of Honduras in return for an export tax reduction applied to bananas. When the payoff was revealed, the president was removed from office.

There are other areas of controversy. Suppose a Canadian subsidiary of a U.S.-based MNC conducts trade with a communist country. Should U.S. policy makers outlaw such activities? The Canadian subsidiary may be pressured by the parent organization to comply with U.S. foreign policy. During international crises, MNCs may rapidly move funds from one financial center to another to avoid losses (make profit) from changes in exchange rates. This conduct makes it difficult for national governments to stabilize their economies. Finally, U.S. policy makers have become increasingly suspicious over the expanding investment by Arab oil ministers in American business and financial institutions, fearing that Arabs on the board of directors might have sufficient voting power to determine the course of business activity of a major corporation.

In a world where national economies are interdependent and factors of production are mobile, the possible loss of national sovereignty is often viewed as a necessary cost whenever direct investment results in control of foreign production facilities. Whether the welfare gains accruing from the international division of labor and specialization outweigh the potential diminution of national independence involves value judgments by policy makers and interested citizens.

Balance of Payments

The United States offers a good example of how a multinational firm can affect a country's balance of payments. In brief, the balance of payments is an account of the value of goods and services, capital movements including direct foreign investment, and other items that flow into or out of a country. Items that make a positive contribution to a country's payments position include exports of goods and services and capital inflows (that is, foreign investment entering the home country), whereas the opposite flows would weaken the payments position. At first glance, we might conclude that when U.S. MNCs make direct foreign investments, it represents an outflow of capital from the United States and hence a negative factor on the U.S. payments position. Although this view may be true in the short run, it ignores the positive effects on trade flows and earnings that direct investment provides in the long run.

When a U.S. multinational firm sets up a subsidiary overseas, it generally purchases U.S. capital equipment and materials needed for running the subsidiary. Once in operation, the subsidiary tends to purchase additional capital equipment and other material inputs from the United States. Both of these factors stimulate U.S. exports, strengthening its payments position.

Another long-run impact that U.S. direct foreign investment has on its balance of payments is the return inflow of income that overseas operations generate. Table 10.5 summarizes U.S. direct investments abroad and inflow of income from the direct investments for selected years. Such income includes earnings of overseas affiliates, interest and dividends, and fees and royalties. These items generate inflows of revenues for the economy and strengthen the balance-of-payments position.

How long does it take for a dollar of new U.S. direct foreign investment to generate offsetting return flows of income? Although empirical studies have not furnished conclusive evidence on this issue, some have estimated that receipts from new investment overseas will pay for the initial negative effect on the balance of payments within 5 to 10 years. The direct investment of MNCs also has an effect on the payments position of host countries. An inflow of direct investment tends initially to benefit the host country's

Table 10.5   Receipts of Income from U.S. Direct Investments Abroad

Year	U.S. Direct Investments Abroad (billions of dollars)	Total Income (billions of dollars)
1972	89.9	8.5
1974	110.1	14.4
1976	136.4	14.8
1978	162.7	25.5
1980	215.5	37.1
1982	221.3	22.9

Source: U.S. Department of Commerce, *Survey of Current Business*, various issues.

balance of payments. As the subsidiary firm repatriates earnings back to the parent country, the payments position of the host country may weaken over the long run.

MNC Taxation

One of the most controversial issues involving MNCs for U.S. policy makers is the taxation of income stemming from direct foreign investment. Labor unions and other groups often contend that U.S. tax laws provide a disincentive to invest at home. When the U.S. Senate conducted its investigation of the U.S. oil companies in response to the energy shortage, it found that an average U.S. oil firm pays only about 5 percent of its total taxable income as federal income taxes, compared with a 48 percent maximum corporate tax rate. Such reductions in tax liability are largely due to the tax concessions offered by the U.S. government on direct foreign investment. These concessions entail (1) foreign tax credits and (2) tax deferrals.

According to U.S. tax law, an MNC headquartered in the United States is permitted *credits* on its U.S. income tax liabilities in an amount equal to its income taxes paid to foreign governments. Assuming a Canadian subsidiary earns $100,000 taxable income and that Canada's income tax rate is 25 percent, it would pay the Canadian government $25,000. But if that income were applied to the parent organization in the United States, the tax bill to the U.S. government would be $48,000, given an income tax rate of 48 percent. Under the tax credit system, the parent organization would pay the U.S. government $23,000 ($48,000 − $25,000 = $23,000). The rationale of the foreign tax credit is to allow MNCs headquartered in the United States to avoid double taxation, whereby the identical income would be subject to comparable taxes in two countries. The foreign tax credit is designed to prevent the combined tax rates of the foreign

host and domestic source governments from exceeding the higher of the two national rates. In this example, should Canada's income tax rate be 48 percent, the parent organization would not pay any taxes in the United States on the income of its Canadian subsidiary.

American-based MNCs also enjoy a *tax deferral* advantage given by U.S. tax laws. The parent firm has the option of deferring U.S. taxes paid on its foreign subsidiary income as long as that income is retained overseas rather than repatriated to the United States. This system amounts to an interest-free loan extended by the U.S. government to the parent firm for as long as the income is maintained abroad. Retained earnings of an overseas subsidiary can be reinvested abroad without being subject to American taxes. No similar provisions apply to domestic investments. Such discriminatory tax treatment encourages foreign direct investment over domestic investment.

U.S. Regulation of Multinational Enterprise

Although multinational enterprise is no new invention, it has become increasingly prominent in the post–World War II era. It has also become more and more controversial for both host and source countries. In efforts to regulate the activities of MNCs, national governments have often adopted controls that regulate the international movement of capital, enterprise, and technology. For the United States, regulating the MNC has largely evolved around its effects on the balance of payments, employment levels, antitrust policy, and taxation. Although policies have been enacted that affect various aspects of MNC behavior, there is still no comprehensive U.S. government policy toward multinationals. This section reviews some of the U.S. policies toward MNCs.

Investment Controls

During the 1960s, there was a popular notion that Europe was becoming "Americanized" by U.S. multinationals. In the United States, official concern was focused on the adverse balance-of-payments effects stemming from the financial outflows associated with U.S. direct investment abroad.

In 1965, the U.S. government enacted voluntary direct investment controls that called on the business community to reduce the financial outflows associated with overseas investment, while expanding exports and the remittance of earnings abroad. The program emphasized the benefits of financing overseas investments through foreign borrowing. Investment curbs were to be placed on foreign investment in industrialized countries, while the U.S. government still promoted direct investment in the less-developed countries. In 1968, U.S. controls on direct investment abroad became mandatory when the Nixon administration tightened up on permitted levels of investment outflows in conjunction with the worsening balance-of-payments deficit of the United States. The restrictions lasted until 1974, when the entire set of U.S. investment controls was lifted after the flood of U.S. direct investment abroad had eased and foreigners were investing more and more in the United States.

Today, the U.S. government influences foreign investment flows by entering into pacts specifying the rights of American investors in given foreign countries. Provisions often relate to property ownership and the right to conduct business abroad.

Tax Law Revisions

In the United States, there has been strong opposition to multinational enterprises by organized labor. Labor's concern rests on the belief that when a U.S.-based firm transfers production to its overseas subsidiaries, exports from the United States become displaced and American workers become unemployed. During the early 1970s, the American Federation of Labor and Congress of Industrial Organizations (AFL-CIO) urged the U.S. Congress to enact programs that would place limits on both U.S. imports and U.S. direct foreign investment. In response to protectionist sentiment, in 1971, Representative Burke and Senator Hartke presented before Congress a bill known as the Foreign Trade and Investment Act of 1972, commonly referred to as the Burke-Hartke bill. The bill called for restrictions on U.S. imports as well as curbs on U.S. direct foreign investment. The bill also proposed the elimination of the foreign tax credit in its entirety and the requirement that all retained earnings of American-controlled foreign subsidiaries be subject to current taxation on the basis that they represent income to their U.S. stockholders.

The Burke-Hartke bill was never passed by Congress, largely because its highly restrictive provisions affected a significant portion of U.S. trade and investment flows. Instead, Congress passed the Trade Act of 1974, a more selective and less restrictive measure. Although efforts to terminate the tax credit and tax deferral features of the U.S. tax laws have not been successful, the taxation of foreign-earned income continues to be a controversial issue facing the president and Congress alike.

Antitrust Policy

According to U.S. antitrust policy, competition is in itself desirable. Antitrust enforcement attempts to regulate the structure of a market and the conduct of business to create a competitive environment that will best promote the interests of society. The Sherman Act of 1890 and the Clayton Act of 1914 are our major antitrust laws. They forbid policies whereby single firms can restrain trade and lessen competition, in addition to joint actions by firms that attempt to monopolize a market.

U.S. antitrust laws are currently applied to firms operating domestically within the United States and U.S.-based firms with international operations. The logic of extending the coverage of antitrust enforcement to the multinationals is that business conduct outside the United States can have anticompetitive effects on U.S. markets and restrain trade flows. In recent years, U.S. firms have been prevented from acquiring certain foreign companies and entering into formal agreements to divide sales territories and fix prices with partially owned foreign subsidiaries.

Application of antitrust policy is difficult to carry out. Part of the problem is that multinationals conduct business in more than one country, sometimes through small local subsidiaries in foreign countries. However, laws pertaining to the public disclosure of financial information generally apply to large domestic corporations. The multinational organization can thus circumvent much of the thrust of these laws. At the international level, the antitrust views of, say, the United States and West Germany or Japan may differ. Standard international antitrust laws would be difficult to enact.

International Trade Theory and Multinational Enterprise

Perhaps the main explanation of the development of multinational firms lies in the strategies of corporate management. The reasons for engaging in international business can be outlined in terms of the comparative advantage principle. Corporate managers see advantages they can exploit in the forms of access to factor inputs, new technologies and products, and managerial know-how. Firms establish overseas subsidiaries largely because profit prospects are best enhanced by foreign production. From a trade

theory perspective, the multinational enterprise analysis is fundamentally in agreement with the predictions of the comparative advantage principle. Both approaches contend that a given commodity will be produced in the low-cost country. The major difference between the multinational firm analysis and the conventional trade model is that the former stresses the international movement of factor inputs, whereas the latter is based on the movement of merchandise among nations.

International trade theory suggests that the aggregative welfare of both the source and host countries is enhanced when multinationals make direct foreign investments for their own benefit. The presumption is that if firms can earn a higher return on overseas investments than can be earned on those at home, resources are transferred from lower to higher productive uses, and on balance an improvement in the world allocation of resources will occur. The analysis of multinationals is essentially the same as the conventional trade theory, which rests on the movement of products among nations.

In spite of the basic agreement between conventional trade theory and the multinational firm analysis, there are some notable differences. The conventional model presupposes that goods are exchanged between interdependent firms on international markets at competitively determined prices. But multinationals are generally vertically integrated firms whose subsidiaries manufacture intermediate goods as well as finished goods. In a multinational organization, sales become *intrafirm* when goods are transferred from subsidiary to subsidiary. Although such sales are part of international trade, that value may be determined by factors other than a competitive pricing system.

A multinational firm involved in intrafirm sales will generally attempt to maximize overall corporate profits rather than those of any single subsidiary. In doing so, corporate management may try to hold costs down by way of *transfer*

)n goods being transferred among sub-ocated in foreign countries, for exam-ple, management might deflate prices to minimize profits on subsidiaries in high-tax countries, while inflating prices that maximize profits for subsidiaries in low-tax countries. Overall corporate tax payments would be held down. In short, the international mobility of factor inputs and the concept of transfer pricing do present conventional trade theory with additional burdens in attempting to explain a world in which multinational enterprise accounts for increasingly large portions of international trade.

Summary

1.   Today, the world economy is characterized by the international movement of factor inputs. The multinational corporation plays a central part in this process.

2.   There is no single agreed-upon definition of what constitutes a multinational corporation. Some of the most identifiable characteristics of multinationals are the following: (1) Stock ownership and management is multinational in character. (2) Corporate headquarters is far removed from where a particular activity occurs. (3) A high ratio of foreign sales to total sales exists.

3.   Multinational firms have diversified their operations along vertical, horizontal, and conglomerate lines.

4.   Among the major factors that influence decisions to conduct direct foreign investment are (1) market demand, (2) trade restrictions, (3) investment regulations, and (4) labor productivity and costs.

5.   In planning to set up overseas operations, a firm must decide on constructing (purchasing) plants abroad or extending licenses to foreign firms to produce its goods.

6.   Some of the more controversial issues involving multinational corporations are (1) employment, (2) national sovereignty, (3) balance of payments, and (4) taxation.

7.   For the United States, regulating the multinational corporation has largely evolved around (1) investment controls used for balance-of-payments purposes, (2) tax law revisions, and (3) antitrust policy.

8.   The theory of multinational enterprise essentially agrees with the predictions of the comparative advantage principle.

9.   There are major differences between the theory of multinational enterprise and conventional trade theory. The conventional model assumes that commodities are traded between independent, competitive firms. However, multinationals are often vertically integrated firms and resort to intrafirm sales. Also, multinationals may use transfer pricing to maximize overall company profits, instead of the profits of any single subsidiary.

Study Questions

1.   Multinational firms may diversify their operations along vertical, horizontal, and conglomerate lines within the host and source countries. Distinguish among these diversification approaches.

2.   What are the major foreign industries in which American firms have chosen to place direct investments? What are the major industries in the United States in which foreigners place direct investments?

3.   Why is it that the rate of return on U.S. direct investments in the developing countries often exceeds the rate of return on its investments in industrial countries?

4.   What are the most important motives behind a firm's decision to undergo direct foreign investment?

5.   What is meant by the term *multinational corporation*?

6. Under what conditions would a firm wish to enter foreign markets by way of extending licenses or franchises to local firms to produce its goods?

7. What are the major issues involving multinational firms as a source of conflict for source and host countries?

8. What methods has the U.S. government used in regulating the conduct of multinational firms?

9. Is the theory of multinational enterprise essentially consistent or inconsistent with the traditional model of comparative advantage?

Notes

1. See Richard Caves, *American Industry: Structure, Conduct, Performance* (Englewood Cliffs, N.J.: Prentice-Hall, 1977), chap. 3.

2. See Stefan H. Robock and Kenneth Simmonds, *International Business and Multinational Enterprise* (Homewood, Ill.: Richard D. Irwin, 1973).

3. See R. Hal Mason, Robert R. Miller, and Dale R. Weigel, *The Economics of International Business* (New York: John Wiley, 1975), pp. 243–245.

4. See Martin C. Schnitzer, *Contemporary Government and Business Relations* (Chicago: Rand McNally, 1978), chaps. 8–9.

Suggestions for Further Reading

Bergsten, C. F., T. Horst, and T. Moran. *American Multinationals and American Interests*. Washington, D.C.: The Brookings Institution, 1978.

Calvet, A. L. "A Synthesis of Foreign Direct Investment and Theories of the Multinational Firm." *Journal of International Business Studies*, Spring–Summer, 1981.

Frank, I. *Foreign Enterprise in Developing Countries*. Baltimore: Johns Hopkins Press, 1980.

Parry, T. G. *The Multinational Enterprise*. Greenwich, Conn.: JAI Press, 1980.

Rugman, A. M. *Inside the Multinationals*. New York: Columbia University Press, 1981.

United Nations. *Transnational Corporations in World Development*. New York, 1980.

U.S. Department of Commerce. *Survey of Current Business*. Washington, D.C.: U.S. Government Printing Office, monthly.

Vernon, R. *Sovereignty at Bay*. New York: Basic Books, 1971.

INTERNATIONAL
MONETARY
RELATIONS

11

THE BALANCE
OF PAYMENTS

Previous chapters have emphasized international trade flows and commercial policies. In this chapter, we examine the monetary aspects of international trade by considering the nature and significance of a country's balance of payments.

The Balance of Payments

Over the course of a year, the residents of one country engage in a variety of transactions with residents abroad. These include payments for goods and services, loans, investments, and gifts. To analyze the economic importance of these transactions, it is necessary to classify and aggregate them into a summary statement.

The *balance of payments* is a record of the economic transactions between the residents of one country and the rest of the world. Because the balance of payments is calculated over the course of a one-year period, it is interpreted as a *flow* concept. A main purpose of the balance of payments is to provide information about a country's international position to its government authorities. An international transaction refers to the exchange of goods, services, and assets between residents of one nation and

those abroad. But what is meant by the term *resident?* Residents include business firms, individuals, and government agencies who make the country in question their legal domicile. Although a corporation is considered to be a resident of the country in which it is incorporated, its overseas branch or subsidiary is not. Military personnel, government diplomats, tourists, and workers who temporarily emigrate are considered residents of the country in which they hold citizenship.

Double-Entry Accounting

The arrangement of international transactions into a balance-of-payments account requires that each transaction be entered as a credit or a debit. A *credit* transaction is one that results in a receipt of a payment from foreigners. A *debit* transaction is one that leads to a payment to foreigners. This distinction is clarified when we assume that transactions take place between U.S. residents and foreigners and that all payments are financed in dollars.

From the U.S. perspective, what types of transactions are credits, leading to the receipt of dollars from foreigners?

1. Merchandise exports
2. Transportation and travel receipts
3. Income received from investments abroad
4. Gifts received from foreign residents
5. Aid received from foreign governments
6. Investments in the United States by overseas residents

Conversely, the following transactions are debits from the U.S. viewpoint because they involve payments to foreigners.

1. Merchandise imports
2. Transportation and travel expenditures
3. Income paid on investments of foreigners
4. Gifts to foreign residents
5. Aid given by the U.S. government
6. Overseas investment by U.S. residents

Although we have spoken of credit transactions and debit transactions, every international transaction involves an exchange of assets and so has both a credit and a debit side. Each credit entry is balanced by a debit entry and vice versa. The recording of any international transaction therefore leads to two offsetting entries. This means that the balance of payments accounts utilize a *double-entry* bookkeeping system.

Even though the entire balance of payments by definition must numerically balance, it does not necessarily hold that any single subaccount or subaccounts of the statement must balance. For instance, merchandise exports may or may not be in balance with merchandise imports. Double-entry accounting assumes only that the total of all the entries on the left-hand side of the statement matches the total of the entries on the right-hand side. The following examples illustrate the double-entry technique.

1. IBM sells $25 million worth of computers to a West German importer. Payment is made by a bill of exchange, which increases the balances of New York banks on their Bonn correspondents. Because the export involves a transfer of American assets abroad for which payment is to be received, it is entered in the U.S. balance of payments as a credit transaction. IBM's receipt of payment held in the West German bank is classified a short-term capital movement, as the financial claims of the United States against the West German bank have increased. The entries on the U.S. balance of payments would appear as follows:

	Credits (+)	Debits (−)
Merchandise exports	$25 million	
Short-term capital movement		$25 million

2. A U.S. resident who owns bonds issued by a Japanese company receives dividend payments of $10,000. With payment, the balances owned by New York banks at their Tokyo affiliate are increased. The impact of this transaction on the U.S. balance of payments would be:

	Credits (+)	Debits (−)
Service exports	$10,000	
Short-term capital movement		$10,000

In short, double-entry accounting in balance-of-payments analysis results in the equality of total debits and credits.

Balance-of-Payments Structure

Besides classifying a country's international transactions according to the direction of payment involved, the balance of payments identifies transactions along functional lines. Balance-of-payments transactions are grouped into several categories: (1) goods and services, (2) unilateral transfers, (3) international capital movements, and (4) official settlements.

Goods and Services

The *goods and services* account of the balance of payments shows the monetary value of all of the goods and services a country exports or imports. It is not difficult to identify exports and imports of merchandise because these transactions are a measure of physical goods that cross a country's boundaries. The dollar value of exports is recorded as a plus, whereas the dollar value of imports is recorded as a minus in this account. Merchandise trade normally represents the major component of the goods and services account.

As for exports and imports of services, a variety of items are covered here. Should U.S. ships carry foreign products or should foreign tourists spend money at U.S. restaurants and motels, valuable services are being provided by U.S. residents, who must be compensated. Such services are considered exports and are recorded as plus items on the goods and services account. Conversely, when foreign ships carry U.S. products or when U.S. tourists spend money at hotels and restaurants abroad, then foreign residents are providing services that require compensation. Because U.S. residents are in effect importing these services, they are recorded as debit items. Insurance and banking services are explained in the same way.

Individuals sometimes have more difficulty understanding dividends and interest from investments, which are thought of as service exports and imports. The value to U.S. residents of investment income earned on foreign government securities of stock in foreign corporations reflects the export of the services of U.S. capital. In return for the value of the services that U.S. capital invested abroad gives foreign residents,

the U.S. investors expect payment. The value of this service rendered is taken to be a plus item on the U.S. goods and services account. In like manner, the amount of investment income paid by U.S. residents to foreigners represents the value of the services rendered by foreign capital in the United States. This results in a minus entry in the U.S. goods and services account.

Just what does a surplus (deficit) balance appearing on the U.S. goods and services account indicate? Should the goods and services account show a surplus, the United States has transferred more resources (goods and services) to foreigners than it received from them over the period of one year. Besides measuring the value of the net transfer of resources, the goods and services balance also furnishes information about the status of a country's gross national product (GNP). This is because the balance on the goods and services is defined essentially the same way as the *net export of goods and services*, which comprises part of a country's GNP.

For a country's GNP, the balance on the goods and services account can be interpreted as follows. A positive balance on the account indicates an excess of exports over imports, the difference of which must be added to the GNP. When the account is in deficit, the excess of imports over exports must be subtracted from GNP. However, should a country's exports of goods and services equal its imports, the account would have a net imbalance of zero and would not affect the status of the GNP. Therefore, depending on the relative value of exports and imports, the balance on goods and services contributes to the level of a nation's national product.

Unilateral Transfers

This balance-of-payments category deals with transactions that are one-sided, reflecting the movement of goods and services in one direction without corresponding payments in the other direction. These one-way transactions represent gifts and payments between the United States and the rest of the world. *Private transfer payments* refer to gifts made by individuals and nongovernmental institutions to foreigners. These might include a remittance from an immigrant living in the United States to relatives back home or a contribution by U.S. residents to relief funds for the underdeveloped nations. *Governmental transfers* refer to gifts or grants made by one government to foreign residents or foreign governments. The U.S. government has made transfers in the form of money and capital goods to the underdeveloped countries, military aid to foreign governments, and remittances such as retirement pensions to foreign workers who moved back home. In some cases, U.S. government transfers have represented payments associated with foreign assistance programs that could be used by foreign governments to finance trade with the United States.

Capital Transactions

Capital transactions involve the exchange of real or financial assets for money. Included are the purchase and sale of stocks and bonds, borrowing and lending, and changes in bank balances. The capital account is a record of the import or export of anything representing a change in financial claims among nations. The capital account is divided into two parts, long term and short term.

Long-term capital represents real and financial assets and liabilities having a maturity of one year or more. *Real* long-term capital, or *direct investment*, refers to the outright construction or purchase abroad of production facilities (manufacturing plants, real estate, land) by domestic residents. *Financial* or *portfolio* long-term capital refers to stocks and bonds as well as bank loans that have a maturity of one year or more. The usual explanations for long-term capital movements include profit rate differentials, the exploitation of foreign markets and raw materials, and the varying technological levels of different nations. The long-term capital account also includes any long-term loans between the U.S. government and a foreign government.

Short-term capital represents financial claims of less than one-year maturity or those payable on demand. Among the types of financial assets frequently involved in short-term capital flows are (1) commercial bank demand deposits and savings (time) deposits; (2) short-term government securities such as 90-day U.S. Treasury bills; (3) commercial paper, which refers to short-term promissory notes of large corporations; (4) bank loans; and (5) banker acceptances, which are promissory notes for which banks guarantee repayment at maturity. The great majority of short-term capital transactions represents bank loans and transfers that finance trade and long-term capital investments. Among the factors that induce people to shift such liquid funds between financial centers are interest rate differentials, political unrest, and the fear that the international value of a country's currency may change over time.

When recording capital transactions in the balance of payments, a plus sign is applied to capital inflows, a minus sign to capital outflows. A capital inflow might occur under the following circumstances: (1) U.S. liabilities to foreigners rise (should a foreign resident purchase the securities of the U.S. government). (2) Claims on foreigners decrease (should a U.S. bank receive repayment for a loan it made overseas). (3) Foreign-held assets in the U.S. rise (should foreigners purchase or build plants in the U.S.). (4) U.S. assets overseas decrease (should U.S. residents sell their foreign plants). A capital outflow would imply the opposite.

The following rule may be helpful in appreciating the fundamental difference between credit and debit transactions that make up the capital account. Any transaction that leads to the United States receiving payments from foreigners can be regarded as a plus item. Capital inflows can be likened to the export of goods and services in the balance-of-payments' current account. Conversely, any transaction that leads to foreigners receiving payment from the United States is considered a minus item. A capital outflow is thus similar in effect to the import of goods and services.

Official Settlements

Suppose the United States registers a deficit in the goods and services account, unilateral transfers account, and capital account as a group. How can this deficit be financed? The answer lies in the official settlements account. To meet the deficit, the United States must make some means of payment that is acceptable to foreigners. This might consist of gold, convertible currencies, or liquid liabilities to foreign central banks.

The *official settlements account* measures the movement of financial assets among official holders, predominantly central banks. These financial assets fall into two categories—*official reserve assets* and *liabilities to foreign official agencies*. Table 11.1 summarizes the official reserve asset position for the United States. One such asset is the stock of gold reserves held by the U.S. government. Next are convertible currencies, such as the West German mark, that are readily acceptable as payment for international transactions and can easily be exchanged for one another. Another reserve asset is the Special Drawing Right (SDR). Last is the reserve position that the United States maintains in the International Monetary Fund.

The official settlements account also includes U.S. liabilities to foreign official holders. These liabilities refer to foreign official holdings with U.S. commercial banks and official holdings of U.S. Treasury securities. Foreign governments

Table 11.1   U.S. Reserve Assets, 1983*

Type	Amount (billions of dollars)
Gold stock	11.1
Special drawing rights	5.5
Reserve positions in International Monetary Fund	9.4
Convertible foreign currencies	7.9
Total	33.9

Source: Board of Governors of the Federal Reserve System, *Federal Reserve Bulletin*, June 1983, p. A55.
*May.

often wish to hold such assets because of the interest earnings they provide. In recent years, U.S. deficits have been financed primarily by increasing official liabilities instead of transferring official reserve assets abroad.

The U.S. Balance of Payments

For the United States, the method the U.S. Department of Commerce uses in presenting balance-of-payments statistics is contained in Table 11.2. This format groups specific transactions together along functional lines to provide analysts with information about the impact of international transactions on the domestic economy. The *partial balances* published on a regular basis include the merchandise trade balance, the balance on goods and services, and the current account balance. Information about transactions in U.S. official reserve assets, as well as foreign official assets in the United States, is also given.

The *merchandise trade balance*, commonly referred to as the *trade balance* by the news media, is derived by computing the net exports (imports) in the merchandise accounts. Owing to its narrow focus on traded goods, the merchandise

Table 11.2   United States Balance of Payments, 1982
(billions of dollars)*

	Amount
Merchandise trade balance	
Exports	211.0
Imports	−247.3
Net	−36.3
Services	
Investment income, net	28.7
Military transactions, net	0.6
Other services, net	6.8
Balance on goods and services	−0.2
Remittances, pensions, and other unilateral transfers	−2.5
U.S. government grants	−5.4
Balance on current account	−8.1
U.S. assets abroad, net**	
Total	−118.3
U.S. official reserve assets	−5.0
Other U.S. government assets	−5.8
U.S. private assets	−107.5
Foreign assets in the U.S., net***	
Total	84.5
Foreign official assets	3.0
Other foreign assets	81.5
Allocations of special drawing rights (SDRs)	0
Statistical discrepancy	41.9

Source: Board of Governors of the Federal Reserve System, *Federal Reserve Bulletin*, June 1983, p. A54. See also *Economic Report of the President* (Washington, D.C.: U.S. Government Printing Office, 1983, pp. 276–277.

*Credits (+), debits (−).

**Increase/capital outflow (−).

***Increase/capital inflow (+).

trade balance offers limited policy insight. The popularity of the merchandise trade balance is largely due to its availability on a monthly basis. Merchandise trade data can be rapidly gathered and reported, whereas measuring trade in services requires time-consuming questionnaires.

As seen in Table 11.2, the United States had a merchandise trade deficit of $36.3 billion in 1982, resulting from the difference between U.S. merchandise exports ($211 billion) and U.S. merchandise imports ($247.3 billion). The United States thus was a net importer of merchandise. Table 11.3 shows the United States consistently faced merchandise trade deficits in the 1970s and early 1980s. This contrasts with the 1950s and 1960s when merchandise trade surpluses were common for the United States.

Trade deficits generally are not popular with domestic residents and policy makers because they tend to exert adverse consequences on the home country's terms of trade and employment levels, as well as on the stability of the international money markets. For the United States, concern over persistent trade deficits has often focused on their possible effects on the terms at which the United States trades with other countries. With a trade deficit, the value of the dollar may fall in international currency markets as dollar outpayments exceed dollar inpayments. Foreign currencies would become more expensive in terms of dollars, so that imports would become more costly to U.S. residents. A trade deficit that induces a decrease in the dollar's international value imposes a real cost on U.S. citizens in the form of higher import costs.

Another potentially harmful consequence of a trade deficit is its impact on local employment levels. A worsening trade balance may injure domestic labor, not only by the number of jobs lost to foreign workers who produce our imports, but also by the employment losses due to deteriorating export sales. It is no wonder that home country labor unions often raise the most vocal arguments about the evils of trade deficits for the domestic economy.

Discussion of U.S. competitiveness in merchandise trade often gives the impression that the United States has consistently performed poorly relative to other industrial countries. However, a merchandise trade deficit is a narrow concept, since goods are only part of what the world trades. Another part of trade is services. The *goods and services balance* is a better indication of the nation's international payments position. Table 11.3 also shows that in 1982, the United States generated a surplus of $36.1 billion on service transactions. Combining this surplus with the merchandise trade deficit of $36.3 billion yields a deficit on the goods and services balance of $0.2 billion for 1982. This means that the United States transferred fewer real resources (goods and services) to other countries than it received from them during 1982.

The growing importance of American trade in services is seen in Table 11.3. The United States had continuous surpluses in its services balance throughout the 1970s and 1980s. These surpluses have sometimes more than offset merchandise trade deficits, resulting in a surplus in the goods and services balance. The major contributor by far to the surplus on services is income earned by Americans on their overseas investments. But other components of service trade such as tourism, shipping, consulting, and construction have often reduced net services income.

Another balance of special interest is the *current account balance*. This balance measures the net export of goods, services, and unilateral transfers by residents of the United States in exchange for financial claims from abroad (for example, bank balances held overseas, commercial paper of foreign corporations, and official reserves). The current account balance is synonymous with net foreign investment in national income accounting. A *current account surplus* means an excess of exports over imports of goods, services, and unilateral transfers. This permits a net receipt of financial claims for U.S. residents. These funds can be used by the United States to build up its financial assets or to reduce its liabilities to the rest of the world, improving its net foreign investment position (that is, net worth vis-à-vis the rest of the world). Conversely, a *current account deficit* implies an excess of imports over exports of goods, services, and unilateral transfers. This leads to an increase in net foreign claims upon the United States. The United States becomes a net demander of funds from abroad, the demand being met through borrowing from other nations or liquidating foreign assets. The result is a worsening of the U.S. net foreign investment position.

As Table 11.2 shows, the United States had a current account deficit of $8.1 billion in 1982.

Table 11.3   U.S. Balance of Payments: Selected Accounts
(billions of dollars)

Year	Merchandise Trade Balance	Services Balance	Goods and Services Balance	Unilateral Transfers Balance	Current Account Balance
1970	2.1	1.5	3.6	−3.1	0.5
1972	−7.0	1.0*	−6.0	−3.8	−9.8
1974	−5.4	9.0	3.6	−7.2	−3.6
1976	−9.4	18.7	9.3	−5.0	4.3
1978	−34.1	23.2	−10.9	−5.1	−16.0
1980	−25.3	33.6	8.3	−6.8	1.5
1982	−36.3	36.1	−0.2	−7.9	−8.1

Source: Board of Governors of the Federal Reserve System, *Federal Reserve Bulletin*, various issues.

This meant an excess of imports over exports—of goods, services, and unilateral transfers—resulted in decreasing net foreign investment for the United States.

The U.S. current account balance in recent years has swung back and forth from deficit to surplus, as seen in Table 11.3. We should not become unduly preoccupied with the current account balance by itself, for it ignores capital account transactions. If foreigners purchase more U.S. real and financial assets in the United States (such as land, buildings, and bonds), then the United States can afford to import more goods and services from abroad. To look at one aspect of a country's international payment position without considering the others is misleading.

Taken as a whole, U.S. international transactions always balance. This means that any force leading to an increase or decrease in one balance-of-payments account sets in motion a process leading to exactly offsetting changes in the balances of other accounts. As seen in Table 11.2, in 1982, the United States had a current account deficit of $8.1 billion. Offsetting this deficit was a combined surplus of $8.1 billion in the remaining accounts, as follows: (1) U.S. assets abroad, deficit of $118.3 billion; (2) foreign assets in the United States, surplus of $84.5 billion; (3) SDR allocation, no change; (4) statistical discrepancy,[2] $41.9 billion inflow.[3]

Balance of International Indebtedness

A main feature of the U.S. balance of payments is that it measures the economic transactions of the United States over the period of one year. The balance of payments is thus a *flow* concept, applying to a given time period. But at any particular moment, a country will have a fixed stock of assets and liabilities against the rest of the world. The statement that summarizes this situation is known as the *balance of international*

indebtedness. Because the balance of international indebtedness is a record of the international position of the United States at a given point in time, it is a *stock* concept.

The U.S. balance of international indebtedness indicates the international investment position of the United States, reflecting the value of U.S. investments abroad as opposed to foreign investments in the United States.[4] The United States is considered a *net creditor* to the rest of the world when U.S. claims on foreigners exceed foreign claims on the United States at a particular time. When the reverse occurs, the United States assumes a *net debtor* position. The history of the U.S. balance of international indebtedness reveals that it was not until World War I that the United States enjoyed a net creditor position. Since then, the U.S. balance of international indebtedness has been positive, with rare exception. The terms *net creditor* and *net debtor* in themselves are not particularly meaningful. We need additional information about the specific types of claims and liabilities under consideration. The balance of international indebtedness therefore looks at the short-term and long-term investment positions of both the private and governmental sectors of the economy. The U.S. balance of international indebtedness is summarized in Table 11.4

Of what use is the balance of international indebtedness? Perhaps of greatest significance is that it breaks down international investment holdings into several categories so that policy implications can be drawn from each separate category about the *liquidity status* of the country. For the short-term investment position, the strategic factor is the amount of short-term liabilities (bank deposits and governmental securities) held by foreigners. This is because these holdings potentially can be withdrawn at very short notice by foreigners, resulting in a disruption of domestic financial markets. The balance of official monetary holdings is also significant. Assume this balance to be negative from the U.S.

Table 11.4   United States Balance of International Indebtedness,
1970–1982 (billions of dollars)*

Type of Investment	1970	1974	1978	1982
U.S. assets abroad	165.5	256.2	447.9	834.2
U.S. government assets	46.6	54.2	14.7	107.9
U.S. private assets	118.8	202.0	433.2	726.3
Foreign assets in the United States	106.8	197.4	371.6	665.5
Foreign official assets	26.1	80.3	173.0	189.2
Other foreign assets	80.7	117.1	198.6	476.3
Net international investment position of the United States	58.7	58.8	76.2	168.7

Source: U.S. Department of Commerce, *Survey of Current Business*, August, 1983, p. 44.
*Figures may not add because of rounding.

viewpoint. Should foreign monetary authorities decide to liquidate their holdings of U.S. government securities and have them converted into official reserve assets, the financial strength of the dollar would be reduced. As for a country's long-term investment position, it is of less importance for the U.S. liquidity position because long-term investments generally respond to basic economic trends and are not subject to erratic withdrawals.

The balance of international indebtedness does provide a useful breakdown of a country's investment position at a particular time, but this statement suffers from a major weakness involving the valuation of a country's assets. Should an asset be carried at its historical value (original cost minus depreciation) or its current market value? Depending on the method employed, an asset's stated value can vary considerably. This valuation problem can be seen in the U.S. balance of international indebtedness, which has traditionally undervalued U.S. foreign asset holdings. Although U.S. portfolio investments are carried at current market value, its direct investments have been carried at historical value, an inaccurate measure of their market value as going concerns. In spite of this valuation problem, the balance of international indebtedness is a useful analytical tool. By breaking down a country's investment position into categories of outstanding claims and liabilities, attention can be focused on a country's overall liquidity status.

Summary

1.   The balance of payments is a record of a country's economic transactions with other nations in the world for a given year. A credit transaction is one that results in a receipt of payments from foreigners, whereas a debit transaction leads to a payment abroad. Owing to double-entry bookkeeping, a country's balance of payments will balance.

2.   From a functional viewpoint, the balance of payments identifies economic transactions as (1) goods and services, (2) unilateral transfers, (3) international capital movements, and (4) official settlements.

3.   The balance on goods and services is important to policy makers, as it indicates the net

transfer of real resources overseas. It also measures the extent to which a country's exports and imports are part of its gross national product.

4. The capital account of the balance of payments shows the international movement of loans and investments. Portfolio investments refer to stocks, bonds, and other financial instruments. Direct investment includes the purchase or construction of a foreign subsidiary. Capital flows can be either long term or short term. Capital inflows (outflows) are analagous to exports (imports) of goods and services, as they result in the receipt (payment) of funds from (to) other countries.

5. Official reserves consist of a country's financial assets: (1) monetary gold holdings, (2) convertible currencies, (3) Special Drawing Rights, and (4) drawing positions on the International Monetary Fund.

6. The current method employed by the Department of Commerce in presenting the U.S. international payments position makes use of a functional format emphasizing the following *partial* balances: (1) merchandise trade balance, (2) balance on goods and services, and (3) current account balance.

7. The international investment position of the United States at a particular time is measured by the balance of international indebtedness. Unlike the balance of payments, which is a flow concept, the balance of international indebtedness is a stock concept.

Study Questions

1. What is meant by the balance of payments?

2. What economic transactions give rise to the receipt of dollars from foreigners? What transactions give rise to payments to foreigners?

3. Why is it that the balance-of-payments statement balances?

4. From a functional viewpoint, a nation's balance of payments can be grouped into several categories. What are these categories?

5. Distinguish between real investment and portfolio investment.

6. What are some examples of short-term capital? How about long-term capital?

7. What financial assets are categorized as official reserve assets for the United States?

8. What is the meaning of a surplus (deficit) on the (1) merchandise trade balance, (2) goods and services balance, and (3) current account balance?

9. Why has the goods and services balance sometimes shown a surplus, while the merchandise trade balance shows a deficit?

10. What does the balance of international indebtedness measure? How does this statement differ from the balance of payments?

Notes

1. See Norman S. Fieleke, *What Is the Balance of Payments?* (Boston: Federal Reserve Bank of Boston, 1976).

2. Statistical discrepancy refers to errors and omissions in reported transactions. It is used as a residual item to ensure that total credits equal total debits in the balance of payments. Statistical discrepancy includes balance-of-payments components for which statistics are least reliable (for example, short-term financial claims).

3. The 1982 statistical discrepancy in the U.S. balance of payments was large by any standard. Being a positive amount (that is, not having a negative sign), statistical discrepancy suggested that the United States experienced unrecorded inflows of $41.9 billion. This reflected the desire on the part of foreigners to acquire dollar-denominated financial assets,

which was probably owing to the strength of the dollar in foreign exchange markets, high interest rates in the United States, and the economic and political problems in other countries.

4. As it applies to the balance of international indebtedness, the term *investment* is the stock counterpart of the flow concept net foreign investment in national income accounting.

Westerfield, J. M. "A Lower Profile for the U.S. Balance of Payments." *Business Review*, Federal Reserve Bank of Philadelphia, November–December 1976.

U.S. Department of Commerce. *Survey of Current Business*. Washington, D.C.: U.S. Government Printing Office, monthly.

Suggestions for Further Reading

Congdon, T. "A New Approach to the Balance of Payments." *Lloyds Bank Review*, October 1982.

Fieleke, N. S. *What Is the Balance of Payments?* Boston: Federal Reserve Bank of Boston, 1976.

International Monetary Fund. *Balance of Payments Yearbook*. Washington, D.C.: International Monetary Fund, annual.

Kemp, D. S. "Balance-of-Payments Concepts—What Do They Really Mean?" *Review*, Federal Reserve Bank of St. Louis, July 1975.

Kuwayama, P. M. "Measuring the U.S. Balance of Payments." *Monthly Review*, Federal Reserve Bank of New York, August 1975.

Lamfalussy, A. "Why Does the Current Account Matter?" *De Economist*, 130, no. 2, 1982.

Meade, J. E. *The Balance of Payments*. London: Oxford University Press, 1951.

"Report on the Advisory Committee on the Presentation of Balance of Payments Statistics." *Survey of Current Business*, June 1976.

Stern, R. M., et al. *The Presentation of the U.S. Balance of Payments*. Essays in International Finance, no. 123. Princeton, N.J.: Princeton University Press, 1977.

Wallich, H. C., and K. Friedrich. "Cyclical Patterns in the U.S. Balance of Payments." *Economies et Sociétés*, April–May 1982.

12

FOREIGN EXCHANGE

Among the factors that make international economics a distinct subject is the existence of different national monetary units of account. In the United States, prices and money are measured in terms of the dollar. The Deutsche mark represents Germany's unit of account, whereas the franc and yen signify the units of account of France and Japan, respectively. A typical international transaction requires two distinct purchases. First, the foreign currency is bought; second, the foreign currency is used to facilitate the international transaction. For example, before an American importer can purchase commodities from, say, a Japanese exporter, he must first purchase yen to meet his international obligation. Making international payments consequently requires some institutional arrangements that permit an efficient mechanism by which monetary claims can be settled with a minimum of inconvenience to both parties. Such a mechanism exists in the form of the foreign exchange market.

Foreign Exchange Market

The *foreign exchange market* refers to the organizational setting within which individuals, business firms, and banks buy and sell foreign currencies and other debt instruments.[1] Unlike stock or commodity exchanges, the foreign exchange market is not an organized structure. It has no centralized meeting place and no formal requirements for participation. Nor is the foreign exchange market limited to any one country. For any currency, such as the U.S. dollar, the foreign exchange market consists of all locations where dollars are bought and sold for other national currencies. The two largest foreign exchange markets in the world are located in New York and London. A dozen or so other market centers also exist around the world, such as Paris and Zurich. Trading is done over the telephone or through the telex.

A typical foreign exchange market, like that in New York, is organized at three levels: (1) the transactions between commercial banks and their commercial customers, who are the ultimate demanders and suppliers of foreign exchange; (2) the domestic interbank foreign exchange market conducted through brokers; and (3) active trading in foreign exchange by New York banks with banks overseas. These three tiers combined constitute the New York foreign exchange market.

Exporters, importers, investors, and tourists buy and sell foreign exchange from and to commercial banks rather than each other. In the United States, about a dozen banks in New York and a dozen banks located in other American

217

cities maintain foreign exchange inventories in the form of working balances with foreign banks to meet the needs of their customers. Those banks that do not trade in foreign exchange can accommodate customers through a correspondent trading bank. The major trading banks thus form the basis of the foreign exchange market. Each bank is a clearinghouse where users and suppliers of foreign exchange are brought together. Not only do these banks deal at the retail level with their customers (corporations and exporters), but they also buy and sell foreign exchange at the wholesale level with other banks. This is because banks typically do not want to maintain excessive foreign exchange holdings.

The major trading banks generally do not deal directly with each other, but instead use the services of foreign exchange brokers. The basic purpose of such brokers is to permit the trading banks to maintain desired foreign exchange balances. If a bank finds that at a particular moment it does not have the proper foreign exchange balances, it can turn to a broker to buy additional foreign currency or sell the surplus. Brokers thus provide a wholesale, interbank market where trading banks can buy and sell foreign exchange. Brokers are paid a commission for their services by the selling bank. In the United States, there are about eight foreign exchange brokers located in New York that serve as intermediaries for trading banks.

The third tier of the foreign exchange market consists of the transactions between the trading banks and their overseas branches or foreign correspondents. Although several dozen U.S. banks trade in foreign exchange, it is the major New York banks that usually carry out transactions with foreign banks. The other inland trading banks maintain correspondent relationships with the New York banks so they can meet their foreign exchange needs. Trading with foreign banks permits the matching of supply and demand of foreign exchange in the New York market. These international transactions are carried on primarily by telephone but also by cable, telegraph, and the mail.

Instruments of Foreign Exchange

The term *foreign exchange* refers to a financial asset that involves a cash claim held by a resident of one country against a resident of another country. Foreign exchange is not a homogeneous product, since several short-term credit instruments can be classified as foreign exchange. Among the most important instruments that banks use in dealing in the foreign exchange market are cable transfers and bills of exchange.[2]

Cable Transfers

The most important instrument of foreign exchange is currently the cable (telegraphic) transfer. A *cable transfer* is an order sent by a bank, say in New York, to its foreign correspondent in Paris, to pay out a specific amount in francs to a designated person or account. For example, when a U.S. importer purchases francs from his New York bank, this bank would cable its foreign correspondent in Paris to transfer the francs from its account to the exporter's account. Similarly, a U.S. exporter who holds franc balances might sell a cable transfer to a New York bank. This means she would cable her Paris bank to transfer the designated amount of francs to the New York bank's account, receiving an equivalent amount of dollars from the New York bank. The cable transfer's main advantage is the speed at which it can be effected. The transfer of funds by cable is normally completed on the first or second day following the purchase or sale.

Bills of Exchange

Another means of financing international transactions is the *bill of exchange*. This document represents an order on, say, a U.S. importer to pay a designated amount of francs to a French exporter at a certain date. Some bills are payable immediately, whereas others are payable 30, 60, 90, or 180 days after a specified date. Most exporters want immediate payment for their goods sold. After drawing up the bill of exchange, the exporter can sell it to his Paris bank for a designated amount of francs, subject to a slight discount for the services furnished by the bank. The exporter thus receives immediate payment for his goods. The Paris bank then sends the bill to its New York correspondent, which in turn presents it to the U.S. importer to be signed *accepted*. Once the bill is accepted by the importer, the Paris bank has two options. It can hold the bill (acceptance) until payment is due by the importer, or it can direct its New York correspondent to sell the bill in the domestic money market for immediate payment. It is also possible that the New York bank may purchase the bill, subject to a discount, from the Paris bank.

Other Foreign Exchange Instruments

In addition to the exchange of deposits, part of the foreign exchange market is made up of *foreign bank notes* (foreign currency) and coins. For a given country, the demand for foreign bank notes largely comes from domestic tourists, and the supply comes from foreign tourists. For the United States, a fairly large number of Canadian bank notes are acquired by U.S. merchants in the border areas. Another foreign exchange instrument is *traveler's checks*, used by tourists as a method of making international payments.

Reading Foreign Exchange Quotations

Most daily newspapers in the United States and other countries give foreign exchange quotations for major currencies. Table 12.1 lists the rates taken from the *Wall Street Journal* for July 22, 1983. Note that the foreign exchange quotations include those of the New York Foreign Exchange Market and the International Monetary Market.

Bank Transfers

The *New York Foreign Exchange Market* includes trading in both bank (cable) transfers and bank notes. In columns 1 and 2 of Table 12.1, the selling prices of bank transfers are listed in dollars. The columns state how many U.S. dollars are required to purchase one unit of a given foreign currency. For example, the quote for the Austrian schilling for Friday was .0549. This means that it required $0.0549 to purchase 1 schilling. Columns 3 and 4 illustrate the foreign exchange rates from the opposite perspective, telling how many units of a foreign currency are required to buy a U.S. dollar. Again referring to Friday, it would take 18.21 Austrian schillings to purchase $1 U.S.

The term *selling rate* in the table's caption refers to the price at which a New York bank or foreign exchange dealer will sell foreign exchange. The reason why the buying price is not given in the table is that it is commonly known by the market participants. For large foreign exchange transactions, a bank's buying price will fall below the selling price by as little as one-tenth of 1 percent or less. This small differential represents the service charge or commission required by the bank for the transaction. For very small foreign exchange sales, a bank may require an additional service charge.

The quotations of Table 12.1 are for bank (cable) transfers. Because the quickest means of

Table 12.1 Foreign Exchange Quotations

New York Foreign Exchange Market

Friday, July 22, 1983

The New York foreign exchange selling rates below apply to trading among banks in amounts of $1 million and more, as quoted at 3 p.m. Eastern time by Bankers Trust Co. Retail transactions provide fewer units of foreign currency per dollar.

Country	U.S. $ equiv. Fri	U.S. $ equiv. Thur	Currency per U.S. $ Fri	Currency per U.S. $ Thur
Argentina (Peso)	.11210	.11210	8.9200	8.920
Australia (Dollar)	.8795	.8750	1.1370	1.1428
Austria (Schilling)	.0549	.0553	18.21	18.08
Belgium (Franc)				
Commercial rate	.0193	.0193	51.79	51.68
Financial rate	.0191	.0192	52.10	51.94
Brazil (Cruzeiro)	.00171	.00171	584.72	584.72
Britain (Pound)	1.5230	1.5247	.6565	.6558
30-Day Forward	1.5233	1.5250	.6564	.6557
90-Day Forward	1.5241	1.5258	.6561	.6553
180-Day Forward	1.5255	1.5268	.6555	.6549
Canada (Dollar)	.8103	.8107	1.2340	1.2334
30-Day Forward	.8107	.8112	1.23335	1.2327
90-Day Forward	.8115	.8120	1.2322	1.2315
180-Day Forward	.8123	.8128	1.2310	1.2302
Chile (Official rate)	.01299	.01299	77.00	77.00
China (Yuan)	.5003	.5003	1.9986	1.9986
Colombia (Peso)	.01284	.01284	77.92	77.92
Denmark (Krone)	.1071	.1074	9.3350	9.3075
Ecuador (Sucre)				
Official rate	.0228	.0228	43.875	43.875
Floating rate	.0127	.0127	78.50	78.50
Finland (Markka)	.1790	.1794	5.5845	5.5730
France (Franc)	.1284	.1287	7.7855	7.7700
30-Day Forward	.1281	.1284	7.8025	7.7870
90-Day Forward	.1271	.1274	7.8645	7.8490
180-Day Forward	.1251	.1250	7.9930	7.9975
Greece (Drachma)	.01185	.01185	84.35	84.35
Hong Kong (Dollar)	.1393	.1396	7.1780	7.1600
India (Rupee)	.0992	.0993	10.08	10.07
Indonesia (Rupiah)	.001025	.001025	975.00	975.00
Ireland (Punt)	1.2198	1.2265	.8198	.8153
Israel (Shekel)	.02127	.02127	47.00	47.00
Italy (Lira)	.000652	.000654	1532.50	1527.50
Japan (Yen)	.00416	.004176	240.00	239.45
30-Day Forward	.00417	.004188	239.32	238.77
90-Day Forward	.00420	.004212	237.90	237.40
180-Day Forward	.00424	.004255	235.48	235.00
Lebanon (Pound)	.2357	.2357	4.2425	4.2425
Malaysia (Ringgit)	.4290	.4293	2.3310	2.3290
Mexico (Peso)				
Floating rate	.00673	.00673	148.50	148.50
Netherlands (Guilder)	.3451	.3456	2.8975	2.8930
New Zealand (Dollar)	.6545	.6540	1.5278	1.5290
Norway (Krone)	.1364	.1368	7.3275	7.3075
Pakistan (Rupee)	.0757	.0757	13.20	13.20
Peru (Sol)	.000606	.000725	1648	1378.48
Philippines (Peso)	.0904	.0904	11.05	11.05
Portugal (Escudo)	.0084	.00839	118.60	119.05
Saudi Arabia (Riyal)	.28985	.28985	3.45	3.4500
Singapore (Dollar)	.4705	.4710	2.1250	2.1230
South Africa (Rand)	.9130	.9125	1.0952	1.0958
South Korea (Won)	.0013	.0013	767	767.00
Spain (Peseta)	.00679	.00676	147.15	147.83
Sweden (Krona)	.1301	.1301	7.6850	7.6825
Switzerland (Franc)	.4750	.4766	2.1050	2.0980
30-Day Forward	.4771	.4786	2.0959	2.0891
90-Day Forward	.4813	.4830	2.0773	2.0702
180-Day Forward	.4883	.4899	2.0478	2.0410
Taiwan (Dollar)	.0250	.0250	39.97	39.97
Thailand (Baht)	.04349	.04349	22.99	22.99
Uruguay (New Peso)				
Financial	.0319	.0319	31.3479	31.3479
Venezuela (Bolivar)				
Official rate	.2329	.2329	4.2930	4.2930
Floating rate	.07692	.07692	13.00	13.00
W. Germany (Mark)	.3862	.3869	2.5890	2.5840
30-Day Forward	.3879	.3886	2.5777	2.5730
90-Day Forward	.3911	.3917	2.5563	2.5528
180-Day Forward	.3958	.3964	2.5260	2.5226
SDR	1.06265	1.06608	.941041	.938017

Special Drawing Rights are based on exchange rates for the U.S., West German, British, French and Japanese currencies. Source: International Monetary Fund.
z-Not quoted.

International Monetary Market

	Open	High	Low	Settle	Change	Lifetime High	Lifetime Low	Open Interest
BRITISH POUND (IMM)—25,000 pounds; $ per pound								
Sept	1.5245	1.5270	1.5290	1.5265	+ .0025	1.6360	1.4460	21,499
Dec	1.5265	1.5285	1.5210	1.5275	+ .0025	1.6425	1.4460	2,141
Mar				1.5285	+ .0025	1.6010	1.4470	1,244
June				1.5295	+ .0025	1.5400	1.5160	15
Est vol 3,412; vol Thurs 5,427; open int 24,899, +21.								
CANADIAN DOLLAR (IMM)—100,000 dlrs.; $ per Can $								
Sept	.8115	.8115	.8105	.8112	+ .0001	.8185	.7960	8,539
Dec	.8121	.8123	.8115	.8120	+ .0001	.8171	.8005	3,041
Mar84				.8125	...	.8169	.8040	1,070
June				.8130	...	.8168	.8100	328
Est vol 861; vol Thur 586; open int 12,978, +5.								
JAPANESE YEN (IMM) 12.5 million yen; $ per yen (.00)								
Sept	.4189	.4195	.4183	.4188	− .0009	.4382	.4140	22,744
Dec	.4232	.4236	.4225	.4229	− .0008	.4416	.4179	3,764
Mar84	.4271	.4271	.4265	.4265	− .0008	.4329	.4221	80
June				.4302	− .0004			3
Est vol 7,936; vol Thur 11,637; open int 37,591, −1,258.								
SWISS FRANC (IMM)—125,000 francs-$ per franc								
Sept	.4798	.4808	.4781	.4795	− .0010	.5428	.4635	30,910
Dec	.4865	.4876	.4848	.4862	− .0009	.5450	.4784	1,697
Mar84				.4918	− .0012	.5170	.4850	73
June				.4985	− .0012	.5045	.4970	7
Est vol 15,145; vol Thur 16,899; open int 32,687, +1,458.								
W. GERMAN MARK (IMM)—125,000 marks; $ per mark								
Sept	.3896	.3901	.3882	.3891	− .0008	.4370	.3873	24,924
Dec	.3946	.3949	.3930	.3939	− .0006	.4400	.3921	2,542
Mar84	.3990	.3990	.3990	.3990	...	.4100	.3970	48
Est vol 6,571; vol Thur 10,001; open int 27,514, −385.								

EURODOLLAR (IMM)—$1 million; pts of 100%

	Open	High	Low	Settle	Chg	Yield Settle	Yield Chg	Open Interest
Sept	89.57	89.59	89.45	89.46	− .14	10.54	+ .14	12,906
Dec	89.21	89.22	89.10	89.10	− .17	10.90	+ .17	11,291
Mar84	89.00	89.00	88.89	88.89	− .17	11.11	+ .17	6,096
June	88.82	88.82	88.72	88.72	− .18	11.28	+ .18	1,501
Est vol 2,203; vol Thur 4,038; open int 31,794, +194.								

international payment is by telecommunications, bank transfers using such technology are today the most important instrument of foreign exchange. New York banks sell bank transfers to those who owe money abroad, such as domestic importers. Conversely, New York banks may purchase bank transfers from holders of foreign exchange balances, such as domestic exporters.

The caption of the table also states at what time during the day the quotation was made. This is because currency prices fluctuate throughout the day in response to changing supply and demand conditions. The *Wall Street Journal* customarily quotes the closing day rates, 3 P.M. eastern time. Next-day readers of the newspaper are thus offered the most recent currency prices.

Futures (Forward) Markets

Foreign exchange can be bought and sold for delivery immediately (the *spot market*) or for future delivery (the *futures* or *forward* market). Futures contracts are normally made by those who will receive or make payment in foreign exchange in the weeks or months ahead. As seen in Table 12.1, the New York Foreign Exchange Market is a spot market for most currencies of the world. Regular futures markets, however, exist only for the more widely traded currencies. Exporters and importers, whose foreign exchange receipts and payments are in the future, are the primary participants in the futures market. The futures quotations for the British pound, Canadian dollar, French franc, Japanese yen, Swiss franc, and West German mark are for delivery 30, 90, or 180 days from the date indicated in the table's caption (July 22, 1983).

Table 12.1 also gives futures quotations for the International Monetary Market (IMM), a division of the Chicago Mercantile Exchange. Founded in 1972, the IMM is an extension of the commodity futures markets in which specific quantities of wheat, corn, and other commodities

are bought and sold for delivery at specific dates. The IMM provides trading facilities for the purchase and sale for future delivery of financial instruments (like foreign currencies) and precious metals (such as gold). The IMM is especially popular with smaller banks and companies. Also, the IMM is one of the few places where individuals can speculate on changes in exchange rates.

Foreign exchange trading on the IMM is limited to major currencies. Contracts are set for delivery on the third Wednesday of March, June, September, and December. Price quotations are in terms of U.S. dollars per unit of foreign currency, whereas futures contracts are of a fixed amount (for example, 25,000 British pounds).

Here is how to read the IMM's future prices in Table 12.1. Column 1 gives the months for which delivery of the currency may be obtained. The next three columns give the opening, highest, and lowest prices of the day. Column 5 gives the *settlement price*, which approximates the last price of the day.[3] Column 6, labeled *change*, shows the difference between the latest settlement price and the one for the previous day. The next two columns give the highest and lowest prices at which each contract month has ever traded. Column 8 is labeled *open interest*, which is the number of contracts outstanding and is a measure of public interest in a contract.

Bank Notes

Besides furnishing quotations for bank transfers, the New York Foreign Exchange Market also deals in foreign bank notes. *Bank notes* refer to the actual currencies of foreign nations. Bank note transactions have several distinct characteristics. First, the prices for bank notes are quoted for the entire day, unlike the bank transfer market, where prices fluctuate throughout the day so that newspapers must indicate the time of the day the quotation was made. Second, rather than having a uniform spread between the buying and selling prices, as in the case for bank transfers, the prices for bank notes vary depending on the currency involved. This in part reflects the costs of transporting bank notes among financial centers.

Third, New York banks generally require a higher service charge for bank note transactions than for transactions in bank transfers. For example, the bank note spread for the French franc may be 10 percent or more. This is because trading in bank notes requires larger transaction expenses for the banks. Not only do bank notes have a greater potential for theft, but they also do not afford banks any interest income while they are stored in their vaults. Consequently, a higher service charge is applied to bank note transactions.

Finally, the selling prices for bank notes are not always identical to those of bank transfers. Selling prices for these two foreign exchange instruments are explained by (1) prevailing supply and demand conditions and (2) the transaction costs of transporting and maintaining holdings of banks notes and deposits. Depending on those conditions, the selling price for bank notes may be slightly above that of bank transfers.

Exchange Rate Determination

The previous discussion focused on the rate of exchange. Now we view the exchange rate from the perspective of the United States, dollars per unit of foreign currency. Since an exchange rate is a price, it would be expected to change over time. An increase in the U.S. exchange rate from $2 = 1 pound to $2.25 = 1 pound suggests the dollar has depreciated against the pound (the pound has appreciated relative to the dollar). This is because more dollars are needed to purchase 1 pound. Conversely, a decrease in the U.S. exchange rate from $2 = 1 pound to $1.75 = 1 pound means the dollar has appreciated against the pound (the pound

has depreciated relative to the dollar). Like other prices, the rate of exchange in a free market is determined by both supply and demand conditions.[4]

Demand for Foreign Exchange

A country's *demand for foreign exchange* is derived from, or corresponds to, the debit items on its balance of payments. For example, the U.S. demand for pounds stems from such factors as its desire to import British goods and services, to make investments in Britain, or to make transfer payments to Britain.

Like most demand curves, the U.S. demand for pounds varies inversely with its price; that is, fewer pounds are demanded at higher prices than at lower prices. This relationship is depicted by line *DD* in Figure 12.1. As the dollar depreciates against the pound (the dollar price of the pound rises), British goods and services become more expensive to U.S. importers. This is because more dollars are required to purchase each pound needed to finance the import purchases. The higher exchange rate reduces the number of imports bought, lowering the number of pounds demanded by U.S. residents. In like manner, an appreciation of the U.S. dollar relative to the pound would be expected to induce larger import purchases and more pounds demanded by U.S. residents. The U.S. demand for pounds is based on the assumption that all relevant factors other than the rate of exchange are given and constant. These other factors include changes in income, prices, interest rates, costs, and tastes and preferences, all of which can induce changes in the debit items of the balance of payments.

Supply of Foreign Exchange

The *supply of foreign exchange* refers to the amounts of foreign exchange that will be supplied at various rates, all other factors held constant. Underlying the supply of foreign exchange

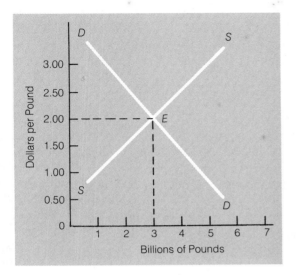

Figure 12.1   Foreign exchange market.

are the credit items of the balance of payments. For example, the U.S. supply of pounds largely depends on the British desire to import U.S. goods and services, to loan funds and make investments in the United States, and to extend transfer payments to U.S. residents.

The U.S. supply of pounds is represented by curve SS in Figure 12.1. It is depicted in the diagram as a positive function of the U.S. exchange rate. As the dollar depreciates (dollar price of the pound rises), U.S. export prices appear low to foreigners because fewer pounds are required to purchase each dollar. This price reduction for dollars induces rising U.S. exports and a larger supply of pounds to U.S. residents. Similarly, an appreciation of the dollar tends to reduce exports, reducing the number of pounds offered to U.S. residents. The supply of pounds depicted in Figure 12.1 is illustrated as a positive function of the exchange rate, rising from left to right. Can we be assured this always occurs? Not necessarily. The outcome depends on the price elasticity of the British demand for U.S. exports and thus for dollars.

Given a depreciation of the dollar against the pound, two opposing forces operate. The dollar depreciation causes the pound price of U.S. exports to fall. This induces an increase in the quantity of U.S. exports demanded. Whether this increases or decreases the quantity of pounds supplied depends on the relative size of the price and quantity changes (elasticity). There are several possibilities.

Should the British demand for U.S. goods be price elastic, a given percentage drop in price would bring forth a greater percentage increase in quantity purchased. The net effect would be more pounds offered to U.S. exporters as the result of the dollar depreciation. The supply of pounds would therefore be upward sloping, varying directly with changes in the exchange rate. This is the situation assumed by curve SS in Figure 12.1.

Should the British demand for U.S. goods be price inelastic, the percentage decrease in price would not be matched by the percentage increase in the quantity of goods bought. The amount of pounds offered to U.S. exporters would decline if the dollar depreciated against the pound. In this case, the U.S. supply of pounds would appear as a negatively sloped (backward sloping) function in Figure 12.1. It is also possible that the British demand for U.S. exports would be unitary elastic with respect to price changes. This means that the percentage decrease in price induced by the dollar depreciation just equals the percentage increase in the quantity of goods purchased. The result is that the same number of pounds would be offered to U.S. exporters after the dollar depreciation. The supply of pounds would appear as a vertical line in Figure 12.1.

Like the demand curve for foreign exchange, the supply curve for foreign exchange is based on the assumption that factors other than the exchange rate are held constant. These are the factors behind the credit items of the balance of payments such as prices, tastes and preferences, interest rates, and income levels.

Equilibrium Rate of Exchange

As long as foreign monetary authorities do not attempt to stabilize exchange rates or moderate their movements, the equilibrium rate of exchange is determined by the intersection of the supply and demand schedules. This occurs at point E in Figure 12.1. At this exchange rate, 3 billion pounds will be traded at a price of $2 per pound. The foreign exchange market is precisely cleared, leaving neither an excess supply nor an excess demand. Given the supply and demand schedules of Figure 12.1, there is no reason for the rate of exchange to deviate from the equilibrium level. But in practice, it is unlikely that the equilibrium exchange rate would remain at the existing level very long. This is because the forces that are assumed to be given and constant in constructing the supply and demand schedules tend to change over time.

Suppose there occurs a rise in the level of U.S. real income relative to that abroad. This would tend to increase the U.S. demand for imports at each exchange rate, thereby increasing the U.S. demand for pounds at each exchange rate. Given a constant supply schedule, the result would be a rise in the exchange rate (a dollar depreciation), as shown in Figure 12.2. The U.S. demand for pounds might similarly rise if the U.S. inflation rate increases relative to that of Britain, making British exports less expensive. An increase in British interest rates relative to those in the United States would tend to reduce capital inflows to the United States and induce capital outflows. The U.S. demand for pounds would increase. Conversely, a fall in U.S. price and income levels, or a rise in its interest rates relative to those of Britain, would tend to result in a decrease in its demand for pounds.

As for the supply schedule of pounds for the United States, it may increase or decrease in response to several factors. Suppose the British rate of inflation rises above U.S. levels. Because U.S. goods would become relatively cheaper, British importers would purchase more U.S. goods at each exchange rate, increasing the amount of pounds offered to the U.S. at each rate of exchange. Given a constant demand for pounds, the United States would find its exchange rate falling (a dollar appreciation) with the increase in the supply of pounds, as illustrated in Figure 12.3. Rising British income levels that encourage additional import purchases from the United States would also add to the U.S. supply of pounds. Should British speculators anticipate an appreciation of the dollar in the near future, they might rush to purchase dollars and thus add to the U.S. supply of pounds.

Measuring the Dollar's International Value

Since 1973, the U.S. dollar has *floated* on the foreign exchange market; this means the value of the dollar in terms of foreign currencies changes daily, in response to market conditions.[5] This makes the measurement of the dollar's international value a confusing task. Financial pages of newspapers have sometimes headlined a sharp rise of the dollar against some currencies and a sharp fall against others. How can one assess the economic significance of such events?

Providing a measure of the dollar's international value in a world of floating exchange rates requires some type of weighted index of the dollar against a selected number of other currencies as a group. This section considers one of these measures, the *Morgan Guaranty Index*, which appears in the financial pages of many newspapers including the *Wall Street Journal*. Table 12.2 illustrates the *trade-weighted value* of the U.S. dollar for July 22, 1983. The index shows changes in the U.S. dollar's value against an index of 15 leading currencies. To reflect the

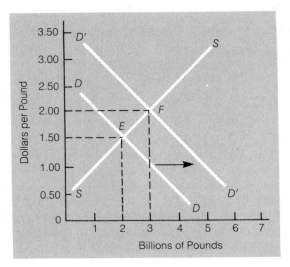

Figure 12.2 The effects of an increase in the demand for foreign exchange.

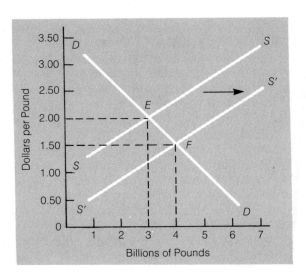

Figure 12.3 The effects of an increase in the supply of foreign exchange.

relative importance of individual currencies in the index, each currency is assigned a weight based on relative shares in trade with the United States.

The Morgan Guaranty Index makes direct comparisons of fluctuations of the dollar against other currencies over time by computing index numbers. These represent percentages of a previous base period (equal to 100), with exchange rates at subsequent time periods expressed as a

percentage of that value. The choice of a base period is usually intended to reflect economic conditions of historic interest. As shown in Table 12.2, the Morgan Guaranty Index identifies three different base periods from which comparisons can be made: (1) May 29, 1970—reflects the economic circumstances immediately preceding the floating of the Canadian dollar (June 1970), which resulted in the first major change

Table 12.2 Trade-Weighted Dollar

NEW YORK—Morgan Guaranty Trust Co. reported the dollar's percentage change in market value, weighted for volume of trade with the U.S., against 15 other currencies, as of noon Eastern time, from the following dates:

	a-May 29, 1970	b-December 18, 1971	c-February 15, 1973
July 22	+ 3.2	+ 14.3	+ 21.2
Week ago	+ 3.5	+ 14.7	+ 21.5
Year ago	− 0.6	+ 10.1	+ 16.7

a-Parities prior to Canadian dollar float. b-Smithsonian Agreement central rates. c-Market rates following dollar devaluation.

Source: *Wall Street Journal*, July 25, 1983.

in the post–World War II international monetary system; (2) December 18, 1971—the date of the historic Smithsonian exchange rate realignments at which the U.S. dollar was officially devalued by 8.57 percent; (3) February 15, 1973—just before the adoption of managed floating exchange rates (March 19, 1973) and immediately following another currency realignment and a 10 percent dollar devaluation (February 12, 1973).

Inspection of Table 12.2 reveals several interesting trends. Compared with the May 29, 1970 base period, the July 22, 1983 value of the dollar rose by 3.2 percent against the trade-weighted values of 15 other national currencies. The dollar's value on July 22, 1983 was 14.3 percent above what it was on December 18, 1971 and 21.2 percent above the level of February 15, 1973.

The purpose of trade-weighted indexes is to permit direct comparisons over a period of time, of the movements of national currency values occurring under a system of floating exchange rates. Such comparisons are used to examine how changes in the value of a country's currency, vis-à-vis other currencies, affect the bilateral trade of that country vis-à-vis these countries. For example, should the West German mark and the Japanese yen appreciate in value relative to the U.S. dollar, the volume of imports to the United States from West Germany and Japan tends to decrease, owing to the American consumer's response to the higher prices of imported goods in terms of the U.S. dollar. Moreover, U.S. exports to West Germany and Japan tend to increase, owing to lower prices of U.S. goods in terms of these currencies.

In addition to bilateral-trade weighted indexes, multilateral (global) trade-weighted indexes have been developed to meet the needs of professional analysts. These indexes consider not only the impact of changes in a country's

exchange rate on the bilateral trade of that country with other countries but also the entire matrix of trade flows between all countries. Referring to the trading example in the preceding paragraph, the multilateral trade-weighted index considers an additional proposition—that the rest of the world's trading countries will find West German and Japanese goods relatively more expensive than U.S. goods as the result of the dollar depreciation, and that as a result, they will tend to shift their purchases to the United States. Multilateral trade-weighted indexes thus consider the impact of exchange rate changes on the country's trade balance with all other countries.

One multilateral trade-weighted index is the *index of effective exchange rates* constructed by the International Monetary Fund. Using 1975 as a base, this index combines the exchange rate changes in each of the fund's member countries' currencies relative to 20 major world currencies. Mathematically, all foreign currencies are not equally important, so it is necessary to weight them. The weights take account of the relative importance of a country's trading partners in its direct bilateral relations with them, of competitive relations with "third countries" in particular markets, of differences in the importance of the foreign sector in the overall economy in affecting the composition of trade, and of estimated elasticities affecting trade flows. The exchange rate index is constructed as the geometric average of individual exchange rates compared with the base period.

Table 12.3 illustrates the effective exchange rate indexes for five industrial countries. Compared with the base year (1975 = 100), an increase in a country's effective exchange rate indicates currency appreciation and a loss in overall price competitiveness. A decrease in a country's effective exchange rate implies the opposite. Compared with 1975, the effective exchange rate of the U.S. dollar fell about 6 percent by

Table 12.3   Effective Exchange Rates*

Year	U.S. Dollar	West German Mark	Japanese Yen	U.K. Pound Sterling	Canadian Dollar
1976	105.2	104.8	104.2	85.6	106.1
1978	95.7	120.1	141.7	81.5	87.8
1980	93.9	128.8	126.5	96.1	84.5
1982	118.1	124.3	134.8	90.5	88.6
1983**	122.5	130.0	145.9	82.7	90.7

Source: International Monetary Fund, *International Financial Statistics*, June 1983.
*Index: 1975 = 100.
**April.

1980. This was followed by a strengthening of the dollar. By 1983, the effective exchange rate of the dollar was more than 22 percent higher than base year levels.

Arbitrage

The preceding section described how the supply and demand for foreign exchange can set the market exchange rate. This analysis was from the perspective of the U.S. (New York) foreign exchange market. But what about the relationship between the exchange rate in the U.S. market and that in other nations? When restrictions do not modify the ability of the foreign exchange market to operate efficiently, normal market forces result in the market exchange rates of all currencies having a consistent relationship with each other. That is to say, if 1 British pound equals $2 in the U.S. foreign exchange market, then $1 will equal half a pound in the British foreign exchange market. The prices for the same currency in different world locations will be identical.

The factor underlying the consistency of the exchange rates is called *exchange arbitrage*. Exchange arbitrage refers to the simultaneous purchase and sale of a currency in different foreign exchange markets in order to profit from exchange rate differentials in the two locations. It is exchange arbitrage that brings about an identical price for the same currency in different locations and thus results in one market.

Suppose that the dollar/pound sterling exchange rate is 1 pound = $2 in New York, but the exchange rate is $2.01 in London. Foreign exchange traders would find it profitable to purchase pounds in New York at $2 per pound and immediately resell them in London for $2.01. A profit of 1 cent would be made on each pound sold, less the cost of the bank transfer and the interest charge on the money tied up during the arbitrage process. This return may appear to be insignificant, but on a $1 million arbitrage transaction it would generate a profit of approximately $5,000! Not bad for a few minutes' work! As the demand for pounds increases in New York, the dollar price of a pound would rise above $2. This arbitrage process will continue until the exchange rate between the dollar and pound in New York is approximately the same as it is in London. Arbitrage between the two currencies unifies the foreign exchange markets.

This example is commonly referred to as *two-point arbitrage*, where only two currencies are traded between two financial centers. A more intricate form of arbitrage involves three currencies and three financial centers. This *three-point arbitrage* involves essentially the same principle. However, in practice, this form of arbitrage takes place less often than two-point arbitrage.

The Futures Market

Foreign exchange markets may be *spot* or *futures* (forward). In the spot market, currencies are bought and sold for immediate delivery, although in practice immediate delivery generally means two business days after the conclusion of the deal. In the futures market, currencies are bought and sold now for future delivery, typically 30, 90, or 180 days from the date of the transaction. The exchange rate is agreed on at the time of the contract, but payment is not made until the future delivery actually takes place. Fewer foreign currencies are traded on the regular futures market than on the spot market, only the most widely traded currencies being included. Individual futures contracts, however, can be negotiated for most national currencies.

The Futures Rate

Exchange rates for forward exchange can be quoted in the same way as spot rates—the price of one currency in terms of another currency. It is customary that either currency can be stated in relation to the spot rate of the two currencies involved. The futures rate is thus quoted as a *premium* or *discount* from the spot rate. According to the New York foreign exchange market quotations of Table 12.1, on Friday, the 30-day forward German mark is selling at $0.3879, whereas the spot price of the mark is $0.3862. Since the futures price of the mark exceeds the mark's spot price, the mark is at a 30-day future premium of 0.17 cents or 0.44 percent (or at a

5.3 percent future premium on an annual basis) against the dollar.[6] Conversely, the French franc's spot rate is $0.1284, whereas the 30-day futures rate is $0.1281. The franc is at a 30-day future discount of 0.03 cents or 0.23 percent (or at a 2.8 percent future discount on an annual basis) against the dollar.

Futures Market Functions

The primary purpose of the futures market is to protect international traders and investors from the risks involved in fluctuations of the spot rate. The process of avoiding or covering a foreign exchange risk is known as *hedging*. Those people who expect to make or receive payments in terms of a foreign currency at a future date are concerned that if the spot rate changes, they must make a greater payment, or receive less in terms of the domestic currency, than expected. This could wipe out anticipated profit levels. The solution is for such traders and investors to eliminate the element of uncertainty of the foreign exchange rate from their transactions.

Consider the situation of a U.S. importer who must pay a certain amount of marks to a German exporter in three months. During this period, the importer is in an exposed or uncovered position. Should the dollar price of the mark rise (the mark appreciates against the dollar), the purchase of the necessary amount of marks will require more dollar outlays than expected. To cover himself against this risk, the importer might buy marks immediately, but this would immobilize his funds for three months. Alternatively, the importer could cover his exposed position by purchasing marks in the forward market at today's forward rate. Not only can the future purchase be made for the exact day the marks are needed to meet the payment obligation, but the purchase does not require an immediate outlay of the importer's funds. The importer has hedged his exchange risk.

What about a U.S. exporter who anticipates receiving a given amount of marks in three months from a German importer? Should the dollar price of the mark fall (the mark depreciates against the dollar) over this period, the exporter's receipts in marks would be worth less in terms of dollars. To cover this exchange risk, the exporter could sell her expected mark receipts in the futures market at today's futures rate. By locking into a set futures exchange rate, the exporter is guaranteed that the value of her mark receipts will be maintained in terms of the dollar, even if the value of the mark should happen to fall. Again, the exchange market risk has been hedged successfully.

The forward market eliminates the uncertainty of fluctuating spot rates from international transactions. Exporters can hedge against the possibility of the foreign currency depreciating against the domestic currency, and importers can hedge against the possibility of the foreign currency appreciating against the domestic currency. Hedging is not limited to exporters and importers. It applies to anyone who is obligated to make a foreign currency payment or who will enjoy foreign currency receipt at a future time. International investors, for example, also make use of the futures market for hedging purposes.

Relation of the Spot Rate and the Futures Rate

One topic that has not been considered is the relation between the spot and futures rates. Referring to the New York Foreign Exchange Market quotations, we see that the U.S. dollar's spot and forward rates are not identical for, say, the German mark. This is also true for the British pound and Japanese yen. Forward exchange normally sells either at a premium over or a discount under the spot rate. What explains this situation?

The relationship between the spot and forward rate is primarily determined by the difference between the short-term interest rates at home and abroad. Generally speaking, the *difference between the spot and forward rates tends to equal the spread between the existing short-term interest rates of the domestic and foreign financial centers*. The following example illustrates this situation.

Suppose the interest rate on three-month Treasury bills is 12 percent in London and 10 percent in New York. The interest spread in favor of London thus equals 2 percent. Suppose also that today's spot rate for the pound is $4, whereas the three-month forward pound sells for $3.99. This means that the three-month forward pound is at a 1 percent discount on a per-annum basis.

U.S. investors could profit by shifting funds from New York to London to take advantage of the interest rate differential on the British securities. This would require the investors to first purchase pounds on the spot market at $4 per pound and then use the pounds to buy the securities. Having done so, the investors are now in an uncovered exchange position. To protect their anticipated profits, investors will immediately sell in the forward market an amount of pounds sufficient to cover their purchase of spot pounds, the forward selling price being $3.99 per pound. When the Treasury bills mature in three months, the investors can convert their pounds into dollars at the contracted forward rate. The cost of the forward cover thus equals the difference between the spot and forward rates, or 1 cent per pound (which equals the 1 percent discount on the pound). The net profit on the transaction equals 1 percent, the interest rate spread (2 percent) less the cost of the forward cover (1 percent discount).

This investment opportunity will not last for long, for the net profit margin will soon disappear. As U.S. investors purchase spot pounds, the spot rate will increase. Concurrently, the sale of forward pounds will push the forward rate downward. The result is a widening of the discount on the forward pounds. This process will continue until the forward discount on the pound widens to 2 percent, at which the profitability of such investments vanishes. The result is that the discount on the pound now equals the interest rate spread between New York and London.

In short, the theory of foreign exchange suggests that the forward discount or premium on one currency against another directly reflects the difference in the short-term interest rates between the two countries. The currency of the higher-interest-rate country should be at a forward discount against the currency of the lower-interest-rate country. The opposite holds equally true.

International differences in interest rates do exert a major influence on the relation between the spot and forward rates. But on any particular day, one would hardly expect the spread on short-term interest rates between financial centers precisely to equal the discount or premium on foreign exchange. One reason for this is that changes in interest rate spreads do not always induce an immediate investor response necessary to eliminate the investment profits. In addition, investors sometimes transfer funds on an uncovered basis. Such transfers do not have an effect on the futures rate. Finally, factors such as governmental exchange controls and speculation may weaken the connection between the interest rate differential and the spot and forward rates.

Speculating in the Foreign Exchange Markets

Besides facilitating the financing of commercial and private transactions, the foreign exchange markets give rise to exchange speculation. *Foreign exchange speculation* refers to the deliberate taking of an uncovered position or foreign exchange risk with the hope of profiting from exchange rate fluctuations. It is the opposite of

hedging. A speculator is a conscious risk bearer. He buys and sells currencies with the expectation of taking advantage of a currency's spot rate changes over time.[7]

Spot and Futures Market Speculation

Speculation can be undertaken on both the spot and futures markets. A speculator who anticipates the spot rate of the German mark appreciating in three months might purchase marks at today's spot rate, hold them for three months, and resell them at a higher rate. Conversely, suppose a speculator expects the spot rate of the mark to depreciate in three months. He could borrow marks and trade them for his domestic currency at today's spot rate. Assuming he is correct, in three months he could profit by repurchasing marks at a lower spot rate in sufficient quantities to repay the loan. However, such speculation is cumbersome because it involves the borrowing of foreign currency or the immobilization of the speculator's funds. Both of these factors require costs in addition to the exchange market risk.

The most widely adopted method of profiting from changes in exchange rates over time is by speculation in the futures market. In this case, the speculator does not have to make a major commitment of funds to gamble on a currency's spot rate. The additional costs that plague spot market speculation can be avoided by speculation in the futures market. Futures market speculation assumes one of two forms. A speculator can assume either a long position or a short position.

Suppose a speculator anticipates that the mark's spot rate in three months will exceed the three-month forward rate as quoted today. The speculator would find it profitable to take a *long position*. This means that she would buy marks for three-month future delivery at today's forward rate. If the speculator is correct, in three months, she can sell her marks in the spot market, collecting the difference between the prevailing spot rate and the contracted futures rate. On the other hand, a speculator who expects the mark's spot rate in three months to fall below today's three-month forward rate would assume a *short position*. He would sell marks for three-month delivery at today's futures rate even though he does not have an equivalent amount of marks at that moment. The expectation is that with his domestic currency, he can buy marks at a lower spot rate when the futures contract matures and use them to fulfill his futures contract obligation. The domestic currency receipts resulting from the transaction would be sufficient for the speculator to realize an overall profit.

In practice, U.S. speculators in foreign exchange often conduct their futures transactions at the International Monetary Market, established in 1972 by the Chicago Mercantile Exchange. Margins run as low as 5 percent or less for established speculators. This means that for a mere $5,000, a U.S. speculator can take an uncovered position in $100,000 worth of a foreign currency. If the speculator guesses right, this financial leverage paves the way for extraordinary profits. But leverage can work both ways. A speculator can get wiped out in hours, or even minutes, if he is on the wrong side of the market. Even if he is right about the general market trends, he can lose because of exchange rate fluctuations. Needless to say, foreign exchange speculation is a very risky business.

Other Forms of Speculation

Besides speculating in the spot markets and futures markets, there are other ways of capitalizing from expectations of currency movements. One such way is to purchase *securities* denominated in a foreign currency. Should a U.S. speculator anticipate that the German mark's spot rate will significantly appreciate in the near future, he might purchase bonds issued by German corporations and expressed in marks. The bonds are paid for in marks, which are purchased by converting dollars into marks at the prevailing spot rate. If the mark goes up, the speculator gets not only the accrued interest from the bond but also its appreciated value, in terms of dollars. The catch is that in all likelihood, others have the same expectations. The overall demand for the bonds may be sufficient to force up the bond's price, resulting in lower interest rates. The speculator is therefore forfeiting interest income. For the speculator to win, the mark's appreciation must exceed the loss of interest income. The problem is that in many cases the exchange rate changes are not large enough to make such investments worthwhile.

Rather than investing in foreign securities, some speculators choose to purchase *stocks* of foreign corporations, denominated in foreign currencies. The speculator in this case is trying to predict the trend of not only the foreign currency but also its stock market. The speculator must be highly knowledgeable about both foreign financial and economic affairs.

For investors who expect that the spot rate of a foreign currency will soon rise, the answer lies in a *savings account* denominated in a foreign currency. For example, a U.S. investor may contact a major New York bank or a U.S. branch of a foreign bank and take out an interest-bearing certificate of deposit expressed in a foreign currency. An advantage of such a savings account is that the investor is guaranteed a fixed interest rate. Provided that the investor has guessed correctly, he also enjoys the gains stemming from the foreign currency's appreciation. However, the investor must be aware of the possibility that governments might tax or shut off such deposits or interfere with the investor's freedom to hold another country's currency.

ulation and Exchange Market Stability

An exchange market speculator deliberately assumes foreign exchange risk with expectations of profiting from future changes in the spot exchange rate. Such activity can exert either a stabilizing or destabilizing influence on the foreign exchange market.

Stabilizing speculation goes against market forces by moderating or reversing a rise or fall in a currency's exchange rate. It occurs when a speculator buys foreign currency with domestic currency when the domestic price of the foreign currency falls, or depreciates. The hope is that the domestic price of the foreign currency will soon increase, leading to a profit. Such purchases increase the demand for the foreign currency, which moderates its depreciation. Stabilizing speculation also occurs when a speculator sells foreign currency when the domestic price of the foreign currency rises, or appreciates, in hope that the price will soon fall. Such sales moderate the appreciation of the foreign currency. Stabilizing speculation performs a useful function for bankers and business people who desire stable exchange rates.

Destabilizing speculation goes with market forces by reinforcing fluctuations in a currency's exchange rate. It occurs when a speculator sells a foreign currency when it depreciates, the expectation being that it will further depreciate in the future. Such sales depress the foreign currency's value. It also occurs when speculators buy a foreign currency when its exchange rate appreciates, the expectation being that it will appreciate even further in the future. Such purchases increase the foreign currency's value. Destabilizing speculation reinforces exchange rate fluctuations and can disrupt international trade and investment.

Should destabilizing speculation against a currency be sufficiently large, it may induce sizable forward discounts on the currency. If speculators view a currency as particularly weak, they may anticipate a significant decline in its value. Immediately they would begin selling the currency forward for future delivery, with the hope of fulfilling their futures contracts at lower spot rates. These sales tend to further weaken the forward rate, causing the forward discount to become larger. When there is a sizable forward discount on a currency, the ability of interest rate differentials to promote order in the exchange market may be limited.

Destabilizing speculation may disrupt international transactions in several ways. Because of the uncertainty of financing exports and imports, the cost of hedging may become so high that international trade is impeded. What is more, unstable exchange rates may disrupt international investment activity. This is because the cost of obtaining forward cover for international capital transactions may significantly rise as foreign exchange risk intensifies.

A slight variant of the concept of exchange market speculation is that of *capital flight*. This is motivated not by the expectation of profit but rather by the fear of exchange market loss. Flight capital movements may be induced by fear of currency devaluation, political instability, or government restrictions on foreign exchange movements. Such short-run monetary flows, sometimes referred to as *hot money*, created marked disruptions in the international monetary system during the late 1960s and early 1970s. Major capital flights out of the overvalued U.S. dollar in 1971 and 1973 touched off not only the termination of the dollar's gold convertibility but also the collapse of the historic Bretton Woods monetary system.

Summary

1. The foreign exchange market provides the institutional framework within which individuals, businesses, and financial institutions purchase and sell foreign exchange. Two of the world's

largest foreign exchange markets are located in New York and London.

2.   Several financial assets are considered to be foreign exchange: (1) cable transfers, (2) bills of exchange, (3) foreign bank notes and coins, and (4) traveler's checks.

3.   The foreign exchange rate is the price of one unit of foreign currency in terms of the domestic currency. From a U.S. viewpoint, the exchange rate might refer to the number of dollars necessary to buy a West German mark. A dollar depreciation (appreciation) is an increase (decrease) in the number of dollars required to buy a unit of foreign exchange.

4.   The *Wall Street Journal's* foreign exchange quotations include those of the New York Foreign Exchange Market and the International Monetary Market located in Chicago. Both spot quotations and forward (futures) quotations are provided.

5.   The equilibrium rate of exchange in a free market is determined by the intersection of the supply and demand schedules of foreign exchange. These schedules are derived from the credit and debit items in a country's balance of payments.

6.   Whereas the demand curve for foreign exchange is normally drawn as downward sloping, the supply curve may be positively sloped or negatively sloped.

7.   Exchange arbitrage permits the rates of exchange in different parts of the world to be kept the same. This is achieved by selling a currency when its price is high and purchasing when the price is low.

8.   Foreign traders and investors often deal in the futures market for protection from possible exchange rate fluctuations. However, speculators also buy and sell currencies in the futures markets in anticipation of sizable profits. In general, interest arbitrage determines the relationship between the spot rate and futures rate.

9.   Speculation in the foreign exchange markets may be either stabilizing or destabilizing in nature.

Study Questions

1.   What is meant by the foreign exchange market? Where is it located?

2.   What are some of the more important instruments of foreign exchange?

3.   Distinguish between a bank transfer and a bank note.

4.   What is meant by the forward (futures) market? How does this differ from the spot market?

5.   The supply and demand for foreign exchange are considered to be derived schedules. Explain.

6.   Explain how the supply of foreign exchange may be upward sloping and backward sloping at various exchange rates.

7.   What factors cause shifts in the supply and demand schedules of foreign exchange?

8.   Why is it that exchange rate quotations stated in different financial centers tend to be consistent with each other?

9.   Who are the participants in the forward exchange market? What advantages does this market afford these participants?

10.   What explains the relationship between the spot rate and futures rate?

11.   What is the strategy of speculating in the futures market? What other ways can one speculate on exchange rate changes?

12.   Distinguish between stabilizing speculation and destabilizing speculation.

Notes

1.   See Gerald H. Anderson, "The Foreign Exchange Market," in *Economic Review* (Cleveland: Federal Reserve Bank of Cleveland, Fall 1976), pp. 3–11.

2. See Talat M. Othman, "How Foreign Exchange Markets Work," in D. R. Mandich, ed., *Foreign Exchange Trading Techniques and Controls* (Washington, D.C.: American Bankers Association, 1976).

3. In commodity markets, the *close* is a period of time, generally less than two minutes, during which a large number of transactions can occur. To obtain a single closing price, exchanges must calculate what the last price of the day would be, if there were one. A common method is to take a single average of the highest and lowest prices during the closing period.

4. Fritz Machlup, "The Theory of Foreign Exchanges," *Economica* (November 1939), pp. 375–397; reprinted in American Economic Association, *Readings in the Theory of International Trade* (Homewood, Ill.: Richard D. Irwin, 1949).

5. Although the U.S. dollar is floating on the foreign exchange market, it is being managed to some degree. Central bankers often intervene to slow or smooth fluctuations in the dollar's international value to keep the market orderly.

6. On a per-annum basis, the percentage of discount or premium in a futures quote is computed by the following formula:

$$\text{Forward premium (discount)}$$

$$= \frac{(\text{Forward rate} - \text{Spot rate})}{\text{Spot rate}}$$

$$\times \frac{12}{\text{Number of months forward}}$$

7. An interesting account of speculation in the foreign exchange markets is given in Richard J. Stinson, "Can You Win at Currency Trading?" *Financial World*, May 15, 1976, pp. 21–24.

Suggestions for Further Reading

Aliber, R. Z., ed. *The International Market for Foreign Exchange*. New York: Praeger, 1969.

Coninx, R. G. F. *Foreign Exchange Today*. New York: Halsted Press, 1977.

Dufey, G., and I. H. Giddy. *The International Money Market*. Englewood Cliffs, N.J.: Prentice-Hall, 1978.

Einzig, P.A. *A Textbook on Foreign Exchange*. New York: St. Martin's Press, 1966.

Henning, C. *International Finance*. New York: Harper & Row, 1958.

Kubarych, R. M. *Foreign Exchange Markets in the United States*. New York: Federal Reserve Bank of New York, 1978.

Machlup, F. "The Forward-Exchange Market: Misunderstandings Between Practitioners and Economists." In G. N. Halm, ed., *Approaches to Greater Flexibility of Exchange Rates*. Princeton, N.J.: Princeton University Press, 1970.

Mandrich, D. E. *Foreign Exchange Trading Techniques, Controls*. New York: American Bankers Association, 1976.

Walker, T. *A Guide for Using the Foreign Exchange Market*. New York: John Wiley, 1981.

Yeager, L.B. *International Monetary Relations*. New York: Harper & Row, 1976.

13

BALANCE-OF-PAYMENTS ADJUSTMENTS: FIXED EXCHANGE RATES

Chapter 11 examined the meaning of a balance-of-payments deficit and surplus. Recall that owing to double-entry bookkeeping, total inpayments (credits) always equal total outpayments (debits) when all of the balance-of-payments accounts are considered. A deficit refers to an excess of outpayments over inpayments for selected accounts grouped along functional lines. For example, a current account deficit suggests an excess of imports over exports of goods, services, and unilateral transfers. A current account surplus implies the opposite.

A nation finances or covers a current account deficit out of its international reserves or by attracting investment (for example, purchases of factories or securities) from its trading partners. However, the capacity of a deficit country to cover the excess of outpayments over inpayments is limited by its stocks of international reserves and the willingness of its trading partners to invest in the deficit country. For a surplus country, once it believes that its stocks of international reserves or overseas investments are adequate—although history shows that this belief may be a long time in coming—it will be reluctant to run prolonged surpluses. In general, the incentive for reducing a payments surplus is not as direct and immediate as that for a payments deficit.

Countries normally prefer to adjust their payments positions over time to move toward long-run equilibrium. The adjustment mechanism works for the return to equilibrium after the initial equilibrium has been disrupted. The process of payments adjustment takes two different forms. First, under certain conditions, there are adjustment factors that automatically promote equilibrium. Second, should the automatic adjustments be unable to restore equilibrium, *discretionary government policies* may be adopted to achieve this objective.

This chapter emphasizes the automatic balance-of-payments adjustment process that occurs under a fixed exchange rate system. The adjustment variables that we examine include *prices*, *interest rates*, and *income*. The impact of *money* on the balance of payments is also considered. Subsequent chapters discuss the adjustment mechanism under flexible exchange rates and the role of government policy in promoting payments adjustment.

Although the various automatic adjustment approaches have their contemporary advocates, each was formulated during a particular period and reflects a given body of economic thought. That the balance of payments could be adjusted by prices and interest rates stemmed from the classical economic thinking of the 1800s and early 1900s. The classical approach was geared toward the existing gold standard associated with fixed exchange rates. That income changes could promote balance-of-payments adjustments reflected the Keynesian theory of income determination that grew out of the Great Depression era of the 1930s. That money plays a crucial role in the long run as a disturbance and adjustment in the nation's balance of payments is an extension of domestic monetarism. This approach originated during the late 1960s and is associated with the Chicago school of thought.

Price Adjustments

The original theory of balance-of-payments adjustment is credited to David Hume (1711–1776), a noted English philosopher and economist.[1] Hume's theory arose from his concern with the prevailing mercantilist view that advocated government controls to ensure a continuous favorable balance of payments. According to Hume, this strategy was self-defeating over the long run, because a country's balance of payments tends automatically to move toward equilibrium over time. Hume's theory stresses the role that adjustments in national price levels play in promoting balance-of-payments equilibrium.

Gold Standards

The classical gold standard that existed from the late 1800s to the early 1900s was characterized by the following conditions: (1) Each member country's money supply consisted of gold or paper money backed by gold. (2) Each member country defined the official price of gold in terms of its national currency and was prepared to buy and sell gold at that price. (3) Free import and export of gold was permitted by member countries. These conditions resulted in a country's money supply being directly tied to its balance of payments. A country with a balance of payments surplus would acquire gold, directly expanding its money supply. Conversely, the money supply of a deficit country would decline as the result of a gold outflow.

The balance of payments can also be directly tied to a country's money supply under a modified gold standard or even a conventional fixed-exchange rate system. A modified gold standard would require that the country's stock of money be fractionally backed by gold at a constant ratio. It would also apply to a fixed exchange rate system in which payments disequilibriums are financed by some acceptable international reserve asset, assuming a constant ratio between the country's international reserves and its money supply is maintained.

Quantity Theory of Money

The essence of the classical price adjustment mechanism is embodied in the *quantity theory of money*. Consider the so-called *equation of exchange:*

$$MV = PQ.$$

M refers to a country's money supply. V refers to the velocity of money—that is, the number of times per year the average currency unit is spent on final goods. The expression MV corresponds to the aggregate demand or total monetary expenditures on final goods. In addition, the monetary expenditures on any year's output can be interpreted as the physical volume of all final goods produced (Q) multiplied by the average price at which each of the final goods is sold (P). As a result, $MV = PQ$.

This equation is an identity. It says that total monetary expenditures on final goods equals the monetary value of the final goods sold. The amount spent on final goods equals the amount received from selling them. The classical economists made two additional assumptions. First, they took the volume of final output (Q) to be fixed at the full employment level in the long run. Second, they assumed the velocity of money (V) was constant, depending on institutional, structural, and physical factors that rarely changed. With V and Q relatively stable, a change in M must induce a *direct and proportionate* change in P. The model linking changes in M to changes in P became known as the quantity theory of money.

Balance-of-Payments Adjustment

The preceding analysis showed how under the classical gold standard, the balance of payments is linked to a country's money supply, which is linked to its domestic price level. This section illustrates how the price level is linked to the balance of payments. Referring to Figure 13.1, suppose that under the classical gold standard, a country finds itself located at point D, where its balance of payments ($X - M$) shows a $40 billion

deficit. The deficit country would experience a gold outflow, which would reduce its money supply and thus its price level. The country's international competitive position would be enhanced, its exports rising and imports falling. This process would continue until its price index had fallen from 180 to 120, ($X = M$) being achieved at point E. On the other hand, a country located at point S would find its $40 billion surplus being eliminated by a persistent gold inflow and an increase in its money supply, until its price index had risen from 60 to 120 where ($X = M$) at point E. These two examples stress how the opposite price adjustment process would be taking place at the same time in each trading partner.

The price adjustment mechanism as devised by David Hume illustrated the impossibility of the mercantilist notion of maintaining a continuous favorable balance of payments. The linkages (balance of payments–money supply–price level–balance of payments) demonstrated to Hume that over time, balance-of-payments equilibrium tends to be achieved automatically.

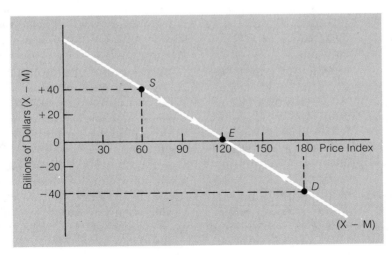

Figure 13.1   Price adjustment mechanism.

Critique of the Price Adjustment Mechanism

With the advent of Hume's price adjustment mechanism, classical economists had a very powerful and influential theory. It was not until the Keynesian revolution in economic thinking during the 1930s that this theory was effectively challenged. Even today, the price adjustment mechanism is a hotly debated issue. A brief discussion of some of the major criticisms against the price adjustment mechanism is in order.

The classical linkage between changes in a country's gold supply and its money supply no longer holds. Central bankers can easily offset a gold outflow (or inflow) by adopting an expansionary (or contractionary) monetary policy. The experience of the gold standard of the late 1800s and early 1900s indicates this was often what occurred in practice. The classical view that full employment always exists has also been challenged. When an economy is far below its full employment level, there is a smaller chance that prices in general will rise in response to an increase in the money supply than if the economy is at full employment. It has also been pointed out that in a modern industrial world, prices and wages are inflexible in a downward direction. If prices are inflexible downward, then changes in M will not affect P but rather Q. A deficit country's falling money supply would bring about a fall in output and employment. Furthermore, the stability and predictability of V has been questioned. Should a gold inflow that results in an increase in M be offset by a decline in V, total spending (MV) and PQ would remain unchanged.

These issues are part of the current debate over the price adjustment mechanism's relevance. They have caused sufficient doubts among economists to warrant a search for additional balance-of-payments adjustment explanations. The most notable include the effect of interest rate changes on capital movements and the effect of changing incomes on trade flows.

Interest Rate Adjustments

Under the classical gold standard, the price adjustment mechanism was not the only vehicle that served to restore equilibrium in the balance of payments. Another monetary effect of a payments surplus or deficit lay in its impact on *short-term interest rates* and hence on short-term private capital flows.

Consider a world of two countries—country A enjoying a surplus, country B facing a deficit. The inflow of gold from the deficit to the surplus country automatically results in an increase in country A's money supply and a decline in the money supply of country B. Induced by a payments surplus, country A enjoys a gold inflow and an increase in its money supply. Given a constant demand for money, this would lower domestic interest rates. At the same time, the opposite forces would be operating in country B. Country B's deficit would result in a gold outflow and a declining money supply, bidding up interest rates. In response to falling domestic interest rates and rising foreign interest rates, the investors of country A would find it attractive to send additional investment funds abroad. Conversely, country B investors would not only be discouraged from sending money overseas, but also might find it beneficial to liquidate foreign investment holdings and put the funds into domestic assets.

This process facilitates the automatic restoration of payments equilibrium in both countries. Because of the induced changes in interest rates, stabilizing capital movements automatically flow from the surplus to the deficit country. The result is that the payment imbalances of both countries are reduced. Although this induced short-term capital movement is of a temporary rather than continuous nature, it nevertheless facilitates the automatic balance-of-payments adjustment process.

During the actual operation of the gold standard, however, central bankers were not totally passive to these automatic adjustments. They instead agreed to reinforce and speed up the interest rate adjustment mechanism by adhering to the so-called *rules of the game*. This required central bankers in a surplus country to expand credit, leading to lower interest rates. Central bankers in deficit countries would tighten credit, bidding interest rates upward. The result is that private short-term capital presumably would flow from the surplus country to the deficit country. Not only would the deficit country's ability to finance its payments imbalance be strengthened, but also the surplus country's gold inflows would be checked.

The Gold Standard in Practice

When analyzing the so-called automatic adjustment mechanism, discussion often turns to the operation of the gold standard during its golden age of 1880–1914. Before World War I, the theoretical conditions for price and interest rate adjustments seemed to prevail. Did the gold standard in practice behave as the theoretical discussion suggests? Today, economic historians generally contend that even during its golden age, the gold standard adjustment mechanism was not all that automatic.

Under the rules of the game, central bankers agreed to react positively to gold flows in order to reinforce and speed up the automatic adjustment mechanism. Surplus countries enjoying gold inflows were to undergo an expansion in their money supplies, and deficit countries facing gold outflows were to contract their money supplies. In practice, the gold standard never operated quite so simply. Gold movements were often divorced from money supply when deficit nations undertook expansionary monetary policies and surplus countries adopted contractionary monetary policies. The Bank of England before World War I had an armory of devices for this purpose. By weakening the linkage between gold flows and

the money supply, such neutralization operations disrupted the automatic gold standard adjustment mechanism.

Even though the rules of the game were not followed precisely during the golden age of the gold standard, an era of balance-of-payments stability occurred. Part of the explanation for this lies in the equilibrating role of international capital movements. During the gold standard, wealthy surplus nations such as Great Britain acted as international bankers by generating a surplus of savings that the less-developed countries could draw on for financing sizable and lasting payments deficits. By easing the financing constraint that deficit nations faced, the capital flows had the effect of making massive gold movements unnecessary.

By disrupting the flow of trade and investments, World War I dealt the gold standard a blow from which it never really recovered. During the war, all major trading nations abandoned the gold standard. The 1920s' return to gold never worked out as satisfactorily as the prewar gold standard. Not only were the rules of the game disregarded, but also beggar-thy-neighbor trade and capital restrictions disrupted the system. Because capital movements were no longer permitted to exert their equilibrating influence, adherence to the rules of the game was critical to an efficient adjustment mechanism. But central bank neutralization policies and other measures undertaken to prevent price and interest rate adjustments paved the way for the gold standard's demise. The Great Depression of the 1930s put an end to the gold standard in Europe as well as in the United States.

Capital Flows and the Balance of Payments

Although not the central focus of their balance-of-payments adjustment theory, the classical economists were aware of the impact of *changes in interest rates on international capital movements*.

With national financial systems closely integrated today, it is recognized that interest rate fluctuations can induce significant changes in a country's capital account and balance-of-payments position.

Recall that the capital account of the balance of payments records net changes in a nation's international financial assets and liabilities, excluding changes in official reserves, over a one-year period. Its size depends on all the factors that cause financial assets to move across national borders. The most important of these factors is *interest rates* in domestic and foreign markets. However, other factors are important, such as investment profitability, national tax policies, and political stability.

Figure 13.2 illustrates the hypothetical capital account curves for the United States. Capital account surpluses (net capital inflows) and deficits (net capital outflows) are measured on the vertical axis. Capital flows between the United States and the rest of the world are

assumed to respond to *interest rate differentials* between the two areas (U.S. interest rate minus foreign interest rate) for a particular set of economic conditions in the United States and abroad.

Referring to capital account curve CA_0, the U.S. capital account is in balance (zero net capital flow) at point A, where the U.S. interest rate is equal to that abroad. Should the United States reduce its monetary growth, the scarcity of money would tend to raise interest rates in the United States compared with the rest of the world. Suppose U.S. interest rates rise 1 percent above those overseas. Investors, seeing higher U.S. interest rates, will tend to sell foreign securities to purchase American securities that offer a higher yield. The 1 percent interest rate differential leads to net capital inflows of $5 billion for the United States, which thus moves to point B on curve CA_0. Conversely, should foreign interest rates rise above those in the United States, the United States will face net capital outflows as

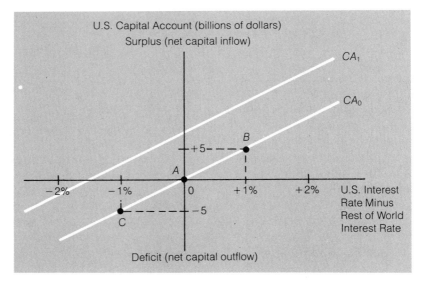

Figure 13.2   Capital account curve for the United States.

investors sell American securities to purchase foreign securities offering a higher yield.

Figure 13.2 assumes that interest rate differentials are the basic determinant of capital flows for the United States. Movements along a given capital account curve are caused by changes in the interest rate in the United States relative to the rest of the world's interest rate. Similarly, there are certain determinants other than interest rate differentials that might cause the United States to import (or export) more or less capital at each possible interest rate differential and thereby change the location of the capital account curve.

To illustrate, assume the United States is located along capital account curve CA_0 at point A. Suppose that rising U.S. income leads to higher sales and increased profits. Direct investment (for example, in an auto assembly plant) becomes more profitable in the United States. Nations such as Japan will invest more in their American subsidiaries, whereas General Motors will invest less overseas. The higher profitability of direct investment leads to more capital flowing into the United States at each possible interest rate differential and an upward shift in the capital account curve (for example, to curve CA_1).

Suppose the U.S. government levies an interest equalization tax, as it did from 1964–1974. This tax was intended to help reverse the large capital outflows that the United States faced when European interest rates exceeded those in the United States. By taxing Americans on dividend and interest income from foreign securities, the tax reduced the net profitability (that is, the after-tax yield) on foreign securities. At the same time, the U.S. government enacted a foreign credit restraint program, which placed direct restrictions on foreign lending by U.S. banks and financial institutions and later on foreign lending of nonfinancial corporations. By discouraging capital flows from the United States to Europe, these policies resulted in an upward shift in the U.S. capital account curve in terms of Figure 13.2, suggesting that less capital would flow out of the United States in response to higher interest rates overseas.

Although the emphasis of this chapter is on balance-of-payments adjustment under a system of fixed exchange rates, the reader may recognize that expectations of future exchange rate movements can influence international capital flows. It is possible that capital could flow between two countries in response to exchange rate expectations, even though the countries' interest rates are identical!

Referring to Figure 13.2, suppose the United States is located at point A along capital account curve CA_0. At this point, the interest rates of the United States and the rest of the world are identical and the United States experiences zero net capital flows. Suppose investors anticipate that in the future, the U.S. dollar will appreciate against foreign currencies. The value of securities denominated in dollars would be expected to rise relative to the value of securities denominated in foreign currencies. Investors will compare the expected return on foreign securities, indicated by the foreign interest rate, against the rate of return on American securities, which includes the rate of interest in the U.S. (assumed to be identical to the foreign interest rate) plus the added return due to the dollar appreciation. Because expectations of a future dollar appreciation result in U.S. securities becoming more attractive, investment funds would flow into the United States. The U.S. capital account curve shifts upward in the figure, suggesting that a greater amount of capital would flow into the United States at each possible interest rate differential.

Income Adjustments

The classical balance-of-payments adjustment theory relied primarily on the price adjustment mechanism, a secondary role being delegated to the effects of interest rates on private short-term capital movements. A main criticism of the classical theory was that it almost completely neglected the effect of income changes on the adjustment process. The classical economists were aware that the income, or purchasing power, of a surplus country rose relative to that of the deficit country. This would have an impact on the level of imports in each country. But the income effect was viewed as an accompaniment of price changes. Largely because the gold movements of the nineteenth century exerted only minor impacts on price and interest rate levels, economic theorists began to look for alternate balance-of-payments adjustment explanations under a fixed exchange rate system. The *theory of income determination* developed by John Maynard Keynes in the 1930s provided such an explanation.[2]

The Keynesian theory suggests that under a system of fixed exchange rates, the influence of income changes in surplus and deficit countries will automatically help restore payments equilibrium. Given a persistent payments imbalance, a surplus country would face rising income levels and thus increased imports. Conversely, a deficit country would experience a fall in income, resulting in a decline in imports. These effects of income changes on import levels would reverse a disequilibrium in the balance of payments.

Income Determination in a Closed Economy

Begin by assuming a *closed economy* with no foreign trade, with price and interest rate levels constant. In this simple Keynesian model, national income (Y) is the sum of consumption expenditures (C) plus savings (S).

$$Y = C + S.$$

Total expenditures on national product are C plus business investment (I). This relationship is given by

$$Y = C + I.$$

The upper part of Figure 13.3 represents the familiar income determination model found in introductory economics textbooks. Consumption is assumed to be functionally dependent on income, whereas investment spending is autonomous—that is, independent of the level of income. The economy is in equilibrium when the level of planned expenditures equals income. This occurs at Y_E, where the 45° line intersects the ($C + I$) curve. At any level of income lower (or higher) than Y_E, planned expenditure would exceed (or fall below) income, and income would rise (or fall).

Combining these relationships yields the following:

$$Y = C + S = C + I.$$

The basic equilibrium condition can be stated as

$$S = I$$

or

$$S - I = 0.$$

This equivalent condition for equilibrium income is illustrated in the lower part of Figure 13.3. Like consumption, saving is assumed to be functionally related to income. Given a constant level of investment, the $S - I$ curve is upward sloping. Savings can be regarded as a leakage from the income stream, whereas investment is an injection into the income stream. At income levels below Y_E, I exceeds S, the level of income rising. The opposite holds equally true. The economy is thus in equilibrium where $S = I$ (or $S - I = 0$). The lower part of Figure 13.3 is later used to illustrate income determination in an open economy.

Suppose an economy that is initially in equilibrium experiences some disturbance, say an

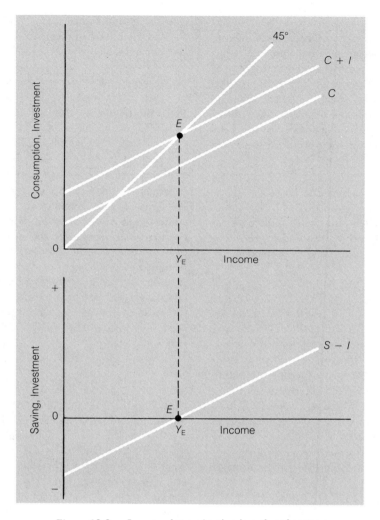

Figure 13.3   Income determination in a closed economy.

increase in investment spending. This would bid up the level of equilibrium income. This comes about by the *multiplier process*—the initial investment sets off a chain reaction that results in greater levels of spending, so that income increases by some multiple of the initial investment. Given an autonomous injection of investment spending into the economy, the induced increase in income is given by

$$\Delta Y = \Delta I \times \text{Multiplier}$$

or,

$$\Delta Y = \Delta I \times (1/\text{marginal propensity to save}).$$

To show how the multiplier is derived for a closed economy, first remember that in equilibrium, an economy will find planned saving equal to planned investment. It follows that any ΔI must be matched by an equivalent ΔS if the economy is to remain in balance. Because it has been assumed that saving is functionally dependent on income, changes in saving will be related to changes in income, or $\Delta S = s\Delta Y$, where s represents the marginal propensity to save out of additional income levels. Given an autonomous increase in investment, the equilibrium condition suggests that

$$\Delta I = \Delta S = s\Delta Y.$$

The multiplier concept shows the induced relationship between I and Y. From the preceding expression, the multiplier can be derived as

$$\Delta Y = \Delta I \times 1/s.$$

Suppose, for example, a country finds that its marginal propensity to save (MPS) is 0.25, and there occurs an autonomous increase in investment of $100. According to the multiplier principle, the induced change in income stemming from the initial increase in investment spending equals the increase in investment spending times the multiplier (k). Since the MPS is assumed to equal 0.25, $k = 1/MPS = 1/0.25 = 4$. The $100 increase in investment expenditure ultimately results in a $400 increase in the level of income.

Income Determination in an Open Economy

Now assume an *open economy* subject to international trade. The condition for equilibrium income, as well as the formulation of the spending multiplier, must both be modified. In an open economy, imports (M), like savings, constitute a leakage out of the income stream, whereas exports (X), like investment, represent an injection into the stream of national income. The condi-

tion for equilibrium income, which relates leakages to injections in an open economy's income stream, becomes

$$S + M = I + X.$$

Rearranging terms, this becomes

$$S - I = X - M.$$

Assume that exports are unrelated to the level of domestic income. Also, assume that imports are functionally dependent on domestic income—that is, $\Delta M = m\Delta Y$, where m represents the marginal propensity to import. We are now in a position to derive what is known as the *foreign trade multiplier*.

First, let the injections and leakages into the income stream rise by the same amount, so that the induced change in income will be of equilibrium magnitude. This yields

$$\Delta S + \Delta M = \Delta I + \Delta X.$$

Since $\Delta S = s\Delta Y$ and $\Delta M = m\Delta Y$, the induced change in income stemming from the changes in injections and leakages can be shown as follows:

$$(s + m)\,\Delta Y = \Delta I + \Delta X.$$

Holding exports constant, the induced change in income is equal to the change in investment times the foreign trade multiplier, or

$$\Delta Y = \Delta I \times 1/(s + m).$$

The preceding expression states that the *foreign trade multiplier equals the reciprocal of the sum of the marginal propensities to save and to import.* In the preceding formulation, an autonomous change in exports, investment remaining fixed, would have an impact on domestic income identical to an equivalent change in investment.

Foreign Trade Multiplier Implications

To show the adjustment implications of the foreign trade multiplier concept, we construct a diagram based on the framework of Figure 13.3. Remember that the $(S - I)$ curve is positively sloped. This is because changes in savings are assumed to be directly related to changes in income, investment being unaffected. Subtracting investment from saving yields an upward sloping $(S - I)$ curve, as shown in Figure 13.4. Similarly it has been assumed that changes in imports are directly related to changes in income, exports remaining constant. When imports are subtracted from exports, the result is a downward sloping $(X - M)$ curve. As before, the equilibrium condition of an open economy with no government requires $(X - M) = (S - I)$.

Starting at equilibrium income level $1,000 in Figure 13.4, suppose a disturbance results in an autonomous increase in exports by, say $200. This is shown by shifting the $(X - M)$ schedule upward by $200, resulting in the new schedule $(X' - M)$. The level of income rises, generating increases in imports and savings. Domestic equilibrium is established at income level $1,400, where $(S - I) = (X' - M)$. The trade account is no longer in balance, for there exists a trade surplus of $100. This surplus is less than the initial $200 rise in exports, because part of the surplus is offset by increases in imports induced by the rise in income from $1,000 to $1,400.

In this example, we can use the foreign trade multiplier concept to determine the effect of the increase in exports on the home economy. Inspection of the $(S - I)$ schedule in Figure 13.4 reveals that the slope of the curve, and thus the marginal propensity to save, equals 0.25. The $(X - M)$ schedule also indicates that the marginal propensity to import equals 0.25. The foreign

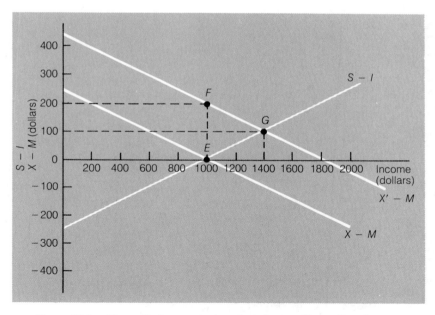

Figure 13.4   Domestic income and trade balance effects of an increase in exports.

trade multiplier has a value of 2.0 (the reciprocal of the sum of the marginal propensities to save and to import). An autonomous increase in exports of $200 would generate a twofold increase in domestic income, equilibrium income rising from $1,000 to $1,400. As for the trade account effect, the $400 rise in domestic income induces a $100 increase in imports, given a marginal propensity to import of 0.25. Part of the initial export-led surplus is neutralized, lowering it from $200 to $100. The increase in imports generated by increased domestic expenditures will over time tend to reduce the trade surplus, but not enough to restore balance-of-payments equilibrium.

Consider another case that illustrates the national income and balance-of-payments effects of a change in expenditures. Assume that owing to improved profit expectations, domestic investment rises autonomously by $200. Starting at equilibrium level $1,000 in Figure 13.5, the increase in investment will displace the $(S - I)$ schedule downward by $200, since the negative term is increased. This gives us the new schedule $(S - I')$. Domestic income rises from $1,000 to $1,400, which stimulates a rise in imports and a trade deficit of $100. Unlike the previous case of export-led expansion, an autonomous increase in domestic investment spending (or government expenditures) increases domestic income, but at the expense of a balance-of-payments deficit. This should serve as a reminder to economic policy makers that under a system of fixed exchange rates, the impact of domestic policies on the balance of payments cannot be overlooked.

Foreign Repercussions

The preceding income adjustment analysis needs to be modified to include the impact that changes in domestic expenditures and income

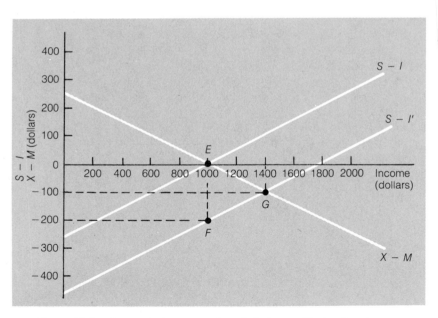

Figure 13.5　Domestic income and trade balance effects of an increase in investment.

levels have on foreign economies. This process is referred to as the *foreign repercussion effect*. Assume a two-country world, the United States and Canada, in which there initially exists balance-of-payments equilibrium. Owing to changing consumer preferences, suppose the United States faces an autonomous increase in imports from Canada. This results in an increase in Canada's exports. According to the multiplier principle, U.S. income would fall and Canada's income would rise. Induced by the fall in its income, the level of U.S. imports falls (and Canada's exports fall). At the same time, the rise in Canada's income induces a rise in Canada's imports (and a rise in U.S. exports). This feedback process is repeated again and again.

The consequence of this feedback process is that both the rise in income of the surplus country (Canada) and the fall in income of the deficit country (United States) are dampened. This is because the autonomous increase in U.S. imports (and Canada's exports) will cause the U.S. income to decrease as imports are substituted for home-produced goods. Given the marginal propensity to import, the decline in U.S. income will generate a reduction in its imports. Because U.S. imports are Canada's exports, the result will be to moderate the rise in Canada's income. From the perspective of the United States, the decline in its income will be cushioned by an increase in exports to Canada stemming from a rise in Canada's income.

The importance of the foreign repercussion effect depends in part on the economic size of a country so far as international trade is concerned. A small country, by increasing its imports from a large country, will have little impact on the large country's income level. The repercussion effect is therefore negligible for a country whose exports and imports are a minor part of world trade. But for major trading nations, the foreign repercussion effect is likely to be significant and must be taken into account when considering the income adjustment mechanism.

Disadvantages of Automatic Adjustment Mechanisms

The preceding sections have considered automatic balance-of-payments adjustment mechanisms under a system of fixed exchange rates. According to the classical school of thought, adjustments take the form of prices and interest rates responding to international gold movements. Keynesian theory emphasized another adjustment process, the effect of changes in national income on a country's balance of payments.

Although elements of price, interest rates, and income adjustments may operate in the real world, these adjustment mechanisms have a major shortcoming. The problem is that an efficient adjustment mechanism requires central bankers to forego their use of monetary policy to promote the goal of full employment without inflation. Each country must therefore be willing to accept inflation or recession when balance-of-payments adjustment requires it. Take the case of a nation that faces a deficit caused by an autonomous increase in imports or decrease in exports. For income adjustments to reverse the deficit, monetary authorities must permit domestic income to decrease and not undertake policies to offset its decline. The opposite applies equally to a country with a balance-of-payments surplus.

To the classical economists, the abandonment of an independent monetary policy would not be considered a disadvantage. This is because classical thought envisioned a system that would automatically move toward full employment over time, as well as placing a high priority on balance-of-payments adjustment. In today's world, unemployment is often the norm. Its elimination is generally given priority over balance-of-payments equilibrium. Modern nations are therefore reluctant to make significant internal sacrifices for the sake of external equilibrium. The result is that reliance on an automatic payments adjustment process is politically unacceptable.

Monetary Adjustments

The previous sections examined how changes in national price, interest rate, and income levels automatically lead to balance-of-payments adjustment. During the 1960s and 1970s, a new theory emerged, called the *monetary approach to the balance of payments*.[3] The monetary approach views disequilibriums in the balance of payments primarily as a monetary phenomenon. Money acts as both a disturbance and an adjustment to the balance of payments. Adjustment in the balance of payments is viewed as an automatic process.

Payments Imbalances Under Fixed Exchange Rates*

The monetary approach emphasizes that balance-of-payments disequilibriums reflect imbalance between the demand and the supply of money. A first assumption is that over the long run, the nation's demand for money is a stable function of *real income*, *prices*, and the *rate of interest*.

The quantity of nominal money balances demanded is directly related to income and prices. Increases in income and/or prices trigger increases in the value of transactions and an increased need for money to finance the transactions, and vice versa. The quantity of money demanded is inversely related to the interest rate. Whenever money is held rather than used to make an investment, the holder of money sacrifices interest that could have been earned on the investment. If interest rates are high, people will try to keep as little money on hand as possible, putting the rest into interest-earning investments. Conversely, a decline in interest rates increases the quantity of money demanded.

*A discussion of the monetary approach under floating exchange rates is presented in Chapter 15.

The nation's *money supply* is a multiple of the monetary base that includes two components. The *domestic component* refers to credit created by the nation's monetary authorities (for example, Federal Reserve liabilities for the United States). The *international component* refers to the foreign exchange reserves of a nation, which can be increased or decreased as the result of balance-of-payments disequilibriums.

The monetary approach maintains that all payments deficits are the result of an excess in the supply of money over the demand for money in the home country. Under a fixed exchange rate system, the excess supply of money promotes a payments deficit, resulting in foreign exchange reserves flowing overseas and a reduction in the domestic money supply. Conversely, an excess demand for money in the home country leads to a payments surplus, resulting in the inflow of foreign exchange reserves from overseas and an increase in the domestic money supply. Balance in the country's payments position is restored when the excess supply of money, or the excess demand for money, has fallen enough to restore the equilibrium condition: *money supply equals money demand*. Table 13.1 summarizes the conclusions of the monetary approach, given a system of fixed exchange rates.

To illustrate, assume that to finance a budget deficit, the Canadian government creates additional money. Considering this money to be in excess of desired levels (excess money supply), suppose Canadian residents choose to increase their spending on goods and services instead of holding extra cash balances. Given a fixed exchange rate system, the rise in home spending will push up the prices of Canadian goods and services relative to those abroad. Canadian buyers will be induced to decrease purchases of Canadian-produced goods and services, as will foreign buyers. Conversely, Canadian sellers will offer more goods at home and fewer abroad, whereas foreign sellers will try to increase sales to Canada. By encouraging a rise in imports and

Table 13.1   Changes in the Supply of Money and Demand for Money Under Fixed Exchange Rates: Impact on the Balance of Payments According to the Monetary Approach

Change*	Impact
Increase in money supply	Deficit
Decrease in money supply	Surplus
Increase in money demand	Surplus
Decrease in money demand	Deficit

*Starting from a position where the nation's money demand equals the money supply and its balance of payments is in equilibrium.

a fall in exports, these forces tend to worsen the Canadian payments position. As Canada finances its deficit by transferring international reserves to foreign nations, the Canadian money supply will fall back toward desired levels. This in turn will reduce Canadian spending and demand for imports, restoring payments balance.

The monetary approach views balance-of-payments adjustment as an automatic process. Any payments imbalance reflects a disparity between actual and desired money balances that tends to be eliminated by inflows or outflows of foreign exchange reserves, which leads to increases or decreases in the domestic money supply. This self-correcting process requires time. Except for implying that the adjustment period will be the long run, the monetary approach does not consider the time period needed to achieve equilibrium. The monetary approach thus emphasizes the economy's final, long-run equilibrium position.

The monetary approach assumes that flows in foreign exchange reserves associated with payments imbalances do exert an influence on the domestic money supply. This is true as long as central banks do not use monetary policies to neutralize the impact of flows in foreign exchange reserves on the domestic money supply. If they do neutralize such flows, payments imbalances will continue, according to the monetary approach.

Policy Implications

What implications does the monetary approach have for domestic economic policies? The monetary approach suggests that economic policy affects the balance of payments through its impact on the domestic demand for and supply of money. A policy that increases the supply of money relative to the demand for money will lead to a payments deficit, an outflow of foreign exchange reserves, and a reduction in the domestic money supply. Policies that increase the demand for money relative to the supply of money will trigger a payments surplus, an inflow of foreign exchange reserves, and an increase in the domestic money supply.

The monetary approach also suggests that nonmonetary policies that attempt to influence a nation's balance of payments (for example, tariffs, quotas, or currency devaluation) are unnecessary, since payments disequilibriums are self-correcting over time. However, in the short run, such policies may speed up the adjustment process by reducing excesses in the supply of money or the demand for money.

For example, given an initial equilibrium, suppose the Canadian government creates money in excess of that demanded by the economy, leading to a payments deficit. The monetary approach maintains that in the long run, foreign exchange reserves automatically would flow out of Canada and the Canadian money supply would decrease. This would continue until the money supply decreases enough to restore the equilibrium condition: money supply equals money demand. To speed up the return to equilibrium, suppose Canada imposes a tariff on imports. The tariff increases the price of imports as well as the prices of nontraded goods (that is, goods produced exclusively for the domestic market, which face no competition from imports), owing to interproduct substitution. Higher Canadian prices trigger an increase in the quantity of money demanded, since Canadians now require additional funds to finance higher-priced purchases. The increase in the quantity of money demanded absorbs part of the excess money supply. The tariff therefore results in a more speedy elimination of the excess money supply and payments deficit than would occur under an automatic adjustment mechanism.[4]

The monetary approach also has policy implications for the growth of the economy. Starting from the point of equilibrium, as the nation's output and real income expand, so do the number of transactions and the quantity of money demanded. If the government does not increase the domestic component of the money supply with the increase in the quantity of money demanded, the excess demand will induce an inflow of funds from abroad and a payments surplus. This explanation often is advanced for the West German payments surpluses that occurred during the late sixties and early seventies, a period when the growth in West German national output and money demand surpassed the growth in the domestic component of the West German money supply.

Summary

1. Because persistent balance-of-payments disequilibriums—be they surpluses or deficits—tend to have adverse economic consequences, there exists a need for adjustment.

2. Balance-of-payments adjustment may be classified as automatic or discretionary. Under a system of fixed exchange rates, automatic adjustments may arise through variations in prices, interest rates, and incomes. The demand for and supply of money can also influence the adjustment process.

3. David Hume's adjustment mechanism was an explanation of the automatic adjustment process that occurs under the gold standard. Starting from a condition of payments balance, any surplus or deficit would automatically be eliminated by changes in domestic price levels. Hume's theory relied heavily on the quantity theory of money.

4. Another important consequence of international gold movements under the classical theory lay in their impact on short-term interest rates. A deficit nation suffering gold losses would face a shrinking money supply, which would force up interest rates, promoting capital inflows and payments equilibrium. The opposite holds true for a surplus country. Rather than relying on automatic adjustments in interest rates to restore payments balance, central bankers often resorted to monetary policies designed to reinforce the adjustment mechanism during the gold standard era.

5. With the advent of Keynesian economics during the 1930s, greater adjustment emphasis was put on the income effects of trade.

6. In an open economy, national income is in equilibrium when savings plus imports just match investment plus exports.

7. The foreign trade multiplier equals the reciprocal of the sum of the marginal propensity to save and the marginal propensity to import.

8. The foreign repercussion effect refers to a situation whereby a change in one country's macroeconomic variables will induce a chain reaction in both countries' economies.

9. There are several main disadvantages of an automatic balance-of-payments adjustment mechanism. Countries must be willing to accept changes in the domestic economy where balance-of-payments adjustment requires it. Policy makers must forego using discretionary economic policy to promote domestic equilibrium.

10. The monetary approach to the balance of payments is presented as an alternative, instead of a supplement, to traditional adjustment theories. It maintains that over the long

run, payments disequilibriums are rooted in the relationship between the demand for and the supply of money. Adjustment in the balance of payments is viewed as an automatic process.

Study Questions

1. What is meant by the term *balance-of-payments adjustment*? Why does a deficit country have an incentive to undergo adjustment? How about a surplus country?

2. Under a fixed exchange rate system, what automatic adjustments promote payments equilibrium?

3. What is meant by the quantity theory of money? How did it relate to the classical price adjustment mechanism?

4. How can adjustments in domestic interest rates help promote payments balance?

5. In the gold standard era, there existed the so-called rules of the game. What were these rules? Were they followed in practice?

6. Keynesian theory suggests that under a system of fixed exchange rates, the influence of income changes in surplus and deficit countries helps promote balance-of-payments equilibrium. Explain.

7. What is the foreign trade multiplier? What factors underlie its size?

8. When analyzing the income adjustment mechanism, one must account for the foreign repercussion effect. Explain.

9. What are some major disadvantages of the automatic adjustment mechanism under a system of fixed exchange rates?

10. According to the monetary approach, balance in a country's payments position is restored when the excess supply of money or the excess demand for money have

fallen to restore the equilibrium condition: money supply equals money demand. Explain.

11. What implications does the monetary approach have for domestic economic policies?

Notes

1. David Hume, "Of the Balance of Trade," reprinted in *International Finance: Selected Readings*, ed. Richard N. Cooper (Harmondsworth, England: Penguin Books, 1969), chap. 1.

2. John Maynard Keynes, *The General Theory of Employment, Interest, and Money* (London: Macmillan, 1936).

3. Having its intellectual background at the University of Chicago, the monetary approach to the balance of payments originated with Robert Mundell, *International Economics* (New York: Macmillan, 1968) and Harry Johnson, "The Monetary Approach to Balance of Payments Theory," *Journal of Financial and Quantitative Analysis* (March 1972).

4. An import quota would promote payments equilibrium by restricting the supply of Canadian imports and increasing their price. The quantity of money demanded by Canadians rises, reducing the excess money supply and the payments deficit. As is discussed in Chapter 14, a currency devaluation also leads to higher-priced imports. This generates higher quantities of money demanded and a shrinking payments deficit, according to the monetary approach.

Suggestions for Further Reading

Aghevli, B. B. "The Balance of Payments and the Money Supply Under the Gold Standard Regime: U.S. 1879–1914." *American Economic Review*, March 1975.

Bryant, R. C. *Money and Monetary Policy in an Open Economy*. Washington, D.C.: The Brookings Institution, 1980.

Dornbusch, R. *Open Economy Macroeconomics*. New York: Basic Books, 1980.

Hawtrey, R. G. *The Gold Standard in Theory and Practice*. London: Longmans, Green, 1947.

Hinshaw, R., ed. *The Economics of International Adjustment*. Baltimore: Johns Hopkins Press, 1971.

Keynes, J. M. *A Treatise on Money*, vol. 2. London: Macmillan, 1930.

Kreinin, M., and L. Officer. *The Monetary Approach to the Balance of Payments*. Studies in International Finance, no. 43. Princeton N.J.: Princeton University Press, 1978.

Krueger, A. O. "Balance of Payments Theory." *Journal of Economic Literature*, March 1969.

Machlup, F. *International Trade and the National Income Multiplier*. Philadelphia: Blakistan, 1943.

Meade, J. E. *The Balance of Payments*. Oxford: Oxford University Press, 1951.

Robinson, R. "A Graphical Analysis of the Foreign Trade Multiplier." *Economic Journal*, September 1952.

Stern, R. M. *The Balance of Payments*. Chicago: Aldine, 1973.

14

ADJUSTABLE EXCHANGE RATES AND THE BALANCE OF PAYMENTS

The previous chapter emphasized that balance-of-payments disequilibriums tend to be reversed by automatic economic adjustments under a fixed exchange rate system. If these automatic adjustments are allowed to operate, however, reversing balance-of-payments disequilibriums may come at the expense of domestic disequilibrium in the form of falling production and income, unemployment, and price deflation. The cure may be perceived as being worse than the disease.

Instead of exclusively relying on automatic adjustment mechanisms to counteract payments imbalances, all contemporary governments attempt to exercise influence over economic transactions with foreigners. One adjustment policy uses *exchange rate management*. Under a system of fixed exchange rates, governments have adopted currency *devaluation* and *revaluation* policies to promote payments equilibrium. This chapter examines the operation and consequences of currency devaluation and revaluation.

Fixed Exchange Rate System

Very few nations have in practice allowed the value of their currencies to be established solely by the forces of supply and demand in a free market. Until the industrialized countries adop-

ted managed floating exchange rates, the practice generally was to maintain a pattern of relatively fixed exchange rates among national currencies. Changes in national exchange rates presumably were to be initiated by domestic monetary authorities when long-term market forces warranted it.[1]

Par Value

To fix an exchange rate, a currency is assigned a par value by domestic monetary authorities. The *par value* is then the official exchange rate of the home currency against foreign currencies. Par values have been set in several different ways. National currencies have been defined against gold, key foreign currencies, or composite units of account such as the Special Drawing Right (SDR). In Figure 14.1, which represents the U.S. foreign exchange market, the dollar's par value might be set equal to, say, $2.40 per pound. Ideally, this official exchange rate is set at or near the long-term market equilibrium rate, so its value reflects existing economic conditions.

Under the Bretton Woods agreement, which governed the world's international financial system from the 1940s until the 1970s, member countries declared the par values of their

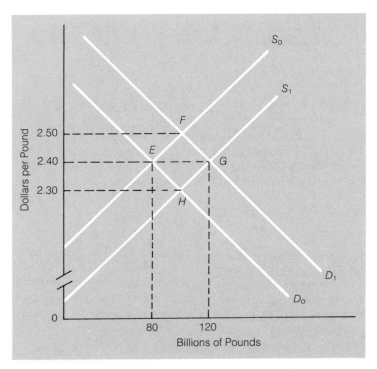

Figure 14.1   Exchange rate stabilization under a fixed exchange rate system.

currencies in terms of gold. Gold was the numeraire or standard by which currencies were compared and exchanged. For example, the official exchange rate between the U.S. dollar and British pound would be at $2.40 = 1 pound as long as the United States would buy and sell gold for $35 per ounce and Britain would value gold at 14.58 pounds per ounce. By agreeing to buy and sell unlimited quantities of gold at the official price, fixed exchange rates had to exist between member nation currencies.

In addition to having gold serve as a numeraire, many countries have chosen to define their par values in terms of certain key currencies such as the U.S. dollar. A *key currency* is one that is widely traded on world money markets, has demonstrated relatively stable values

over time, and has been widely accepted as a means of international settlement. Under this arrangement, the monetary authority first defines its official exchange rate in terms of the key currency. It then defends the fixed parity by purchasing and selling its currency for the key currency at that rate. Assume, for example, that Bolivian central bankers fix their peso at 20 pesos = $1 U.S., whereas Ecuador's sucre is set at 10 sucres = $1 U.S. The official exchange rate between the peso and sucre becomes 1 peso = ½ sucre.

One reason why various nations have opted to maintain parities in terms of key currencies is that they are widely used as a means of international settlement. Consider a Norwegian importer who wants to purchase Argentinian beef over the next year. If the Argentine exporter is unsure of what the Norwegian krone will purchase in one year, he might reject the krone in settlement. Similarly, the Norwegian importer might doubt the value of Argentina's peso. One solution is for the contract to be written in terms of a key currency such as the U.S. dollar. Generally speaking, smaller countries with relatively undiversified economies and large foreign trade sectors have been inclined to peg the value of their currency to one of the key currencies. The majority of the less-developed countries have, for example, maintained fixed links with the currency that they traditionally use to intervene in the exchange market—typically dollars, pounds, and francs.

Perhaps the greatest problem associated with fixing a national currency's parity against a single currency is that the value of the numeraire currency may fluctuate over time. Such fluctuations induce changes in the exchange rates of all national currencies quoted against it. To avoid this problem, a domestic monetary authority may set the parity of its currency in terms of some average or composite of a group of major currencies. These composites have been chosen to reflect the trading pattern of a given country.

Exchange Rate Stabilization

A first requirement for a country participating in a fixed exchange rate system is to determine a par value for its currency. The next step is to set up a mechanism by which the official exchange rate can be defended against changing market conditions.[2] This requires the country to establish an *exchange stabilization fund*, which the monetary authorities can use in pegging the exchange rate. The *pegging technique* requires the monetary authority to supply at the official rate all of the nation's currency that is demanded at that rate and to demand at the official rate all the nation's currency that is offered to it.

Referring to Figure 14.1, suppose an increase in U.S. incomes results in a rise in the demand for British exports. Starting at the official exchange rate of $2.40 per pound, let the induced increase in the demand for pounds be from D_0 to D_1. Under free market conditions, the dollar would depreciate from $2.40 per pound to $2.50 per pound. But under a fixed exchange rate system, the monetary authority will attempt to defend the official rate. At $2.40 per pound there exists an excess amount of pounds demanded equal to 40 billion pounds, from the U.S. point of view. This means that the British face an excess supply of dollars by the same amount. To keep the exchange rate from depreciating beyond $2.40 per pound, the U.S. exchange stabilization fund is used to purchase the excess supply of dollars for an equivalent amount of pounds. This in effect increases the supply of pounds from S_0 to S_1, resulting in the exchange rate being stabilized at $2.40 per pound. Conversely, during times of a dollar appreciation, the stabilization process would require the U.S. stabilization fund to purchase foreign currency with dollars.

These cases illustrate how an exchange stabilization fund undertakes its pegging operations. But from time to time, the par value and long-term equilibrium rate may move apart, reflecting changes in fundamental economic conditions—income levels, tastes and preferences, and technological conditions. In the case of a fundamental disequilibrium, the cost of defending the established par value may become prohibitive.

Take the case of a deficit country that finds its currency depreciating in the exchange market. To maintain the official rate may require the exchange stabilization fund to purchase sizable quantities of its currency with foreign currencies or other reserve assets. This may impose a severe drain on the deficit country's stock of international reserves. Although the deficit country may be able to borrow reserves from other countries or from the International Monetary Fund to continue the defense of its exchange rate, such borrowing privileges are generally of limited magnitude. At the same time, the deficit country will be undergoing internal adjustments to curb the disequilibrium. These measures will likely be aimed at controlling inflationary pressures and at raising interest rates to promote capital inflows and discourage imports. If the imbalance is persistent, the deficit country may view such internal adjustments as too costly in terms of falling income and employment levels. Rather than continually resorting to this measure, the deficit country may decide that the reversal of the disequilibrium calls for an adjustment in the exchange rate itself. Under a system of pegged exchange rates, a chronic imbalance may be counteracted by a currency devaluation in the case of a deficit country and a revaluation in a surplus country's case.

Devaluation and Revaluation

Under a pegged exchange rate system, a country's monetary authority may decide to pursue balance-of-payments equilibrium by adopting a currency devaluation or revaluation. Technically speaking, a *devaluation* implies an increase in the exchange rate (stated as the value of foreign currencies in terms of the domestic currency) from one par value to another. The purpose of devaluation is to cause the home currency to depreciate in value, so that the home currency's price falls in terms of foreign currencies. This policy is normally used by countries desiring to remove payments deficits. A *revaluation* suggests a decrease in the exchange rate from one par value to another. By causing the home currency's exchange rate to appreciate in value against foreign currencies, such a policy removes a payments surplus. Table 14.1 gives examples of currency devaluations and revaluations that occurred under the historic Bretton Woods system of fixed exchange rates.

The terms *devaluation* and *revaluation* technically refer to a legal redefinition of a currency's par value under a system of pegged exchange rates. The terms *depreciation* and *appreciation* are typically used to refer to the actual impact on the market exchange rate caused by a redefinition of a par value or to changes in an exchange rate stemming from changes in the supply of or demand for foreign exchange.

Devaluation and revaluation policies are considered to be *expenditure-switching* instruments. This is because they work on relative prices to switch domestic and foreign expenditures between home and foreign goods. By raising the home price of the foreign currency, a devaluation makes the home country exports cheaper to foreigners in terms of the foreign currency, while making the home country's imports more expensive in terms of the home currency. Expenditures are diverted from foreign to home goods as home exports rise and imports fall. In like manner, a revaluation discourages home country

Table 14.1 Selected Devaluations and Revaluations, 1946–1970

Year	Country	Percentage Change in Par Value
Devaluations		
1949	Australia	31
1949	United Kingdom	31
1949	Netherlands	30
1954	Mexico	30
1957	Finland	28
1958	France	18
1967	United Kingdom	14
Revaluations		
1961	West Germany	5
1961	Netherlands	5
1969	West Germany	9

Source: International Monetary Fund, *International Financial Statistics*, December 1971, p. 6.

exports and encourages its imports, diverting expenditures from home goods to foreign goods.

The policy measures of devaluation and revaluation differ from freely floating (market-determined) exchange rates in a number of ways. Before implementing a devaluation or revaluation, the monetary authority must decide (1) if an adjustment in the official exchange rate is necessary to correct a payments disequilibrium, (2) when the adjustment will occur, and (3) the size of the adjustment that will take place. Because exchange rates are not determined by the free market forces of supply and demand, exchange rate decisions may be incorrect—that is, ill-timed and of improper magnitude. In making the decision to undergo a devaluation or revaluation, monetary authorities generally attempt to hide behind a veil of secrecy. Just hours before the decision is to become effective, public denials of any such policies by official government representatives are common. This is to discourage currency speculators, who try to profit by shifting funds from a currency falling in value to one rising in value. Given the destabilizing impact that massive speculation can exert on financial markets, it is hard to criticize monetary authorities for being secretive in their actions. However, the need for devaluation tends to be obvious to outsiders as well as to government officials, and in the past has nearly always resulted in heavy speculative pressures.

Legal Versus Economic Implications

Both currency devaluations and revaluations are used in conjunction with a fixed exchange rate system, whereby the monetary authority changes a currency's exchange rate by decree and usually by sizable amounts at a time. Just how is such a policy carried out in practice? To understand this process, we must keep in mind both the legal and economic implications of currency devaluations and revaluations.

Under a fixed exchange rate system, the home currency is assigned a par value by the nation's monetary authorities. The par value is the amount of a nation's currency that is required to purchase a fixed amount of gold, a key currency, or the Special Drawing Right. Gold, key currency, or SDR represents the legal numeraire, or the unit of contractual obligations. By comparing various national currency prices of the numeraire, the official rate of exchange is determined for the currencies. In the legal sense, a devaluation or revaluation occurs when the home country redefines its currency price of the official numeraire, changing the par value. Assuming other trading nations retain their existing par values, a change in the home country's exchange rate occurs. The home country's exchange rate moves from one par value to another. The economic effect of the legal redefinition of the par value is the impact on the market rate of exchange. One would expect an official devaluation of a currency to result in a depreciation in its exchange rate against other currencies, whereas a currency revaluation would lead to an appreciation in the home country exchange rate.

Figure 14.2 illustrates the *legal and economic implications* of devaluation-revaluation policies.[3] For historical perspective, let gold serve as the numeraire by which the value of individual currencies relative to each other can be defined. The diagram's vertical axis denotes the U.S. dollar's price of an ounce of gold, and the horizontal axis depicts the British pound's (representative of the rest of the world currencies) price of an ounce of gold. Three price ratios are illustrated by each point in the figure: (1) the dollar price of gold, (2) the pound price of gold, and (3) the dollar price of the pound, indicated by the value of the slope of a ray connecting the origin with any point in the figure.

Suppose the United States sets its par value at $35 per gold ounce, whereas the British par value equals 14.58 pounds per gold ounce.

Connecting these two prices yields point Q in the diagram. Relative to each other, the official exchange rate between the dollar and pound is $2.40 = 1 pound, denoted by the slope of the ray *OQ*. Assume now that the United States wishes to devalue the dollar by, say, 10 percent to correct a payments deficit. Starting at point Q, this would be achieved by having the United States raise the official price of gold from $35 to $38.50 per ounce, a 10 percent increase. This results in a movement from point Q to point R. Corresponding to the slope of ray *OR*, the new exchange rate is $2.64 = 1 pound. The dollar devaluation thus results in its depreciating against the pound by 10 percent ($2.64 exceeds $2.40 by $0.24, or 10 percent). Conversely, suppose the United States revalues the dollar 10 percent to reverse a payments surplus. Starting at point Q in Figure 14.2, the United States would lower

the official price of gold from $35 to $31.50. The value of the dollar against the pound would increase from $2.40 = 1 pound to $2.16 = 1 pound, an appreciation of 10 percent.

To change the dollar/pound exchange rate, it is not merely sufficient for the United States to redefine the dollar's par value. It is also required that the par value of Britain remain constant or be altered by a smaller fraction. A change in the dollar/pound exchange rate requires a change in the slope of ray *OQ*. The United States acting by itself can only establish the vertical position in the diagram. Since Britain determines the horizontal position, any redefinition of the U.S. par value can be neutralized by an equivalent change in the British par value. This means that Britain can offset any change in the slope of the ray that the United States may wish to undertake. For example, let us start at point Q, where the

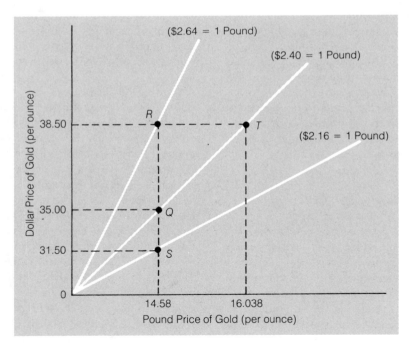

Figure 14.2   Devaluation-revaluation: legal versus economic implications.

exchange rate is set at $2.40 = 1 pound. Facing a payments deficit, suppose the United States devalues the dollar 10 percent by increasing the official price of gold from $35 to $38.50 an ounce. This would cause a movement from point Q to R in the diagram, where the exchange rate would be $2.64 = 1 pound. But what if Britain feels that the dollar devaluation gives the United States an unfair competitive advantage? Suppose Britain immediately retaliates by devaluing the pound 10 percent, increasing the official price of gold from 14.58 pounds to 16.038 pounds. A movement from point R to point T in the diagram would result. Although both currencies have been officially devalued 10 percent, the exchange rate remains constant at $2.40 = 1 pound. The conclusion is that a devaluation in the legal sense does not necessarily ensure a devaluation in the economic sense (in which there is a depreciation in the exchange rate). This will occur only if other nations do not retaliate by initiating offsetting devaluations of their own.

Currency devaluations do have foreign repercussions similar to those of domestic economic policies. The larger and more significant is the devaluing country, the greater are the economic effects transmitted abroad. A country that devalues to initiate an export-led economic recovery may be the cause of recession in its trading partners. This was often the case during the Great Depression of the 1930s, where competitive devaluations and other forms of beggar-thy-neighbor policies were widespread. It is no wonder that when currency realignments involving devaluations and revaluations are called for, they usually require intense negotiations and the harmonization of economic interests among participating countries.

Trade and Income Implications

This section considers the relationship between devaluation or revaluation and the impact on the balance of payments and level of domestic income. In Figure 14.3, assume the United States is initially located at point E, where domestic income equals $1,200 and there is a payments deficit of $100. The United States could attempt to correct the deficit by officially devaluing the dollar. The devaluation tends to discourage home imports by making them more expensive, while encouraging exports by making them less expensive overseas. With the rise in exports and fall in imports, the trade balance schedule $(X - M)$ rises to $(X - M)'$, a position such that $X = M$ at point G. The dollar devaluation is therefore intended to promote balance-of-payments equilibrium.

Besides having a balance-of-payments effect, a currency devaluation can also affect the level of domestic income. In the preceding example, the dollar devaluation leads to an upward shift in the trade balance schedule by $200. This represents an autonomous injection of spending into the U.S. economy. The associated rise in income from $1,200 to $1,500 reflects the multiplier effect of this injection. A devaluation's income effect means that the overall improvement in a country's payment position tends to be less than the amount the trade balance schedule is displaced. In the example, eliminating a payments deficit of $100 requires that the trade balance schedule be shifted upward by $200. This is because the rise in income causes imports to rise by $100, which reduces the initial improvement in the trade balance.

Figure 14.3 can also be used to illustrate the balance-of-payments and income effects of currency revaluation for a surplus country. Suppose the United States finds itself located at point H, with a surplus of $100 and domestic income equal to $1,800. The surplus could be corrected by a dollar revaluation that would lead to a downward shift in the $(X - M)''$ trade balance curve, so that $(X - M)'$ would intersect the unchanged $(S - I)$ schedule at income level $1,500. The elimination of a $100 surplus requires the trade balance schedule to shift downward by $200. As the trade balance schedule

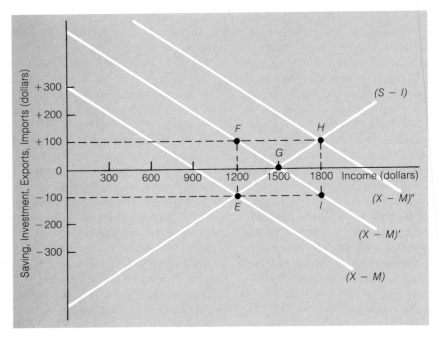

Figure 14.3   Devaluation-revaluation: trade and income implications.

shifts downward, domestic income contracts and leads to a decline in imports, which counteracts a portion of the revaluation's initial effect. One might expect the balance of payments to be the usual target of devaluations and revaluations. However, these policy instruments are sometimes used to influence the level of domestic income. Such was the case of West Germany's upward revaluations in 1961, 1969, and 1971, the primary objective having been to slow down an overheated economy so the rate of inflation could be brought under control.

U.S. Dollar Devaluations

This section discusses some situations in which official changes in par values have been used. The U.S. dollar devaluations of 1971 and 1973 furnish examples.

Bretton Woods System

According to the agreements reached by the International Monetary Fund countries in 1944 at Bretton Woods, New Hampshire, international trade was to be conducted under a system of essentially fixed exchange rates. Many governments maintained fixed exchange rates by setting the par values for their currencies in terms of the U.S. dollar. They bought and sold their currencies in exchange for dollars to defend their official exchange rates. The United States did not have to fix the value of the dollar in terms of other currencies as long as the other currencies' values were fixed against the dollar. The obligation that the United States assumed was (1) to set the dollar value of gold for transactions with foreign central banks and (2) to freely exchange gold for dollars or dollars for gold with foreign central bankers at the established official price (originally fixed at $35 per ounce).

Under the *Bretton Woods system*, countries were to use international reserves to finance temporary deficits in international payments. Any imbalance viewed as a fundamental disequilibrium was to be corrected by changes in the exchange rate. The term *fundamental disequilibrium* apparently indicated a long-run continuous imbalance (in practice, a deficit) that appeared unlikely to be reversed by domestic economic policies. According to IMF rules, a nation could automatically change its par value up to 10 percent without permission of the fund. (This rule was not strictly followed in practice.)

Although these arrangements were intended to provide an effective adjustment mechanism, several problems limited the system's efficiency. One problem was that there was an adjustment asymmetry between surplus and deficit countries. Because surplus countries could better postpone equilibrating adjustments than could deficit countries facing falling reserve levels, a *devaluation bias* was present under the Bretton Woods system. But deficit countries found it politically embarrassing to undergo devaluation. The belief evidently was that such a policy implied an admission to the world of financial irresponsibility. Because the United States was the reserve center nation, it lacked the ability to determine its exchange rate policy. Not only was the dollar's exchange rate set by the practice of other governments fixing their currencies' values against the dollar, but also it was generally contended that any unilateral decision by the United States to adjust its par value would be offset by other countries' counteracting exchange rate adjustments. The consequence of these factors was that the Bretton Woods system was without an adequate adjustment mechanism.

This problem became particularly acute by the late 1960s and early 1970s when the U.S. payments position deteriorated rapidly. The U.S. trade balance, which had been in surplus by some $8.6 billion in 1964, registered a surplus of less than $1 billion in 1969, a deficit of $2.7 billion in 1971, and an even greater deficit of $6.4 billion in 1972. The deterioration of the U.S. trade position reflected more rapid productivity advances abroad and rising inflation in the United States. One thing was apparent by 1970—given the existing world exchange rate structure, the dollar was an overvalued currency.

Countries with balance-of-payments surpluses, notably Japan and West Germany, might have revalued their undervalued currencies upward in light of the fundamental disequilibrium that prevailed. However, surplus countries were reluctant to revalue because of the negative impact on employment that would ensue in their export industries. On August 15, 1971, the Bretton Woods system was suspended when the United States allowed the overvalued dollar to float in the exchange markets. This was intended to create incentives for exchange rate changes. This situation illustrates the inherent problem of the Bretton Woods system, namely, that the IMF rules did not set up a procedure for making frequent and timely exchange rate adjustments. Such adjustments were instead to occur only in response to fundamental disequilibriums. When exchange rate adjustments did occur, they usually came too late and in very large amounts.

The Smithsonian Agreement

A major objective of the United States' going off the Bretton Woods system of fixed exchange rates in August 1971 was to permit the depreciation of its overvalued dollar against the undervalued currencies, specifically Japan's yen and West Germany's mark. In December 1971, a conference was conducted at the Smithsonian Institution in Washington, D.C., to restructure the exchange rate system among the 10 largest industrial countries of the Western world (the Group of Ten, consisting of Belgium, Canada, France, West Germany, Italy, Japan, the Netherlands, Sweden, the United Kingdom, and the United States).

Foreign governments demanded an official devaluation of the U.S. dollar for several reasons. Politically it represented an admission of laxness on the part of the United States, which had not practiced domestic financial responsibility and maintained control of its inflation rate. A dollar devaluation also implied an across-the-board dollar depreciation against all other currencies that maintained existing par values. This was a significant concession to Japan, whose yen was notably undervalued against the dollar. Japan contended that the dollar devaluation across the board would result in the adjustment burden being shared more uniformly among U.S. trading partners, rather than falling primarily on itself.

On December 18, 1971, the *Smithsonian Agreement* was reached by the Group of Ten countries. The United States agreed to adjust its long-standing parity against gold from $35 to $38 per ounce. This act initiated a formal devaluation of the dollar of approximately 8.57 percent. In return for the dollar devaluation, the nine other members of the Group of Ten countries agreed to realign their exchange rates against the dollar. The results are summarized in Table 14.2.

According to the Smithsonian Agreement, a new exchange rate structure emerged in roughly four categories. First, some countries—the United Kingdom and France—maintained existing official parities. The currencies of these countries appreciated against the dollar by the full amount of the devaluation. Second, the bloc composed of West Germany, Japan, Belgium, and the Netherlands agreed to revalue their currencies officially in addition to the U.S. devaluation. Their currencies appreciated relative to the dollar by an amount exceeding the U.S. devaluation. Third, Sweden and Italy officially devalued their currencies by 1 percent, thereby appreciating against the dollar by some 7.5 percent. Last, rather than undergoing an official adjustment in its par value, Canada permitted its dollar to float in the exchange markets.

The Dollar Devaluation of 1973

The initial reactions to the Smithsonian currency realignments were quite optimistic. It was expected that the new exchange rate structure

Table 14.2   Changes in Exchange Rates of Group of Ten Currencies Against the U.S. Dollar: January 1, 1971 to December 31, 1971

Currency	Units per U.S. Dollar (January 1971)	Units per U.S. Dollar (December 1971)	Change in Terms of U.S. Dollars (percent)
Japanese yen	360.00	308.00	16.88
West German mark	3.66	3.22	13.58
Netherland guilder	3.62	3.24	11.57
Belgian franc	50.00	44.82	11.57
French franc	5.55	5.12	8.57
United Kingdom pound	0.42	0.38	8.57
Swedish krona	5.17	4.81	7.49
Italian lira	625.00	581.50	7.48
Canadian dollar*	1.01	1.00	1.00

Source: International Monetary Fund, *International Financial Statistics*, November 1973, pp. 2–3.
*Because Canada maintained a system of floating exchange rates, it did not adjust its parity.

would result in an average 12 percent depreciation of the dollar against the Group of Ten currencies, except for the floating Canadian dollar. This amount was initially felt to be sufficient to correct the fundamental disequilibrium of the U.S. balance of payments. However, the $6.4 billion trade deficit of the United States in 1972 led to renewed pessimism over that country's trade position.

After intensive negotiations, the United States persuaded the countries in payments surplus to permit an appreciation of their currencies against the dollar. On February 12, 1973, the United States devalued the dollar approximately 10 percent. This was accomplished by changing the dollar's value in terms of gold from $38 to $42.22 per ounce. In spite of this second dollar devaluation and the subsequent exchange rate realignments among the Group of Ten currencies, the international monetary system faced considerable uncertainty in March 1973. The result was that the industrialized nations terminated the long-lasting system of fixed exchange rates and adopted a managed floating exchange rate system.

When Is Devaluation Successful?

The previous discussion emphasized the effect that currency devaluations and revaluations may have on a country's balance of payments and income level, but considered only the intended effects rather than what may actually occur in practice. Another question that must be answered is under what conditions a currency devaluation (or revaluation) will be successful in bringing about balance-of-payments adjustment. The discussion is confined to a currency devaluation, but the conclusions analogously apply for currency revaluation.

Several approaches to devaluation are analyzed. The *elasticity approach* emphasizes the relative price effects of devaluation and suggests in general that devaluation works best when demand elasticities are high. The *absorption approach* deals with the income effects of devaluation. The implication is that a decrease in domestic expenditure relative to income must occur for devaluation to promote payments equilibrium. The *monetary approach* stresses the effects devaluation has on the purchasing power of money balances and the resulting impact on domestic expenditure levels.

Devaluation: The Elasticity Approach

One way in which devaluation affects a country's balance of payments is through changes in the relative prices of goods and services internationally. A deficit country may be able to reverse the imbalance by lowering its prices so that exports are encouraged while imports decline. One way of accomplishing this is by adjusting the exchange rate by currency devaluation. The ultimate outcome of a currency devaluation depends on the price elasticity of demand for a country's imports and the price elasticity of demand for its exports.

Elasticity of demand refers to the responsiveness of buyers to changes in price. It indicates the percent change in the quantity demanded stemming from a 1 percent change in price. Mathematically, elasticity is the ratio of the percent change in the quantity demanded to the percent change in price. This may be symbolized as:

$$\text{Elasticity} = \frac{\Delta Q}{Q} \div \frac{\Delta P}{P}.$$

The elasticity coefficient is stated numerically, without regard to the algebraic sign. If the preceding ratio exceeds 1, a given percent change in price results in a larger percent change in quantity demanded. This is referred to as relatively elastic demand. If the ratio is less than 1, demand is said to be relatively inelastic because the percent change in price exceeds the percent change in quantity demanded. A ratio precisely equal to 1 denotes unitary elastic demand, meaning that the percent change in price just matches the percent change in quantity demanded.

The following analysis investigates the effects of a devaluation on a country's balance of trade—that is, the value of its exports minus imports. Suppose the monetary authorities of Britain decide to devalue the pound by 10 percent to correct a payments deficit against the United States. Whether the British trade balance will be improved depends on what happens to the dollar inpayments for its exports as opposed to the dollar outpayments for its imports. This depends on whether the U.S. demand for British exports is elastic or inelastic and whether the British demand for imports is elastic or inelastic.

Depending on the size of the demand elasticities for British exports and imports, Britain's trade balance may improve, worsen, or remain unchanged in response to the pound devaluation. The general rule that determines the actual outcome is commonly known as the *Marshall-Lerner Condition*.[4] The Marshall-Lerner Condition says: (1) Devaluation will improve the trade balance if the devaluing country's demand elasticity for imports plus the foreign demand elasticity for the country's exports exceeds 1. (2) If the sum of the demand elasticities is less than 1, devaluation will worsen the trade balance. (3) The trade balance will be neither helped nor hurt if the sum of the demand elasticities equals 1. The Marshall-Lerner Condition may be stated in terms of the currency of either the country undergoing a devaluation or its trading partner, but it cannot be expressed in terms of both currencies simultaneously. Our discussion is confined to the currency of the devaluing country, Great Britain.

Case 1: Improved Trade Balance

Referring to Table 14.3, assume the British demand elasticity for imports equals 2.5, whereas the United States' demand elasticity for British exports equals 1.5. To improve its payments position, suppose that Britain officially devalues the pound by 10 percent, which leads to a depreciation of the pound against the dollar by the same amount. To assess the overall impact of the devaluation on Britain's payments position, the devaluation's impact on import expenditures and export receipts must be identified.

Table 14.3   British Devaluation: Improved Trade Balance

Assumptions

British demand elasticity for imports = 2.5 ⎫
Demand elasticity for British exports = 1.5 ⎬ Sum = 4.0
Pound devaluation = 10%   ⎭

Trade Balance Effect

Sector	Change in Pound Price	Change in Quantity Demanded	Net Effect (in pounds)
Import	+ 10%	− 25%	− 15% Outpayments
Export	0	+ 15%	+ 15% Inpayments

If prices of imports remain constant in terms of foreign currency, then a devaluation increases the home currency price of goods imported. Because of the devaluation, the pound price of British imports rises 10 percent. British consumers would thus be expected to reduce their purchases from abroad. Given an import demand elasticity of 2.5, the devaluation triggers a 25 percent decline in the quantity of imports demanded. The 10 percent price increase in conjunction with a 25 percent quantity reduction results in approximately a 15 percent decrease in British outpayments in pounds. This cutback in import purchases actually reduces import expenditures, which reduces the British deficit.

How about British export receipts? The devaluation results in British goods being sold for fewer dollars than before, whereas the pound price of the exports remains constant. Consumers in the United States find British exports are falling in price in terms of dollars, so they expand their foreign purchases. Given a U.S. demand elasticity of 1.5 for British exports, the 10 percent British devaluation will stimulate foreign sales by 15 percent, so that export receipts in pounds increase by approximately 15 percent. This strengthens the British payments position. The 15 percent reduction in import expendi-

tures coupled with a 15 percent rise in export receipts means that the pound devaluation reduced the British payments deficit. With the sum of the elasticities exceeding 1, the devaluation strengthens Britain's trade position.

Case 2: Worsening Trade Balance

In Table 14.4, let the British demand elasticity for imports be 0.2 and the U.S. demand elasticity for British exports equal 0.1, the combined total being 0.3. The 10 percent British devaluation raises the pound price of imports 10 percent, inducing a 2 percent reduction in the quantity of imports demanded. Contrary to case 1, under relatively inelastic conditions, the devaluation contributes to an increase, rather than a decrease, in import expenditures in pounds of some 8 percent. As before, the pound price of British exports is unaffected by the devaluation, whereas the dollar price of exports falls 10 percent. U.S. purchases from abroad thus rise 1 percent, resulting in an increase in pound receipts of about 1 percent. With expenditures on imports rising 8 percent while export receipts increase only 1 percent, the British deficit would tend to worsen. The Marshall-Lerner Condition holds that *devaluation will cause*

Table 14.4   British Devaluation: Worsened Trade Balance

Assumptions

British demand elasticity for imports = 0.2
Demand elasticity for British exports = 0.1 } Sum = 0.3
Pound devaluation = 10%

Trade Balance Effect

Sector	Change in Pound Price	Change in Quantity Demanded	Net Effect (in pounds)
Import	+ 10%	− 2%	+ 8% Outpayments
Export	0	+ 1%	+ 1% Inpayments

a deterioration in a country's trade position if the sum of the elasticities is less than 1.

Case 3: No Change in Trade Balance

Suppose that Britain's import demand elasticity and the U.S. demand elasticity both equal 0.5, the combined sum being 1.0. As before, a 10 percent devaluation of the pound is assumed. For Britain, the devaluation leads to a 10 percent rise in the pound price of imports, which causes the quantity of imports demanded to drop 5 percent, as shown in Table 14.5. The result is that import expenditures in pounds rise approximately 5 percent. Although the devaluation leaves unchanged the pound price of British exports, it forces the dollar price of the exports downward by 10 percent. This induces a 5 percent rise in sales abroad and an increase in export receipts of some 5 percent. Devaluation therefore brings about an equal rise in import expenditures and export receipts. The implication is that a country's *trade balance remains unaffected by devaluation if the sum of the demand elasticities equals 1.*

Although the Marshall-Lerner Condition gives a general rule about when a currency devaluation will be successful in restoring payments equilibrium, it depends on some simplifying as-

sumptions. For one, it is assumed that a country's trade balance is in equilibrium when the devaluation occurs. This is because if there is initially a very large trade deficit, with imports exceeding exports, then a devaluation might cause import expenditures to change more than export receipts, even though the sum of the demand elasticities exceeds 1. What is more, the analysis assumes no change in the sellers' prices in their own currency. But this may not always be true. To protect their competitive position, foreign sellers may lower their prices in response to a home country devaluation. Or domestic sellers may raise home currency prices so that the devaluation's effects are not fully transmitted into lower foreign exchange prices for their goods. However, neither of these assumptions invalidates the Marshall-Lerner Condition's spirit, which suggests that devaluations work best when demand elasticities are high.

Empirical Measurement: Import-Export Demand Elasticities

The Marshall-Lerner Condition illustrates the price effects of a country's devaluation (revaluation) on its trade balance. The extent by which price changes affect the volume of goods traded

Table 14.5   British Devaluation: Unchanged Trade Balance

Assumptions

British demand elasticity for imports = 0.5 ⎱ Sum = 1.0
Demand elasticity for British exports = 0.5 ⎰
Pound devaluation = 10%

Trade Balance Effect

Sector	Change in Pound Price	Change in Quantity Demanded	Net Effect (in pounds)
Import	+ 10%	− 5%	+ 5% Outpayments
Export	0	+ 5%	+ 5% Inpayments

depends on the elasticity of demand for imports. If the elasticities were known in advance, it would be possible to determine the proper exchange rate policy to restore payments equilibrium. Without such knowledge, countries often have been reluctant to change the par values of their currencies.

During the 1940s and 1950s, there was considerable debate among economists concerning the empirical measurement of demand elasticities. Several early studies suggested low demand elasticities, close to unity or even less. Those findings led to the formation of the *elasticity pessimist* school of thought, which contended that currency devaluations and revaluations would be largely ineffectual in promoting changes in a country's trade balance. By the 1960s, most economists considered themselves *elasticity optimists*, estimating the demand elasticities for most

countries to be rather high. Consider the Houthakker-Magee study, whose findings are generally consistent with past analysis. Houthakker and Magee's objective was to estimate the price elasticities for both imports and exports. Table 14.6 contains the price elasticities for total imports and exports by country. The calculated elasticities in general are quite high. This means that the value of exports and imports would be expected to respond significantly to price (exchange rate) changes that may occur. Table 14.7 illustrates the price elasticities for U.S. imports and exports from and to other countries. A comparison of the tables indicates that the U.S. price elasticity against individual countries is larger than for the world as a whole. Perhaps this is explained by a high degree of substitution between countries. Substitution arises because consumers are quick to shift their purchases of a good to the country with the lowest prices.

Table 14.6   Price Elasticities for Total Imports and Exports of 15 Industrial Countries (annual data, 1951–1966)

Import Price Elasticity	Country	Export Price Elasticity
.83	Australia	−.21
−1.02	Belgium-Luxembourg	.42
−1.46	Canada	−.59
−1.66	Denmark	−.56
.17	France	−2.27
−.24	West Germany	−1.25
−.13	Italy	−1.12
−.72	Japan	−.80
.23	Netherlands	−.82
−.78	Norway	.20
−.52	South Africa	−2.41
−.79	Sweden	−.47
−.84	Switzerland	−.58
−.21	United Kingdom	−1.24
−1.03	United States	−1.51

Source: H.S. Houthakker and S. P. Magee, "Income and Price Elasticities in World Trade," *Review of Economics and Statistics*, 51 (May 1969), pp. 111–125. See also H. Robert Heller, *International Monetary Economics* (New York: Prentice-Hall, 1974), p. 27.

Table 14.7   Price Elasticities for Total United States Trade with Selected Countries (annual data, 1951–1966)

U.S. Import Price Elasticity	Country	U.S. Export Price Elasticity
−4.69	Australia	−8.10
−2.08	Belgium-Luxembourg	−2.38
.49	Canada	−1.45
−6.05	Denmark	−.47
−4.58	France	−3.14
−8.48	West Germany	−2.39
−3.82	Italy	−2.04
−4.96	Japan	−.41
−2.47	Netherlands	−.35
−1.82	Norway	−2.26
−3.10	South Africa	−2.68
−2.49	Sweden	.73
−.04	Switzerland	−2.01
−4.25	United Kingdom	−1.69

Source: Houthakker and Magee, pp. 111–125. See also Heller, p. 28.

Time Path of Devaluation

Empirical estimates of price elasticities in international trade in part have been aimed at answering whether, according to the Marshall-Lerner Condition, devaluation would improve a country's trade balance. Most recent empirical studies are affirmative on this point. A basic problem, however, in measuring world price elasticities is that there tends to be a *time lag* in the process between changes in exchange rates and their ultimate effect on real trade. One popular description of the time path of trade flows is the so-called **J**-Curve effect. This view suggests that in the very short run, a currency devaluation will lead to a worsening of a country's trade balance. But as time passes, the trade balance will likely improve. This is because it takes time for new information about the price effects of devaluation to be disseminated throughout the economy and for economic units to adjust their behavior accordingly.

J-Curve Effect

A currency devaluation affects a country's trade balance by its net impact on export receipts in conjunction with import expenditures. Export receipts and import expenditures are calculated by multiplying the commodity's per-unit price times the quantity being demanded. The process by which devaluation influences export receipts and import expenditures is shown in Figure 14.4.

The immediate effect of devaluation is a change in relative prices. If a country devalues 10 percent, it means that import prices initially increase 10 percent in terms of the home currency. The quantity of imports demanded would then fall according to home demand elasticities. At the same time, exporters will initially receive 10 percent more in home currency for each unit of foreign currency they earn. This means they

Figure 14.4   Devaluation flowchart.

can become more competitive and lower their export prices measured in terms of foreign currencies. Export sales would then rise in accordance with foreign demand elasticities. The problem with this illustration is that for devaluation to take effect, time is required for the pricing mechanism to induce changes in the volume of exports and imports sold.

The time path of the response of trade flows to a devaluation can be described in terms of the **J**-Curve effect. The *J-Curve effect* contends that the trade balance continues to get worse for a while after devaluation (sliding down the hook of the **J**) before it gets better (moving up the stem of the **J**). This is because the first effect of devaluation is an increase in import expenditures, since the volume is unchanged owing to prior commitments while the home currency price of imports has risen. As time passes, the quantity adjustment period becomes relevant, whereby import volume is depressed while exports become more attractive to foreign buyers.

Advocates of the J-Curve effect use the 1967 devaluation of the British pound as an example. As seen in Figure 14.4, the British balance of payments showed a $1.3 billion deficit in 1967. To improve its payments position, Britain devalued the pound by 14.3 percent in November

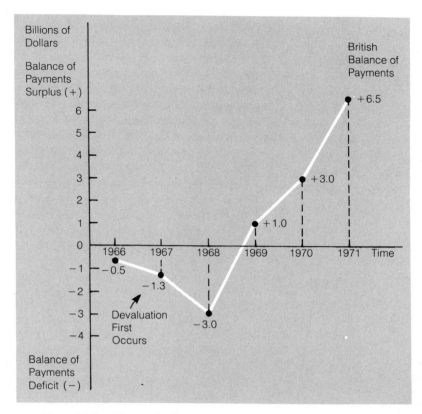

Figure 14.5   Time path of British balance of payments in response to
pound devaluation. (Source: U.S. Department of Commerce,
International Economic Indicators, February 1975, p. 72.)

1967. The initial impact of the devaluation was
negative, for by 1968, the British balance of
payments showed a $3 billion deficit. After a lag,
however, the British balance of payments improved, having a reduction in the growth of
imports and a rise in the growth of exports. By
1969, the British balance of payments showed a
$1 billion surplus followed by a $6.5 billion surplus by 1971.

What factors might explain the time lags in a
devaluation's adjustment process? The types of
lags between the response of goods traded to
changes in relative prices include the following:

1. *Recognition* lags of changing competitive
   conditions
2. *Decision* lags in forming new business con-
   nections and placing new orders
3. *Delivery* lags between the time new orders
   are placed and their impact on trade and
   payment flows
4. *Replacement* lags in using up inventories
   and wearing out existing machinery before
   placing new orders
5. *Production* lags involved in increasing the
   output of commodities for which demand
   has increased

Empirical evidence suggests that the trade balance effects of devaluation do not materialize until years afterward. Adjustment lags may be four years or more, although the major portion of adjustment takes place in about two years. One study made the following estimates of the lags in the devaluation adjustment process for trade in manufactured goods: (1) The response of trade flows to relative price changes stretched out over a period of some four to five years. (2) Following a price change, almost 50 percent of the full trade flow response occurs within the first three years, and about 90 percent takes place during the first five years.[5]

Devaluation: The Absorption Approach

According to the elasticities approach, currency devaluation offers a price incentive to reduce imports and increase exports. But even if elasticity conditions are favorable, whether the home country's trade balance will actually improve may depend on how the economy reacts to the devaluation. The *absorption approach*[6] provides insights to this question by considering the impact of devaluation on the spending behavior of the domestic economy and the influence of domestic spending on the trade balance.

The absorption approach starts with the idea that the value of total domestic output (Y) equals the level of total spending. Total spending consists of consumption (C), investment (I), government expenditures (G), and net exports ($X - M$). This can be written as

$$Y = C + I + G + (X - M).$$

The absorption approach then consolidates $C + I + G$ into a single term, A, which is referred to as absorption, while letting net exports ($X - M$) be designated as B. Total domestic output thus equals the sum of absorption plus the level of net exports, or

$$Y = A + B.$$

This can be rewritten as

$$B = Y - A.$$

This expression suggests that the balance of trade (B) equals the difference between total domestic output (Y) and the level of absorption (A). If national output exceeds domestic absorption, the economy's trade balance will be positive. Conversely, a negative trade balance suggests that an economy is spending beyond its ability to produce.

The absorption approach predicts that if a currency devaluation is to improve an economy's trade balance, national output must rise relative to absorption. This means that a country must increase its total output, reduce its absorption, or do some combination of the two. The following examples illustrate these possibilities.

Assume that an economy faces unemployment as well as a trade deficit. With the economy operating below maximum capacity, the price incentives of devaluation would tend to direct idle resources into the production of goods for export, in addition to encouraging spending away from imports to domestically produced substitutes. The impact of the devaluation is to expand domestic output as well as to improve the trade balance. It is no wonder that policy makers may view currency devaluation to be an effective tool when an economy faces unemployment with a trade deficit.

In the case of an economy operating at full employment, however, there are no unutilized resources available for additional production. National output is at a fixed level. The only way in which devaluation can improve the trade balance is for the economy to somehow cut domestic absorption, freeing resources needed to produce additional export goods and import substitutes. For example, domestic policy makers could decrease absorption by adopting restrictive fiscal and monetary policies in the face of higher prices resulting from the devaluation. But this would result in sacrifice among those who bear the burden of such measures. Devaluation may thus be considered inappropriate when an economy operates at maximum capacity.

The absorption approach goes beyond the elasticity approach, which views the economy's trade balance as distinct from the rest of the economy. Instead, devaluation is viewed in relation to the economy's utilization of its resources and level of production. The two approaches are therefore complementary.

Devaluation: A Monetary Approach

A survey of the traditional approaches to devaluation reveals a major shortcoming. According to the elasticities and absorption approaches, monetary consequences are not associated with balance-of-payments adjustment, or to the extent that such consequences exist, they can be neutralized by domestic monetary authorities. The elasticities and absorption approaches apply only to the trade account of the balance of payments, neglecting the implications of capital movements. The *monetary approach* to devaluation addresses this shortcoming.[7]

According to the monetary approach, currency devaluation exerts an impact on the purchasing power (that is, real value) of money balances, which affects expenditure levels and the balance of payments. (Figure 14.6)

The example following illustrates the operation of the monetary approach to devaluation.[8]

Starting from a balance-of-payments equilibrium, suppose the home country undergoes a

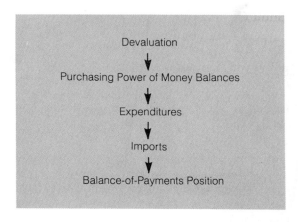

Figure 14.6   The monetary approach to devaluation.

devaluation of its currency. Because it would now require more units of the home currency to purchase a given amount of foreign goods, the devaluation raises domestic prices. As a result, the purchasing power of domestic resident money balances declines. To replenish the purchasing power of their money balances, local residents must increase the level of saving. But this would reduce domestic consumption, resulting in an excess supply of goods. As for the rest of the world, the opposite effects would occur. With the devaluation, fewer units of the rest of the world's currency are now needed to purchase a unit of the devaluing country's currency. Foreigners find that the prices of the goods imported from the devaluing country have fallen. The purchasing power of their money balances rises, which encourages them to expand expenditures on goods relative to their income. In addition to purchasing goods they produce, the rest of the world's nations would tend to increase their demand for the devaluing country's goods. Combining these effects, the devaluation results in a payments surplus for the devaluing country and a payments deficit for the rest of the world.

ary

1. In a fixed, or pegged, exchange rate system, the monetary authorities assign a par value to the domestic currency. This represents the nation's official exchange rate. The par value ideally should be set at the long-term equilibrium rate so its value is consistent with existing economic trends. Par values are stated in terms of some numeraire such as gold, key currencies, or Special Drawing Rights.

2. The defense of the par value may require the monetary authorities to intervene in foreign exchange markets. If the market price of the home currency is falling, monetary authorities will purchase the currency, supporting its value. Conversely, a currency whose value is rising will be sold on the foreign exchange market.

3. Should a country face a chronic payments disequilibrium, it may decide to revalue its currency (in the case of a surplus country) or devalue it (in the case of a deficit country) to restore payments balance.

4. The terms *devaluation* and *revaluation* refer to a legal redefinition of a country's par value under a system of fixed exchange rates. A country could devalue (revalue) its currency by increasing (decreasing) the official price of gold or some other numeraire. All else being equal, this would result in a change in the market exchange rate.

5. Owing to balance-of-payments problems, the United States formally devalued the dollar in 1971 and 1973.

6. A currency devaluation may affect a country's trade position through its impact on relative price levels, incomes, and purchasing power of money balances.

7. According to the elasticities approach, devaluation works best when demand elasticities are high. Recent empirical studies in general indicate that the estimated demand elasticities for most countries are quite high.

8. The time path of currency devaluation can be explained in terms of the J-Curve effect. According to this concept, the response of trade flows to changes in relative prices increases with the passage of time.

9. The absorption approach emphasizes the income effects of devaluation. According to this view, a devaluation may initially stimulate a country's exports and production of import-competing goods. But this will promote excess domestic spending unless real output can be expanded or domestic absorption reduced. The result would be a return to a payments deficit.

10. The monetary approach to devaluation emphasizes the effect that devaluation has on the purchasing power of money balances and the resulting impacts on domestic expenditures and import levels.

Study Questions

1. How does a country go about establishing a fixed exchange rate system?

2. What is meant by the term *par value*?

3. How do central banks stabilize exchange rates?

4. Distinguish between a currency devaluation versus depreciation and revaluation versus appreciation.

5. How can it be that two countries that simultaneously devalue their currencies find that neither currency depreciated (or appreciated) in terms of the other?

6. How does a currency devaluation affect a country's balance of payments?

7. Several major approaches analyze the economic impacts of a currency devaluation: (1) elasticities approach, (2) absorption approach, and (3) monetary approach. Distinguish among the three.

8. What is meant by the Marshall-Lerner Condition? Do recent empirical studies suggest that world elasticity conditions are sufficiently high to permit successful devaluations and revaluations?

9. How does the J-Curve effect relate to the time path of devaluation?

10. According to the absorption approach, does it make any difference whether a country devalues its currency under conditions where the economy is operating at less than full capacity versus full capacity?

11. How can devaluation-induced changes in household real money balances promote payments equilibrium?

Notes

1. See Henry C. Wallich, "The Case for Fixed Exchange Rates," in *The United States Balance of Payments*, Hearings Before the Joint Economic Committee, 88th Cong., 1st Sess., Washington, D.C., part 3, pp. 495–499.

2. For a *balance sheet* approach to exchange rate stabilization, see Anatol B. Balbach, "The Mechanics of Intervention in Exchange Markets," *Review*, Federal Reserve Bank of St. Louis (February 1978), pp. 2–7.

3. See Robert A. Mundell, "Should the United States Devalue the Dollar?" *Western Economic Journal* (September 1968), pp. 247–259.

4. A more rigorous treatment of the Marshall-Lerner Condition can be found in Charles P. Kindleberger and Peter H. Lindert, *International Economics* (Homewood, Ill.: Richard D. Irwin, 1978), chap. 15.

5. Helen Junz and Rudolf R. Rhomberg, "Price Competitiveness in Export Trade Among Industrial Countries," *American Economic Review* (May 1973), pp. 412–419. See also Robert A. Feldman, "Dollar Appreciation, Foreign Trade, and the U.S. Economy," *Quarterly Review*, Federal Reserve

Bank of New York (Summer 1982), pp. 1–9.

6. Sidney S. Alexander, "Effects of a Devaluation on a Trade Balance," *IMF Staff Papers* (April 1952), pp. 263–278.

7. See Donald S. Kemp, "A Monetary View of the Balance of Payments," *Review*, Federal Reserve Bank of St. Louis (April 1975), pp. 14–22 and Thomas M. Humphrey, "The Monetary Approach to Exchange Rates: Its Historical Evolution and Role in Policy Debates," *Economic Review*, Federal Reserve Bank of Richmond (July–August 1978), pp. 2–9.

8. This example is based on several assumptions. First, domestic residents and foreigners have command over money balances as well as commodities. Second, people wish to hold money balances in some fixed proportion to their income levels. Third, monetary authorities do not control the domestic money supply, as they cannot neutralize the impact on the money supply of international reserve movements stemming from trade balance surpluses or deficits. Last, monetary prices are assumed to be flexible, falling when supply exceeds demand in the market, rising when demand exceeds supply.

Suggestions for Further Reading

Bryant, R. *Money and Monetary Policy in an Open Economy*. Washington, D.C.: The Brookings Institution, 1980.

Burton, D. "Expectations and the Dynamics of Devaluation." *Review of Economic Studies*, October 1981.

Cheng, H. S. "Depreciation = Inflation?" Federal Reserve Bank of San Francisco, *Business and Financial Letter*, May 20, 1977.

Cornes, R., and A. Dixit. "Comparative Effects of Devaluation and Import Controls on Domestic Prices." *Economica*, February 1982.

Dornbusch, R. "Devaluation, Money, and Non-traded Goods." *American Economic Review*, December 1973.

Einzig, P. *Leads and Lags: The Main Cause of Devaluation*. New York: St. Martin's Press, 1968.

Frenkel, J., and H. G. Johnson. *The Monetary Approach to the Balance of Payments*. London: Allen & Unwin, 1975.

Jones, R. W. "Depreciation and the Dampening Effects of Income Changes." *Review of Economics and Statistics*, February 1960.

Magee, S. P. "Currency Contracts, Pass-Through, and Devaluation." Brookings Papers on Economic Activity, no. 1, 1973.

Marshall, A. *The Pure Theory of Foreign Trade*. London: London School of Economics, 1879.

Orcutt, G. H. "Measurement of Price Elasticities in International Trade." *Review of Economics and Statistics*, May 1950.

Schmid, M. "Devaluation: Keynesian Trade Models and the Monetary Approach." *European Economic Review*, January 1982.

Williamson, J. "A Survey of the Literature on the Optimal Peg." *Journal of Development Economics*, August 1982.

15

FREELY FLOATING
EXCHANGE RATES

The system of freely floating exchange rates has many notable proponents among economists, such as Milton Friedman. But freely floating exchange rates have traditionally been unpopular with actual practitioners—central bankers, finance ministers, commercial bankers, traders, and investors. What is more, other academic economists have recently formulated sophisticated arguments that have challenged the traditional views on freely floating rates. This chapter describes the operation of freely floating rates and presents arguments and evidence supporting and negating the case for freely floating rates. The student is cautioned to be skeptical when reading these arguments, because there is no consensus among economists on the subject.

How the System Works

By *flexible or floating exchange rates*, we mean currency prices that are established daily in the foreign exchange market, without restrictions imposed by government policy on the extent to which prices can move. The basic idea underlying this mechanism is that some equilibrium exchange rate exists that equates the demand for and supply of the home currency. Changes in the

exchange rate will ideally correct a payments imbalance by bringing about shifts in imports and exports of goods, services, and short-term capital movements. The exchange rate will respond to forces that cause a surplus or deficit in the balance of payments. A payments deficit induces a depreciation in the home currency's exchange rate, whereas a payments surplus causes the home currency to appreciate in value. As the exchange rate responds to these imbalances, it will induce changes in the level of trade flows and capital movements that will correct the imbalances.

To appreciate how freely floating exchange rates would ideally operate, consider Figure 15.1, which illustrates the foreign exchange market position of the United States. Starting at equilibrium point E, suppose a rise in U.S. income causes it to demand more West German products and thus an increase in its demand for marks from D_0 to D_1. Initially there is a tendency toward disequilibrium, because the U.S. demand for marks exceeds the supply by some 10 billion at the exchange rate $\$0.40 = 1$ mark. But as U.S. consumers purchase marks to satisfy their demand for imports, the dollar will begin to depreciate against the mark. This will cause the export prices in terms of the mark to fall, stimulating U.S. sales abroad. Concurrently, the

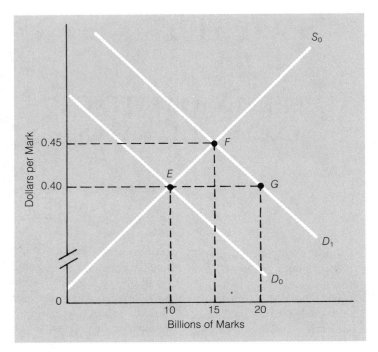

Figure 15.1   Payments adjustment under freely floating exchange rates.

dollar price of imports increases, which induces a reduction in home consumption. Given sufficiently high elasticities, the dollar depreciation will cause export receipts to rise relative to import expenditures, balance-of-payments equilibrium being restored. This is indicated in Figure 15.1 by a dollar depreciation from $0.40 to $0.45 per mark, exchange market equilibrium being achieved at point F.

A dollar depreciation would not immediately be expected to generate a large improvement in U.S. commodity trade with West Germany. This is because time is required to substitute the products of the depreciating country for those of the appreciating country. The adjustment time path depends on such factors as the mobility of factor inputs, whether excess productive capacity exists, the degree that buyers can shift purchases

to new suppliers, and the size of the depreciation-induced price change. Initially the quantity response of trade flows to the change in price would be minor. As time passes, the dollar depreciation would cause U.S. exports to rise and imports to fall, correcting the payments disequilibrium.

Unlike a system of pegged exchange rates, a freely floating system is not characterized by par values and official exchange rates. Floating rates are determined by market supply and demand conditions rather than set by central bankers. Although freely floating rates do not have an exchange stabilization fund to maintain existing rates, it does not necessarily follow that floating rates must fluctuate erratically. They will tend to do so if the underlying market forces become unstable.

Arguments for Freely Floating Rates

The case for freely floating rates parallels the advantages claimed for a free market economy—that is, an *efficient allocation of resources at least cost*. It is quite apparent that those who advocate the adoption of freely floating rates, such as Milton Friedman, tend to attach great importance to the social benefits of decentralized government and personal freedom. In other words, they prefer market solutions over government solutions to economic problems.[1] This being the case, consider the advantages claimed for floating rates.

Simplicity

A first advantage claimed for freely floating rates is their simplicity. Being sensitive to supply and demand conditions, floating rates respond quickly to market forces, clearing the market of shortages or surpluses of a given currency. Instead of having formal rules of conduct among central bankers governing exchange rate movements, floating rates are market determined. They operate under simplified institutional arrangements that are relatively easy to enact and administer. Furthermore, because the exchange rate is the easiest variable affecting the supply of and demand for a given currency to modify, it represents the least costly method of achieving the proper adjustment.

Owing to an economic downturn abroad, suppose there is a decline in the demand for the home country's export product that results in a payments deficit for the home country. The disequilibrium could be corrected in the following ways. First, holding the exchange rate constant, contractionary monetary adjustments could induce falling domestic price and spending levels. Second, adjustment could come about by directly altering one price, the exchange rate, holding constant the average level of domestic prices. Instead of modifying thousands of domestic money prices, isn't it more convenient to directly alter but one price? This situation has been likened to the decision to adopt daylight saving time during the summer months. Instead of rescheduling all our daily activities one hour earlier in accordance with the sun's daily cycle, why not simply set the clock forward one hour? The lower adjustment cost of resetting the clock parallels the benefits of directly altering the exchange rate instead of thousands of domestic money prices.

Continuous Adjustment

Since a free exchange rate is sensitive to changing market conditions, a floating exchange rate system permits continuous adjustment. The daily adjustment of market-determined rates suggests that the adverse effects of prolonged disequilibriums will be eliminated. This is unlike the Bretton Woods system of pegged exchange rates, which was characterized by sizable disequilibriums over extended time periods. The Bretton Woods system purportedly did not promote efficient adjustment of imbalances between surplus and deficit countries. When exchange rate adjustments did occur, they came about abruptly and in very large amounts. Conversely, floating rates permit smooth adjustments as supply and demand conditions change. Gradual changes in exchange rates would eliminate the sudden shocks and abrupt adjustments that may characterize pegged exchange rate systems.

Independent Domestic Policies

It has also been argued that floating rates at least partially insulate the home economy from external forces. This means that governments will not have to restore payments equilibrium by undergoing painful inflationary or deflationary adjustment policies as would be called for under pegged exchange rates. Switching to floating rates thus frees a country from having to adopt policies that perpetuate domestic disequilibrium as the cost of maintaining a satisfactory balance-of-payments position. Countries have greater freedom under floating rates to pursue policies that promote domestic balance than would occur under pegged exchange rates.

Suppose a country, because of high levels of inflation, faces a balance-of-payments deficit. Under a pegged rate system, proper adjustment policy would call for monetary contraction and falling domestic price and income levels. A floating rate system, however, would relieve this adjustment burden. This is because the deficit country's currency would depreciate in value against other currencies, offsetting the effects of inflation on the balance of payments. Monetary authorities tend to have more freedom under floating rates to formulate domestic policies independently of balance-of-payments considerations. The desire of countries to avoid large and erratic exchange rate fluctuations, however, may restrict their independence in pursuing domestic objectives.

Increased Effectiveness of Monetary Policy

Another advantage of floating rates is that they tend to make monetary policy more effective for domestic stabilization. The reason is that under floating rates, monetary policy affects the domestic economy through commodity trade movements as well as domestic spending levels. Suppose that domestic monetary authorities lower interest rates to combat a recession. Under pegged exchange rates, the economic expansion would take the form of increased levels of investment spending, reacting to lower interest rates. Under floating rates, this monetary policy would also operate on commodity trade flows. The decrease in domestic interest rates tends to cause investors to put their funds abroad where interest rates are more favorable. Such capital outflows depreciate the home currency's exchange rate, which stimulates home exports and discourages home imports. The improving trade balance stimulates domestic income and spending levels through the multiplier process. The change in the trade balance thus serves to reinforce the purely domestic effects of lower interest rates and helps to combat the recession. The opposite chain of events occurs when monetary policy is used to combat domestic inflation.

Reduction of Need for Reserves

Not only do floating exchange rates help solve the adjustment problem, but they also reduce the problem of reserve adequacy. The need for reserves is the result of pegging operations by exchange stabilization funds. With market-determined exchange rates, any holdings of international reserves would be for working balances rather than for maintaining a given rate of exchange for any currency.

Arguments Against Freely Floating Rates

The advantages of floating rates to many academic economists are undeniable. For actual practitioners such as bankers and business people, who must live with and operate in whatever exchange rate system is in existence, this system is often considered to be of limited usefulness. This section points out the leading economic and political arguments against floating rates.[2]

Elasticity Pessimism

Floating rates theoretically can be thought of as reasonably stable, because exchange markets are highly competitive and the basic supply and demand factors are sensitive to changes in price.

Given these elastic conditions, it would take a relatively small proportionate change in the exchange rate (price) to generate a sizable response in the quantities of goods traded. But if demand conditions are inelastic, the quantity response to the change in the exchange rate (price) is minor. It would take a relatively large change in the exchange rate to initiate significant changes in trade flows.

For a depreciation (devaluation) to correct a deficit, it is necessary for export receipts to rise relative to import expenditures. This requires that the Marshall-Lerner Condition be met—the sum of the demand elasticity for a country's imports plus the world demand elasticity for its exports must exceed 1. Unless the sum of the demand elasticities is significantly greater than 1, it would take a large proportionate change in the exchange rate to bring about proper adjustment. The contention of the elasticity pessimists is that the demand elasticities are low, so that currency depreciations are of limited, if any, benefit to deficit countries. Proponents of floating exchange rates, however, point out that there is little empirical evidence to support the view that demand elasticities are low. In fact, current empirical studies generally conclude that demand elasticities are relatively high.

Disorderly Exchange Markets

According to the opponents, perhaps the chief disadvantage of floating rates results from the discouragement to foreign trade and investment. In these areas, floating rates add to existing financial risks resulting from price and revenue uncertainties. Critics cite the 1974 experience of the U.S. dollar under the existing managed floating system. Although central bankers agreed to maintain orderly exchange market conditions, the dollar in 1974 fell 17.5 percent against West Germany's mark, only to rise 9.5 percent and then fall to a new low by the end of the year! It has been

pointed out that such movements could hardly be explained by the dollar's underlying value. Jarring fluctuations like these add an important additional risk to international transactions.

It is often argued that exchange risk can be minimized when business people buy and sell currencies in the forward exchange markets. But the exchange risk that can be covered is of a very specific type—that is, the risk that profit on a particular transaction will be reduced as the result of fluctuating exchange rates. But some transactions are either difficult or impossible to hedge. For many frequently recurring transactions, there is no way of guarding against such a risk; and companies that contract sales or deliveries more than one year in advance often find forward markets very thin. Moreover, the cost of hedging can get expensive. By increasing the cost of obtaining forward cover on international commercial and financial transactions, floating rates may stifle commodity trade flows and capital movements.

It is also possible that floating rates may be conducive to destabilizing speculation, magnifying fluctuations in exchange rates. Economic downturns or political unrest might lead to hot-money movements and capital flight that would distort exchange rates away from normal levels. Once an exchange rate begins to depreciate, speculators might interpret this as a signal for future depreciation. Acting on these expectations, they will sell the depreciating currency and cause it to decline in value even more. Such large swings in exchange rates act as an impediment to trade and capital movements. Critics point to the exchange market instability of a few weeks in mid-1973 when the U.S. dollar greatly declined in value. Although this is possible and may sometimes occur, floating rate proponents counterargue that floating rates may lessen speculative activity by introducing more risk. This is because a speculator must always face the risk that a currency may become overbought or oversold and reverse its direction.

Reckless Financial Policies

Floating rates in theory are supposed to allow governments to set independent monetary and fiscal policies. But this may cause a problem of another sort, as floating rates may result in the domestic economy being subject to an inflationary bias. This is because monetary authorities may lack the sense of financial discipline required by a fixed exchange rate system.

Suppose a country faces relatively high rates of inflation compared with the rest of the world. Unlike fixed exchange rates, the inflation will have no negative impact on the country's trade balance under floating rates, since its currency will automatically depreciate in the exchange market. However, a protracted depreciation of the currency would result in persistent increasing import prices and a rising price level, making inflation self-generating and the depreciation continuous. Since there is greater freedom for domestic financial management under floating rates, there may be less resistance to overspending and its subsequent pressure on wages and prices.

Do Floating Rates Cause Inflation?

With the downfall of the Bretton Woods system of pegged exchange rates in 1973, the emerging international monetary order adopted the floating rate arrangement. Rather than a pure, or free, float, a managed float was adopted, in which central bankers still exerted some influence in keeping exchange rates orderly. During the first two years of the system, worldwide inflation became rampant. In the United States, consumer prices rose 22 percent and wholesale prices increased almost 40 percent over the two-year period 1973–1975. The fact that inflation intensified just as managed floating rates were

adopted made some economists question the conventional view of floating rates.

There is a view held by some economists that although the fundamental cause of the 1970s inflation was the growth in the money supply, floating exchange rates are a structural factor that ratchets the inflation spiral upward. This section first considers the conventional wisdom concerning inflation and currency depreciation and then investigates the contrasting view.[3]

Inflation Leads to Depreciation

The traditional view of inflation and currency depreciation concludes the following: (1) Domestic inflation causes adjustments in exchange rates. (2) It is the domestic policies of each country, rather than exchange rates, that are the cause of inflation. The traditional view thus focuses attention of the inflationary policies of the individual national economy rather than on an integrated world economy.

To illustrate the traditional view that inflation leads to depreciation, consider an example based on the following assumptions: (1) The United States produces television sets for $100, while importing television sets from West Germany that sell at the identical dollar price. (2) The exchange rate between the dollar and mark is at $1 = 5 marks. Suppose that the U.S. inflation rate rises to 25 percent, whereas that of West Germany remains at zero. We would expect the price of U.S.-produced television sets to rise from $100 to $125 per unit. Being relatively attractive at $100, more West German television sets would be demanded by U.S. consumers. As more marks are purchased to buy the television set imports, the dollar price of marks will rise—that is, the dollar's exchange rate will depreciate. The value of the dollar will decrease 25 percent from $1 = 5 marks (1 mark = 20 cents) to $1 = 4 marks (1 mark = 25 cents), reflecting the U.S.

rate of price inflation. Concurrently, the domestic inflation will force up the price of U.S. exports, making them less attractive to foreigners. As foreign demand decreases, the dollar further depreciates against the mark.[4]

The conventional view of how inflation causes a currency to depreciate recognizes that modern industrial economies are interdependent. But it does not accept the notion that changes in exchange rates significantly influence domestic prices. Instead, some economists think the causation works in the other direction.

Depreciation Leads to Inflation

The conventional wisdom maintains that domestic inflation can lead to exchange rate depreciation. However, immediately following the industrialized countries' adoption of almost-floating exchange rates in 1973, global inflation accelerated. Some economists have challenged the conventional view by attempting to demonstrate how currency depreciation leads to inflation. The challengers contend that because of downward price inflexibility, a ratchet effect results in an inflationary bias, both for individual countries and for the world economy, under a system of floating exchange rates.

Assume the United States and West Germany both produce calculators and television sets for domestic consumption. The United States exports calculators, and television sets are exported by West Germany. As the result of changing American tastes, suppose American imports of West German television sets increase. Under floating exchange rates, this leads to an increased U.S. demand for marks and a depreciation of the dollar relative to the mark. More dollars are now required to purchase West German television sets and fewer marks to purchase U.S. calculators.

The dollar depreciation results in U.S. goods becoming better bargains than West German

goods. As U.S. consumers purchase more domestic television sets, home producers will permit their prices to drift upward toward the prices of West German imports. The reason for this is that in an integrated economic world, arbitragers exploit price differentials to make a profit. They would profit by purchasing television sets cheap in U.S. markets and selling them dear in West Germany. But this process tends to be short-lived, since relative prices approach equality as U.S. prices are bid up toward foreign levels. At the same time, the dollar depreciation makes U.S. calculators a good bargain overseas. But as West Germans purchase additional calculators, U.S. producers increase calculator prices in their domestic market as well as export market, again reflecting the arbitrage process that transmits higher prices of imports and exports throughout an integrated world market. The dollar depreciation therefore generates a higher level of prices in the United States.

Given that the dollar depreciation against the mark causes prices to increase in the United States, wouldn't it follow that any mark appreciation against the dollar would push West German prices downward? Not so, contend the challengers. Owing to national institutions such as trade associations and labor unions, prices move up more easily than down. Prices are rigid in a downward direction. If there were no downward price rigidities and the dollar depreciated against the mark, half the adjustment would show up as higher nominal prices in the United States and half as lower nominal prices in West Germany. But owing to downward rigidities, a disproportionate share of adjustment takes the form of price inflation in the depreciating country. To illustrate, if the dollar depreciates in six months by 10 percent against the mark, prices would rise in the United States while remaining quite constant in West Germany. But if West Germany's mark depreciates over the next six months by 10 percent, prices will rise in West

Germany while not noticeably falling in the United States. At year's end, the exchange rates are unchanged, but nominal prices are higher in both countries.

Given the foregoing analysis, the challengers to the conventional wisdom reach a number of unorthodox conclusions about the merits of floating exchange rates as well as currency devaluations. First, they maintain that currency depreciations (devaluations) are unable to improve a country's trade balance. Any short-run price advantage gained by a currency depreciation is soon neutralized by a higher-than-average inflation rate in the depreciating country. Changes in exchange rates therefore do not provide a country any real competitive advantage. Second, currency depreciations do have more of an inflationary impact than the conventional wisdom suggests.

The Monetary Approach Under Floating Exchange Rates

Recall that Chapter 13 discussed the monetary approach to balance-of-payments adjustment under a fixed exchange rate system. The monetary approach also has adjustment implications for a floating exchange rate system.

This chapter emphasizes how currency depreciation or appreciation can bring about balance-of-payments equilibrium under a system of floating exchange rates. The result is no change in a country's foreign exchange reserves. The domestic money supply remains constant unless national monetary authorities initiate policies to change it. Any imbalance between the domestic supply of and demand for money will be eliminated by changes in the demand for money. According to the monetary approach, currency depreciation or appreciation will remove such imbalances.

To illustrate, given an initial equilibrium in the money market and the foreign exchange market, suppose the Federal Reserve increases the money supply of the United States. The monetary expansion would make it easier for individuals and companies to borrow money. A rise in domestic spending and income would occur, leading to increased imports and a rise in the demand for foreign currency. The monetary expansion also would result in lower interest rates, assuming the absence of inflationary expectations. Lower interest rates motivate Americans to invest overseas, again increasing the demand for foreign currency. With the demand for foreign currency now exceeding the supply, the U.S. dollar would depreciate in value under floating exchange rates. The dollar depreciation would induce higher domestic prices. Higher-priced transactions result in an increase in the demand for money. The adjustment process would continue until the excess supply of money was eliminated.

The monetary approach thus emphasizes that, under a system of floating exchange rates, movements in currency values play a primary role in restoring equilibrium between money demand and money supply. Table 15.1 summarizes the impact of changes in the money supply and money demand on domestic currency values, according to the monetary approach.

Table 15.1 Changes in Money Supply and Money Demand Under Floating Exchange Rates: Impact on the Exchange Rate According to the Monetary Approach

Change*	Impact
Increase in money supply	Depreciate
Decrease in money supply	Appreciate
Increase in money demand	Appreciate
Decrease in money demand	Depreciate

*Starting from the point of equilibrium between the money supply and money demand.

Summary

1.   A freely floating exchange rate system incorporates a direct extension of the institutions of a free market into international transactions. Under this system, exchange rates are established by the free-market forces of supply and demand, with no active intervention by monetary authorities. A freely floating system is not characterized by par values or official exchange rates.

2.   Among the most important arguments for freely floating exchange rates are the following: (1) simplicity, (2) continuous adjustment, (3) independent domestic policies, (4) increased effectiveness of monetary policy, and (5) reduced needs for international reserves.

3.   Several arguments against freely floating exchange rates stress the following issues: (1) world demand elasticities for traded goods, (2) disorderly exchange markets, and (3) reckless financial policies on the part of governments.

4.   Some economists maintain that changes in currency values over time do not affect relative prices of goods. Any short-run price advantage gained by depreciation of a currency is soon offset by inflation in the country undergoing currency depreciation.

5.   The monetary approach to balance-of-payments adjustment maintains that under a floating exchange rate system, currency depreciation or appreciation tends to remove imbalances between the domestic supply of and demand for money, promoting balance-of-payments equilibrium.

Study Questions

1.   How does a freely floating exchange rate system operate?

2.   Why is it that international reserves needed under a floating exchange rate system?

3.   Does the Marshall-Lerner Condition apply to floating exchange rates?

4.   Under what conditions may exchange rates become disorderly?

5.   Compare the alleged strengths and weaknesses of a fixed versus floating exchange rate system.

6.   Do floating exchange rates cause inflation?

7.   Under a system of floating exchange rates, how does currency depreciation or appreciation lead to balance-of-payments equilibrium, according to the monetary approach to the balance of payments?

Notes

1.   See Milton Friedman, "The Case for Flexible Exchange Rates," in American Economic Association, *Readings in International Economics* (Homewood, Ill.: Richard D. Irwin, 1968), pp. 413–437.

2.   See Henry C. Wallich, "The Case for Fixed Exchange Rates," in *The United States Balance of Payments*, Hearings Before the Joint Economic Committee, 88th Cong., 1st Sess., Washington, D.C., part 3, pp. 495–499.

3.   See Arthur Laffer, "Do Devaluations Help Trade?" *Wall Street Journal*, February 5, 1973, p. 10 and "The Bitter Fruits of Devaluation," *Wall Street Journal*, January 10, 1974, p. 14. Jude Wanniski summarizes this view in "The Mundell-Laffer Hypothesis: A New View of the World Economy," *The Public Interest* (Spring 1975).

4.   Janice M. Westerfield, "Would Fixed Exchange Rates Control Inflation?" *Business Review*, Federal Reserve Bank of Philadelphia (July–August 1976), pp. 3–10.

Suggestions for Further Reading

Bautista, R. M. "Exchange Rate Changes and LDC Export Performance Under Generalized Currency Floating." *Weltwirtschaftliches Archiv*, 117, no. 3, 1981.

Calderon-Rossell, J. R., and M. Ben-Horim. "The Behavior of Foreign Exchange Rates." *Journal of International Business Studies*, Fall 1982.

Caves, R. E. "Flexible Exchange Rates." *American Economic Review*, May 1963.

Friedman, M., and R. Roosa. *The Balance of Payments: Free Versus Fixed Exchange Rates*. Washington, D.C.: American Enterprise Institute, 1967.

Helpman, E., and A. Razin. "Dynamics of a Floating Exchange Rate Regime." *Journal of Political Economy*, August 1982.

The International Adjustment Mechanism. Proceedings of a Monetary Conference. Boston: Federal Reserve Bank of Boston, 1970.

Lanyi, A. *The Case for Floating Exchange Rates Reconsidered. Essays in International Finance*, no. 72. Princeton, N.J.: Princeton University Press, 1969.

Machlup, F. *On Terms, Concepts, Theories and Strategies in the Discussion of Greater Flexibility of Exchange Rates. Princeton Reprints in International Finance*, no. 14, 1970.

Morgan, E. V. "The Theory of Flexible Exchange Rates. *American Economic Review*, June 1955.

Persson, T. "Global Effects of National Stabilization Policies Under Fixed and Floating Exchange Rates." *Scandinavian Journal of Economics*, 84, no. 2, 1982.

Sohmen, E. *Fluctuating Exchange Rates: Theory and Controversy*. Chicago: University of Chicago Press, 1961.

16

CHOOSING AN EXCHANGE
RATE SYSTEM

During the quarter century following World War II, the trading nations of the West operated under a largely uniform system of fixed exchange rates for their currencies. But the 1960s witnessed a series of crises in the foreign exchange market that disrupted the confidence of international traders and investors in the fixed exchange rate system. During the early 1970s, a combination of disruptions in commodity markets and large differences among inflation rates in trading nations made it all but impossible to maintain a system of fixed exchange rates.

Today, individual nations choose the exchange rate policies most compatible with their own economic objectives. As outlined in Figure 16.1, the range of options in exchange rate systems is broad.

In choosing an exchange rate system, the decision a country must make is whether to allow its currency to float or to be pegged against some standard of value. Should a country adopt a float, it must decide whether to float independently, in unison with a group of other currencies, or to crawl according to a predetermined formula such as relative inflation rates. The decision to peg a currency includes the options of pegging to a single currency, to a basket of currencies including the SDR, or to monetary

gold. In Figure 16.1, monetary gold is included as a standard of value only for historical interest. Since 1971, the technique of expressing a par value in terms of gold has been unjustifiable. This is because the United States withdrew its commitment to the free purchase and sale of gold, in effect downplaying the role of gold as an official reserve asset.

This chapter considers the major present and historic exchange rate practices that have been in operation during the post–World War II era. The discussion focuses on the nature and operation of actual exchange rate systems and identifies economic factors that influence the choice between exchange rate systems.

Floating Versus Pegging

Since the termination of the Bretton Woods system of fixed exchange rates in 1973, member countries of the International Monetary Fund (IMF) have been free to follow any exchange rate policy that conforms to three principles: (1) Exchange rates should not be manipulated to prevent effective balance-of-payments adjustments or to gain an unfair competitive

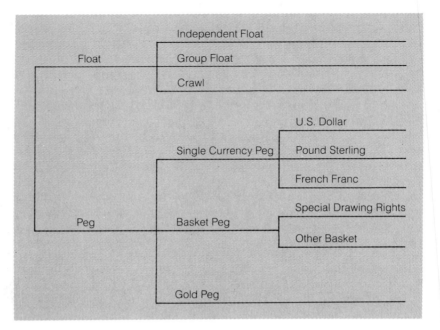

Figure 16.1   Exchange rate system alternatives.

advantage over other members. (2) Members should act to counter disorderly conditions in exchange markets of a short-term nature. (3) When members intervene in exchange markets, they should take into account the interests of other members. The IMF is authorized to play a surveillance role and to consult with any member that is suspected of violating these principles.

As seen in Table 16.1, 93 members of the IMF chose to peg their currencies in some manner in 1983, out of a total of 146 IMF countries. The importance of floating exchange rates, however, should not be underestimated. Although fewer than one-third of IMF countries floated their currencies in 1983, as a group they accounted for four-fifths of world exports.[1]

Pegging Alternatives: Single Currency Versus Currency Basket

Despite the importance of floating exchange rates for international trade and investment, many nations peg their currencies to some relatively stable standard. Pegged exchange rates, used primarily by small nations (generally the less-developed countries), are assumed to encourage both world trade and investment by reducing the risks of transacting in foreign countries. Small countries choose to peg their currencies to either a single currency or a currency basket.[2]

Pegging to a *single currency* is generally used by small nations whose trade and financial relationships are mainly with a single trading partner. For example, Ivory Coast, which trades

Table 16.1   Exchange Rate Arrangements of
IMF Members, 1983

Exchange Rate Regime	Number of Countries
Pegged rates: currency pegged to	
U.S. dollar	37
French franc	13
Other national currencies	5
Special Drawing Right	14
Other currency composite	24
Joint floating	8
Exchange rate adjusted to a Set of Indicators	5
Managed floating	22
Independently floating	8
Other	10
Total	146

Source: International Monetary Fund, *International Financial Statistics*, June 1983, p. 15.

primarily with France, pegs the value of its currency to the French franc. A small nation, by pegging the value of its currency to that of its trading partner, can reduce changes in the prices of imports and exports that result from changes in the value of its currency relative to that of its trading partner. The result could be greater stability of output and employment in exporting and importing sectors, which could have favorable effects on the country's economic development.

Small countries with more than one major trading partner often desire to peg the value of their currencies to a group or *basket of currencies*. The basket is composed of prescribed quantities of foreign currencies in proportion to the amount of trade done with the country pegging its currency. Once the basket is selected, the currency value of the country is computed using exchange rates of the foreign currencies in the basket. By pegging the domestic currency value of the basket, fluctuations in export or import prices caused by exchange rate movements can be averaged out. The effects of exchange rate changes on the domestic economy thus are reduced.

Tanzania and Malta use a basket of currencies of their major trading partners in the management of their exchange rates. In addition to developing countries, some developed nations with small economies peg their currencies against a basket of currencies. Sweden, for example, uses a basket of 15 currencies of its major trading partners in the management of its exchange rate.

Rather than constructing their own currency basket, many nations peg the value of their currencies to the Special Drawing Right (SDR), a currency basket defined by the International Monetary Fund. The SDR is composed of the currencies of the five IMF members having the largest exports of goods and services during the period 1975–1979—the United States, West Germany, France, Japan, and Great Britain. Nations pegging their currencies to the SDR tend to trade with these countries, whose currencies are represented in the SDR's value.

The idea behind the SDR basket valuation method is to make the SDR's value more stable than the foreign currency value of any single national currency. The SDR is valued according to an index based on the moving average of those currencies in the basket. Should the values of the basket currencies either depreciate or appreciate against each other, the SDR's value would remain in the center. The SDR would depreciate against those currencies that are rising in value and appreciate against the currencies whose values are falling. Nations desiring exchange rate stability are attracted to the SDR as a currency basket against which to pay their currency values.

Table 16.2 illustrates the basket valuation of the SDR as of April 30, 1981. On the basis of

Table 16.2 Computation of SDR Value, April 30, 1981

Currency	National Currency Unit per SDR		Exchange Rate: Foreign Currency Unit per U.S. Dollar		U.S. Dollar Value*
U.S. dollar	0.54	÷	1.0000	=	0.540
Deutsche mark	0.46	÷	2.2145	=	0.208
French franc	0.74	÷	5.2540	=	0.141
Japanese yen	34.00	÷	215.1300	=	0.158
Pound sterling	0.07	×	2.1404	=	0.152
				=	1.199
			U.S. dollar value of SDR	=	$1.199
			SDR value of 1 U.S. dollar	=	0.834

Source: International Monetary Fund, *Annual Report*, 1981, p. 95.
*All of the exchange rates in column 4 are in foreign currency units per dollar, except for the British pound, which is dollars per pound.

weights calculated for the five currencies in the currency basket,[3] the amount of each currency in the SDR is indicated in column 2 of the table. The value of the SDR on a national currency basis thus equals

$$1 \text{ SDR} = 0.54 \text{ dollars} + 0.46 \text{ marks}$$

$$+ 0.74 \text{ francs} + 34 \text{ yen}$$

$$+ 0.07 \text{ pounds.}$$

The SDR's value in terms of the U.S. dollar is given in column 4 of the table, determined by adjusting column 2 for the exchange rates of column 3. As of 1983, 14 developing nations chose to peg their currency values to the SDR. However, the SDR has a long way to go before it will be a strong competitor to major national currencies as a standard against which to peg currency values.

Exchange Rate Forecasting: The Purchasing Power Parity Doctrine

Throughout the post–World War II era, most national authorities have exercised some management of exchange rate movements. Under the Bretton Woods system of 1946–1971, governments periodically devalued or revalued their currency units to restore balance-of-payments equilibrium. Under the managed floating system of the 1970s and 1980s, authorities have attempted to create a stable environment for international trade by buying and selling foreign exchange for the purpose of moderating fluctuations in exchange rate movements.

Determining the *long-run equilibrium value* of an exchange rate (the value toward which the actual rate would tend to move, given current economic conditions and policies) is important for successful exchange rate management. For example, if a country's exchange rate rises above the level warranted by economic conditions, becoming an overvalued exchange rate, the country's costs will no longer be competitive and a balance-of-payments deficit will likely occur. An undervalued currency would have the opposite effect. National authorities have tried to forecast the long-run equilibrium rate and initiate exchange rate adjustments to keep the actual rate in line with the forecasted rate. The purchasing power parity approach is a popular method for such exchange rate forecasting.

According to the *purchasing power parity* theory, changes in relative national price levels determine changes in exchange rates. A currency maintains its purchasing power parity if it depreciates by an amount equal to the excess of domestic inflation over foreign inflation. Conversely, a currency maintains its purchasing power parity if it appreciates by an amount equal to the excess of foreign inflation over domestic inflation. If either of these possibilities occurs, the purchasing power of the domestic currency remains unchanged compared with the purchasing power of the foreign currency—thus the expression "purchasing power parity."

For example, if the domestic inflation rate in the United States is 5 percentage points higher than the rate of inflation in Switzerland, the purchasing power parity theory maintains that the dollar will tend to depreciate on the foreign exchange market at a rate of 5 percent relative to the Swiss franc under a system of flexible exchange rates. It follows from the theory that the way to strengthen a currency's external value is to strengthen its internal value by lowering the domestic rate of inflation. In the preceding example, the way to prevent the dollar's depreciation against the Swiss franc is to bring the U.S. inflation rate down to equality with the lower Swiss rate. When both currencies experience the same rate of inflation, their purchasing power will remain constant and the exchange rate will stabilize.

The purchasing power parity theory can be used to predict long-run levels of exchange rates and to forecast approximate levels to which currency values should be changed, if it becomes necessary to change them. Letting 0 be the base period and 1 represent period 1, the purchasing power theory[4] is given in symbols as

$$S_1 = S_0 \frac{P_{U.S._1}/P_{U.S._0}}{P_{WG_1}/P_{WG_0}} ,$$

where S_0 equals the equilibrium exchange rate existing in the base period and S_1 equals the estimated target at which the actual rate should be in the future.

For example, let the price indexes of the United States and West Germany be

$$P_{U.S._0} = 100, P_{U.S._1} = 200, P_{WG_0} = 100,$$

$$P_{WG_1} = 100, \text{ and } S_0 = \$0.50.$$

Putting the figures into the above equation, we can determine the new equilibrium exchange rate for period 1:

$$S_1 = \$ .50 \left(\frac{200/100}{100/100}\right)$$

$$= \$ .50 \quad (2)$$

$$= \$1.00$$

Over the course of the two periods, the U.S. inflation rate rose 100 percent, whereas West Germany's inflation rate remained unchanged. Maintaining purchasing power parity between the dollar and the mark requires the dollar to depreciate against the mark by an amount equal to the difference in the percent rates of inflation in the United States and West Germany. The dollar must depreciate by 100 percent, from 50 cents per mark to $1 per mark, to maintain its purchasing power parity. Had the example assumed instead that West Germany's inflation rate doubled while the U.S. inflation rate remained unchanged over the course of the two periods, the dollar would appreciate to a level of 25 cents per mark, according to the purchasing power parity theory.

An application of the purchasing power parity concept is provided in Table 16.3, which gives the dollar-peso exchange rate over the period 1975–1979, during which Argentina experienced very high price inflation. From 1975 to 1979, the U.S. inflation rate rose by almost 35 percent, whereas Argentina's inflation rate skyrocketed by well over 10,000 percent. Applying the purchasing power parity formula to the figures, we would expect the dollar to appreciate against the peso, from $0.0164 per peso to $0.0002 per peso, owing to the relative decline in the peso's domestic purchasing power. Actually the dollar appreciated to $0.0006 per peso, not far from the forecasted rate.

Although the purchasing power parity theory can be helpful in forecasting appropriate levels to which currency values should be adjusted, it is not an infallible guide to exchange rate determination. For instance, the theory overlooks the fact that exchange rate movements may be influenced by capital flows (for example, foreign investment). The theory also faces the problem of choosing the appropriate price index to be used in price calculations (such as consumer prices or wholesale prices) and determining the equilib-

rium period to use as a base. Moreover, government policy may interfere with the operation of the theory, as did the U.S. policy of high interest rates in 1983, which caused the dollar to appreciate. In spite of these problems, the purchasing power parity theory is useful as a partial guide for exchange rate management.

The Adjustable Peg

In 1944, delegates from 44 members of the United Nations met at Bretton Woods, New Hampshire, to create a new international monetary system. The delegates were aware of the unsatisfactory monetary experience of the 1930s, during which the international gold standard collapsed as the result of the economic and financial crises of the Great Depression and nations experimented unsuccessfully with freely floating exchange rates, managed floating exchange rates, and exchange controls. The delegates wanted to establish international monetary order and avoid the instability and nationalistic practices that occurred during the pre–World War II era.

The international monetary system that was created became known as the Bretton Woods system. The founders of the Bretton Woods

Table 16.3   Purchasing Power Parity in Action: 1975–1979

	1975	1976	1977	1978	1979
U.S. index of consumer prices	100	105.8	112.7	121.2	134.9
Argentina index of consumer prices	100	543	1,500	4,131	10,721
Actual exchange rate (dollar per peso)	0.0164	0.0036	0.0017	0.0010	0.0006
Forecasted exchange rate (dollar per peso)	——	0.0032	0.0012	0.0005	0.0002

Source: International Monetary Fund, *IMF Financial Statistics*, November 1980, pp. 59, 407.

system felt that neither completely fixed exchange rates nor freely floating exchange rates were optimal systems. Instead, some kind of managed exchange rate system seemed appropriate. The result was the adoption of adjustable pegged exchange rates as part of the Bretton Woods system, which lasted from 1944 until 1973.[5]

The essential idea of *adjustable peg* is that currencies are tied to each other to provide stable exchange rates for commercial and financial transactions. When the balance of payments moves away from its long-run equilibrium position, the country may repeg its exchange rate by moving it from one par value to another (devaluation or revaluation). Although the adjustable peg accepts the principle of limited exchange rate flexibility, this does not mean that exchange rates are unalterably fixed.

Exchange Rate Bands

According to the adjustable pegged system adopted by the Bretton Woods system, each member country set the par value of its currency in terms of gold or, alternatively, the gold content of the U.S. dollar in 1944. Market exchange rates were almost but not completely fixed, kept within a band of 1 percent on either side or parity for a total spread of 2 percent. National exchange stabilization funds were used to maintain the band limits.

Suppose the Belgian monetary authorities set the franc's par value at 50.0 francs per dollar. Under the IMF rules, the Belgian stabilization fund would have to take action to defend the actual fluctuation of its exchange rate within a margin of 50.5 francs per dollar and 49.5 francs per dollar, a band of 2 percent around parity, as shown in Figure 16.2. Within these limits, the exchange rate can fluctuate freely according to prevailing market conditions. Now suppose a rise in Belgian incomes results in an increase in that country's demand for U.S. exports and thus a rise in the demand for dollars from D_0 to D_1. Under free market conditions, the price of dollars would rise to 51 francs per dollar. At this point, the franc would have depreciated by 2 percent. The Belgian exchange stabilization fund must therefore intervene to defend the band's limits. At the band's limit, there is an excess demand for dollars of GH. The fund would enter into the market and increase the supply of dollars from S_0 to S_1, maintaining the exchange rate within the prescribed ranges.

Under the original IMF agreement, the U.S. dollar was pegged to gold, whereas other member countries were obligated to maintain their exchange rates against the dollar within 1 percent on either side of parity. According to the Smithsonian Agreement, the exchange support margins were widened to 2.25 percent on either side of parity. The widening of exchange rate margins was intended to offer several advantages. First, greater flexibility in exchange rates would eliminate payments imbalances by setting in motion corrective trade and capital movements. Second, widening exchange rate margins would introduce greater uncertainty into the returns from short-term capital transactions, discouraging the movement of short-term funds that had plagued the Bretton Woods system in 1971. However, the negative balance-of-payments figures in 1972 created widespread suspicion that the wider margins of the Smithsonian Agreement were not working. With the collapse of the Bretton Woods system in 1973, the Smithsonian Agreement was terminated and managed floating rates became widespread.

Cross Rates

The United States was placed in a central position under the Bretton Woods system, in which other currency parities were expressed in terms of the dollar, which itself was tied to gold. By

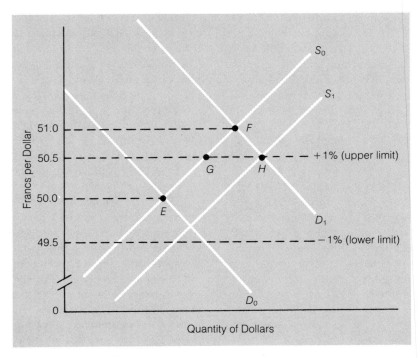

Figure 16.2   Exchange rate stabilization under the Bretton Woods system.

having parities maintained against the dollar, the permissible exchange spread between two nondollar currencies was double the width of the band between the dollar and a foreign currency. Under the original Bretton Woods arrangements, for example, the dollar's rate could fluctuate up to 2 percent against other currencies, whereas the potential spread (cross rate) between two nondollar currencies, vis-à-vis the dollar, was 4 percent.

Assume the U.S. dollar serves as the common denominator against which par values are measured and that Great Britain and West Germany are peripheral countries. Suppose national par values are set at 1 pound = 200 cents and 1 mark = 100 cents. According to the Bretton Woods limits, the following ranges are established:

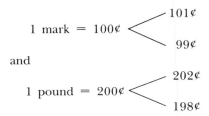

and

The potential cross rates between the mark and the pound fall within the limits of

Lower bound in terms of pound

$$\frac{198¢}{101¢} = 1.96 \text{ marks per pound}$$

Upper bound in terms of pound

$$\frac{202¢}{99¢} = 2.04 \text{ marks per dollar}$$

The spread thus becomes 0.08 mark. Let us use the midpoint of the range in terms of marks between the weakest and strongest position of the mark as a base—that is, 2 marks. The permissible variation in the cross rate between the mark and pound becomes 4 percent ($0.08/2 = 0.04$). The potential cross rate between currencies not used as a common denominator for expressing par values is 4 percent rather than 2 percent.

Adjustment Efficiency

The rationale for the Bretton Woods system's adoption of the adjustable peg was to permit the advantages of stable rates without the need to completely sacrifice the exchange rate as a policy instrument. Member countries agreed in principle to defend existing par values as long as possible in times of balance-of-payments disequilibrium. They were expected to use fiscal and monetary policies first to correct payments imbalances. But reversing a persistent payments imbalance might come at the expense of severe disruption to the domestic economy in terms of inflation or unemployment. Member countries could then correct this fundamental disequilibrium by repegging their currencies up to 10 percent without permission of the IMF. The adjustable peg system thus attempts to avoid both the destabilizing effects of wildly fluctuating exchange rates and the worst consequences of completely fixed exchange rates.

Although adjustable pegged rates are intended to promote a viable balance-of-payments adjustment mechanism, they have been plagued with operational problems. In the Bretton Woods system, adjustments in prices and incomes often conflicted with domestic stabilization objectives. Also, currency devaluation was undesirable, since it seemed to indicate a failure of domestic policies and a loss of international prestige. On the other hand, revaluations were most unacceptable to exporters, whose livelihoods were vulnerable to such policies. Repegging exchange rates only as a last resort often meant that when adjustments finally did occur, they were of sizable amounts. Furthermore, adjustable pegged rates pose difficulties in estimating the equilibrium rate to which a currency should be repegged. Finally, once the market exchange rate reaches the margin of the permissible band around parity, it in effect becomes a rigid fixed rate that presents speculators with a one-way bet. For example, at the band's lower limit, and given persistent downward pressure, speculators would have the incentive to move out of a weakening currency that is expected to depreciate further in value as the result of official devaluation.

Managed Floating Exchange Rates

The adoption of managed floating exchange rates by the industrialized countries in 1973 followed the breakdown of the international monetary system based on the Bretton Woods par value system. Before the 1970s, only a handful of economists gave serious consideration to a general system of floating rates. But owing to the defects in the decision-making process stemming from procedural difficulties and political biases, adjustments of par values under the Bretton Woods system were often delayed and discontinuous. It was recognized that exchange rates should be adjusted more promptly and in small but continuous amounts in response to evolving market forces.

By 1973, there was accelerating worldwide inflation, a recessionary tendency in some leading industrial countries, and a world commodity boom, as well as other political and economic uncertainties. It was inevitable that the widespread floating of exchange rates by industrial nations in March 1973 would continue for an indefinite period. A move to a free floating system was unrealistic at this time, since governments would not relinquish to the market forces all control over a variable as important as the exchange rate. A managed floating system was adopted instead under which informal guidelines were established by the International Monetary Fund for coordination of national exchange rate policies.

Why Guidelines?

Conceptually there are two extreme types of floating exchange rate systems. First is a *free float*, in which only market forces determine exchange rate movements. Second is a completely *managed float*, whereby monetary authorities manage the exchange rate so it changes in a predetermined manner. Between these poles lie a host of exchange rate systems based on varying degrees of government intervention. What emerged in 1973 was a change in the political setting of the decision-making process that deemphasized decisions about exchange rate policy. The result was a system of managed floating rates where informal guidelines were formulated for the modification of exchange rate behavior.

The motivation for the formulation of guidelines for floating arose from two concerns. The first was that countries might intervene in the exchange markets to avoid alterations of their exchange rates that would weaken their competitive position. When the United States suspended its gold convertibility pledge and allowed its overvalued dollar to float in the exchange markets, it hoped that a free market adjustment would result in a depreciation of the dollar against other undervalued currencies. Rather than permitting a *clean float* (free market solution) to occur, Japan's central bank refused to permit the dollar depreciation against the yen by purchasing dollars for yen on the exchange market. The United States considered this a *dirty float*, as the free market forces of supply and demand were not allowed to achieve their equilibrating role. A second motivation for floating guidelines was that free floats may over time lead to a nonoptimal behavioral pattern of exchange rates. This means that exchange market conditions become disorderly, which leads to erratic fluctuations in exchange rates. Such destabilizing factors may create an uncertain business climate and lower levels of world trade. These concerns—about the consequences of competitive alterations in exchange rates, as well as disorderly exchange markets—lay behind the desire of the participating IMF countries to develop guidelines for managed floating exchange rates.

Guidelines for Management of Floating Rates

With the introduction of managed floating, the need for management guidelines was recognized by most central bankers. In 1975, the Guidelines for the Management of Floating Exchange Rates were adopted by the International Monetary Fund. The term *guidelines* rather than *rules* was used to indicate their tentative and experimental character. The guidelines have been based on the assumption that avoiding disorderly fluctuations in exchange rates is desirable and that governmental behavior with respect to exchange rates should be a matter of consultation. Although not legally binding, the guidelines were formulated in three main areas: (1) the stability of exchange markets in the very short term (day-to-day and week-to-week fluctuations); (2) fluctuations in exchange rates over periods of several months or quarters; and (3) the adjustment of exchange rates to underlying changes in balance-of-payments positions.

Concerning day-to-day and week-to-week exchange rate movements, a primary objective has been to prevent the emergence of erratic exchange rate fluctuations. The potential for such disruptive conditions was clearly seen in June and July of 1973, when speculative pressures intensified in the exchange markets. During this period, the U.S. dollar depreciated against some European currencies by as much as 4 percent in a single day and 10 percent in a single week. Another case was the January 1974 experience, when the U.S. dollar appreciated by more than 6 percent against several European currencies in a single week, only to depreciate rapidly the following week. Such erratic exchange rate fluctuations over a short time period can increase the cost of hedging and disrupt trade patterns. According to the guidelines, a member should intervene as necessary to prevent sharp and disruptive exchange rate fluctuations from day to day and week to week. Such an exchange rate policy involves *leaning against the wind*—intervening to reduce short-term fluctuations in exchange rates without attempting to adhere to any particular rate over the long run.

The second guideline for floating embodies the same general principle as the first guideline, but it is based on a longer time perspective. The reasoning is that it may be beneficial to smooth out short-term fluctuations in exchange rates and to offer some resistance to market pressures in the slightly longer run, especially when they are leading to unduly large fluctuations in the exchange rate. The guideline also suggests that members should not act aggressively with respect to their currency exchange rates—that is, they should not enhance the value when it is appreciating or depress the value when it is depreciating.

Over the longer run, exchange rate movements depend largely on factors underlying long-term capital flows and conditions determining competitiveness of an economy. Long-term capital flows respond to such factors as relative costs, location, and prevailing monetary and fiscal policies. An economy's competitiveness may be influenced by the availability of productive inputs, taste and preference conditions, and the availability of substitute goods. During periods in which countries are experiencing inflation at widely divergent rates, changes in relative costs of production tend to influence exchange rates significantly.

Under the managed float, some nations choose *target exchange rates* and intervene to support them. Target exchange rates are intended to reflect long-term economic forces that underlie exchange rate movements. One way for managed floaters to estimate a target exchange rate is to follow statistical indicators that respond to the same economic forces as the exchange rate trend. Then, when the values of indicators change, the exchange rate target can be adjusted accordingly. Among these indicators are rates of inflation in different countries, levels of official foreign reserves, and persistent imbalances in international payments accounts. For example, Portugal has revised its exchange rate by using an indicator formula based on inflation differentials between Portugal and its major trading partners.

One measure that the International Monetary Fund has used in assessing an economy's competitiveness is the relative prices of a country's manufactured goods, adjusted for inflation and changes in exchange rates. The relative competitiveness of five industrial countries is summarized in Figure 16.3. For each country, the price index line plotted is the price level of the nation in question, relative to the weighted average of the major industrial countries as a group. The weights reflect the relative shares of world trade in manufactured goods. The price index lines assume the base year to be 1980 = 100. For the time period in question, the manufacturing sectors of the United States and Japan became less competitive, as their export prices rose relative to the average of the major industrial countries. Conversely, the manufacturing sectors of Canada, West Germany, and Belgium were gaining in competitive strength.

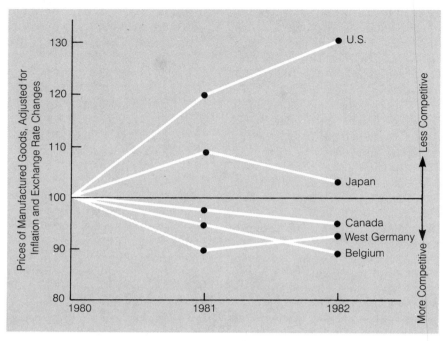

Figure 16.3   Relative export competitiveness of five industrial countries (1980 = 100). (Source: International Monetary Fund, *International Financial Statistics*, June 1983, pp. 48–49.)

The use of export prices or costs as guidelines for exchange rate movements is suggested by their relationship to an economy's international competitiveness. However, there are several problems in using prices or costs as indicators. Not only does the coverage of domestic price and cost indexes vary among countries, but also comprehensive data become available only after a considerable time lag. Also, the base period of Figure 16.3 was 1980 = 100. Because one cannot assume that the pattern of exchange rates was in equilibrium at that time, any interpretation of the figure should be approached with caution. Finally, price and costs as indicators are limited, as they relate primarily only to a portion of a country's payments position, the trade account.

Any overall assessment of the merits of managed floating rates requires comparing the way monetary authorities would have coped with economic developments under alternative exchange rate systems. Overall, it appears that exchange markets have functioned and that the types of monetary crises that plagued the Bretton Woods par value system have been avoided. Erratic fluctuations in exchange rates have taken place and floats at times may have become rather dirty, but the record indicates that world trade has continued to expand. Because the managed float seems to be working reasonably well, the IMF nations have proceeded rather slowly in reaching any formal arrangements for the international payments adjustment mechanism.

Joint Floating

Besides individual countries independently floating their currencies, the international monetary system has been characterized by currencies that float under mutual intervention arrangements. As of 1984, there were seven European countries—Belgium, Denmark, West Germany, France, Ireland, Italy, and the Netherlands—whose currencies were pegged to each other, while floating as a unit against nonmember countries. This European *joint float* is illustrated in Figure 16.4.

The Snake in the Tunnel

A primary objective of the European Economic Community (EEC) has been to achieve a high degree of monetary union. Such an arrangement, it was believed, would help the EEC nations pursue their goals of economic and political integration, at the same time establishing a major currency bloc that would rival the U.S. dollar. Such a move calls for the adoption of fixed exchange rates among member currencies and ultimately the adoption of a common currency. In 1970, the specifics of monetary integration were outlined in the Werner Report, based on the work of Pierre Werner, prime minister of Luxembourg. It called for a reduction and eventual elimination of exchange rate fluctuations among EEC currencies and complete liberalization of capital movements. Although the plan was not adopted formally, many of the principles it set forth became embodied in subsequent programs. The Werner Report's influence was reflected in the adoption of narrow margins for EEC currencies following the Smithsonian Agreement of 1971.

According to the Smithsonian Agreement, member currencies were permitted to float against the U.S. dollar within a band whose maximum width was 4.5 percent (plus or minus 2.25 percent) around the dollar's par value. However, this arrangement called for greater exchange rate flexibility than was desired by EEC nations. The result was that the maximum potential fluctuations between EEC currencies were reduced to 2.25 percent around the dollar's par value. The EEC currencies were permitted to float jointly, subject to the limits of the outer Smithsonian band. This arrangement became known as the *snake in the tunnel*. The tunnel's maximum width represented the greatest possible spread of EEC exchange rates against the dollar as permitted by the Smithsonian Agreement. The snake's maximum width signified the greatest possible exchange rate spread between EEC currencies.

The European snake consisted of the member currencies jointly floating against the dollar subject to the constraints of the Smithsonian Agreement, with a maximum spread of 2.25 percent between the dollar rates of the strongest and weakest member currencies. The internal pegging within the snake was carried out by *multiple currency intervention*. The central bank of each member country would conduct stabilization operations in its own market with the currencies of the other member countries to defend the peg. The members of the joint float also agreed to stay with a band of 4.5 percent around the dollar's par value. To maintain this peg, European central bankers would intervene in their markets with dollars when the snake reached the limits of the tunnel. This two-tier pegging procedure gave rise to the so-called snake in the tunnel.

These arrangements were to be consistent with the EEC's goal of eliminating exchange rate fluctuations between member currencies. The outer limits of the snake presumably would be reduced gradually, until a fixed exchange rate system was complete. At the same time, the EEC nations wanted the benefits of greater exchange rate flexibility between their currencies and the dollar. Thus, the inner band of EEC currencies floated jointly within the outer Smithsonian tunnel.

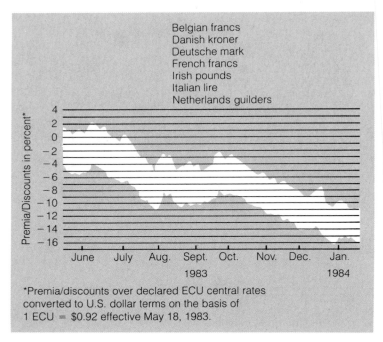

Belgian francs
Danish kroner
Deutsche mark
French francs
Irish pounds
Italian lire
Netherlands guilders

*Premia/discounts over declared ECU central rates
converted to U.S. dollar terms on the basis of
1 ECU = $0.92 effective May 18, 1983.

Figure 16.4   The European monetary system. (Source:
International Money Fund, *IMF Survey*, February 6,
1984, p. 48.)

The Snake Without a Tunnel

The April 1972 adoption of the snake-in-the-tunnel scheme was initially interpreted as a sign of success for the forces moving the EEC toward monetary union. Then renewed currency crises developed in 1972. By March 1973, the Smithsonian bands could no longer be maintained, and on their termination, the snake floated against the dollar with no preconceived limits. The world found itself with something new—an unlimited joint float among European currencies. By 1974, the Arab oil embargo had created new political and exchange rate strains within the EEC. Several members dropped out of the joint float rather than sacrifice national sovereignty to gain

the uncertain advantages of such an arrangement. The history of recent international monetary integration in Europe has not been a successful story. Membership in the joint float does not coincide with membership in the EEC. Although the joint float was intended as a basis for unalterable fixed exchange rates, major currency adjustments have occurred.

The European Monetary System

In spite of differing cultures, politics, and economic structures, Europeans have continued to press for monetary union. A step in this direction was taken in 1979 when eight countries agreed to establish the *European Monetary System* (EMS). The original members included West Germany, Belgium, Denmark, France, Ireland, Italy, Luxembourg, and the Netherlands. Alone among the Common Market members, Britain decided to remain outside the EMS, at least for a time. The impetus for the initiation of the EMS stemmed from the unstable exchange market conditions of 1977 and 1978. Europeans feared that continued exchange market disruptions would hamper international trade flows. To create a zone of monetary stability for Europe, two major objectives were outlined for the EMS: (1) to link European currencies together by virtually fixed exchange rates and (2) to establish a European Monetary Fund which would help members with balance-of-payments problems. The EMS was intended to be a refinement and extension of the EEC snake, in which a group of European currencies floated in unison against the U.S. dollar.

To facilitate linkage of the member currencies, the EMS has favored the *European Currency Unit* (ECU). Such an asset would serve as the numeraire of the EMS exchange rate mechanism and as a means of settlement among member central banks. The ECU's value is a composite, reflecting the values of the EMS member currencies as a group in which the West German mark weighs most heavily. Under the EMS, member country exchange rates are normally to be maintained within a band of plus or minus 2.25 percent around the ECU, which floats around the U.S. dollar. However, a weak currency nation like Italy can petition to have its currency value stray 6 percent either way around the ECU. The pact also called for the initiation of the *European Monetary Fund*. It was agreed that financing should come from a pooling of European monetary reserves with contributions by member countries. The fund loans reserves to needy members to finance payments aimed at keeping their currencies in line with the currency bloc.

In addition to the immediate objective of providing a stabilizing influence on the exchange markets, the EMS over the longer term may move toward European economic and political unity. By agreeing to maintain exchange rates within a narrow band, member countries implicitly recognize the need to coordinate their national economic policies. However, such a blending of divergent economic systems requires member countries to surrender a high degree of national sovereignty. Skeptics of European integration are quick to point out that under the former arrangements, members such as France withdrew from the community snake during times of adverse economic pressure. Such withdrawals would certainly damage the EMS chances for monetary union.

The Crawling Peg

Since 1968, the Brazilian government has announced a change in the par value of the cruzeiro several times a year. The frequent adjustments in Brazil's exchange rate occur in response to the following indicators: (1) the movement in prices in Brazil relative to that of its main trading partners, (2) the level of foreign exchange reserves, (3) export performance, and (4) the overall balance of payments position. These exchange rate adjustments are an application of a mechanism dubbed the crawling peg. Not only has Brazil adopted this system, but it also has been used by countries including Argentina, Chile, Israel, and Peru.

The crawling peg system is a compromise between fixed and floating rates. As illustrated in Figure 16.5, the crawling peg system means that a country makes small, frequent changes in the par value of its currency to correct balance-of-payments disequilibriums. Deficit and surplus countries both keep adjusting until the desired exchange rate level is attained. The term *crawling peg* reflects the fact that par value changes are implemented in a large number of small steps to make the process of exchange rate adjustment

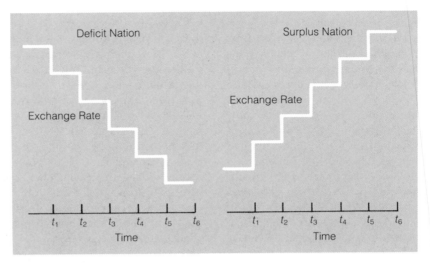

Figure 16.5   The crawling peg. The exchange rate refers to the foreign price of the domestic currency.

continuous for all practical purposes. The peg thus crawls from one par value to another. The crawling peg mechanism has been used primarily by countries having high rates of inflation. Some developing countries, mostly South American, have recognized that a pegging system can operate in an inflationary environment only if there is provision for frequent changes in the par values. Associating national inflation rates with international competitiveness, these countries generally have used price indicators as a basis for adjusting crawling pegged rates. In these countries, the primary concern is the criterion that governs exchange rate movements, instead of the currency or basket of currencies against which the peg is defined.

The crawling peg contrasts with the system of adjustable pegged rates. Under the adjustable peg, currencies are presumably tied to a par value that changes infrequently but suddenly, and usually in large jumps. The idea behind the crawling peg is that a country can make small, frequent changes in par values so that they creep along slowly in response to evolving market conditions. Supporters of the crawling peg argue that the system offers the flexibility of floating rates with the stability usually associated with fixed rates. They contend that a system providing continuous and steady adjustments is more responsive to changing competitive conditions and avoids the problem of adjustable pegged rates, whereby changes in par values are frequently wide of the mark. Moreover, small and frequent changes in par values made at random intervals frustrate speculators with their irregularity.

In recent years, the crawling peg formula has been used by developing countries facing rapid and persistent inflation. But the International Monetary Fund has generally contended that such a system would not be in the best interests of countries like the United States or West Germany, which bear responsibilities for international currency levels. The IMF has felt that it would be hard to apply such a system to the industrialized nations whose currencies serve as a source of international liquidity. Although even the most ardent proponents of the crawling peg admit that the time for its widespread adoption has not yet come, the debate over its potential merits is bound to continue.

Exchange Controls

The exchange rate mechanisms discussed so far have an important characteristic in common. They are all based on the principle of a free exchange market and automatic market forces. True, monetary authorities may modify the exchange rate outcome by purchasing and selling national currencies, but the foreign exchange transactions conducted among private exporters and importers are free from government regulation. The result is that a private foreign exchange market exists. If governments do not wish to permit a free foreign exchange market, they can set up a system of exchange measures to enable a government to keep its balance of payments under control when the exchange rate moves away from its equilibrium level. Various devices have been used to achieve this objective, including direct control over balance-of-payments transactions and multiple exchange rates. *Exchange controls* achieved prominence during the economic crises of the late 1930s and immediately following World War II, and it was not until the late 1950s that the industrialized countries of Western Europe considered themselves financially stable enough so that most controls could be dismantled and a high degree of freedom provided for many international transactions. Exchange controls are still widespread today in the less-developed countries of Africa, South America, the Far East, and the Near East.

At one extreme, a government may desire to gain control over its payments position by directly circumventing market forces through the imposition of direct controls on international transactions. For example, a government having a virtual monopoly over foreign exchange dealings may require that all foreign exchange earnings be turned over to authorized dealers. The government then allocates foreign exchange among domestic traders and investors at prices set by the government. The advantage of such a system is that the government can influence its payments position by regulating the amount of foreign exchange allocated to imports or capital outflows, limiting the extent of these transactions. Exchange controls also permit the government to encourage or discourage certain transactions by offering different rates for foreign currency for different purposes. Furthermore, exchange controls may give domestic monetary and fiscal policies greater freedom in their stabilization roles. By controlling the balance of payments through exchange controls, a government can pursue its domestic economic policies without fear of balance-of-payments repercussions.

A related method of gaining control of the balance of payments is the practice of *multiple exchange rates*. Used primarily by the developing nations, multiple exchange rates attempt to ensure that necessary goods are imported and less essential goods are discouraged. Essential imports like raw materials or capital goods are subsidized when the government sets a low exchange rate for these commodities, resulting in lower prices to home buyers. For the less desirable imports such as luxury products, a higher price will be set when the government makes foreign exchange available only at a high rate. Multiple exchange rates can thus be used to subsidize or tax import purchases so that a country's scarce supply of foreign exchange will be rationed among only the most essential commodities. Obviously the implementation of such a mechanism requires an elaborate classification system, as well as strict penalties against smuggling and black markets.

Dual Exchange Rates

A major factor that has plagued the operation of the world financial system has been international capital flows. Short-term capital tends to move across national borders in response to anticipated changes in exchange rates and interest rate differentials. Such movements may result in monetary authorities being unable to pursue policies that are insulated from balance-of-payments considerations or even to defend official exchange rates. One method of controlling international capital movements is for a country to adopt a system of *dual (two-tier) exchange rates*. Such a mechanism has been used, not only in the less-developed countries, but also in such industrial countries as Belgium, France, and Italy.[6]

The basic idea of dual exchange rates is to insulate a country from the balance-of-payments effects of capital flows, while providing a stable business climate for commercial (current account) transactions involving merchandise trade and services. This is accomplished by having separate exchange rates for commercial and capital transactions. Commercial transactions must be conducted on a market where exchange rates are officially pegged by national monetary authorities, whereas capital transactions occur in a financial market in which exchange rates are floating. Although history gives no example of a dual exchange rate system where complete segregation of commercial and capital transactions has occurred, the experiences of Belgium, France, and Italy have approximated such a mechanism.

To carry out the segregation of commercial and capital transactions, a distinction between these activities must be made. For example, the Belgian dual exchange rate system requires that all current transactions involving the export and import of goods and services must pass through the commercial market. All financial transactions must pass through the capital market. The French

system, however, permitted several current account transactions—those relating to tourism, profit, and interest—to pass through the financial market. The essence is that the distinction between the markets does not require a uniform classification system for all countries; the market eligibility of any given transaction depends on the objectives of a particular country.

Dual Rates in a Single Country

Under dual rates, a floating financial rate is intended to keep the capital account in balance. The following example illustrates this point for a dual-rate country, Belgium. Starting at equilibrium, suppose that Belgium finds that in the financial market, the foreign demand for its franc has decreased, leading to a depreciation of the franc against other currencies. Because each franc exchanges for less foreign currency, the profitability of Belgian investments abroad falls. As Belgian investors contract foreign operations, the quantity of francs supplied in the financial market for foreign currency declines. Because a given amount of foreign currency exchanges for more francs, foreign investment in Belgium would become more profitable and would rise, leading to an increased amount of foreign currency being exchanged for a greater number of francs. The quantity of francs demanded in the financial market would increase as foreigners expand investments in Belgium. The combined effect of these two flows is to eliminate any net movement of capital into or out of the dual-rate nation.

Evaluation

With dual rates, the capital account would always be in balance and any balance-of-payments disequilibriums would stem from commercial transactions. Although dual exchange rate systems have recently been used by countries whose financial structures are particularly sensitive to short-term capital flows, several factors limit dual rates as a cushion.

One problem of dual rates is the disruptive effect on trade and capital flows when the commercial and financial rates split apart. Should the demand for a country's currency in the financial market continually decline, its financial rate might depreciate enough to fall below its commercial rate. Administration of the commercial rate would become increasingly difficult as fraudulent intermarket transfers of funds became more profitable. Also, investor expectations concerning the future financial rate would govern the extent to which equilibrating capital flows would respond to exchange rate changes. Should speculators interpret a country's financial rate falling below its commercial rate as indicating a further decline in the financial rate, they might continue selling the weakening currency. This would put greater downward pressure on the financial rate and disrupt the exchange markets.

Dual rates are also unable to cope with a type of speculation known as *commercial leads-and-lags*. This involves speeding-up import payments and delaying export receipts in anticipation of a currency depreciation; the opposite holds for an expected currency appreciation. Dual rates are designed to moderate speculative flows of capital in the financial market. In times of speculative pressure, traders of goods may attempt to change the timing of their basic transactions or payments to gain extra profits from changes in the price of foreign exchange. Under these conditions, dual rates would be unable to cope with exchange market speculation.

The experience of dual exchange rates also indicates that countries do not have much more independence in their monetary policies than under a single-rate, pegged system. This is because a divergence of the commercial and financial rates might occur if a country attempt determine its interest rates independent., or other countries. Should a dual-rate country attempt to set its interest rates higher than those of its trading partners, there would be an inducement for capital flows into the country, and this would likely lead to an appreciation of the financial rate above the commercial rate. Belgium's decision to adopt a monetary policy that maintains its interest rates consistent with those abroad apparently reflects concern over the disruptive consequences that diverging rates have for a dual-rate system.

Probably the main benefit of dual exchange rates for a single country is that they may provide a temporary cushion against the destabilizing effects of speculative capital flows on the balance of payments. However, dual rates cannot cope with the speculative activity of commercial leads and lags. If speculation persists, the maintenance of dual rates may require monetary intervention or other direct controls to prevent the two rates from significantly splitting apart. Thus, dual rates have not been widely adopted by trading nations.

Summary

1.   Most countries in practice maintain neither completely fixed nor freely floating exchange rates. Most contemporary exchange rate systems embody some features of each of these standards.

2.   Small countries often peg their currencies to a single currency or a currency basket. Pegging to a single currency is generally used by small countries whose trade and financial relationships are mainly with a single trading partner. Small countries with more than one major trading partner often peg their currencies to a basket of currencies.

3.   The SDR is a currency basket composed of five currencies of IMF members. The basket

valuation technique attempts to make the SDR's value more stable than the foreign currency value of any single currency in the basket. Developing nations often choose to peg their exchange rates to the SDR.

4. The purchasing power parity theory is used to estimate the long-run equilibrium exchange rate. This information is useful for central bankers who are planning on devaluing or revaluing their currencies.

5. The adjustable pegged exchange rate system came out of the Bretton Woods Agreement of 1944. The idea was to provide participating countries with stable but flexible exchange rates. The system broke down in the early 1970s.

6. With the breakdown of the Bretton Woods par value system, the major industrialized nations adopted a system of managed floating exchange rates. Central bank intervention in the foreign exchange markets is intended to prevent disorderly market conditions.

7. As part of their efforts to achieve monetary union, members of the European Monetary System have adopted a joint float of their currencies.

8. Under a crawling pegged exchange rate system, a country makes frequent small devaluations (or revaluations) of its currency to restore payments balance. Developing countries suffering from high inflation rates have been the major users of this mechanism.

9. Exchange controls are sometimes used by governments in an attempt to gain control of the balance of payments. The government may ration foreign exchange to domestic traders and investors to limit imports. Multiple exchange rates are sometimes used in an attempt to ensure that only necessary goods will be imported.

10. Countries such as Belgium have resorted to dual exchange rates to insulate the balance of payments from short-term capital movements while providing exchange rate stability for commercial transactions.

Study Questions

1. What factors underlie a country's decision to adopt floating exchange rates or pegged exchange rates?

2. Policy makers are often concerned about identifying the long-term equilibrium of an exchange rate. What methods are available to forecast such a rate?

3. How do managed floating exchange rates operate? Why were they adopted by the industrialized nations in 1973?

4. Of what significance is a joint float for members of the European Monetary System?

5. Discuss the philosophy and operation of the Bretton Woods system of adjustable pegged exchange rates.

6. Why have nations such as Brazil adopted a crawling peg exchange rate system?

7. What is the purpose of exchange controls? Are they still being used today?

8. How do dual exchange rates attempt to provide a steady environment for commercial transactions while also insulating the balance of payments from destabilizing capital movements?

9. Why do small countries adopt currency baskets against which to peg their exchange rates?

10. What advantage does the SDR offer small countries who desire to peg their exchange rates?

Notes

1. See H. Robert Heller, "Choosing an Exchange Rate System," *Finance and Development* (June 1977), pp. 23–27.

2. Nicholas Carlozzi, "Pegs and Floats," *Business Review*, Federal Reserve Bank of

Philadelphia (May–June, 1980), pp. 13–23. See also Leslie Lipschit and V. Sundararajan, "Pegging to a Currency Basket in a World of Floating Rates," *Finance and Development* (June 1980), pp. 25–28.

3. The weights for the five currencies reflect the relative importance of these currencies in international trade and finance based on the value of exports of goods and services of the members issuing the currencies for the period 1975–1979. The weights used in the computation of the SDR's value are as follows: (1) U.S. dollar = 42 percent, (2) West German mark = 19 percent, (3) French franc = 13 percent, (4) Japanese yen = 13 percent, and (5) British pound = 13 percent. The list of currencies and their weights in determining the value of the SDR is revised every five years to reflect changing trade patterns.

4. This chapter presents the so-called relative version of the purchasing power parity theory, which addresses changes in prices and exchanges over a period of time. Another variant is the absolute version of the purchasing power parity theory, which states that the equilibrium exchange rate will equal the ratio of domestic to foreign general price levels at one point in time. See Lawrence H. Officer, "The Relationship Between Absolute and Relative Purchasing Power Parity," *Review of Economics and Statistics*, 60 (November 1978), pp. 562–568.

5. In addition to adopting adjustable pegged exchange rates, the Bretton Woods system created two institutions: the International Monetary Fund and the International Bank for Reconstruction and Development (now referred to as the World Bank).

6. Philip Rushing, "The Two-Tier Exchange Rate System," *New England Economic Review* (March–April, 1974), pp. 13–22.

Suggestions for Further Reading

Artus, J. R., and J. H. Young. "Fixed and Flexible Exchange Rates: A Renewal of the Debate." *IMF Staff Papers*, December 1979.

Basevi, G. "When the Snake Gets Out of the Tunnel." *Metroeconomica*, September–December, 1972.

Blackhurst, R., and J. Tumlir. *Trade Relations Under Flexible Exchange Rates*. GATT Studies in International Trade, no. 8, Geneva, 1980.

Carbaugh, R. J., and L. S. Fan. *The International Monetary System*. Lawrence: University Press of Kansas, 1976.

Cohen, B. J. *The European Monetary System*. Essays in International Finance, no. 142, Princeton, N.J.: Princeton University Press, 1981.

Halm, G. *Approaches to Greater Flexibility of Exchange Rates*. Princeton, N.J.: Princeton University Press, 1970.

Howle, E., and C. Moore. "Richard Cooper's Guiding Parities: A Proposed Modification." *Journal of International Economics*, November 1971.

Kenen, P. B. "Floats, Guides, and Indicators: A Comparison of Methods for Changing Exchange Rates." *Journal of International Economics*, May 1975.

Page, S. A. B. "The Development of the EMS." *National Institute Economic Review*, November 1982.

Tosini, P. A. *Leaning Against the Wind: A Standard for Managed Floating*. Princeton Essays in International Economics, December 1977.

Williamson, J. "A Survey of the Literature on the Optimal Peg." *Journal of Development Economics*, August 1982.

17

INTERNATIONAL LIQUIDITY

Under a system of fixed exchange rates or managed floating exchange rates, governments may attempt to moderate fluctuations in the international values of currencies. The historic Bretton Woods system, for example, saw central bankers agreeing to maintain market exchange rates within a band of plus or minus 1 percent around a currency's par value. Under the managed floating system, central bankers in conjunction with the International Monetary Fund have agreed in principle to preserve orderly exchange markets to provide a stable environment for commercial and financial transactions.

A currency's international value can be affected in a number of ways by national governments. Commercial policies such as tariffs, quotas, and subsidies may be used to modify the demand and supply schedules of goods and services. Central bankers may intervene in foreign currency markets and purchase (or sell) national currencies with (or for) international reserves. International reserves facilitate central banker exchange market operations. This chapter deals with the nature and significance of *international reserves*. The demand, or need, for international reserves is first investigated, followed by a discussion of the supply, or sources, of international reserves. Finally, an assessment of the

economic consequences of international reserves for the world monetary order is given.

Nature of International Reserves

A country's need for international reserves is quite similar to a householder's desire to hold cash balances (currency and demand deposits). At both levels, monetary reserves are intended to bridge the gap between monetary receipts and monetary payments. Suppose a householder finds that his or her income is received in equal installments every minute of the day and expenditures for goods and services are likewise evenly spaced over time. The householder would require a minimum cash reserve to finance purchases, since no significant imbalances between cash receipts and cash disbursements would exist. This is rarely the situation for householders in general.

Most householders in practice want to hold some portion of their assets in the form of cash balances. This is because they usually purchase goods and services on a fairly regular basis from day to day, yet receive paychecks only at weekly or monthly intervals. A certain amount of cash is therefore required to finance the discrepancy that arises between monetary receipts and payments. When a householder initially receives a paycheck, her cash balances are high. But as time progresses, her holdings of cash may fall to virtually zero just before the next paycheck is received. Householders are thus concerned over the amount of cash balances that, on average, are necessary to keep them going until the next paycheck becomes due. Although it is true that householders desire cash balances primarily to fill the gap between monetary receipts and payments, this desire is influenced by a number of other factors. The need for cash balances may become more acute, the greater is the absolute dollar volume of transactions, because larger imbalances may result between receipts and payments. Conversely, to the extent that householders can finance their transactions on credit, the less they require cash in hand.

Like an individual householder's desire to hold cash balances, national governments have a need for international reserves. The chief purpose of international reserves is to enable countries to *finance disequilibriums* in their balance of payments positions. When a country finds its monetary receipts falling short of its monetary payments, the deficit is settled by international reserves. Eventually the deficit must be eliminated, since countries tend to have limited stocks of reserves. The advantage of international reserves from a policy perspective is that they enable countries to sustain temporary balance-of-payments deficits, so that acceptable adjustment measures can operate to correct the disequilibrium. Holdings of international reserves facilitate effective policy formation, as corrective adjustment measures need not be implemented prematurely. Should a deficit country possess abundant stocks of reserve balances, however, it may be able to resist unpopular adjustment measures that make eventual adjustments even more troublesome.

Demand for International Reserves

When a country's international monetary payments exceed its international monetary receipts, some means of settlement is required to finance its payments deficit. Settlement ultimately consists of transfers of international reserves among nations. Both the magnitude and longevity of a balance-of-payments deficit that can be sustained in the absence of equilibrating adjustments are limited by a country's stock of international reserves. On a global basis, the demand for international reserves largely depends on two related factors: (1) the monetary value of international transactions and (2) the disequilibriums that can arise in balance-of-payments positions. The demand for international reserves is also contingent on such things as the speed and strength of the balance-of-payments adjustment mechanism and the overall institutional framework of the world economy.

Exchange Rate Flexibility

One factor commonly associated with the need for international reserves is the degree of *exchange rate flexibility* of the international monetary system. This is because exchange rate flexibility in part underlies the efficiency of the balance-of-payments adjustment process. Let Figure 17.1 represent the exchange market position of the United States in trade with Great Britain. Starting at equilibrium point E, suppose that an increase in imports increases the U.S. demand for pounds from D_0 to D_1. The prevailing exchange rate system will determine the quantity of international reserves needed to bridge the gap between the amount of pounds demanded and the amount supplied.

If exchange rates are fixed or pegged by the monetary authorities, international reserves play a crucial role in the exchange rate stabilization

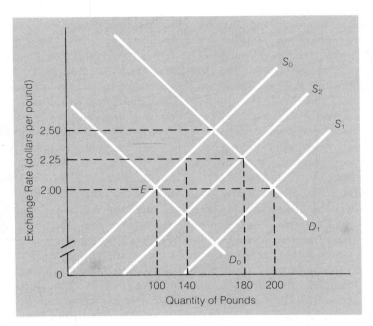

Figure 17.1   The demand for international reserves and exchange rate flexibility.

process. Suppose the exchange rate is pegged at $2 in Figure 17.1. Given a rise in the demand for pounds from D_0 to D_1, the United States would face an excess demand for pounds equal to 100 pounds at the pegged rate. If the U.S. dollar is not to depreciate beyond the pegged rate, the monetary authorities must enter the market to supply pounds (in exchange for the dollar) in an amount necessary to eliminate the disequilibrium. In the figure, pegged rate $2 could be maintained if the monetary authorities would supply 100 pounds on the market. Coupled with the existing supply curve S_0, the added supply would result in a new supply curve at S_1. Market equilibrium would be restored at the pegged rate.

Rather than operating under a rigidly pegged rate system, suppose a country makes an agreement to foster some automatic adjustments by allowing market rates to float within a narrow band around the official exchange rate. *Limited exchange rate flexibility* would be aimed at correcting minor payments imbalances, whereas large and persistent disequilibriums would require other adjustment measures. Referring to Figure 17.1, assume that $2 per pound represents the U.S. official exchange rate, while the upper limit of the band of permissible exchange rate fluctuations is set at $2.25 per pound. Given a rise in the U.S. demand for pounds, the value of the dollar would begin to decline. Once the exchange rate depreciates to $2.25 per pound, domestic monetary authorities would supply 40 pounds on the market to defend the band's outer limit. This would have the effect of shifting the market supply curve from S_0 to S_2. The main point is that under a system of limited exchange rate flexibility, movements in the exchange rate serve to reduce the payments disequilibrium. Smaller amounts of international reserves are required for exchange rate stabilization purposes under this system than in the case where exchange rates are completely fixed by monetary authorities.

A fundamental purpose of international reserves is to help facilitate government interventions in exchange markets to stabilize currency values. The more active a government's stabilization activities, the greater the need for reserves. Virtually all exchange rate standards today involve some stabilization operations and require international reserves. However, if exchange rates were allowed to float freely without government interference, theoretically there would be no need for reserves. This is because a floating rate would serve to eliminate an incipient payments imbalance, negating the need for stabilization operations. Referring to Figure 17.1, suppose the exchange market is initially in equilibrium at rate $2 per pound. Given an increase in the demand for foreign exchange from D_0 to D_1, the home currency would begin to depreciate. It would continue to weaken until rate $2.50 per pound was reached, at which exchange market equilibrium would be restored. The need for international reserves would therefore be nonexistent under freely floating rates.

Other Determinants

The lesson to be learned from the previous section is that changes in the degree of exchange rate flexibility are *inversely* related to changes in the quantity of international reserves demanded. In other words, a monetary system characterized by more rapid and flexible exchange rate adjustments requires smaller reserves, and vice versa. Figure 17.2 depicts such a relationship.[1] The quantity of international reserves is placed on the diagram's horizontal axis and an index representing the degree of exchange rate flexibility is

located on the vertical axis. The index of flexibility would in the limit have a value equal to one under a freely floating exchange rate system, whereas its value would equal zero under fixed exchange rates. The demand for reserves is downward sloping, reflecting the inverse relationship between the need for reserves and the degree of exchange rate flexibility.

In constructing a demand curve such as D_0 in Figure 17.2, the assumption is that exchange rate flexibility is the crucial factor underlying the amount of international reserves demanded. But variables other than exchange rate flexibility can and do exert an impact on the desire for reserves. Construction of a given demand curve requires that there are other factors that are assumed to be held constant. When these determinants undergo changes, the demand curve will shift outward to the right or inward to the left.

What are the major determinants of the demand for international reserves other than the

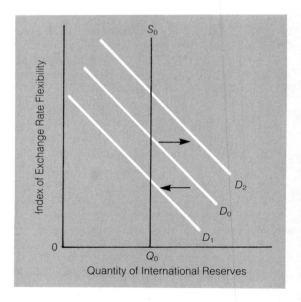

Figure 17.2 International reserves: supply and demand.

exchange rate? Among the most important are (1) automatic adjustment mechanisms that respond to payments disequilibriums, (2) economic policies used to bring about payments equilibrium, and (3) the international coordination of economic policies. Our earlier analysis has shown that adjustment mechanisms involving prices, interest rates, incomes, and monetary flows automatically tend to correct balance-of-payments disequilibriums. A payments deficit or surplus initiates changes in each of these variables. The more efficient each of these adjustment mechanisms are, the smaller and more short-lived market imbalances will be and the fewer reserves will be needed. The demand for international reserves therefore tends to be smaller (shifts leftward in Figure 17.2), the speedier and more complete the automatic adjustment mechanisms.

The demand for international reserves also is influenced by the choice and effectiveness of government policies adopted to correct payments imbalances. Unlike automatic adjustment mechanisms, which rely on the free market to identify industries and labor groups that must bear the adjustment burden, the use of government policies involves political decisions. All else being equal, the greater a country's propensity to apply commercial policies (including tariffs, quotas, or subsidies) to key sectors, the less would be its need for international reserves. This assumes these policies are effective and would reduce payments disequilibriums. Because of uncertainties about the nature and timing of payments disturbances, however, countries are often slow in initiating such trade policies and find themselves requiring international reserves to weather periods of payments disequilibriums.

The international coordination of economic policies is another determinant of the demand for international reserves. A primary goal of economic cooperation among financial ministers is to reduce the frequency and extent of payments imbalances and hence the demand for international reserves. Since the end of World War II, countries have moved toward the harmonization of national economic objectives by establishing programs through such organizations as the International Monetary Fund and the Organization of Economic Cooperation and Development. Another example of international economic organization has been the European Economic Community, whose goal is to achieve a common macroeconomic policy and full monetary union. By reducing the intensity of disturbances to payments balance, such policy coordination would reduce the need for international reserves.

Other factors influence the demand for international reserves. The quantity demanded is positively related to the level of world prices and income. One would normally expect rising price levels to inflate the market value of international transactions and therefore the potential demand for reserves. It would also be expected that the need for reserves would tend to rise with the level of global income and trade activity.

In summary, central banks need international reserves to bridge a possible or expected excess of payments to other nations at some future time. How many international reserves are demanded directly relates to the size and duration of payments gaps. If a nation with a payments deficit is willing and able to initiate quick actions to increase receipts or decrease payments, the amount of reserves needed will be relatively small. Conversely, the demand for reserves will be relatively large if nations initiate no actions to correct payments imbalances or adopt policies that prolong such disequilibriums.

Supply of International Reserves

The analysis so far has emphasized the demand for international reserves. But what about the supply of reserves? For simplicity, assume that in Figure 17.2, the quantity of reserves is given and constant at OQ_0. The supply curve of reserves is denoted by the vertical line S_0 in the figure. This assumption corresponds well to reality if there are reserve assets, such as gold or Special Drawing Rights, whose sources are independent of the monetary system's degree of exchange rate flexibility.

The total supply of international reserves consists of two distinct categories, *owned* reserves and *borrowed* reserves. Reserve assets such as gold, acceptable foreign currencies, and Special Drawing Rights are generally considered to be directly owned by the holding nations. But if countries with payments deficits find their stocks of owned reserves falling to unacceptably low levels, they may be able to borrow international reserves as a cushioning device. Lenders may be foreign nations with excess reserves, foreign financial institutions, and international agencies such as the International Monetary Fund.

Foreign Currencies

International reserves are a means of payment used in financing foreign transactions. As long as they are generally acceptable to foreign payees, reserve assets can be an effective medium of exchange. One such asset is holdings of *national*

currencies (foreign exchange). As seen in Table 17.1, the largest share of international reserves today consists of national currency holdings, which currently account for almost 80 percent of total international reserves. The table also shows that following the otherwise modest growth of foreign currency holdings during the 1960s, the 1970s witnessed explosive growth in these reserve assets.

Over the course of the 1900s, two national currencies in particular have gained prominence as means of financing international transactions. These currencies, the U.S. dollar and the British pound, have been considered *reserve currencies*, as trading nations have traditionally been willing to hold them along with gold as international reserve assets. Since World War II, the U.S. dollar has been the dominant reserve currency. Next in importance has been the British sterling pound, the remaining holdings consisting largely of German marks, French francs, Japanese yen, and a few other currencies that are acceptable in payment for international transactions. One reason why currencies like the mark and yen have not assumed reserve currency status is that their governments have not permitted the large and sustained payments deficits that would encourage foreign nations to increase their holdings of these currencies.

Table 17.1   International Reserves, 1960–1983 (billions of SDRs)

End of Year	Gold	Foreign Exchange	IMF Reserve Positions	SDRs	Total Reserves
1960	37.7	19.9	3.6	——	61.2
1965	41.5	25.4	5.4	——	72.3
1970	37.0	45.4	7.7	3.1	93.2
1975	35.5	137.8	12.6	8.8	194.7
1980	33.4	296.7	16.8	11.8	358.7
1983 (May)	33.1	296.0	32.2	17.8	379.1

Source: International Monetary Fund, *International Financial Statistics*, various issues.

For years, countries have considered holdings of British pounds as part of their international reserves. The role of the pound as a reserve currency has been due largely to events that occurred during the late 1800s and early 1900s. Not only did Britain at this time assume a dominant role in world trade, but also the efficiency of London as an international money market was widely recognized. This was the golden age of the gold standard, and the pound was freely convertible into gold. Traders and investors felt confident financing their transactions with pounds. With the demise of the gold standard and the arrival of the Great Depression during the 1930s, Britain's commercial and financial status began to deteriorate and the pound lost some of its international luster. Today, the pound still serves as an important international reserve asset, but its status as the most prestigious reserve currency has been replaced by the U.S. dollar. The emergence of the U.S. dollar as a reserve currency stemmed from a different set of circumstances. Coming out of World War II, the U.S. economy not only remained unharmed but also actually became stronger. Because of the vast inflows of gold into the United States during the 1930s and 1940s, the dollar was in a better position than was the pound to assume the role of a reserve currency.

The mechanism that supplied the world with dollar balances was the balance-of-payments deficits of the United States. These deficits stemmed largely from U.S. foreign aid granted to Europe immediately following World War II, as well as the flow of private investment funds abroad from U.S. residents. The early 1950s were characterized as a *dollar shortage* era when the massive developmental programs of the European nations resulted in an excessive demand for the dollars used to finance such efforts. As the United States began to run modest payments deficits during the early 1950s, the dollar outflow was appreciated by the recipient nations.

By the late 1950s, the U.S. payments deficits had become larger. As foreign nations began to accumulate larger dollar balances than they were accustomed to, the dollar shortage era gave way to a *dollar glut*. Throughout the 1960s, the United States continued to provide reserves to the world through its payments deficits. However, the persistently weak position of the U.S. balance of payments increasingly led foreigners to question the soundness of the dollar as a reserve currency. By 1970, the amount of dollar liabilities in the hands of foreigners was several times as large as U.S. reserve assets. Lack of confidence in the soundness of the dollar inspired several European nations to exercise their rights to demand that the U.S. Treasury convert their dollar holdings into gold, which in turn led to the United States suspending its gold convertibility pledge to the rest of the world in 1971.

The important implication of the dollar as a reserve currency was that the supply of international reserves varied with the payments position of the United States. During the 1960s, this situation gave rise to the so-called *liquidity problem*, which involved the following dilemma. To preserve confidence in the dollar as a reserve currency, the United States had to strengthen its payments position by eliminating its deficits. But a correction of the U.S. deficits would mean an elimination of additional dollars as a source of reserves for the international monetary system. The creation in 1970 of Special Drawing Rights as reserve assets and their subsequent allocations have been intended as a solution for this problem.

Gold

The historical importance of gold as an international reserve asset should not be underemphasized. At one time, gold served as the key monetary asset of the international payments mechanism, while also comprising the basis of many nations' money supplies. As an international money, gold fulfilled several important functions. Under the historic gold standard, gold directly served as an international means of payments. It also provided a unit of account against which commodity prices as well as the parities of national currencies were quoted. Although gold holdings have not yielded interest income, gold has generally been able to serve as a viable store of value in spite of inflations, wars, and revolutions. Perhaps the greatest advantage of gold as a monetary asset has been its overall acceptability, especially when compared with other forms of international monies.

Today, the role of gold as an international reserve asset has declined. Over the past 30 years, gold has fallen from nearly 70 percent to less than 9 percent of world reserves. Private individuals rarely use gold as a medium of payment and virtually never as a unit of account. Nor do central banks currently use gold as an official unit of account for stating the parities of national currencies. The monetary role of gold is currently recognized only by a few countries, mostly in the Middle East. In most countries outside the United States, private residents have been able to purchase and sell gold as they would any other commodity. On December 31, 1974, the U.S. government revoked a 41-year ban on U.S. citizens' ownership of gold. The monetary role of gold today is only a glittering ghost haunting efforts to reform the international monetary system.

International Gold Standard

Under the international gold standard, which reached its golden age during the 1880–1914 period, the values of most national currencies were anchored in gold. Gold coins circulated within these countries as well as across national boundaries as generally accepted means of pay-

ment. Monetary authorities were concerned about maintaining the public's confidence in the paper currencies that supplemented gold's role as money. To maintain the integrity of paper currencies, governments agreed to convert them into gold at a fixed rate. This requirement was supposed to prevent monetary authorities from producing excessive amounts of paper money. The so-called *discipline* of the gold standard was achieved by having the money supply bear a fixed relation to the monetary stock of gold. Given the cost of producing gold relative to the cost of other commodities, a monetary price of gold could be established to produce growth in monetary gold—and also in the money supply—at a rate that corresponded to the growth in real national output.

Over the course of the gold standard's era, the importance of gold began to decline, whereas both paper money and demand deposits showed marked increases. From 1815 to 1913, gold as a share of the aggregate money supply of the United States, France, and Britain fell from about 33 percent to 10 percent. At the same time, the proportion of bank deposits skyrocketed from a modest 6 percent to about 68 percent. By 1913, paper monies plus demand deposits accounted for approximately 90 percent of the U.S. money supply. After World War I, popular sentiment favored a return to the discipline of the gold standard, partly owing to the inflation that gripped many economies during the war years. The United States was the first to return to the gold standard, followed by several European nations. Efforts to restore the prewar gold standard, however, ended in complete collapse during the 1930s. In response to the economic strains of the Great Depression, nations one by one announced they could no longer maintain the gold standard.

As for the United States, the Great Depression brought an important modification of the gold standard. In 1934, the Gold Reserve Act gave the U.S. government title to all monetary gold, and citizens turned in their private holdings to the U.S. Treasury. This was done because the government wanted to end the pressure on U.S. commercial banks to convert their liabilities into gold. The U.S. dollar was also devalued in 1934 when the official price of gold was raised from $20.67 to $35 per ounce. The dollar devaluation was not specifically aimed at defending the U.S. trade balance. The rationale was that a rise in the domestic price of gold would encourage gold production, adding to the money supply and the level of economic activity. The Great Depression would be solved! In retrospect, the devaluation may have had some minor economic effects, but there is no indication that it did anything to lift the economy out of its depressed condition.

Gold Exchange Standard

Emerging from the discussions among the world powers during World War II was a new international monetary organization, the International Monetary Fund. A main objective of the fund was to reestablish a system of fixed exchange rates, with gold serving as the primary reserve asset. Gold became an international unit of account when member countries officially agreed to state the par values of their currencies in terms of gold or, alternately, the gold content of the U.S. dollar. The post–World War II international monetary system as formulated by the fund countries was nominally a *gold exchange standard*. The idea was to economize on monetary gold stocks as international reserves, which could not expand as fast as international trade was growing. This required the United States, which emerged from the war with a dominant economy in terms of productive capacity and national wealth, to assume the role of a world banker. The dollar was to become the international monetary system's chief reserve currency. The coexistence of both dollars and gold as

international reserve assets led to this system being dubbed the *dollar-gold* system.

As a world banker, the United States assumed responsibility for buying and selling gold at a fixed price to foreign official holders of dollars. The dollar was the only currency that was made convertible into gold, and other national currencies were pegged to the dollar. The dollar was therefore regarded as a reserve currency that was good as gold, since it was thought that the dollar would retain its value relative to other currencies and remain convertible into gold. As long as the monetary gold stocks of the United States were large relative to outstanding dollar liabilities abroad, the confidence in the dollar as a viable reserve currency remained intact. Immediately following World War II, the U.S. monetary gold stocks peaked at $24 billion, about two-thirds of the world total. But as time passed, the amount of foreign dollar holdings rose significantly owing to the U.S. payments deficits, while our monetary gold stock dwindled as some of the dollars were turned back to the U.S. Treasury for gold. By 1965, the total supply of foreign-held dollars exceeded our stock of monetary gold. With the United States unable to redeem all outstanding dollars for gold at $35 per ounce, our ability as a world banker to deliver on demand was questioned.

These circumstances led to speculation that the United States might attempt to solve its gold shortage problem by devaluing the dollar. By increasing the official price of gold, a dollar devaluation would lead to a rise in the value of our monetary gold stocks. To prevent speculative profits arising from any rise in the official price of gold, the United States along with several other nations in 1968 established a *two-tier* gold system. This consisted of an *official tier*, in which central banks could buy and sell gold for monetary purposes at the official price of $35 per ounce, and a *private market*, where gold as a commodity could be traded at the free market price. By separating the official gold market from the private gold market, the two-tier system was a step toward the complete demonetization of gold.

Demonetization of Gold

The formation of the two-tier gold system was a remedy that could only delay the inevitable collapse of the gold exchange standard. By 1971, the U.S. stock of monetary gold had declined to $11 billion, only a fraction of our dollar liabilities to foreign central banks. The U.S. balance-of-payments position was also deteriorating in a dramatic manner. In August 1971, President Nixon announced that the U.S. was suspending its commitment to buy and sell gold at $35 per ounce. The closing of the gold window to foreign official holders brought an end to the gold exchange standard, and the last functional link between the dollar and monetary gold was severed.

It took several years for the world's monetary authorities to formally demonetize gold as an international reserve asset. On January 1, 1975, the official price of gold was abolished as the unit of account for the international monetary system. National monetary authorities could enter into gold transactions at market-determined prices, whereas the use of gold was terminated by the International Monetary Fund. It was agreed that one-sixth of the fund's gold would be auctioned at prevailing prices, the profits being distributed to the less-developed countries.

As for the United States, a 41-year ban on gold ownership for U.S. residents was severed on January 1, 1975. Within a few weeks, the U.S. Treasury was auctioning a portion of its gold on the commodity markets. These actions were a signal by the United States that it would treat gold in the same way it treats any other commodity. Throughout the 1970s and early 1980s, the market price of gold fluctuated between $200 and $800 per ounce. As of August 1983, it stood at about $420 per ounce.

Special Drawing Rights

The liquidity and confidence problems of the gold exchange standard that resulted from reliance on the dollar and gold as international monies led in 1970 to the creation of a new reserve asset by the International Monetary Fund, termed *Special Drawing Rights* (SDRs). The objective was to introduce into the payments mechanism a new reserve asset, in addition to the dollar and gold, which could be transferred among participating countries in settlement of payments deficits. By having the fund manage the stock of SDRs, world reserves would presumably grow in line with world commerce.

SDRs are unconditional rights to draw currencies of other countries. When the fund creates a certain amount of SDRs, they are allocated to the member countries in proportion to the relative size of their fund quotas. Countries can then draw on their SDR balances in financing their payments deficits. The key point is that certain surplus countries are designated by the fund to trade their currencies for an equivalent amount of SDRs to deficit countries in need of foreign exchange reserves. Countries whose currencies are acquired as foreign exchange are not required to accept more than three times their initial SDR allotments. SDRs pay interest to surplus countries on their net holdings (the amount by which a country's SDR balance exceeds its allocation as determined by its fund quota.) Interest payments come from deficit countries that draw their SDR balances below their original allotments. The SDR interest rate is periodically adjusted in line with the short-term interest rates in world money markets. It is reviewed quarterly and adjusted on the basis of a formula that takes into account the short-term interest rates of the United States, the United Kingdom, West Germany, France, and Japan.

The objective behind the creation of the SDR was to provide a source of owned reserves for fund countries. The initial allocation totaled 9.3

billion SDR and was issued over three installments in 1970–1972 to members of the fund in proportion to their fund quotas. An additional 12 billion SDR were issued to fund members in 1979–1981. As of 1983, SDRs accounted for about 5 percent of total international reserves.

When the SDR was initially adopted, it was agreed that its value should be maintained at a fixed tie to the U.S. dollar's par value, which was then expressed in terms of gold. The value of the SDR was originally set at $1 U.S. But this linkage became unacceptable following several monetary developments. With the suspension of U.S. gold convertibility in 1971, it was doubted whether the gold value of the dollar should serve as the official unit of account for international transactions. The United States was also making it known at that time that it wished to phase out gold as an international monetary instrument. Furthermore, the dollar's exchange rate against gold fell twice as the result of U.S. devaluations in 1971 and 1973. Finally, under the system of managed floating exchange rates, which was adopted by the industrialized countries in 1973, it became possible for the SDR's value to fluctuate against other currencies while still bearing a fixed tie to the dollar's value. In view of these problems, in 1974, a new method of SDR valuation was initiated—the *basket valuation*.

As discussed more fully in Chapter 16, basket valuation is intended to provide stability for the SDR's value under a system of fluctuating exchange rates, making the SDR more attractive as an international reserve asset. The SDR is called a basket currency since it is based on the value of five currencies—the U.S. dollar, German mark, Japanese yen, French franc, and British pound. An appreciation, or increase in the value, of any one currency in the basket in terms of all other currencies will raise the value of the SDR in terms of each other currency. Conversely, a depreciation, or decline in the value, of any one currency will lower the value of the SDR in terms of each other currency. Since the movements of some currencies can be offset or moderated by the movements of other currencies, the value of the SDR in terms of a group of currencies is likely to be relatively stable.

Besides helping countries finance balance-of-payments deficits, SDRs have a number of other uses. Some of the fund's member countries peg their currency values to the SDR. The SDR is the unit of account for IMF transactions and is used as a unit of account for individuals, such as exporters, importers, or investors, who desire protection against the risk of fluctuating exchange rates.

For example, several major banks in London offer certificates of deposit (CDs) denominated in SDRs. The major attraction of SDR-denominated CDs is that they offer investors a financial instrument that is less susceptible to exchange rate fluctuations than financial assets denominated in any single currency. Although the SDR-denominated CDs are sold for and repaid in dollars, their dollar value at, or any time before, maturity depends on the dollar-SDR exchange rate. Because the dollar-SDR rate is a weighted average of the dollar exchange rates relative to other currencies in the SDR basket, the exchange rate gains or losses over the term of the deposit will be less than that for any one of the currencies making up the SDR. Therefore, by purchasing an SDR-indexed CD, an investor will reduce his overall exchange rate risk, since any eventual losses on one currency may be offset by gains on another in the SDR basket.

Since its adoption in 1970, the SDR has gained in importance as an acceptable international reserve asset. Today, SDRs possess all the qualities of a genuine money and represent a net addition to international reserves as useful as dollars and gold. With the monetary future of gold in doubt, SDRs have become enhanced as a primary reserve asset because of the following attractive features.

The creation of SDRs has represented a first major step in providing a means of internationally controlled reserves for the world. The SDR is unlike the dollar, whose supply stemmed from the balance-of-payments deficits of the United States under the gold exchange standard. Nor is it like gold, the supply of which has often fluctuated owing to speculative and technological factors. Unlike gold, SDRs as bookkeeping entries are virtually costless to produce. Moreover, SDRs benefit the world in terms of the resources saved in bypassing gold production.

The use of SDRs also gives the world a more equitable method of distributing resources than does either the dollar or gold. When money is widely accepted as a means of payment, the issuer of money may benefit from what is referred to as *seigniorage*. This represents the value of resources that accrue to the issuer of money by virtue of the fact that money's face value exceeds the cost of producing it. Under the gold exchange standard, the United States as the principal issuer of international money (dollars) was widely criticized for enjoying an exorbitant financial privilege. The United States could attain considerable seigniorage benefits by running persistent deficits in its balance of payments. Under a pure gold standard, seigniorage gains accrued to gold-producing nations to the degree that the cost of producing gold was less than its official price. In contrast, the seigniorage gains of SDR creation have been distributed to participating countries in compliance with internationally determined standards.

Facilities for Borrowing Reserves

The discussion so far has considered the different types of *owned* reserves—national currencies, gold, and SDRs. Various facilities for *borrowing* reserves have also been implemented for countries with weak balance-of-payments positions. Borrowed reserves do not eliminate the need for owned reserves, but they do add to the flexibility of the international monetary system by increasing the time available for countries to correct payments disequilibriums. The following section examines the major forms of international credit.

Fund Drawings

One of the original purposes of the International Monetary Fund, founded in 1944 at the Bretton Woods Conference, was to help member countries finance balance-of-payments deficits. The fund has furnished a pool of revolving credit for countries in need of reserves. Temporary loans of foreign currency are made to deficit countries, which are expected to repay them within a stipulated time. The transactions by which the fund makes foreign currency loans available are called *drawings on the fund*.

Deficit countries do not borrow from the fund. Instead they "purchase" with their own currency the foreign currency required to help finance deficits. When the country's balance-of-payments position improves, it is expected to reverse the transaction and make repayment by repurchasing its currency from the fund. The fund currently allows members at their own option to purchase other currencies up to the first 50 percent of their fund quotas, which are based on the country's economic size. Special permission must be granted by the fund if a country is to purchase foreign currencies in excess of this figure. The fund extends such permission once it is convinced the deficit country has enacted reasonable measures to restore payments equilibrium.

Since the early 1950s, the fund has also fostered liberal exchange rate policies by entering into *standby arrangements* with interested member countries. These agreements guarantee that a member nation may draw specified amounts of foreign currencies from the fund over given time periods. The advantage is that participating countries can count on credit from the fund

hould it be needed. It also saves the drawing
ountry from administrative time delays when
he loans are actually made.

General Arrangements to Borrow

During the early 1960s, the question was raised
whether the fund had sufficient amounts of foreign currencies to meet the exchange stabilization needs of its deficit member countries. Owing to the possibility that large drawings by major
countries might exhaust the fund's stocks of foreign currencies, the *General Arrangements to Borrow* were initiated in 1962. Ten leading industrial
nations, the Group of Ten, originally agreed to
lend the fund up to a maximum of $6 billion. In
1964, the membership expanded when Switzerland joined the group. By serving as an intermediary and guarantor, the fund could use these
reserves to offer compensatory financial assistance to one or more of the participating countries. Such credit arrangements presumably
would be used only when the deficit country's
borrowing needs exceeded the amount of assis-
ance that could be provided under the fund's
own drawing facilities.

Table 17.2 illustrates the General Arrangements to Borrow setup by identifying the participating countries and the amounts they have
pledged to lend the fund in the case of need. As
of June 30, 1983, the fund's resources totaled
some 5.6 billion SDRs. Although the General
Arrangements to Borrow do not provide a permanent increase in the supply of world reserves
once the loans are repaid and world reserves
revert back to their original levels, these arrangements have made world reserves more flexible
and adaptable to the needs of deficit countries.

Swap Arrangements

During the early 1960s, there occurred a wave of
speculative attacks against the U.S. dollar, which
was expected by many to be devalued in terms of

Table 17.2 Fund Borrowing Agreement
Under the General Arrangements to Borrow,
June 30, 1983

Country	Amount Pledged (millions of SDRs)
United States	1,872
Canada	164
Japan	1,151
Belgium	142
France	340
Germany	947
Italy	213
Netherlands	237
Sweden	64
United Kingdom	514
Total	5,644

Source: International Monetary Fund, *International Financial Statistics*, August 1983, p. 16.

other currencies. To help offset the flow of
short-term capital out of the dollar into stronger
foreign currencies, the U.S. Federal Reserve
agreed with several European central banks in
1962 to initiate reciprocal currency arrangements, commonly referred to as swap arrangements. Today, the swap network on which the
United States depends to finance its interventions in the foreign exchange market includes
the central banks of 15 nations and the Bank for
International Settlements.

Swap arrangements are bilateral agreements
between central banks. Each government provides for an exchange, or swap, of currencies to
help finance temporary payments disequilibriums. If the United States, for example, is short
of marks, it can ask the German Federal Bank to
supply them in exchange for dollars; conversely,
the German Federal Bank can ask for dollars. A
drawing on the swap network is usually initiated
by telephone, followed by an exchange of wire
messages specifying terms and conditions. The
actual swap is in the form of a foreign exchange

contract, the sale of dollars by the Fed for the currency of a foreign central bank. The country requesting the swap presumably will use the funds to help ease its payments deficits and discourage speculative capital outflows. Swaps are to be repaid (reversed) within a stipulated period of time, normally within 3 to 12 months. The total swap facilities available to the United States as of January 31, 1983, shown in Table 17.3, are more than $30 billion. Use of the swap network was quite heavy during the early 1970s as central banks drew on the lines to finance exchange market interventions during waves of currency crises. Since the adoption of managed floating exchange rates by the industrial nations in 1973, swaps have increasingly been used to temper and smooth abrupt changes in market exchange rates.

A number of factors have enhanced swaps as credit instruments compared with the fund's drawing facilities. Not only are fund drawings relatively costly for borrowing nations, but also gaining aid from the fund is quite visible to the public. A large drawing from the fund may signal economic weakness and touch off adverse speculative activity. Swap transactions are also made on an unconditional basis, whereas borrowing from the fund (in excess of 50 percent of a country's quota) may require substantial justification. Finally, swap operations involve minimal administrative lags and can be executed on extremely short notice.

Compensatory Financing of Exports

In 1963, the International Monetary Fund approved a special credit facility to aid the less-developed countries. The idea was to extend the fund's balance-of-payments assistance to member countries suffering from fluctuations in receipts from exports of primary products owing to circumstances beyond their control. Borrowings from the so-called *compensatory financing*

Table 17.3   Federal Reserve Reciprocal Currency Arrangements, January 31, 1983

Institution	Amount of Commitment (millions of U.S. dollars)
Austrian National Bank	250
National Bank of Belgium	1,000
Bank of Canada	2,000
National Bank of Denmark	250
Bank of England	3,000
Bank of France	2,000
German Federal Bank	6,000
Bank of Italy	3,000
Bank of Japan	5,000
Bank of Mexico	1,025
Netherlands Bank	500
Bank of Norway	250
Bank of Sweden	300
Swiss National Bank	4,000
Bank for International Settlements	
Swiss francs-dollars	600
Other authorized European currencies-dollars	1,250
Total	$30,425

Source: Federal Reserve Bank of New York, *Quarterly Review* (Spring 1983), p. 56. Reprinted by permission.

facility are separate from, and in addition to, a country's regular borrowing privileges from the fund. A country facing temporary declines in its commodity export earnings can under this facility borrow an amount up to 50 percent of its fund quota.

Oil Facility

In 1974, the International Monetary Fund established a special facility to help member countries meet the impact on their balance of payments of the skyrocketing costs of oil imports generated by the OPEC price increases of 1973–1974.

Under the *oil facility*, fund resources are made available to members as a supplement to other fund drawing arrangements. Although the oil facility has been used primarily by the less-developed countries, industrialized countries including Italy and the United Kingdom have borrowed reserves under these arrangements.

Buffer Stock Financing Facility

A major concern of the less-developed nations has been erratic fluctuations in their commodity export prices. To correct such disturbances, commodity producers have often banded together and formulated price stabilization schemes based on buffer stocks. Consider the case of the International Tin Agreement, which was initiated by the major tin exporters in 1956. The buffer stock consists of supplies of tin. Should market prices fall below the accepted floor level, the buffer stock manager must purchase tin to support its price. Conversely, the buffer stock manager would sell tin to prevent market prices from rising above accepted ceiling levels. In this manner, the price of tin is stabilized.

Consistent with the International Monetary Fund's support of commodity price stabilization for the less-developed countries, in 1969, the fund established a facility to aid members in financing their contributions to buffer stocks. Under this scheme, a member country with a balance-of-payments need can obtain financial assistance from the fund in amounts up to the value of the country's buffer stocks calculated at the floor price of the agreement or at the average market price of these stocks should the market price fall below the floor price. Borrowing under the *buffer stock facility* cannot exceed 50 percent of a member's fund quota. Like the fund's compensatory financing facility, buffer stock arrangements are separate from, and additional to, normal fund facilities for dealing with balance-of-payments difficulties. The

borrowings are generally expected to be repaid within a period of three to five years after the date of the loan.

Established in 1969, the fund's buffer stock facility was initially used only in connection with the International Tin Agreement. From 1969 to 1978, the participating tin-producing countries obtained an equivalent of 30 million SDRs of credit under this arrangement. Since 1978, the fund has also made its buffer stock facility available to finance special stocks of sugar under the 1977 International Sugar Agreement. The scheme provides financing for a buffer stock arrangement consisting of sugar stocks that are nationally owned but internationally controlled as a means of stabilizing world sugar prices. Such buffer stock financing is intended to help stabilize both prices and earnings of the commodity-producing, less-developed countries.

The International Debt Problem

Much concern has been voiced over the volume of international lending in recent years. At times, the concern has been that international lending was insufficient. Such was the case following the oil shocks in 1974–1975 and 1979–1980, when it was feared that some oil-importing, developing countries might not be able to obtain loans to finance trade deficits resulting from the huge increases in the price of oil. It so happened that many oil-importing countries were able to borrow dollars from commercial banks. They paid the dollars to OPEC nations, who redeposited the money in commercial banks, which then relent the money to oil importers, and so on. In the 1970s, the banks were part of the solution, for if they had not lent large sums to the developing countries, the oil shocks would have done far more damage to the world economy.

By the 1980s, however, commercial banks were viewed as part of an international debt problem, because they had lent so much to developing countries. Flush with OPEC money after the oil price increases of the 1970s, the banks actively sought borrowers and had no trouble finding them among the developing countries. Some countries borrowed to prop up consumption, since their living standards were already low and hit hard by oil price hikes. Most countries borrowed to avoid cuts in developmental programs and to invest in energy projects. It was generally recognized that banks were successful in recycling their OPEC deposits to developing nations following the first round of oil price hikes in 1974–1975. But the international lending mechanism encountered increasing difficulties beginning with the global recession of the early 1980s. In particular, some developing countries were unable to pay their external debts on schedule.

Table 17.4 summarizes the magnitude of the international debt problem of the developing countries. From 1973 to 1983, the external debt of the nonoil developing countries rose at an annual rate exceeding 20 percent. By 1983, the debt of developing countries to private creditors, mainly multinational banks, was more than 50 percent of total external debt. Latin America, the largest debtor by area, accounted for more than 43 percent of total external debt of nonoil developing countries. The ratio of external debt to the national output (gross domestic product) of nonoil developing countries rose from 22.4 percent in 1973 to 34.7 percent in 1983. Moreover, the ratio of external debt to exports rose from 115.4 percent to 144.4 percent over the period 1973–1983. Concerning the capacity of an economy to service its debt (to pay interest and to refinance principal), developing-country *debt service ratio* rose from 15.9 percent in 1973 to 19.3 percent in 1983. This measure represents the scheduled interest and principal

Table 17.4   Nonoil Developing Countries: Long-Term External Debt

	1973	1983
Outstanding debt	$111.8 billion	$571.6 billion
Official creditors	51.0	218.6
Private creditors	60.8	353.0
Outstanding debt by area		
Latin America	$ 44.4 billion	$274.4 billion
Asia	30.0	131.7
Africa	14.2	75.0
Europe	14.5	73.8
Middle East	8.7	43.7
Ratio of external debt to gross domestic product	22.4%	34.7%
Ratio of external debt to exports of goods and services	115.4%	144.4%
Debt service ratio	15.9%	19.3%

Source: International Monetary Fund, *World Economic Outlook*, 1983, Tables 32, 33, 35, pp. 200, 201, 204.

payments on long-term debt as a percentage of exports of goods and services.

By the early 1980s, it was apparent that many developing countries were encountering increasing difficulties in servicing their debt. The major borrowers in difficulty included Argentina, Brazil, and Mexico. A country may experience debt-servicing problems for a number of reasons: (1) It may have pursued improper macroeconomic policies that contribute to large balance-of-payments deficits. (2) It may have borrowed excessively or on unfavorable terms. (3) It may have been affected by adverse economic events that it cannot control.

Although there are marked differences among the developing countries, a common set of factors appeared to have been behind the debt-servicing problems of the developing countries. The world recession of the early 1980s was one such cause. Because of stagnant or declining demand, the prices of the developing countries' exports declined, and declined more rapidly than the less flexible prices of the goods they import. The recession thus made it more difficult for developing countries to obtain the foreign exchange required to service their debt. The sharp rise in interest rates also made it more costly for developing countries to borrow funds. What is more, the rise in the value of the U.S. dollar during the early 1980s resulted in increased costs of debt repayment, since most developing-country debt is denominated in dollars. These factors resulted in commercial banks losing confidence that the loans would be repaid promptly.

A country facing debt-servicing difficulties has several options. First, it may cease repayments on its debt. Such an action, however, undermines confidence in the country, making it difficult (if not impossible) for it to borrow in the future. Furthermore, there is a possibility of the country being declared "in default," whereby its assets (for example, ships and aircraft) may be confiscated and sold to discharge the debt. As a group, however, developing countries in debt might have considerable leverage in winning concessions from their lenders. A second option is for the country to try to service its debt at all costs. To do so may require the restriction of other foreign exchange expenditures, a step that may be viewed as socially unacceptable. Finally, a country may seek debt rescheduling, which generally involves a stretching out of the original payment schedule of the debt. There is a cost, as the debtor country must pay interest on the amount outstanding until the debt has been repaid.

By 1983, there was a sharp increase in the number of countries with balance-of-payments problems and debt-servicing difficulties. Either the debts were rescheduled or the countries began the process of negotiating the rescheduling of their debt with commercial banks. These countries included Argentina, Brazil, and Mexico.

In addition to obtaining credit from commercial banks, member countries may obtain emergency loans from the International Monetary Fund. By insisting on *conditionality*, or restraints on domestic economies, the IMF tries to ensure that the loans it extends to troubled nations will be paid back. Borrowers are asked to adopt austerity programs to shore up their economies and order their muddled finances. Such measures have resulted in the slashing of public spending, private consumption, and in some cases capital investment. Borrowers also must cut imports and expand exports. The IMF views austerity programs as a necessity, because with a sovereign debtor, there is no other way to make it pay back its loans. The IMF faces a difficult situation in deciding how tough to get with borrowers. If it goes soft and offers money on easier terms, it sets a precedent for other debtor nations. But if it miscalculates and requires excessive austerity measures, it risks triggering political turmoil and possibly a declaration of default.

The Eurodollar Market

One of the most widely misunderstood topics in international finance is the nature and operation of the Eurodollar market. To the nonpractitioner, the Eurodollar market may seem like a financial black box into which goes the money of U.S. residents and from which comes credits for foreigners. Academic economists even disagree about the market's operations and economic impact. This section considers some of the basic questions about what the Eurodollar market is and how it functions.

Nature of the Eurodollar Market

Eurodollars are deposits, denominated and payable in dollars, in banks outside the United States, primarily in London, the market's center. Depositors may be foreign exporters who have sold products in the United States and have received dollars in payment. They may also be U.S. residents who have withdrawn funds from their accounts in the United States and put them in a bank overseas. Dollar deposits in foreign banks are generally for a specified time period and bear a stated yield, because most Eurodollar deposits are held for investment purposes rather than as transaction balances. The market, often termed the *Eurocurrency* market, deals in currencies other than the dollar, most notably West Germany's mark and the Swiss franc, but because most transactions are denominated in dollars, we employ the term Eurodollar.

Borrowers come to Eurodollar banks for a variety of purposes. When the market was first developed, borrowers were primarily corporations that required financing for international trade. But other lending opportunities have evolved with the market's development. Loans are currently made to borrowers such as communist governments, the British government, and U.S. banks.

The purpose of the Eurodollar market is to operate as a financial intermediary, bringing together lenders and borrowers. It serves as one of the most important tools for moving short-term funds across national borders. When the Eurodollar market first came into existence in the 1950s, its volume was estimated to be approximately $1 billion. The size of the Eurocurrency market in 1982 was estimated to be $2,055 billion, as seen in Table 17.5. With Eurodollars estimated to make up 72 percent of gross Eurocurrency liabilities, the gross size of the Eurodollar market was approximately $1,480 billion in 1982.[2]

Eurodollar Market Development

Although several hundred banks currently issue Eurodollar deposits on investor demand, it was not until the late 1950s and early 1960s that the market began to gain prominence as a major source of short-term capital. Several factors contributed to the Eurodollar market's growth.

Table 17.5　Eurocurrency Market Size

Year	Gross Eurocurrency Liabilities (billions of dollars)
1973	315
1975	485
1977	740
1979	1,235
1981	1,860
1982	2,055

Source: Morgan Guaranty Trust Company of New York, *World Financial Markets*, July 1983, p. 15.

One factor was fear that deposits held in the United States would be frozen by the government in the event of an international conflict. The Eastern European countries, notably Russia, were among the first depositors of dollars in European banks, because during World War II, the United States impounded Russian dollar holdings located in U.S. banks. Russia was thus motivated to maintain dollar holdings free from U.S. regulation.

Ceilings on interest rates that U.S. banks could pay on time deposits was another reason for the Eurodollar market's growth. This is because the ceilings limited the U.S. banks in competing with foreign banks for deposits. During the 1930s, the Federal Reserve System under Regulation Q established ceiling rates to prevent banks from paying excessive interest rates on saving accounts and thus being forced to make risky loans that would generate high earnings. By the late 1950s, when London was paying interest rates on dollar deposits that exceeded the levels set by Regulation Q, it was profitable for U.S. residents and foreigners to transfer their dollar balances to London. Large American banks directed their foreign branches to bid for dollars by offering higher interest rates than those allowed in the United States. The parent offices then borrowed the money from their overseas branches. To limit such activity, the Federal Reserve in 1969 established high reserve requirements on head office borrowings from abroad. In 1973, the Federal Reserve System made large-denomination certificates of deposit exempt from Regulation Q ceilings, further reducing the incentive to borrow funds from overseas branches.

Throughout the 1970s and early 1980s, the Eurodollar market continued to grow. A major factor behind the sustained high growth of the market has been the risk-adjusted interest rate advantage for Eurocurrency deposits relative to domestic deposits. This reflected the increases in the level of dollar interest rates and the reduc-tions of the perceived riskiness of Euromarket deposits. One policy that may lessen the future growth of the Eurodollar market occurred in 1981 when the Federal Reserve permitted American banks to establish *International Banking Facilities* (IBF), which are exempt from interest rate ceilings and reserve requirements. IBFs are permitted to transact only with foreigners, either in dollars or foreign currency. The rationale is to help American-based banks capture part of the business in the Eurocurrency markets.

Financial Implications

Eurodollars have significant implications for international finance. By increasing the financial interdependence of countries involved in the market, Eurodollars help facilitate the financing of international trade and investment. They also may reduce the need for official reserve financing, as a given quantity of dollars can support a large volume of international transactions. On the other hand, it is argued that Eurodollars may undermine a country's efforts to implement its monetary policy. Volatile movements of these balances into and out of a country's banking system complicate a central bank's attempt to hit a monetary target.

Another concern is that the Eurodollar market does not face the same financial regulations as do the domestic banking systems of most industrialized countries. Should the Eurodollar banks not maintain sound reserve requirements or enact responsible policies, the pyramid of Eurodollar credit might collapse. Such fears became widespread in 1974 with the failure of the Franklin National Bank in the United States and the Bankus Herstatt of West Germany, both of which lost huge sums speculating in the foreign exchange market. Finally, it is feared that the Eurodollar market may be a potential monetary engine of inflation, given its ability to generate credit on a worldwide basis.

ry

e purpose of international reserves is to permit countries to bridge the gap between monetary receipts and payments. Deficit countries can use international reserves to buy time in order to postpone adjustment measures.

2. The demand for international reserves depends on two major factors: (1) the monetary value of international transactions and (2) the size and duration of balance-of-payments disequilibriums.

3. The need for international reserves tends to become less acute under a system of floating exchange rates than under a system of fixed rates. The more efficient is the international adjustment mechanism and the greater the extent of international policy coordination, the smaller is the need for international reserves.

4. The supply of international reserves consists of owned and borrowed reserves. Among the major sources of reserves are the following: (1) foreign currencies, (2) monetary gold stocks, (3) Special Drawing Rights, (4) IMF drawing positions, (5) the General Arrangements to Borrow, and (6) swap arrangements.

5. A Eurodollar deposit is a dollar deposit in a bank outside the United States. The Eurodollar market has grown at a phenomenal rate to become one of the world's leading money markets. It also is an important mechanism whereby short-term funds can be moved across national boundaries.

mine a country's demand for international reserves?

3. The total supply of international reserves consists of two categories: (1) owned reserves and (2) borrowed reserves. What do these categories include?

4. In terms of volume, which component of world reserves is currently most important? Which is currently least important?

5. What is meant by a reserve currency? Historically, which currencies have assumed this role?

6. What was the so-called liquidity problem that plagued the operation of the Bretton Woods system?

7. What is the current role that gold plays in the international monetary system?

8. What advantages do a gold exchange standard have over a pure gold standard?

9. What are Special Drawing Rights? Why were they created? How is their value determined?

10. What facilities exist for trading nations that wish to borrow international reserves?

11. What caused the international debt problem of the developing countries in the 1980s? Why did this debt problem threaten the stability of the international banking system?

12. What is a Eurodollar? What are the major sources and uses of Eurodollars? How did the Eurodollar market develop? Do Eurodollars pose a threat to the stability of the international monetary system?

Study Questions

1. A country's need for international reserves is similar to a householder's desire to hold cash balances. Explain.

2. What are the major factors that deter-

Notes

1. See Herbert G. Grubel, *The International Monetary System* (Baltimore: Penguin Books, 1969), pp. 31–33.

2. The most common definition of the Eurocurrency market is referred to as *gross*

Eurocurrency liabilities. This measure includes the total foreign currency liabilities of banks in major European countries, the Bahamas, Bahrain, Cayman Islands, Netherlands Antilles, Panama, Canada, Japan, Hong Kong, and Singapore. However, much of this constitutes interbank deposits. Adjusting gross Eurocurrency liabilities for interbank deposits gives *net Eurocurrency liabilities*. In 1982, net Eurocurrency liabilities totaled $940 billion, significantly less than the $2,015 billion of gross Eurocurrency liabilities.

Schwartz, A. J. "Reflections on the Gold Commission Report." *Journal of Money, Credit, and Banking*, part 1, November 1982.

Southard, F. A. *The Evolution of the International Monetary Fund*. Essays in International Finance, no. 135. Princeton, N. J.: Princeton University Press, 1979.

Wellons, P. A. *World Money and Credit: The Crisis and Its Causes*. Cambridge, Mass.: Harvard Business School, 1983.

Williamson, J. "International Liquidity: A Survey." *Economic Journal*, September 1973.

Suggestions for Further Reading

Bell, G. *The Eurodollar Market and the International Financial System*. New York: Halsted Press, 1973.

Carlozzi, N. "Regulating the Eurocurrency Market: What Are the Prospects?" *Business Review*, Federal Reserve Bank of Philadelphia, March–April 1981.

Coats, W. L. "The SDR as a Means of Payment." *International Monetary Fund Staff Papers*, September 1982.

Coombs, C. A. *The Arena of International Finance*. New York: John Wiley, 1976.

Flemming, J. M. *Towards Assessing the Need for International Reserves*. Essays in International Finance, no. 58. Princeton, N. J.: Princeton University Press, 1967.

Little, J. S. "The Eurodollar Market: Its Nature and Impact." *New England Economic Review*. Federal Reserve Bank of Boston, May–June 1969.

Nowzed, B. *The IMF and Its Critics*. Essays in International Finance, no. 146. Princeton, N. J.: Princeton University Press, 1981.

Roosa, R., et al., *Reserve Currencies in Transition*. New York: Group of Thirty, 1982.

18

INTERNATIONAL
ECONOMIC POLICY

The previous chapters examined adjustment policies in an international economy and the economic consequences of these policies. We now turn our attention to the actual choice among the various policy instruments that promote equilibrium for an economy. The government of a single country selects its economic policies in view of its own goals. In an interdependent world, the consequences of one country's activities will be felt by its trading partners. The result is the need for policy coordination among national authorities so that a given country will not adopt trade policies that significantly lessen the welfare of other economies. This chapter investigates the domestic and international implications of economic policy. The discussion takes into account how a single country may adopt policies in pursuit of its own objectives, as well as how, in an interdependent world, a country must consider foreign repercussions when forming economic policy. The importance of policy coordination at the international level is emphasized throughout the discussion.

International Economic Policy

International economic policy as a subject encompasses the activities of national governments that have an impact on the movement of trade and factor inputs among nations. Included are not only the obvious measures such as import tariffs and quotas but also domestic measures such as monetary and fiscal policies. Economic policies that are undertaken to improve the conditions of one sector tend to have repercussions that spill over into other sectors. A policy, for example, that improves a country's trade balance may also favorably affect domestic employment and income. Since an economy's internal (domestic) sector is tied to its external (foreign) sector, we cannot designate government economic policies as purely domestic or purely foreign. Rather, the effects of economic policy should be viewed as being located on a continuum between two poles—an *internal effects* pole and an *external effects* pole. The primary impact of an import tariff may be on a country's trade balance, but such a policy also may have secondary effects on the domestic sector. Most economic policies are located between the external and internal sector poles rather than falling directly on either one.

Economic Objectives of Nations

To this point, our discussion of international economic policy has emphasized choosing economic policies to fulfill national objectives. But what are the national objectives that international policies may be geared toward? Since the

Great Depression of the 1930s, the stability of an economy at full employment generally has been pursued by national monetary authorities. Such an objective, commonly referred to as *internal balance*, has two dimensions: (1) a fully employed economy and (2) price stability. Nations traditionally have considered internal balance to be the key economic objective and have therefore geared international economic policy to domestic problems. For example, measures to regulate trade and capital movements are undertaken in accordance with their effects on the state of domestic economic activity.

Although the attainment of internal balance may be a worthy national objective, a country eventually must face up to disequilibriums in its balance of payments. In the post–World War II era, balance-of-payments crises have affected virtually every country in the world. The United States, for example, witnessed a deteriorating payments position during the 1960s and 1970s that led the president to recognize the reversal of these deficits as a national priority. When a country faces persistent balance-of-payments deficits, it may find itself running low on international reserves and must switch priority to external balance (balance-of-payments equilibrium) when forming economic policy. Given the fact that most industrialized countries in recent years have found their trade sectors making larger contributions to the levels of gross national product, we can hardly ignore the significance of *external balance* as a national goal.

Nations also have economic targets other than the promotion of internal and external balance. The less-developed countries of Latin America, Africa, and Asia are desperately pressed with the problems of economic development. Achieving a reasonably equitable distribution of income has also been an objective of national economic policies. The desire to be nationally self-sufficient has gained priority during periods of international political crises or armed conflicts among nations. Although these commitments may influence international economic policies, the following discussion is confined to the desire to obtain *overall balance* for an economy—that is, internal balance plus external balance.

Policy Instruments

International economic policy is carried out through various policy instruments. Among the most important policy tools available to a nation are the so-called *expenditure-changing* instruments. Such tools cause changes in the level of spending and the resulting impact on the level of output and the balance of payments. Expenditure-changing policies can be implemented by fiscal policy, in which government changes its expenditures or modifies tax levels, and by monetary policy, which changes the money supply and affects interest rates and spending levels. Depending on the direction of change, expenditure-changing policies are either *expenditure increasing* or *expenditure reducing* in nature.

Other policy instruments include the so-called expenditure-switching policies. A country, for example, may resort to currency devaluation (or revaluation), tariffs, or quotas to eliminate a payments disequilibrium. These instruments are termed *expenditure switching* because they are aimed at diverting expenditure away from foreign goods to home goods. The success of these measures largely depends on switching demand in the proper direction and amount, as well as on the capacity of the home economy to meet the additional demand by supplying more goods and services.

International economic policy may also use direct controls, which interfere with the operation of market forces. In August 1971, a system of mandatory price and wage controls was applied by the U.S. government to its economy to control inflationary trends and help enhance the U.S. international competitive position. Another case occurred when the U.S. government in

1968 adopted a system of mandatory investment controls designed to curb additional flows of investment funds out of the United States (these controls were subsequently lifted in 1974 when the U.S. foreign investment position improved). Governments may also use various exchange controls to regulate their balance of payments.

Institutional Constraints and the International Monetary Order

The formation of economic policy is subject to *institutional constraints* that are largely political in nature. These constraints stem from the tolerance limits of policy makers concerning the extent to which an economy can deviate from one policy target in its pursuit of another target. For example, to what extent is a country willing to accept contractionary adjustments in income, output, and employment in its attempt to lower home imports and restore balance-of-payments equilibrium? The outcry of the adversely affected groups within the economy might well be more than sufficient to convince policy makers not to adopt such measures. Not only do institutional constraints bear on the formation of economic policy for a single country, but also a government cannot ignore the impact that its economic policies will have on foreign nations. The result is that policy formation in a worldwide system is characterized by negotiations and compromise.

Figure 18.1 can be used to illustrate how institutional constraints relate to the formation of domestic economic policy for a single country, as well as to its international economic policy.[1] Let the country in question be the United States in trade with ROW (the rest of the world nations considered as a group). Referring to the upper portion of the figure, note the following relationships. First, the vertical axis of the diagram designates the extent of balance-of-payments deficits or surpluses. External balance is reached at the diagram's origin, with neither surplus nor deficits being attained. Second, the horizontal axis indicates the extent of recession or inflation. Full employment (zero recession) without inflation (internal balance) is also achieved at the diagram's origin. An economy reaches overall balance when both its internal sector and external sector are in equilibrium.

With respect to an economy's internal balance, initially assume that as a country moves toward full employment, the price level remains constant until full employment is attained. But modern economies often find that prices rise before full employment is achieved and may increase faster the closer a country approaches full employment. A country may therefore face the problem of inflation along with unemployment. This case is considered later in the chapter.

One other feature of Figure 18.1 should be mentioned. Because it is assumed that trade occurs in a two-country world, it follows that any balance-of-payments surplus achieved by one country will be offset precisely by the other country's deficit. This means that in the diagram, the vertical coordinates of one country are identical in magnitude, but opposite in sign to, the other country's vertical coordinates. Suppose the U.S. economy is located at point $U.S._1$ in the figure, where it faces a payments surplus of OS_0 along with domestic inflation. It follows that the ROW economy experiences a payments deficit. This could occur at, say, point ROW_4, where ROW faces a deficit of OD_0, which equals the U.S. surplus.

Expenditure-Switching Policies: Overall Balance

One avenue that governments can pursue to promote overall economic balance is to enact various expenditure-switching policies. Although these measures generally are used to modify a country's international payments position, they

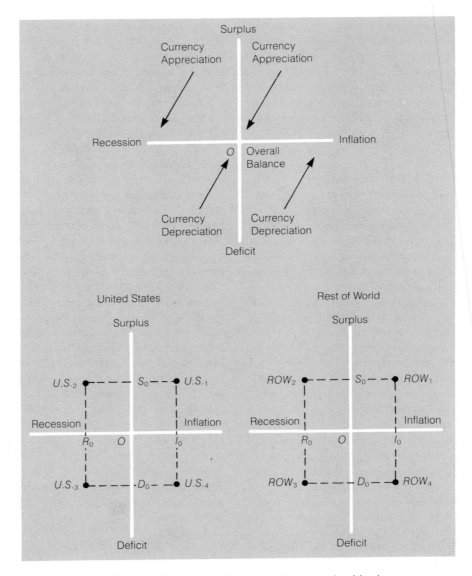

Figure 18.1   Achieving overall balance in economic objectives.

do have secondary impacts on an economy's internal sector. We now discuss one such expenditure-switching instrument, the exchange rate, and illustrate how various institutional political and economic constraints can modify use of this policy tool.

Returning to Figure 18.1, a currency depreciation (devaluation) results in movement in a northeasterly direction, whereas a currency appreciation (revaluation) results in movement in a southwesterly direction. Suppose the United States is located at point $U.S._3$ in the lower portion of the figure, facing both a payments deficit and a domestic recession. By permitting its currency to depreciate against ROW currency, the United States would find its exports rising as they become more competitive, and this would help correct the U.S. deficit. By supplying an injection of spending into the home economy through export sales, the currency depreciation would also help reverse the domestic recession. Conversely, suppose ROW is located at point ROW_1 in the figure, facing a payments surplus with domestic inflation. Should its currency appreciate in value, its exports would fall as they become less competitive, reversing the payments surplus. With export sales down, ROW would find domestic spending shrinking, which in turn would help correct the domestic inflation. Exchange rate changes thus result in northeasterly-southwesterly movements, or vice versa, in the diagram.

In our two-country model, the degree of freedom that a country has in initiating changes in its exchange rate is subject to international negotiations and policy coordinations. This is because in a two-country world, only one exchange rate exists. A currency depreciation for one currency necessarily implies an appreciation of the other currency. Furthermore, an exchange rate policy initiated by one country influences not only both its external and internal sectors but also those of its trading partners. This clearly indicates the need for the harmonization of economic policies. In an international economic order, one country cannot achieve overall balance single-handedly by use of its own policy tools. Other countries can easily upset a country's movement toward overall balance by enacting retaliating changes in the exchange rate, as occurred during the Great Depression of the 1930s.

International Policy Coordination

In a world of fixed exchange rates or managed floating rates, countries from time to time will consult over emerging exchange rate patterns. In some situations, affected countries may recognize that a realignment of exchange rates may aid them in the pursuit of overall economic balance. In other situations, countries may be reluctant to enter into international agreements on exchange rate levels because their efforts to achieve overall economic balance may be frustrated. The following analysis examines some of the potential problems in formulating international economic policy.

Referring to Figure 18.1, suppose the United States and ROW are initially located at $U.S._3$ and ROW_1. To correct its payments deficit, the United States would find it advantageous to propose a dollar depreciation (devaluation). Not only would this policy help enhance its export sales, but the resulting injection of spending into the domestic economy would counteract the recession. From the viewpoint of surplus country ROW, an appreciation (revaluation) of its currency would also be beneficial. As export sales drop off, home spending levels are curtailed, which helps curb the level of domestic inflation. Given these favorable circumstances, both countries could easily accept such an exchange rate realignment, for this would help restore both countries' overall economic balances.

These circumstances characterized the conditions leading up to the historic Smithsonian Currency Realignments of 1971. Facing a huge payments deficit as well as domestic recession, the United States sought a devaluation of its dollar. What is more, countries like West Germany and Japan, with persistent payments surpluses and inflationary booms occurring at the same time, desired a revaluation of their currencies. The ensuing currency realignment therefore was seen as providing benefits to both sides of the exchange rate negotiations. Actual bargaining centered on issues relating to the magnitude and timing of the exchange rate realignment, rather than on the direction in which exchange rate changes should take place.

Consider a situation where both the United States and ROW would likely find exchange rate adjustments unacceptable in restoring overall balance. In Figure 18.1, suppose the United States faces a payments deficit and domestic inflation at $U.S._4$, while ROW experiences domestic recession and a payments surplus at ROW_2. The correction of both countries' external disequilibriums would call for a depreciation of the U.S. dollar—alternately stated, an appreciation of the ROW currency. Although such an exchange rate realignment would promote external balance, it very well might be considered politically unacceptable. This is because the reversal of the external disequilibrium involves a cost for each country. Because the dollar depreciation induces a northeasterly movement in the figure, the cost of reversing the U.S. payments deficit

would be greater inflation. Moreover, since the ROW currency appreciation induces a southwesterly movement in the figure, ROW would have to tolerate a greater recession for its economy. Given the importance that industrialized nations attach to internal balance as a policy objective, the achievement of such an exchange rate realignment would be very much in doubt.

Table 18.1 summarizes the economic effects of various exchange rate policies for the United States and ROW. Because of the interdependence of domestic economies and the political importance that governments attach to the objectives of internal and external balance, institutional constraints limit the degrees of freedom possible for the international monetary system. A country considering a corrective exchange rate policy must be aware of the probable impact on its internal and external sectors, as well as the resulting effect on its trading partners' overall balances. The attempt to construct some kind of compromise between an ideal and a workable international exchange rate realignment may

Table 18.1   Exchange Rate Policies and Overall Balance

Domestic Economic Problem	Exchange Rate Policies	Effect on Overall Balance
$U.S._1/ROW_3$	U.S. appreciation ROW depreciation	U.S. overall balance enhanced ROW overall balance enhanced
$U.S._1/ROW_4$	U.S. appreciation ROW depreciation	U.S. overall balance enhanced ROW inflation worsened
$U.S._2/ROW_3$	U.S. appreciation ROW depreciation	U.S. recession worsened ROW overall balance enhanced
$U.S._2/ROW_4$	U.S. appreciation ROW depreciation	U.S. recession worsened ROW inflation worsened
$U.S._3/ROW_1$	U.S. depreciation ROW appreciation	U.S. overall balance enhanced ROW overall balance enhanced
$U.S._3/ROW_2$	U.S. depreciation ROW appreciation	U.S. overall balance enhanced ROW recession worsened
$U.S._4/ROW_1$	U.S. depreciation ROW appreciation	U.S. inflation worsened ROW overall balance enhanced
$U.S._4/ROW_2$	U.S. depreciation ROW appreciation	U.S. inflation worsened ROW recession worsened

involve conditions where there may be little room for agreement by affected nations.

Overall Balance with Fixed Exchange Rates

Recent history has shown that for a variety of reasons, monetary authorities may be reluctant to change their exchange rates. Under the historic Bretton Woods system, members of the International Monetary Fund agreed to maintain fixed exchange rates in the absence of fundamental disequilibrium. Given fixed exchange rates, can any other policy measure be undertaken to promote both internal and external balance? It may be that overall balance can be achieved by policy mixes that do not include exchange rate adjustment. A government, for example, may use fiscal and monetary expenditure-changing policies for this purpose.

Based on the analysis of the preceding section, Figure 18.2 illustrates the economic alternatives confronting domestic economic policy makers. Line MM represents the effects of an expenditure-increasing or an expenditure-reducing monetary policy, and line FF illustrates the effects of an expenditure-increasing or an expenditure-reducing fiscal policy. Both monetary and fiscal policies result in northwesterly and southeasterly movements in the figure. Suppose the home economy faces a recession and a payments surplus at point A in the figure. A policy that increased domestic spending levels, whether by monetary or fiscal means, would have the initial impact of reversing the domestic recession. As the economy advanced and higher levels of domestic income were attained, the country's imports would rise according to its marginal propensity to import. This would reverse the payments surplus, the result being a southeasterly movement in the figure. Conversely, expenditure-reducing monetary and fiscal policies would induce a northwesterly movement in the figure.

An interesting question is whether under a system of fixed exchange rates, both monetary policy and fiscal policy are equally well suited in promoting external balance. The answer is no. In fact, the response of a country's payments position to monetary policy is greater than its response to fiscal policy. This means that the monetary change required to induce a given response in a country's payments position is less than that of an equivalent change in fiscal policy. That is why line MM is steeper than line FF in Figure 18.2. Assume the home economy is located at point A in Figure 18.2, facing a payments surplus and domestic recession. The reversal of the overall imbalance would call for expansionary monetary and/or fiscal policy. The economic effects of each policy are considered in the following paragraphs.

Suppose the domestic monetary authorities expand the money supply to reverse the disequilibrium. With an increase in the supply of money relative to its demand, interest rates will decline and the quantity of money borrowed for investment spending will increase. The domestic economy will expand toward full employment levels. For the economy's external sector, the monetary expansion will exert effects on trade flows and international capital movements. As the monetary expansion stimulates the home economy, domestic income rises. This bids up the level of imports, which in turn reverses the payments surplus. Concurrently, as the monetary expansion forces down home interest rates relative to those abroad, domestic investors will find it profitable to transfer funds abroad. Again, the payments surplus is counteracted. The point is that both the *trade effect* and *capital flow effect* of an expansionary monetary policy reverse the home country's payments surplus.

As for fiscal policy, suppose the home government encourages domestic spending by adopting expansionary government expenditure and tax measures. As before, the increase in spending will move the economy toward internal balance.

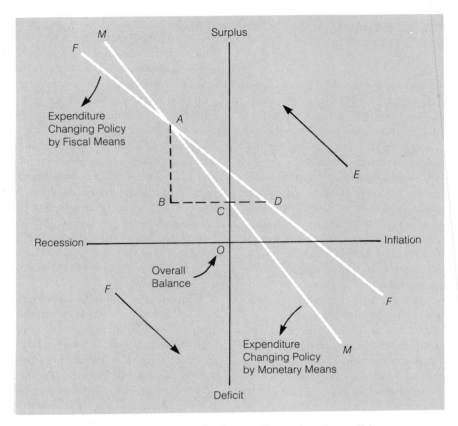

Figure 18.2   Monetary-fiscal expenditure changing policies.

With the economic expansion, domestic income rises, bidding up imports and correcting the payment surplus. But an expansionary fiscal policy will be accompanied by an increase in the amount of money demanded for transactionary purposes. This tends to induce higher domestic interest rates, which encourage capital inflows and further promote the payments surplus. The trade effect and capital flow effect of an expansionary fiscal policy thus contradict each other.

The result of the foregoing two examples is that to achieve an equivalent reduction in a payments surplus, the fiscal policy must be more expansionary than the monetary policy! In terms of Figure 18.2, suppose the home country

desires to lower its payment surplus by some amount, say AB. This could be achieved by an expansionary monetary policy of BC or an expansionary fiscal policy of BD, provided that each policy was used by itself. The amount of required fiscal policy thus exceeds that of required monetary policy by CD, as shown in the diagram.[2]

Policy Conflict

Suppose a country faces an overall disequilibrium in terms of a *payments surplus coupled with a domestic recession*, denoted by point A in

Figure 18.2. An expansionary monetary policy and/or fiscal policy would tend not only to correct the recession but also to reverse the surplus. The opposite also holds true. A contractionary monetary policy and/or fiscal policy would simultaneously tend to correct both a *domestic inflation and payments deficit*. These two disequilibrium cases represent a relatively favorable situation for policy makers. The balance of payments does not act as a constraint on the pursuit of internal balance, nor do domestic employment and income effects present a constraint on the attempt to attain external balance. A given economy can thus promote overall balance by simultaneously eliminating two sources of disequilibrium. Not all cases of overall imbalance are favorable for policy makers. In some situations, the attempt to reverse one source of disequilibrium may aggravate another sector of the economy. A policy conflict thus arises over which source of disequilibrium should be attacked. Such a conflict situation occurs when the domestic economy faces either a *domestic inflation plus payments surplus* or a *domestic recession plus payments deficit*.

Suppose a country is located at point *E* in Figure 18.2, where a payment surplus exists as well as domestic inflation. To eliminate the inflation, monetary authorities might attempt to reduce domestic spending by tightening credit. The resulting higher interest rates, however, would tend to attract more foreign capital into the home economy while reducing capital outflows abroad. Such net capital inflows would further aggravate the payments surplus. A contractionary fiscal policy would result in less government spending to halt inflation. But as domestic income falls, so do imports. Again, the payments surplus would be aggravated. A contractionary monetary or fiscal policy would move point *E* toward the vertical axis (internal balance), although it would be unable to move closer to the point of overall balance. West Germany faced this type of conflict throughout the 1960s and early 1970s. From 1967 to 1972, Japan faced a similar circum-

stance, registering high balance-of-payments surpluses as well as an overheating economy.

Suppose a country is located at point *F* in Figure 18.2, facing a domestic recession coupled with a payments deficit. Once again, a policy conflict exists. An expansionary monetary policy might be aimed at the recession target, but as credit conditions ease and domestic interest rates fall, other forces encourage net capital outflows from the home country. What is more, an expansionary fiscal policy that promotes higher levels of domestic income would induce rising imports. The pursuit of internal balance as a policy target would therefore have a cost in the form of a worsening payments balance. In the diagram, point *F* would be prevented from moving toward overall balance. This was often the U.S. situation in the early 1960s.

Given external balance and internal balance as policy objectives, the ultimate choice among the alternatives is largely a political one. Policy makers generally have favored internal balance over external balance as a policy objective. This was clearly reflected in Great Britain's economic programs during the 1960s and also was evident in the historic *Kennedy tax cut* of 1964. During the early 1960s, the United States found itself facing a domestic recession coupled with a payments deficit. The Kennedy administration was considering whether to adopt expansionary fiscal policy to correct the domestic recession. Despite the possible adverse consequences that such a policy might have on the existing deficit payments position of the United States, the administration considered the internal disequilibrium to be the primary policy target. As a result, the historic tax cut became effective in 1964.

Resolving Policy Conflicts

Table 18.2 summarizes the conclusions reached in the preceding analysis. It has been shown that policy makers in the pursuit of overall balance

Table 18.2   Policy Requirements for Attaining Overall Balance*

External Disequilibrium	Domestic Policy Requirement	Internal Disequilibrium	Domestic Policy Requirement	Domestic Policy Agreement or Conflict
Surplus	Expansion	Inflation	Contraction	Conflict
Deficit	Contraction	Recession	Expansion	Conflict
Surplus	Expansion	Recession	Expansion	Agreement
Deficit	Contraction	Inflation	Contraction	Agreement

*The domestic policies here refer to the expenditure-changing instruments of monetary policy and fiscal policy.

face two targets: (1) balance-of-payments equilibrium, or external balance, and (2) full employment without inflation, or internal balance. The pursuit of these two targets is carried out by manipulation of the economy's level of total spending (aggregate demand), whether the targets be achieved by fiscal measures or monetary measures. Policy makers have but one policy instrument—total spending—to apply to the fulfillment of two objectives.

When the domestic economy is confronted with disequilibriums of recession-plus-surplus or inflation-plus-deficit, the policy variable of total spending can be used to simultaneously eliminate both internal and external problems. However, should the economy face disequilibriums in the form of inflation-plus-surplus or recession-plus-deficit, a policy conflict exists, as the policy instrument of total spending cannot simultaneously achieve both internal and external balance. A policy maker is similar to a marksman who has but one arrow (total spending) to shoot at two targets (internal balance and external balance). Resolution of policy conflicts calls for the use of additional policy tools to match the number of targets. For policy makers to achieve a given number of independent targets, they must have at their command an equivalent number of policy instruments. Each separate target can be lined up with a policy instrument, but should the number of targets exceed the number of policy instruments, some targets may not be attained.

Besides the tool of total spending, policy makers have an arsenal of other instruments. These include the exchange rate, trade policies such as tariffs and quotas, restrictions on foreign travel and tourist expenditures abroad, and limitations on capital outflows and overseas investments. Because each of these policy tools has a different impact on the various policy objectives, government officials must formulate a mix of policies in view of the total economic picture.

Suppose a country faces a conflict in the form of a domestic recession coupled with a payments deficit. Combating the recession would call for an expansion of total spending. But as national income rises, home imports will increase to further aggravate the payments deficit. Policy makers might impose import quotas or tariffs to improve the external balance. In this manner, each policy target is matched up with a policy instrument and both policy objectives can be met at the same time.

In United States history, the Federal Reserve has been involved in attempting to line up policy instruments with targets during conflict situations. During the early 1960s, the conflict was domestic recession plus payments deficit. The Federal Reserve attempted to match instruments with targets by manipulating the structure of domestic interest rates in a program called Operation Twist. *Operation Twist* referred to the modification of the U.S. structure of interest rates so that short-term rates would be used primarily for external balance and long-term rates would be used primarily for internal balance. By keeping short-term interest rates high, short-term funds from abroad would be attracted, aiding the home country payments position. Low long-term rates presumably would stimulate domestic investment spending, correcting the recession. At best, Operation Twist was only partially successful in promoting overall balance. The policy initially appeared to be successful in keeping short-term rates above long-term rates, but as time passed, the differential between them disappeared as inflation pushed both short-term and long-term rates upward, moderating the program's success.

Inflation with Unemployment

So far, we have looked at internal balance under special circumstances. We have assumed that as the economy advances to full employment, domestic prices remain unchanged until full employment is actually reached. Once the nation's capacity to produce has been achieved, further increases in domestic spending pull prices upward. This type of inflation is commonly referred to as *demand-pull inflation*. Under these conditions, the policy objective of internal balance (full employment with stable prices) can be viewed as a single target that requires but one policy instrument. However, industrial economies in recent years have often faced another state of affairs. This is the simultaneous occurrence of inflation and unemployment. Modern economies have sometimes found domestic prices rising before full employment has been achieved. This type of inflation, which may not be totally related to the level of domestic spending, is referred to as *structural (cost-push) inflation*. Given structural inflation, the objectives of full employment and stable prices cannot be

considered as one and the same target. Rather, attainment of full employment and price stability are recognized as two independent targets that require two distinct policy instruments. Achieving overall balance thus involves three separate targets—external balance, full employment, and price stability. A third policy instrument may be needed to ensure that all three objectives can be achieved simultaneously.

This situation confronted the United States in the 1970s. By 1971, the Nixon administration was facing simultaneous problems of inflation and recession as well as a payments deficit. It was thought that increasing domestic spending to achieve full employment would intensify inflationary pressures. The president therefore initiated a comprehensive system of wage and price controls with the hope of eliminating domestic inflation as a constraint preventing expansionary total spending as a means of pursuing full employment. By the year's end, the United States entered into the Smithsonian Agreement, in which the dollar's value fell by some 12 percent on the average against the currencies of its major trading partners. This was intended to help the United States solve its balance-of-payments difficulties. It was the administration's view that these problems could not be eliminated with only the aggregate demand, fiscal, and monetary policies.

Summary

1.   A major economic objective of modern nations is achievement of overall economic balance. One aspect of overall balance is internal balance, which consists of domestic full employment with price stability. The other aspect involves external balance, which consists of balance-of-payments equilibrium.

2.   A nation's international economic policy refers to the various government activities that

influence trade patterns among nations. Included are the following policy tools: (1) monetary and fiscal policy, (2) exchange rate adjustments, (3) tariff and nontariff trade barriers, (4) foreign exchange controls and investment controls, and (5) export promotion measures.

3. Although exchange rate adjustments are normally intended to influence a country's payments position, they have secondary impacts on the domestic economy. Achieving one policy objective may or may not come at the expense of fulfilling other objectives.

4. A depreciation of one country's exchange rate implies an appreciation of another country's exchange rate. International policy negotiations are thus essential whenever exchange rate adjustments are deemed necessary by trading nations.

5. By influencing the level of total spending, monetary and fiscal policies can be used to counteract recession or inflation. However, these instruments have secondary effects on the balance of payments.

6. Assuming a system of fixed exchange rates, for a given impact on domestic expenditures, monetary policy has a greater impact on the balance of payments than does fiscal policy.

7. The theory of economic policy reasons that with at least two policy objectives, it is necessary to have a minimum of two policy instruments for both objectives to be completely attained. Each policy instrument should be aimed at that objective on which it has the strongest impact.

3. What is meant by an expenditure-changing policy? How about an expenditure-switching policy? Give some examples of each.

4. What institutional constraints bear on the formation of economic policy for trading nations?

5. Under what conditions is a currency revaluation or devaluation successful in eliminating a surplus or deficit in a country's payments position?

6. Assume that a country faces a surplus in its balance of payments as well as high levels of domestic inflation caused by excess domestic spending. How could expenditure-changing policies be used to correct the problem of inflation? What would be the likely impact on the balance-of-payments surplus?

7. Under a system of fixed exchange rates, which tool is better suited for promoting external balance—monetary policy or fiscal policy?

8. What is meant by policy conflict? Why is this a problem for trading nations?

9. What does the theory of economic policy have to say about the relationship between policy objectives and policy tools?

10. Although changes in exchange rates are used primarily to restore external balance, they tend to have secondary impacts on a country's internal balance. Explain.

Study Questions

1. Distinguish among external balance, internal balance, and overall balance. As policy objectives, are these measures mutually exclusive or complementary?

2. What are the most important instruments of international economic policy?

Notes

1. See A. C. Day, "Institutional Constraints and the International Monetary System," in R. Mundell and A. Swoboda, eds., *Monetary Problems of the International Economy* (Chicago: University of Chicago Press, 1969), pp. 333–342.

2. See Robert A. Mundell, "The Appropriate Use of Monetary and Fiscal Policy Under Fixed Exchange Rates," *IMF Staff Papers* (March 1962), pp. 70–77.

Suggestions for Further Reading

Cooper, R. N. *The Economics of Interdependence*. New York: McGraw-Hill, 1967.

Corden, W. M. "The Geometric Representation of Policies to Attain Internal and External Balance." *Review of Economic Studies*, vol. 28, 1960.

Dornbusch, R. *Open Economy Macroeconomics*. New York: Basic Books, 1980.

Emminger, O. *The D-Mark in Conflict Between Internal and External Equilibrium*. Essays in International Finance, no. 122. Princeton, N. J.: Princeton University Press, 1977.

Johnson, H. G. "The Objectives of Economic Policy and the Mix of Fiscal and Monetary Policy Under Fixed Exchange Rates." In W. Fellner, F. Machlup, and R. Triffin, eds., *Maintaining and Restoring Balance in International Payments*. Princeton, N. J.: Princeton University Press, 1966.

Jones, R. W. "Monetary and Fiscal Policy for an Economy With Fixed Exchange Rates." *Journal of Political Economy*, July–August 1968.

Meade, J. E. *The Theory of Economic Policy*, vol. 1. London: Oxford University Press, 1951.

Mundell, R. A. *International Economics*. New York: Macmillan, 1968.

Swan, T. W. "Longer-Run Problems of the Balance of Payments." In American Economic Association, *Readings in International Economics*. Homewood, Ill.: Richard D. Irwin, 1968.

Tinbergen, J. *On the Theory of Economic Policy*. Amsterdam: North-Holland, 1952.

INDEX